Ordering
International
Politics

Janice Bially Mattern

Ordering International Politics

Identity, Crisis, and Representational Force

ROUTLEDGE   New York • London

Published in 2005 by
Routledge
270 Madison Avenue
New York, NY 10016
www.routledge-ny.com

Published in Great Britain by
Routledge
2 Park Square
Milton Park, Abingdon
Oxon OX14 4RN U.K.
www.routledge.co.uk

10 9 8 7 6 5 4 3 2 1

Library of Congress Cataloging-in-Publication Data

Bially Mattern, Janice.
    Ordering international politics : identity, crisis, and representational force /
Janice Bially Mattern.
        p. cm.
    Includes bibliographical references and index.
    ISBN 0-415-94896-7 (hb : alk. paper) – ISBN 0-415-94897-5 (pb : alk.
paper)
1. International relations. 2. World politics. I. Title.
    JZ1305.M345 2004
    327.1– dc22   2004008434

To Matthew, my best friend

Table of Contents

Preface

During the last 200 years, the blackbird has abandoned the woods to
become a city bird . . . and yet no one dares to interpret the last two
centuries as the history of the invasion of man's cities by the blackbird. All of us have become prisoners of a rigid conception of what
is important and what is not, and so we fasten our anxious gaze on
the important while from a hiding place behind our backs, the
unimportant wages its guerrilla war, which will end in surreptitiously changing the world and pouncing on us by surprise.
 — *Milan Kundera,* The Book of Laughter and
Forgetting *(1996, 267–8)*

International Relations (IR) is a discipline that fancies itself essential to understanding the world, but, embarrassingly, IR scholars have, as Kundera puts
it, been pounced on by surprise time and again by the considerable changes
occurring in the very world they purport to know. From the end of the Cold
War and the abrupt collapse of the Soviet Union, to backlash against globalization, 9/11, and the rise of terrorism and transnational crime, IR scholars
have been caught off guard. This project—an investigation into the sources of
stability and change in international order—begins with the conviction that
one reason for IR's poor track record is that the anxious gaze of IR scholars
has, for too long, been fastened too exclusively on the important forces of material power politics and state interests. So dominant have analyses of power
politics and state interests been in the literature that other processes and practices have been all but ignored—rejected as unimportant. By putting international identity—or more so, narrative, subjectivity, and language-power—at
the center of my analysis, my aspiration has been to highlight the way in which
the unimportant offers a very different, and sometimes, very compelling lens
through which to view the world. It is, put differently, my effort to offer an account of international order from a blackbird's-eye view.

I am acutely aware that my ambition to see like a blackbird outstrips my actual ability to do so, but in the too-long process of researching and writing this book, I have been lucky to have had many people that helped me stay on track—some by reminding me of where and how the important matters and others by showing me where my focus on the unimportant has been too limited and too polluted by my own biases.

My greatest debt is to four particular mentors who have unflaggingly supported my effort—Michael Barnett, Iver Neumann, Ann Tickner, and Alexander Wendt. While none of them ever really seem to agree with me (or at least, not as much as I think they should!), they have all always encouraged me to think hard and to think for myself. Alex Wendt especially has been patiently nurturing this project (and me) since 1996, when I began working on it as my dissertation under his direction at Yale. It was he who gave me the courage to be ambitious in the first place, and although there have been plenty of times when I wished he would have talked me into doing something easier, I cannot thank him enough for teaching me to trust my intellectual instincts and to indulge my creativity. He has been steadfast, constructive, and generous.

I have also had the good fortune to have excellent colleagues and students. At Temple University between 2000 and 2003, I benefited greatly from ongoing conversations with Richard Deeg, Geoffrey Herrera, Richard Immerman, Lynn Miller, Joe Schwartz, and Lucan Way. The participants in the Temple University graduate seminar in IR theory in Spring 2003—especially William Petti and Adam Lusk—helped me develop and try out a variety of new arguments. Bryan Tiley, Justin Gollub, and Sheri Sunderland provided me with invaluable research assistance and editing help. At Lehigh University, where this book was completed, I have enjoyed and very much appreciated the enthusiastic support of Henri Barkey, Jo Engel, Marian Gaumer, Rajan Menon, and Oles Smolansky. I also profited from the incisive commentaries of Chaim Kaufman, and from spirited conversations with Bruce Moon.

I am especially grateful to Emanuel Adler, Ann Baker, Andreas Behnke, Linda Bishai, Roland Bleiker, Mlada Bukovansky, François Debrix, Rod Hall, Tony Lang, Tom McNaugher, Nick Onuf, Richard Price, Allan Stam, and Wesley Widmaier, all of whom have offered thoughtful reflections, extensive written comments, useful conversation, and/or intellectual support more generally.

I owe Alex Montgomery special thanks for his incredible generosity in the form of both comments on multiple drafts and assistance with the visual presentation of my empirical data.

Although they probably do not realize it (nor would I assume that they necessarily want to accept responsibility for it), James Davis and Friedrich Kratochwil made it possible for me to conceive of actually finishing this book. By requiring that I sharpen my arguments for a precursor article that I published under their editorship in the *European Journal of International Relations,* they forced me to rethink the logic and trajectory of my argument in ways that made ideas that had, by then, become old hat seem interesting to me once again.

I also want to express my deep appreciation to the graduate students at the University of Chicago who attended my presentation at the PIPES workshop, and then engaged me and my work in a spirited and deeply intellectual fashion (especially Xavier Guillame, Jennifer London, and Jacob Schiff). I learned more about my work from them in those two hours than I have in the combined hours of other workshops over the years. That I have not been able to resolve the issues they raised reminds me just how hard it is to understand the world from a different perspective, one that is *really* outside of our rigid conceptions of what is important.

As far as helping me develop my intellectual agenda goes, Patrick Jackson and Daniel Nexon are in a category of their own. Beyond the obvious point that they are both such unique people that they belong in their own category anyway, Patrick and Dan are also the kind of academic comrades without whom I would have felt very alone. Not only has their work influenced me immensely—especially by attuning me to the importance of process—but their intellectual company has kept me from getting jaded.

Whereas Patrick and Dan helped me appreciate process from an intellectual standpoint, John Heussy taught me how to live in it, especially in the context of writing. Without him, I might not have bothered.

Finally, I want to thank my family and friends. My parents, Phyllis and Theodore, have been curious but patient; my sisters, Sharon and Allison, knew better than to ask; and my friends, especially the Morinettis, Carmen and Edna Belucci, Conrad Weiler and Ginny Kelly, Mlada Bukovansky (again), Linda Bishai (again), and Richard Deeg (again), kept me company and helped distract me. And of course, I want to acknowledge my daughter, Kalin Rose Mattern, who was born just as I was finishing this book and who, unlike this book, is simply perfect.

Most of this book was written during the summers of 2001 and 2002 in ramshackle, unfurnished rental apartments in Brigantine Beach, New Jersey. During these writing retreats (generously financed by Temple University), I happily retreated from Philadelphia, which unhappily meant being separated from my husband during the weekdays. It is to him that I dedicate this work. Matt has done much more than just unconditionally support my neurotic, intensive two-year "writing spree" (although he has certainly done that as well, even to the point of meticulously reading and editing *every* draft). He has, over our years together, also given me the very things that Kundera, in *The Book of Laughter and Forgetting,* reminds us to appreciate: the freedom to laugh, the courage to forget, and the love that makes it possible to do both.

Introduction

CHAPTER 1

Toward an Identity Turn?

> The enemies of liberty and our country should make no mistake,
> America . . . [is] shaping a balance of power that favors freedom.
> —*U.S. President George W. Bush*

> More active cooperation between our countries . . . will enhance
> our efforts in *building* a multipolar world and *establishing* a fair, ra-
> tional international order.
> —*Former Chinese President Jiang Zemin*[1]

Statesmen, for all of their here-and-now practicality, are fantastic vi-
sionaries. One commonly hears or reads about some representative of state
holding forth a vision—a fantasy—about an ideal international political
order.[2] While the content of the fantasy invariably differs from statesman to
statesman, state to state, the general aspiration is the same: to construct the
relationships among states so that they are guided by particular expectations and behaviors that will bolster one's own perceived national interests.
Of course, during the Cold War, such fantasies were considered foolish.
One could speak of containing threats or of managing particular international interactions, but to speak of shaping, building, or establishing the
whole of international order in the manner that George W. Bush or Jiang
Zemin freely have was implausible. Since the end of the Cold War, however,
fantasizing about how to order international politics—and openly talking
about it—has come very much into style.[3] In fact, in the more powerful
states, particularly the United States, the trend is toward actively trying to

3

post cold war phenomenon

translate fantasy into reality; it is toward implementing policies geared toward *ordering international politics* in the desired fashion.

But how exactly would one go about the monumental task of ordering international politics? Through what, if any, practice is it possible to design the relations among states?[4] At an applied level, this is a study into the mechanics of getting from fantastic vision (here) to live political reality (there). My premise is that if one endeavors, rightly or wrongly, to accomplish this, the greatest asset in that venture will be knowledge of the origins of order. A concerted ordering of international politics, that is, is much more likely to succeed if its practitioners know what makes international order, as a general phenomenon, possible in the first place. In this way, getting the mechanics right demands getting the theory of order right. Thus, at a more fundamental, and actually more vital, level, this is a study into the sources of international order. It is an investigation into how scholars can best model international order so as to best inform international practice.

International Relations (IR) scholars have been puzzling over the sources of international order for decades, at least partly because they recognize the practical utility of this information for statesmen and other practitioners of foreign affairs. Over the years, scholars have more or less reached a consensus that the sources of international order come in two genres: power politics and common interests. While the former is a realist-inspired view that emphasizes the order-producing effects of material threat systems, the latter is an institutionalist view that emphasizes the order-producing effects of cooperation in pursuit of mutual goals. Both power politics and common interests have become practical cornerstones in the international political fantasies of the world's most powerful leaders. For instance, George W. Bush has broadly called upon power politics to do the order-producing work in his vision. The dissemination of American values, he has argued, must be advanced through the balance of power. In contrast, Jiang Zemin and his successor, Hu Jintao, have called upon common interests, particularly by connecting cooperation among states to the realization of their desired multipolar international order.[5]

But, against scholarly consensus and the apparent confidence of practitioners in it, I am skeptical that power politics and common interests are sources of order in any analytically or practically valuable sense. There is an important distinction, I argue, between *sources* of international order and *factors* that contribute to international order, and recognizing this distinction helps explain my skepticism. A source is some manner of phenomena —process, substance, dynamic, representation, agent, and so on—that can create order out of disorder. A source of order will turn a situation in which stable, shared expectations and behaviors are nonexistent or damaged beyond reliability into one characterized by stable, shared expectations and behaviors. In short, a source of order is *sufficient* for international order—any international order. A contributing factor, in contrast, is not sufficient. It can specify and fortify the particular practices that states should enact to adhere to some order, but on its own cannot create order out of disorder. Contributing factors are not sufficient for shared stable expectations and behaviors.

When applied analytically, this distinction reveals that neither power politics nor common interests are sources of order. They are both contributing factors. Neither power politics nor common interests can create stable, shared expectations and behaviors among states in a context where such expectations and behaviors were previously absent, disrupted, or unreliable. The reason is that neither power politics nor common interests speak for themselves. States can interpret the demands of these stimuli in myriad different ways, which implies that even if states interpret them similarly (a best-case scenario), they may not recognize that they have done so. In this way, expectations and behaviors would not be shared in any meaningful or reliable sense. Rather, if power politics or common interests are to trigger stable, shared expectations and behaviors among states, a *prior* international order must exist: an order of shared knowledge among states about the "essence" and meaning of those stimuli—an epistemological order.[6] In light of this, power politics and shared interests are not sufficient for international order; their contribution to order depends upon something prior.

The "uncovery"* that power politics and common interests are factors, not sources, suggests that perhaps scholars have unwittingly misled practitioners about the most efficacious policies for getting from their fantastic visions of international order to international political realities. The record of success for order-building plans predicated on power politics and common interest models of order certainly appears scant. For instance, it was not long after Bush's upbeat speech about spreading American values through power politics that some of the very enemies who were supposed to be coerced into capitulation by those tactics mocked them with low-tech attacks on the World Trade Center and the Pentagon, the very emblems of American values. As for China, the leadership's efforts to parlay cooperative treaties and regimes, such as the "friendship treaty" with Russia and the

---

*As opposed to a discovery, which implies a new, previously untouched fact of the world. An uncovery implies an excavation from underneath layers of ossified or never-problematized knowledge. This insight was stimulated by Greenblatt (1991).

Association of Asian Parliaments, into the bases for a multipolar international order have essentially stalled in their tracks.[7] To be sure, all kinds of other factors and dynamics have contributed as well to the disappointments of these plans. But given the magnitude of the political and social hope vested in such plans, some reconsideration of the conventional wisdom that international order is built upon power politics and common interests seems warranted.

So if power politics and common interests are not sources, but factors, what *are* the sources of international order? From where does the shared international knowledge that signifies power politics and common interests come? I propose that one source of international order is international identity. Broadly speaking, identity refers to the cognitive, sociological, emotional, and other nontangible bonds among states that constitute their roles in relation to one another and so endows states with a self-definition or concept (Ashmore and Jussim 1997, 7). In this way, international identities amount to knowledge shared among states—intersubjective knowledge—about their situation relative to each other. States can develop any variety of identities with each other, ranging from collective knowledge of positive self-other bonds (friends) to collective knowledge of negative self-other bonds (enemies) (Wendt 1999). But identities are never fixed or finished. Rather than a condition, identity is a relationship that is *always in process,* whether that means emerging, evolving, or breaking down (Connolly 1991). Crucially, whenever states are collectively involved in the process of an international identity (no matter what its content), they are also collectively implicated in an international order. After all, intersubjective meanings about one another situate states so they know what to expect from one another. It follows that where disorder exists, the emergence of an identity would replace an unstable and uncertain environment with precisely the kind of shared epistemological backdrop from which stable expectations and behaviors are forged. International identity, in short, is sufficient for international order; it is what enables states to make sense of contributing factors like power politics and shared interests.

Quite a bit is at stake in the argument that international identity, or more exactly, the identity process (I use the two interchangeably), is a source of international order.[8] Inasmuch as it is borne out, this uncovery would demand an identity turn along a number of dimensions of conventional wisdom about international order. Take IR theory: If identity is a source of international order, then IR scholars are beckoned to integrate their theories of the tangible world of material power and interests with more ideational theories. After all, if identity is a source of international order, then it follows that those international orders, that were previously thought to be founded on material power politics and common interests, are more fundamentally rooted in the stable expectations and behaviors constituted by international identities and the epistemological orders engendered in them. As such, theorizing those identities—and all of the ideational processes they entail—is crucial to more enlightened accounts of international order.

An identity turn would also be called for in the study of international history, particularly in the form of revisionist readings of key orders and systems. For instance, an identity-as-source approach to international order gives rise to a rather different view of the Cold War than does a traditional power and interests approach. For instance, it suggests that the mutually assured destruction (MAD) order during the Cold War was not borne of nuclear arms, per se, but of the enmity between the Soviet Union and United States. That enmity constituted stable expectations among both sides that the other would actually *use* its nuclear weapons, thus demanding appropriate defense preparation (Campbell 1992). Certainly the nuclear weapon itself was the defining factor in producing the particular characteristics of that defense preparation. For example, it specified that states could stably expect each other to seek to maintain second-strike capability. But the very meaning of the nuclear weapon as a threatening artifact derived not from the weapon itself or even its distribution—after all, asymmetrical distributions often fail to engender any perception of threat, no less arms races, as for instance with the U.S. and Britain. Rather, the meaning of that weapon as threatening was constituted by identity, and the United States and Soviet Union shared knowledge of each other as enemies. Similarly, one might reread the breakdown of that order not as a product of power imbalances and dominance, but of transformations in the identity of enmity. Applying this type of identity-first analysis to other orders as well would likely prompt some productive rethinking of international history.

Finally, recognizing identity as a source of international order puts quite a different spin on the how-to of getting from fantasy to reality. Crafting international order becomes less about wielding power politics or constructing common interest regimes, per se, than about spreading an appropriate identity for engendering the desired reaction to different tangible stimuli.[9] For Bush, whose fantasy appears to be an international order organized in the likeness of American values and policed through American military power, the practical implication of an identity turn is that he ought to implement policies designed to engender a collective knowledge structure among states in which all understand that none are immune from American military power. American military might must be signified as universally threatening. This could be accomplished, for instance, by constructing the United States as a cool, distant, and indiscriminate unilateralist, one whose military power would be brought to bear even on its closest allies if they were diverging from American values. Such internationally shared knowledge might even make power politics a more credible threat to terrorists by signaling that there really is *no* safe hiding place from an American strike, even within the borders of countries that are American allies.[10] Of course, this means that the Bush administration has to put a stop to its tendency to toggle back and forth between imagery of the United States as a ruthless unilateralist and as a multilateral team player.[11] Only the former is likely to engender the kind of fear among other states that would be necessary to sustain the material power-based, American-centered international order about which Bush fantasizes.

Different advice would need to be offered to the Chinese leadership who perceive the Chinese national interest as served by a multipolar international order in which power is dispersed among great powers like China, Russia, India, and the United States. In this case, one might advise the leadership to implement policies designed to engender a collective knowledge structure among states that they all share an interest in cooperating to preserve their own spheres of influence. It likely requires some kind of international identity in which states perceive themselves as rival, but not necessarily predatory, competitors. If so, it seems that currently the Chinese are cultivating the wrong knowledge structures. On the one hand, they are engaging in the construction of a friendship with Russia (rather than competitive rivalry), while on the other, they are muddling through with the United States, interspersing a productive logic of rivalry with a counterproductive logic of hostility.[12] An adviser informed by an identity turn might counsel the Chinese leadership that crafting the international multipolar order about which they fantasize will be served well by neither friendship nor hostility. Its identity-cultivating strategies ought to be restructured.

Theorizing Identity

An identity turn promises dramatic change in how scholars and practitioners understand international order. But the extent to which such a turn is called for depends entirely on whether international identity can be shown to be a source of international order. Making this case then—that identity is sufficient to impose order upon disorder—constitutes the bulk of this book. Primarily, this entails developing and presenting a theory of identity that is nuanced enough to illuminate the dynamics of the international identity-international order connection; one transparent enough to allow investigation into the assertion of "sourceness." There are many readily available starting points in IR. Indeed, in recent years, various IR scholars have sought to demonstrate how identity matters for international politics by analyzing an array of puzzles through the lens of identity. For instance, the discipline has seen the application of primordialist approaches to identity to questions of war and conflict (Huntington 1996), of social identity theory to questions of reputation and weapons acquisition (Mercer 1995; Hymans 2000), of rational choice approaches to identity to questions of ethnic violence (Fearon and Laitin 2000), and of social constructivist approaches to identity to questions surrounding anarchy, sovereignty, and the constitution of the modern states system (Wendt 1992; Weber 1995; Ruggie 1998; Reus-Smit 1999; Philpot 2001).[13]

While any of these could prove useful as a starting point for theorizing the connection between identity and international order, the social constructivist approach is particularly appropriate when it comes to discerning the dynamics that produce stable, shared expectations and behaviors among states. Advanced most comprehensively by Alexander Wendt (1999), constructivism (a term I use in the conventional rather than the technical sense)** holds that international identity amounts to shared knowledge structures among states regarding their relationships to one another. These knowledge structures are produced through repeated interaction and social learning and have productive or constitutive effects for state behavior and international outcomes. Because of the constructivist emphasis on the link between intersubjective knowledge and state behavior, this conceptualization of identity lends itself directly to exploring the connections between epistemological orders among states and international order.

But the constructivist view of identity also has important limitations when it comes to exploring international identity as a source of international order. It begins by recognizing that identities are not natural facts, but social constructions that are always in process. Accordingly, the primary burden of the theory is to model when and how the intersubjective meanings that constitute an identity are formed and maintained among states, and then how that identity matters for outcomes. In formulating that account, however, constructivism adopts an assumption of stability as a necessary condition of the environment in which identities are formed and maintained. Put a bit differently, constructivism theorizes about international identity as though it

---

**In IR, the term "constructivism" is semantically fraught. Though the term technically refers to any theory that begins with the assumption that identities are not natural facts, the convention in IR has been to associate this term with one theoretical subset in particular—the subset I discuss here. Moreover, while this subset is not internally monolithic, nor is Wendt's the only formulation, there are basic similarities among them that warrant grouping the variety together for heuristic purposes. I address this more fully in Chapter 2.

develops only in situations where states *already* share an epistemological order, that is, where they are *already mutually oriented* toward each other's "nature" or "essence" (Wendt 1996; Adler and Barnett 1998). In this way, the constructivist model of identity takes for granted what Ann Swidler has called a socially *settled* time of shared basic truths (Swidler 1986).

The problem (aside from assuming part of that which is allegedly being explained) is that by assuming a socially settled foundation, the constructivist model leaves no analytic leverage for thinking about how international identities may form or persist during international crises. This is noteworthy because international crises amount to moments of disorder among states. They amount to moments in which shared expectations and behaviors cease to be shared. Crises are particular events that, for a variety of contextual, socially constructed reasons, reverberate on interstate relations in such a way that prior formal and informal understandings among states are, if not altogether erased, obscured to the point that they are inaccessible as foundations for decision making and behavior (Guthrie 1935). In this way, crises are more than just disagreements, conflicts, or arguments. They are socially *unsettled* times.*** Because they are such times of disorder, they provide an exceptional opportunity for exploring the process by which order is imposed upon disorder, for interrogating how that process works and, in turn, for discerning whether and in what capacity identity is entailed in that process. Crises provide a clear window from which to look closely into the sourceness of international identity for international order.

But when it comes to the relationship among crises, identity, and the imposition of order, the constructivist model of identity is actually more obfuscating than illuminating. In fact, it counsels by the requirement of settledness that identity has nothing to do with the resolution of crises; that it cannot. For constructivism, the identity-formation and maintenance process takes place only against the backdrop of settled social facts, so it logically follows that when those social facts are unsettled—during crises— identity formation and maintenance cannot occur. Thus, if one proceeds from the constructivist model, the only logical conclusion is that international identity cannot be a source of international order. It makes no sense

---

***This is not to say that crises must disrupt *all the* shared understandings among states to produce an unsettled or disorderly time, although conceivably they can, and there are likely empirical instances in which they have. Rather disorder and unsettledness can be wrought within certain modules of shared meanings among states without necessarily unsettling others. Whether or not crises in one clump of shared meanings wreaks unsettledness in another depends on the degree to which they are interrelated and overlapping. I discuss this in Chapter 2.

to think that identity could be sufficient to impose order upon disorder if identity cannot even exist during moments of disorder.

Given that constructivism is allegedly the most promising identity model for probing the identity-order connection, its blind spot toward unsettled times is discouraging. One need not be a skeptic about identity to want to throw up one's hands and conclude that the effort of exploring an identity turn ought to be abandoned, perhaps even in favor of deeper investigation into power politics and common interests. However, that would surely prove unsatisfying. Years of exploration into power politics and common interests have still only resulted in incomplete models of international order that suffer logical and empirical ellipses (see Chapter 2). At the least, this suggests that there must be more to the story than researchers can gain access to through continued attention to those material factors.

Moreover, as Wendt himself notes, it simply seems incorrect to maintain that international identities break down during international crises. Empirically speaking, identities do seem relatively stable, or at least many of them seem able to withstand crises. Thus, a second response, and that which constructivists themselves seem to have adopted, is to resist the implied position of their own theoretic apparatus that identities cannot survive during crises. In this spirit Wendt, in a near-repudiation of the logic of his own constructivist apparatus, has argued that identities *can* survive crises because they are extricable at some level from the processes from whence they are constituted. They are social constructions, he maintains, but not "all the way down." Just *almost* all the way down (Wendt 1999). Thus, during crises, when the constitutive processes of identities are unsettled, identities can still persist.[14] Unfortunately, this "almost all the way down" approach amounts to an ontological assumption about the fundamental corporality of state identity, a move which does not shed much light on the process by which order is imposed upon disorder. As critics note, Wendt's move really just posits another layer of unexplained settledness that allegedly kicks in during crises. Not only does this logic sit in awkward tension with his own constructivism, but it is a move that ends up bracketing or "black boxing" the very questions it is intended to answer (Doty 2000; Behnke 2001; Zehfuss 2001). It leaves the investigation into the sourceness of international identity for international order no further along.

Yet there is a third response, the tack I take here, which is to abandon the assumption of settledness as a precondition for the formation and maintenance of identity. This seemingly small theoretic move produces considerable improvement in the analytic tools available for investigating the identity-order connection. Specifically, building on the significant insights of constructivism while relaxing its restrictive conditions yields a *post-constructivist* model of identity. The model is "post" in a few regards. First, it is post because in relaxing the assumption of a settled backdrop for identity formation and maintenance, this model embraces a *post*structuralist "ontology", one that refuses a corporate account of state identity. (Though, as I argue later, this post account is also distinct in certain ways from poststructuralist theories of IR.) Second, it is post because this model marks a sort of second generation of constructivist identity theory, distinguished from the first generation by its ability to inquire into the fate of identity during times of crisis. Finally, this model is post because its theoretic apparatus leads to different conclusions than implied by the extant version of constructivism about the sourceness of international identity for international order. In contrast to that variant, the postconstructivist model indicates that international identity can well be a source of international order, sufficient to impose order upon disorder.

The starting point for this postconstructivist account of international order is that, although a settled foundation may facilitate the ease with which international identities can be constructed and maintained, settledness is not required.[15] To ground this logic, I draw on the poststructuralist linguistic and political insights of Jean François Lyotard, which I develop into an account of international identities as power-laden narrative constructs. Narrative is a particular process of representation through which an author tells events. Narratives, as such, are under the control of their authors; they are owned processes (Lyotard 1988; Cobley 2001, 6). On Lyotard's view, it is narrative and narrative alone that constitutes identity; the entirety of what makes international identity real is the shared stories among the people who represent or speak on behalf of states about who they are in the world and who they are in relation to one another. Because narrative is what makes an identity real, it follows that an identity is only as enduring as its constitutive narrative is stable, intersubjectively held, and legitimate among those who have been written explicitly in or out as members. In this way, an identity's narrative is the key to discerning the integrity of an identity, as well as to evaluating the relationship between identity and order.

But precisely because identity is nothing but narrative, it lasts only as long as authors keep authoring it, sharing it with others, and collectively believing in it. And yet, there is no particular reason they need to do so. After all, on this view identities are not externally determined by some truth about the character of a self-other relationship. Nor are they passively constructed through repeated social interactions. Rather, identities are the product of *authors* who *choose* to inscribe the narratives that form and maintain them. Authors acquire the will or agency to make such choices through their own *subjectivity*, understood as the extant complex of multiple, specific, and often interconnected identity narratives that constitute a being's overriding or encompassing sense of Self. Subjectivity or Self, thus, is the product of a being's multiple intersubjectively constituted self-other relations. Importantly, then, in the event that one (or more) of the particular identities that constitutes an author's Self ceases to resonate with the rest of the self-other narratives in that complex, an author may choose to no longer narrate the offending identity. In fact, an author may even feel the dissonance wrought within his subjectivity so acutely that he needs to openly narrate dissent from the offensive identity. When an author does dissent from one of his identities in this way, the effect is to challenge, and sometimes altogether dissolve, the logic of that identity narrative, not just for the dissident, but for all the others who share that identity with him. In other words, dissent can unravel shared self and other knowledge; it can dissolve identity. When it does, the order engendered by that knowledge dissolves into disorder.

Significantly, international crises are one class of events that can create dissonance within states' Selves, provoking those who author on behalf of states to dissent from and dissolve the offending identity narratives. After all, international crises are defined by the fact that they provoke deep-seated rifts among states, in the process offering ample fuel for authors to construct dissenting narratives. To the extent that authors find resonance with the dissident opportunities entailed by a crisis, they will narrate their rebellion, thus dissolving the status quo narrative and interrupting the process of identity and the "sharedness" of self-other knowledge.[16] So along with the (denied and repudiated) constructivist position, but for different reasons, I argue that identities *do* break down during crises.

Yet, and significantly, in this postconstructivist account the dissolution of identity during a crisis does not logically rule it out as a source of order, as it does in the constructivist account, precisely because in this model, identity is *not dependent* on settled foundations for its constitution. Identity can (if authors so choose) be *re-produced* in the midst of a crisis; from its dissolved state, it can be produced all over again as if starting from scratch.[17]

So how does re-production happen? It is in this regard that the power-laden aspect of narrative becomes important. As Lyotard relentlessly emphasizes, narrative is not just about authors telling events, it is also about authors constructing those very events as they tell them. In this way, narrative creates "reality." Because it does, narrative—indeed, all language—expresses power. There are a variety of different kinds of language-power[18] that authors might wield in the telling of their narratives, and precisely because authors own their decisions about what and how to narrate, they can choose which forms to wield in their narrative. For instance, they may choose to narrate with authoritative language-power, persuasive language-power, or a whole host of other forms. But during crises, I argue, former members of a now-dissolved identity may well choose to wield the strongest type of language-power, *representational force*, in an effort to re-produce the status quo narrative. Representational force is expressed through the content and structure of the language that authors deploy in their narratives. It is clear when an author has used representational force because unlike any other form of language-power—authority, persuasion, attraction, manipulation, or so on—representational force inscribes a blunt, self-interested, and nonnegotiable threat to its listeners via its narrative. More specifically, representational force constructs a challenge so grave to a victim's subjectivity that the victim ends up trapped in a position of either abandoning his dissent and complying with the demands of the force-wielder or suffering subjective death. Such a choice really confronts the victim as a "nonchoice." In this way, representational force works like a linguistic "gun" to the head. It does not allow argument, dialogue, bargaining, or other forms of communicative exchange. Representational force is a do-or-die command.

When deployed to repair a dissolved identity, representational force re-produces the process through which self-other knowledge is shared. But its effects go beyond repairing dissolved epistemological orders. Because it is forceful and mortally threatening to its victims, representational force *fastens* or cements the identity, so that members have no choice but to keep on instantiating that same status quo narrative over and again for as long as the threat lodged at them through representational force remains compelling. This means that representational force leaves its victims no choice but to *live the experience* of the re-produced identity. Therefore, representational force not only re-produces the epistemological order, but also the expectations and behaviors, and so the international order, that derive from them. Identity, as such, can impose order upon disorder; it can be a source of order. But at least during crises, it does so through force. It *forces order*.

It is in this focus on identity as an agent-driven narrative-in-process infused with language-power that postconstructivism moves beyond constructivism.[19] Constructivism begins with a settled foundation, layered over with socially constructed identities that have somehow been passively produced through repeated interactions. The postconstructivist account begins and ends with narratives and their authors. The emphasis on narrative and power, and the agency of authors to wield both, is what enables postconstructivism to explore the sourceness of identity where constructivism simply falls silent.

[margin handwritten note: representational force versus norm entrepreneur)]

It is also precisely in this emphasis on narrative and power, however, that postconstructivism begins to seem indistinguishable from the poststructuralist approach that informs it. Indeed, all the key theoretical moves in this account are borrowed from Lyotard, a central figure in poststructuralism. But there is at least one crucial feature of postconstructivism that merits the distinct appellation. Whereas poststructuralists in IR have primarily used insights about narrative and power to facilitate genealogical or deconstructive analyses of political practices in the international domain or the study of IR itself (for instance Ashley 1988; Walker 1990; Campbell 1992), in this study I use those same insights to self-consciously construct a theory. This is significant because theory, no matter how contextualized and sensitive to process, is anathema to poststructuralist thinkers. Indeed, the hallmark of the poststructuralist approach to politics—popularized by Lyotard himself (1979) among others[20]—is relentless skepticism toward grand narratives because they "posture as value-free mechanism(s) for resolving . . . aporias, ambiguities, and ironies" (Agger 1992:94). In light of this, any attempt to write theory, no less to discern the source of order through a criteria of sufficiency, is sure to be seen as complicit in camouflaging the world's elusiveness.

This is why I signify this argument as postconstructivist: I am at once an advocate of theory building and entirely sympathetic to the importance of deconstructing grand narratives. After all, theory is needed to make sense of the world, but deconstruction is needed to keep theory from becoming ossified. By distinguishing the argument presented here from poststructuralism, I hope to create the theoretical room for using poststructuralist tools to openly produce new grand narratives while still preserving the logic of the deconstructive, critical project normally associated with poststructuralism.

Forcing Order During the Suez Crisis

The bottom line of the postconstructivist model of identity is that (the process of) identity *can* provide the shared knowledge sufficient to impose international order upon disorder. In turn, an identity-informed reconsideration of the study of international order—from its theory to its history to the policies statesmen use in the effort to order international politics—is vital. This raises a number of key questions. For instance, how do statesmen and politicians actually use representational force in their narrative exchanges, and how effective is it for re-producing the relevant narratives of international identity during moments of disorder or crises? What does representational force look like anyway? And, finally, who wields representational force to construct an international identity during the midst of an international crisis and why?

These are all questions that I pursue through a detailed analysis of the internal dynamics of the Anglo-American order during the Suez Crisis. In particular, I explore how the longstanding international order enjoyed between the United States. and Britain broke down into disorder during the Suez Crisis, but was quickly repaired. By focusing on this passage from order to disorder and back to order, I develop an empirically contextualized and situated postconstructivist model of international identity and its relationship to international order.

For a variety of reasons, the Anglo-American international order during the Suez Crisis provides an extraordinarily useful foil for developing and grounding a postconstructivist model of the international identity-order connection. First, the United States and Britain have long enjoyed a unique international order with one another. In particular, they share a normative expectation and behavioral prohibition on threats or use of physical force when it comes to resolving conflict with one another. Such regimes of physical nonviolence are what Karl Deutsch refers to as security communities. And as Emanuel Adler and Michael Barnett have persuasively argued, these types of international orders exist *only* among states that share a particular type of international identity (Deutsch et al. 1957; Adler and Barnett 1998).[21] As characterized by Adler and Barnett, that identity, "we-ness," exists when states share values, trust, and a sense of common fate (especially in the domain of security). In practice then, we-ness looks rather like the friendship end of the spectrum of international identities; it involves an "extension between [s]elf and [o]ther" (Wendt 1996, 386). It is precisely because of these affective bonds—this particular self-other relationship—that states can mutually and reliably expect nonviolence. In this way, security communities provide a clear illustration of the theoretic logic by which identity is a source of international order.

What is more, security communities offer a particularly useful foil because they are relatively uncontroversial as empirical examples of this theoretic logic. Of course the argument of this study, and of any identity turn it may imply, is that international identity can be a source of *any* type of international order. But the fact remains that beyond security communities, most scholars are unwilling to entertain identity as a source of international order (Mearsheimer 1995). For instance, most scholars still maintain that the balance-of-power order finds its source in material power (Schweller 2001). But in the case of the security community, the idea that identity somehow does matter in *some way* has been more readily accepted, especially because research increasingly has demonstrated how hard it is to talk about these regimes at all without reference to we-ness (Williams 2001; Kuhonta 2002). As a result, less theoretic ground clearing is required to legitimize further interrogation into the sourceness of identity in the case of the security community than it would in, say, the balance of power. The fact that this makes the security community an "easy case" does not undermine its utility. Understanding the operative principles among representational force, identity, and order in the more obvious cases is likely to prove helpful in discerning these principles at work in subtle, and therefore more difficult, instances.

Given that security communities provide a useful international order from which to perform an identity analysis, the Anglo-American security community is particularly so. The Anglo-American relationship is the ultimate instance of a security community. For one, the claim that the United States and Britain experience a shared we-ness identity is one that rests on an unusually well-documented body of evidence. Decades of analysis of an abundance of primary archival resources reveal that British and American leaders have, since World War II, regularly and openly represented their relationship to each other as one predicated on shared ideals, values, cultures, affection, trust, fate, and friendship.[22] In stark contrast to their mutually suspicious and hostile nineteenth-century relations, by 1945 Anglo-American we-ness had even been given a life of its own in the nickname coined by Winston Churchill—"The Special Relationship." Importantly, the Special Relationship—the narrative of which still exists today—and the shared knowledge of friendship that constitutes it, is regularly invoked by British and American policymakers when considering the acceptability of various behaviors toward each other, including military force (Bowie and Immerman 1998; Danchev 1998). In short, it is relatively clear that during socially settled times, we-ness works as theorized in the Anglo-American case.

But what about during unsettled times or crises? In this regard, there is yet another benefit of analyzing the identity-order connection through the lens of a security community. In the case of this form of international order, it is relatively easy to determine empirically when stable expectations and behaviors have broken down, and thus it is possible to pinpoint crises historically. This is not the case with all international orders. As a point of comparison, consider the balance of power order: In that regime violence, imbalances, and shifts in power polarity are theoretically reasoned to be part of the stable expectations and behaviors that constitute order. The problem is that given the breadth of such practices, virtually any expectation among states and any behavior in which they might engage can be interpreted as orderly. This raises an intractable question about when disorder actually exists, and so augments the conceptual problems surrounding the decision of which historical moments are relevant for exploring the question of how order is imposed on disorder.

In contrast, the security community involves clearly specified criteria for when order has broken down. Because the regime can be said to exist only when we-ness constitutes a normative prohibition on threats or use of physical violence, then it follows that when either we-ness has broken down or one party has threatened or used violence with another, the security community order can be said to have broken down into disorder. While it may not be long before a new order with new expectations emerges through some other identity or alternative source, it remains the case that, by definition, the security community must have broken down. In turn, *something* must happen between the end of the security community order and the inception of the next regime of order. It is in that gap that a window of disorder worthy of examination can be discerned, and through which it becomes possible to explore how order is imposed upon disorder.

The Suez Crisis provides one such window of disorder between the United States and Britain. During that 1956 crisis, the Anglo-American security community order broke down. The incident began when the British and Americans found themselves in bitter disagreement over how to handle Egyptian President Nasser's nationalization of the Suez Canal. In fact, the differences between the two went so deep that the British secretly colluded with the French and Israelis to invade Egypt even as it denied these actions to the United States. The result was mutual disaffection of unparalleled proportions between the British and Americans. The Americans felt that the British had behaved in a deceitful and bellicose manner, while the British felt the Americans, in their failure to support British interests, had betrayed them. Ultimately, the disaffection became so intense that both sides publicly negated the Anglo-American we identity; they repudiated the Special Relationship. It produced nothing short of a complete break in the narrative of their identity; an erasure of the narrative of specialness (Risse-Kappen 1995). According to the logic of a security community, then, that particular form of order failed. Because the we-ness identity was disrupted, there was no longer a basis from which to reliably expect nonviolence from one another. In fact, as then Secretary of State John Foster Dulles was quick to note, it was a time of stark uncertainty about what to expect from one another.[23] It was a time of disorder.

As a window of disorder in the previously orderly Anglo-American relationship, the Suez Crisis is particularly interesting because it was resolved between the United States and Britain without even the threat of violence. In other words, it was resolved in a manner completely consistent with the demands of security community even though we-ness, reliable expectations for nonviolence, and so the security community itself had broken down. The question, and one that persists unanswered by political scientists, is why? Consider the circumstances. As the Americans perceived it, the stakes of the situation were dreadfully high, both in terms of the larger Cold War context and in terms of their own wounded ego vis-à-vis their duplicitous allies. In order to lower the stakes, the Americans desperately wanted the British and French to withdraw from the Canal Zone, and to do so immediately. But the two resisted with vigor; they stalled and even outright lied about their intentions. And yet the United States never threatened their fallen allies with their considerable military might. Instead, the United States relied on sanctions and diplomatic pressure. In fact, military force was never even discussed as an option. Given the lack of a security community to constrain such a decision, and the increasingly antagonistic Anglo-American identity, it is more than a little bit hard to understand why.

Some have sought to resolve the puzzle of this outcome by suggesting that force just did not make sense from a cost-benefit perspective; domestic interests, the Cold War context, and the anticipated efficacy of diplomacy and sanctions made this so (Neustadt 1970; Parmar 1995). But under scrutiny, none of these accounts offer much explanatory power. They regularly fail in the face of their own logical lapses, empirical oversights, or tendency to smuggle in extratheoretical references to the normative commitments of the Anglo-American friendship, in order to buttress the account of nonviolence (Bartlett 1992; Risse-Kappen 1995; Bially Mattern 2003). In other words, such accounts smuggle in precisely the Anglo-American we-ness that was, by all accounts, defunct. The question thus remains, why nonviolence? Why this outcome that was coherent with the prior Anglo-American order when that order had dissolved?

The answer, I suggest, is that the old security community order was forced back upon disorder. Drawing on the postconstructivist insights about identity, I theorize that the nonviolent outcome between the United States and Britain in Suez can be linked to a process through which Anglo-American we-ness was quickly and effectively re-produced through campaigns of representational force waged by statesmen and diplomats on both sides of the Atlantic. As the identity was re-produced, so too were the norms and behaviors of nonviolence that followed it—that is, the security community. In this way, the nonviolent outcome of the Suez Crisis was indeed made possible by the security community, and as a form of order, that security community did have its source in identity. But the identity itself was not just remembered or accidentally relearned through repeated Anglo-American interaction (as a constructivist model would hold). It was forcefully fastened through representational force. The security community was actively, intentionally, and forcefully ordered by statesmen.

In order to empirically illustrate this process, I develop a discourse-analytic method for discerning the role of representational force in re-producing the Special Relationship and the Anglo-American order during the Suez Crisis. This method locates representational force in the structure of the language that statesmen and politicians from both countries used in their communication with each other, and it specifies how to determine the effectiveness of those linguistic practices for actually fastening the identity. Drawing on primary historical documents from the Suez Crisis, I show that after the Anglo-American identity dissolved, key actors on both sides of the Atlantic re-produced it forcefully. They deployed representational force systematically in a way that eradicated each side's dissent from the Anglo-American friendship, thus fastening the Anglo-American collective we and, in the process, forcing the security community order back upon the two countries.

Of course, this finding begs a final question: Why would they do such a thing? Why would the same British and American leaders who felt so disaffected with one another that they repudiated the Special Relationship then feel compelled to repair it? Moreover, why did they need to use a forceful form of language-power to do so? In considering these issues, I return once again to the logic of identity as a narrative construct, specifically highlighting that subjectivity (Self) is a product of a states' overlapping identities (narratives of self-other). Drawing on the British and American history of that period, I demonstrate how the Self of each (Britain and the United States) was constituted of various additional identities, the narratives of which were interconnected with, and so in important part dependent upon, the narrative of the Anglo-American international identity (the Special Relationship). Thus, for both sides, the demise of the latter had an unexpected and unpleasant destabilizing domino effect on their entire subjectivity. For each, preserving their Self meant sustaining the narrative of the Special Relationship. The result was a situation in which both countries had an interest (related to subjectivity, not to materiality) in reconstituting the Special Relationship.

However, things were further complicated because beyond the aspects of British and American Self that were dependent on the Special Relationship, there were also other identity narratives constitutive of the British and American Selves that pitted the two countries against each other in a competition for the right to claim leadership of the West in the context of the East/West struggle and the Cold War. Thus, for exactly the same reason that each had an interest (subjective Self-preservation) in re-producing the Special Relationship that had been destroyed, each side also had an interest in forcing the other side to accept blame for the Suez debacle. Thus, for reasons of subjectivity, actualized as the stability of the narratives that constituted their Selves, each side had to find a way to *force* the other to succumb to its version of the Suez story in a way that would enable the repair of the Special Relationship. More benign forms of language-power would not do, because they could fail to persuade the other to succumb.

The result was that key British and American authors each turned to representational force. Each used campaigns of representational force in an attempt to settle the disputes over the Suez Crisis in a way that reinforced the integrity of their competitive identities as leaders of the West, while at the same time repairing the Special Relationship. While each side was successful to varying degrees at the former goal (the British obviously lost their bid to legitimately lay claim to being *the* leader of the West), the reproduction of we-ness was an unmitigated success. As we-ness was fastened, nonviolent order was imposed upon disorder. Identity—re-produced and back in process as a lived Anglo-American experience—provided the source of order.

Theoretical Twists, Historical Revisions, and Practical Cautions

The case of the Anglo-American international order during the Suez Crisis illustrates that international identity *can* be a source of international order. While this says nothing about *the extent* to which this logic travels to other cases, other types of identities, or other forms of order, the implications are nevertheless significant. For one, it counsels that, to some degree, an identity turn *is* in order across various dimensions of the study of international order after all. Even more, it demands a rethinking of the character of that identity turn in light of language-power, and especially representational force. Indeed, an identity turn, animated by a postconstructivist model of identity, implies some interesting theoretical twists, historical revisions, and practical cautions beyond what seemed called for at the first pass.

Revisit for a moment the theoretical implications of an identity turn. Because identity is a source of order, a shift toward ideational theories and frameworks for thinking about international order seems called for.

ıowever, also called for is some rethinking of what it means to shift toward ideas in theorizing about international politics. For instance, implied in the constructivist position is that to shift toward ideas—to put identity first— is to shift power and interests to a status of secondary importance, in the sense that they follow from identity. As Adler and Barnett note, it is a shift away from the realist imagery of power politics (Adler and Barnett 1998, 5). But inasmuch as the postconstructivist approach becomes a useful way to think about international order, putting ideas first hardly means putting power and interests second. Rather, identities *are constituted* of power and interests; that is, of language-power and actors' interests in the preservation of their subjectivity. To be sure, on the postconstructivist account, material power and interests do recede to a secondary status, derivative of identity. But nonmaterial power and interests become the very core of identity itself. In this way, the imagery of power politics does not recede at all; it just occurs on a discursive, subjective plane. It becomes a *power politics of identity*. In fact, this emphasis on power and interests suggests that realists, who emphasize precisely these same concepts though in a material form, may have much to talk about with scholars who conceptualize identity along postconstructivist lines. After all, as Machiavelli, Carr, and Morgenthau all noted in different words, there are important continuities between material power and language-power (Morgenthau 1951; Carr 1964; Machiavelli 1984). In this way, an identity turn in theory may be more a return to the realist roots of IR with a new perspective than a turn away from traditional thought. It may be a turn toward a realist-inspired constructivism.

The historical dimensions of an identity turn also take on a new hue when identity is read through a postconstructivist lens. Reconsider the Cold War story. The first pass at an identity-as-source approach to that order called for a focus on the shared self-other knowledge of enmity between the Soviet Union and United States. It implied a history that traced out how that shared knowledge made sense of various material realities over the course of Cold War history. A postconstructivist rereading would go deeper than this. The story would begin, not with the relationship between shared enmity and behavior but before that, with the production and re-production of that shared enmity over time among the relevant representative authors of the United States and Soviet Union. It would not simply link enmity to MAD or other expected Cold War behaviors, but would examine how authors inscribed, perpetuated, and legitimated their narratives of self and other in a way that made MAD seem natural. In fact, whereas most histories of the Cold War—including a constructivist approach—problematize periods of détente or rapprochement (how, they ask, was it possible for the United States and the Soviet Union to take the risk of cooperation, given their enmity and so the threatening nature of each others' power?), a postconstructivist lens problematizes the enduring persistence of the enmity identity and the MAD order to which it gave rise. From a postconstructivist perspective, the changes embodied in detente, rapprochement, and even the breakdown of the Cold War are altogether understandable in terms of authors' attempts to narrate differently the content of the self-other knowledge between the United States and the Soviet Union. The real puzzle revolves around the persistent enmity all those years. Why did they narrate the same identity for so long? In pursuing answers to that question, a postconstructivist history would focus not on the enduring material incentives, nor on the entrenched settledness of enmity identity, but on the types of language-power that authors were using to re-produce the U.S.-Soviet enmity. In this vein, it would be especially interesting to learn whether the U.S. and Soviet authors relied upon representational force—a power politics of identity—to fasten the reality of their hostile order against dissent and dissolution.

Finally, taking an identity turn through a postconstructivist lens counsels some rather different practical advice for statesmen interested in ordering international politics to their national advantage. It still counsels that getting from here (fantasy) to there (reality) may well be better served by shifting from plans centering around material power politics and common interests to plans that center around the spreading identity. But it articulates more specific strategies through which statesmen might do that. Rather than vaguely suggesting that leaders ought to disseminate appropriate knowledge structures to engender the identities that serve their vision, a postconstructivist account informs that spreading identity is an agent-driven and power-laden process of narration. In fact, it further advises that the kind of language-power that an author chooses to deploy in his different narratives makes the narrative more or less resistible to its target. Given that representational force is the most potent and irresistible, a postconstructivist identity turn suggests to statesmen who are eager to order international politics in their own vision, that their fantasies may be best served by forcing order. Ordering international politics, that is, may be best accomplished through a linguistic gun-to-the-head or do-or-die commands issued through power politics of identity.

In this last suggestion, though—that representational force may be the most efficacious way to concertedly order international politics—the normative implications of attempting such a project become impossible to avoid. The larger normative question is whether it is just or moral for states to seek such control over each other and the international system. But, as I argue in the conclusion, since there is no compelling account of how states can avoid the ethically perilous side effects of order, the question is really about the least immoral fantasies and the least immoral ways for states to pursue them. To be certain, it seems more normatively appealing to seek to design international order by spreading identity than it does by, say, relying on physical power politics. But it is worth taking seriously that spreading identity is not benign either. Language-power in general, though especially representational force, can wield a kind of an identity-oppression. It functions like a weapon of its own sort. This would be true even of the promotion of nice values abroad, like democracy and liberty. In advising policymakers on the logic and mechanisms through which identity constitutes international order, scholars ought to pay attention to these dynamics and explore their potential implications over the longer run.

Theorizing Identity

CHAPTER 2
Sources of Order

For the statesman who divines to order international politics in a manner that serves his country's perceived national interests, a first step must be to understand international order in general. What are the sources of international order? Why and how do states develop and sustain order? Such questions—which are often asked about social units at other levels of social life as well—have come to denote the problem of order. In the study and practice of international politics, the problem of order has been central: because states are, at least formally, sovereign and unaccountable to one another, the question of how organized patterns of interaction emerge is central to the discipline. And yet, in spite of the centrality of this problem to IR, there has been surprisingly little progress made when it comes to solving it. The *sources* of order—the key to understanding, building, and manipulating order—remain inaccessible.

The purpose of this chapter is to present an argument for why the sources of order remain elusive, and to offer identity as a way to move forward. I do so in four sections. In the first, I explore the very notion of international order so that in the second, I can evaluate extant accounts of its sources. I argue that the scholarship of IR has converged on two sources—power politics and common interests—but that neither are truly sources. Neither are sufficient to impose order upon disorder, and so both are better understood as factors that contribute to international order. Yet because scholars have largely failed to recognize the distinction between sources and factors, power politics and common interests have been regularly mistaken for the former. In turn, the study of international order has gotten stuck. In the third section, I heed the distinction between source and factor as I argue that international identity is a potential source of international order. In the final section, however, I argue that as promising as identity may seem for prompting progress in the study of international order, the current state of identity theory actually stands in the way of that possibility. Further theoretical development of identity is necessary before the character of the international identity–international order connection, and thus the demands of an identity turn, can be evaluated in any meaningful way.

What Is International Order?

What is international order? More precisely, what does this notion mean to the scholars who have been working to apprehend its sources? Interestingly —or perhaps curiously—there is little consensus on what exactly international order is and so what its sources are.[1] As Randall Schweller writes, the discussion about international order amounts to a "rigged game" in which scholars build into their definition the very conclusions they would like to reach about its sources. Thus, rather than a productive discussion, research on international order has become largely divided into seemingly incommensurable camps that amount to different ends on a conceptual spectrum. On one end of the spectrum are accounts that conceive of international order as the intentional, cooperative pursuit of shared values among states; on the other are accounts in which order can be unintentional, a mere stable pattern of behavior among states (Bull 1977; Waltz 1979). In other words, at one end are prosocial orders; at the other, "invisible-hand" orders that appear not to require sociality (Wrong 1994). Given this struggle over foundational concepts, one "definition of international order simply excludes from consideration . . . [the] competing models of international order" (Schweller 2001, 171, 169). The insights of one research effort appear irreconcilable with others such that the whole research program on international order has reached an impasse.

But upon closer inspection, these different definitions of international order are not so incompatible. After all, the different conceptions of international order lie on a *spectrum* of continuity with one another, not in dichotomous relationships. By mining the consistencies along the spectrum, it becomes possible to "un-rig" the game of conceptualizing and studying international order.[2] There are, in fact, quite a few consistencies. For instance, all along the spectrum it appears clear that the words "international order" refer specifically to a particular type of *relationship* among *states* (Agnew and Corbridge 1995). States are the units of international order, and what is orderly about them is found in their relationships with each other. International order, therefore, really means interstate order. There are many different types of orders in world politics, many of which are not exclusively constituted of the relationships among states and many of which may not directly involve states at all. For instance, orders can emerge out of the relationships between states and nonstate actors (for example, nongovernmental organizations, or NGOs) or through the relationships among different types of nonstate actors (for example, NGOs and multinational corporations). But as the phrase "international order" is used among IR scholars, it refers only to orders that emerge among states.[3]

A second consistency along the spectrum is that an international order *need not be universal*. In other words, it need not be populated by all states in the world. In fact, most scholars researching international order focus their investigations on particular orders formed among a specific subset of states at given historical points (Koh and Acharya 1998; Jervis 1985; Acharya 2001). Thus, while there may be, as Kenneth Waltz argues, one overarching international system, the structure of which gives rise to one universal international order, scholars also agree that there can simultaneously be multiple pockets of order among specific states within that larger order.

But it is perhaps a third strain of continuity along the conceptual spectrum of international order that is the most interesting: scholars explicitly or implicitly consider order a *normative good*. This is true not just among those who accept the normative foundations of social science (Rengger 2000), or among those who are expressly engaged in trying to theorize a better international order (Falk 1993); it is also true (even if inadvertently so) among those who maintain that they are sustaining a rigid positive or normative distinction (Rengger 2000). Some argue that order is valuable because it provides states with ontological moorings (Baumann 1992). Others argue that order is valuable because it creates a level of certainty that allows states to make decisions about how to best pursue their goals (McKinley and Little 1986). Still others concentrate on the benefits of international order for helping scholars and analysts explain and understand international politics (Waltz 1979). Regardless of precisely why it is considered valuable, international order is perceived to be a good thing.

What is interesting about this is that it gestures toward some crucial nugget of commonality regarding the nature of international order—at least as IR scholars understand and conceptualize it. In other words, something about order makes it good from all perspectives on the conceptual spectrum. So what is it? My suggestion is that the quality or characteristic that makes order so valuable to scholars, no matter where they fall on the conceptual spectrum, is that it engenders regularity and predictability. Order is valuable because it embodies stable, shared understandings among states about what they can expect from one another. After all, if order was not constituted of such a stability of shared understandings, none of the normative goods called up—ontological moorings, certainty, or analytic leverage—would emerge. Stability of interstate relations is required for any of these normative goods to develop. As such, it seems that no matter what else one builds into the definition of international order, one common defining characteristic all along the spectrum of conceptions is that order embodies stable shared understandings of expectations and behaviors among states.

Taken together, then, I suggest that there are at least three useful definitional uniformities along the conceptual spectrum of international order: that international order refers to the relationships among states; that international order need not be universal in membership; and that international order is characterized by stable, shared understandings of expectations and behaviors. These three uniformities can be synthesized into a conceptualization of international order as *a relationship among specific states that produces and reinforces shared understandings of expectations and behaviors with respect to one another.* This definition violates none of the requirements of any particular position on the spectrum, and so avoids the tendency to "rig" the game of studying international order in a way that feeds incommensurable models. In this manner, it is a definition that allows a way forward in thinking about the sources of international order.

Three analytic points that derive from this definition mark the direction forward and are therefore worth highlighting. First, because international order is conceived as a relationship based on shared understandings of expectations and behaviors, it follows that social knowledge among states must matter significantly with regards to international order. After all, in this definition, order is a function of interstate relationships and the kind of shared knowledge those relationships produce about expectations and accepted behaviors. In this way, sociality and learning are likely appreciable as components in the production of order. This insight applies just as much to "antisocial" orders like the Cold War bipolar balance of power or hegemonic orders, in which states share stable expectations of violence from one another at predictable junctures, as it does to "prosocial" orders like the Anglo-American security community, in which states share stable expectations of nonviolence. As Wrong puts it, just because the expectations and behaviors demanded by some order are antisocial in the colloquial sense does not mean that the order is antisocial in the sense of being devoid of social content or sociality (1994, 12).

The second useful point, related to the first, is that because order is defined in terms of stable shared expectations, the substantive *content* of particular expectations and behaviors is irrelevant. No particular shared expectations and behaviors are ruled out from becoming the "stuff" of an order. Order can be violent or nonviolent, competitive or cooperative, and anything in between.[4] The content does not matter as long as the expectations and behaviors are shared, and stably so. Certainly some forms of international order may be more appealing than others as ways of life. States implicated in security community orders, for instance, enjoy an order of nonviolent conflict resolution (Deutsch et al. 1957) whereas balance-of-power and hegemonic orders imply violence, threatened or actual. Indeed, in the balance-of-power order, war is held off only by regular practices of power politics among states (Waltz 1979), while in the hegemonic order, war is part of the orderly interactions in which states engage (Gilpin 1981).[5] Thus, compared to balances of power or hegemonies, security communities may be normatively appealing as a vision of the good life. However, in terms of their status as forms of international order, all three are equal. Violent or not, all three are relationships among states that produce shared stable expectations and behaviors.

The last analytic point arising from the conceptualization of order offered here regards the difference between order and disorder. Given that the content of allowable behaviors for international order is infinite—or at least irrelevant—there is a risk that the very category of order can become meaningless. And yet, it is possible to put a conceptual boundary on the phenomenon by recognizing the distinction between order and disorder. That boundary, in fact, is already implicit in the definition of international order. Because order is defined by an interstate relationship characterized by stable shared understandings about expectations and behaviors, international disorder can be defined as a situation in which the relationship among states degenerates (or fails to materialize) to such a degree that states are uncertain about what to think of one another or hold false, unshared expectations. In that case, confusion prevails and international order cannot exist (Agnew and Corbridge 1995, 16).

It is useful to note that while anarchy (a lack of formal authority) may facilitate disorder by making it harder for states to feel certain about their shared knowledge, there is no necessary reason that anarchy must be disorderly. Anarchy allows for both order and disorder. It is also noteworthy that just like order, disorder does not entail specific behaviors; its set of possible actualizations is infinite. For instance, even though violence is often associated with disorder, disorder can be nonviolent as well. After all, shared expectations and behaviors can be disrupted without giving way to violence. The same can be said of competitive interests. Even though disorder is commonly associated with competing and incommensurable state interests, this need not be the case. All that is necessary is that states be unsure or confused about the commensurability of their interests to the degree that a lack of shared understanding exists about how to engage one another. The key is that order rests upon shared understandings of expectations and behaviors, and disorder lacks them. Subsequently, an obvious question is what makes the difference between order and disorder.

Sources and Factors

To ask about the process through which disorder is transformed into order is to return to the question: What are the sources of order? There has been no shortage of works dedicated to discerning the sources of order, but those that have been traditionally revered among scholars and practitioners are faulty. The reason is that in performing their research and analysis, scholars of international order have overlooked an important distinction between *sources* of international order and *factors* that contribute to it. In fact, most have regularly mistaken sources for factors and so, in trying to discern what makes the difference between order and disorder, much of the extant scholarship has obscured rather than facilitated deeper understanding of international order (especially scholarship in the traditions of Bull 1977, Waltz 1979, and Keohane 1984). The models of order to which they give rise simply give weight to the wrong things.

To see this, consider the distinction between source and factor. A source is something (anything) that can turn an unstable relationship among states (that is, a relationship in which states are uncertain about what to expect from each other) into a stable one (one in which states develop shared understandings about what to expect from each other). Hence, sources are defined by their ability to impose order upon disorder. Contributing factors to international order, in contrast, do not impose order upon disorder because they are phenomena that cannot, on their own, cultivate stable, shared understandings among states where they were previously absent. As Patrick Jackson and Daniel Nexon formulate it, factors amount to the observable material and physical phenomena one sees in the world while sources are the stuff that produce the webs of underlying relations that give meaning to those phenomena (shared understandings, in this case). Therefore, factors are foils for enacting shared understandings among states in the form of particular behaviors and expectations. But without the shared understandings produced by sources, the significance of particular factors, and so the expectations and behaviors they should trigger, would be unintelligible to states (Jackson and Nexon 1999, 315).

A second way to think about the different functions of sources and factors for international order is that sources are *causally sufficient* for order while factors are not. Causal sufficiency requires that wherever the "something" exists, so should the outcome in question (international order, in this case). Something fails the test of sufficiency if it can exist in the absence of the outcome (Ragin 2000, 90–6). By definition, a source accounts for the difference between order and disorder and is therefore sufficient.

In contrast, given that a factor requires a source if it is to contribute to international order, it is by definition *insufficient* to produce international order. In other words, when a factor is untouched or left out by the social signifying effects of shared meanings (and whatever their source is), it is unintelligible to states in terms of its relevance to their international relationships. So that factor cannot make the difference between order and disorder—it must be insufficient for international order. Importantly though, insufficiency does not mean irrelevance; it simply means that with respect to international order, a factor's contribution depends on the presence of something prior—shared understandings among states and whatever it is that gives rise to those.

Thinking about the process by which international order emerges in terms of factors and sources, causal sufficiency and insufficiency, amounts to a shift in the mode of inquiry into international order. For one, in contrast to widely accepted and emulated research methods in IR, this logic of sufficiency does not aspire to discern Hempelian-covering laws in which particular independent and dependent variables are found to exist in some universally applicable relationship to one another (Hempel 1966; King, Keohane, and Verba 1994). The latter, which reflects a positivist approach to causality, focuses on *causation,* meaning an exact (though nuanced) connective device between ontologically distinct and epistemologically self-evident variables. In contrast, the sufficiency approach recognizes that beyond such positivist causality there are other forms of causality as well. For instance, while the logic of sufficiency can help tap into positivist causative relationships between variables,[6] it is also sensitive to *constitutive* forms of causality. Often associated with postpositivism, constitutive forms of causality focus on "whole/part relationships"—the whole and parts of an object of study are not taken as ontologically distinct and self-evident variables, but rather each is only interpretable in relation to the others (Pietroski 2000, 6).

The benefits of adopting an open-ended approach to causality—that is, one that is indifferent toward whether it has captured constitutive or causative forms of causality—is best appreciated in light of what philosopher of science Peter Kosso calls the "risky business" of reading the book of nature. By this, Kosso means that it is presumptuous to claim to have "found" a true instance of some particular kind of causality (Kosso 1992, 186). The problem is that the book of nature, or in this case, the book of international politics, does not reveal itself easily even through sophisticated modes of inquiry. The logic of sufficiency allows us to recognize productive relationships in the social world without imposing on those relationships a particular and possibly ill-suited narrative of causative versus constitutive causality or positivism versus postpositivism. Thinking in terms of sufficiency, sources, and factors allows us to explore the underlying processes of international order without falling prey to the dogmatic presumptions of science.

But thinking about international order through the logic of sufficiency, sources, and factors is not an approach that IR scholarship has recognized, much less internalized. In fact, IR scholars have long used the phrase "source" to refer to what, by the logic of sufficiency, must be factors. "Source" has been used to signify material, tangible things or conditions rather than to designate the processes that give rise to shared understandings among states. Kenneth Boulding offers a case in point. According to Anatol Rapoport, Boulding contends that there are really only two viable sources of international order: power politics and common interests.[7] Yet both power politics and common interest are precisely the kinds of things that, on their own, *cannot* inform stable shared expectations and behaviors. Their significance among states is not self-evident without a prior shared, publicly recognized meaning among states—a prior epistemological order. As such, both power politics and common interests are insufficient for international order; likewise, neither of these are sources. A closer look at each illustrates why.

rational choice

Power Politics

Consider power politics as an alleged source of international order. This story, told primarily by IR realists, begins with an assumption about the logic of anarchy. Specifically, the assumption holds that anarchy engenders uncertainty, and since by nature states are rational, self-interested actors, in the face of anarchy they are left with no choice but to compete with one another if they wish to survive and flourish. To trust another state under anarchy would be to subject oneself to the whim or goodwill of an unaccountable and self-interested other. For a rational, self-interested state, this could not be an option; therefore; international politics becomes a domain of self-help (Morgenthau 1948).

As Waltz points out, however, self-help anarchy is not chaotic. The logic of anarchy, he argues, will naturally lead states to engage in power politics. Power politics are strategic threat systems that states deploy in order to boost their competitive position in the quest for power and interest satisfaction. Two common power-political strategies are deterrence and compellance, but any threat system intended to ameliorate a state's relative power position in a given context can be thought of as power politics (Baldwin 1993; Rengger 2000; Walton 2000). There is, to be sure, some disagreement among realists about precisely when the stakes become high enough for states to deploy power politics. For instance, while Waltz argues that states respond to other states' relative power, Stephen Walt argues that states respond to perceived threats (Waltz 1979; Walt 1987). But both agree on the key point: Power politics is a source of international order.[8] Power politics is thought to be sufficient to create stable, shared understandings of expectations and behaviors among states. The logic of precisely why deserves detailed attention.

The issue is, what is it about these threat systems that should lead states into a relationship that produces and reinforces shared understandings of expectations and behaviors with respect to one another? After all, as Douglas Walton points out, threat systems are ubiquitous in everyday life, ranging from actual physical ones, like power politics, to communicative ones expressed through speech and writing. But not all of these threat systems produce stability of expectations among perpetrators and victims, even when they are iterated over time (Walton 2000). So why should power politics ably do so?

According to Thomas Schelling, what makes power politics sufficient for order is that the particular type of threat systems engendered by power politics are *forceful* (Schelling 1966). It is the forcefulness of the threats it entails that makes power politics sufficient for order; power politics *force order*.[9]

Force is a particular form of power that is characterized by its blunt intention to radically limit the options of its subjects (Connolly 1974). It is distinguishable from other forms of power along three dimensions. First, force is blunt, meaning the force-wielder's intent is obvious. Manipulation, to offer a contrasting example, is a form of power that is not blunt because the power-wielder conceals his intent from the subject. Second, force is wielded for self-interested purposes in that the perpetrator's intention is to settle in his favor what he perceives to be a zero-sum conflict. In contrast, authority, for instance, is not a form of power that can be wielded solely for the self-interest of the perpetrator lest he undermine his own legitimacy. Finally, force is nonnegotiable in that it leaves the victim with no viable alternative options other than compliance or unthinkable loss or suffering. In contrast, persuasion is a form of power that is necessarily negotiable since the recipient is not constrained by considerations of penalties (Wrong 1988).[10] In fact, both manipulation and authority are negotiable as well: the former because the power-wielder must be willing to make some compromises if he is to succeed without revealing himself; and the latter because legitimacy rests upon approval. Manifestations of power that are simultaneously blunt, self-interested, and nonnegotiable are forceful. Those that lack any of these qualities are not. Power politics are forceful because they are blunt, self-interested, and nonnegotiable—they deploy unmistakably destructive weapons as a means to give a victim no viable choice but to comply.

Yet it is also worth noting that the type of force wielded through power politics is coercive rather than brute. This distinction, formulated first by Schelling, highlights how brute force limits the options of its subject through conquest—by overcoming the victim's strength—while coercive force limits the options of its subject by making the victim so afraid of some pain or loss that he succumbs in order to avoid it. Consequently, coercive force works like a trap, whereas brute force works like an attack (Schelling 1966, 3–4). Power politics wield coercive force; rather than actually deploying violence they generate a credible threat to "exploit a capacity for hurting and inflicting damage."[11] Their threat systems are simply that—threats rather than acts. But their threats are effective because they leave the victim with an unsavory "nonchoice" between incurring the damage of the destructive weapons pointed at them, or succumbing to demands of the force-wielder.

As the realist story goes, because power politics are force-laden, they are expedient for producing and reinforcing shared understandings of expectations and behaviors among states—order. As long as its victims coexisting in anarchy are rational (meaning as long as they are unwilling to die for their cause), and the forceful threat lodged by a campaign of power politics is credible, they will succumb. They can succumb either by complying without contestation or by participating in a cycle of counter-threats. While the latter will lead to a balance-of-power order, the former will lead either to hegemony or outright domination. But either way, shared expectations and behaviors emerge. This same logic might be put somewhat differently: When disorder threatens—when states digress from expected behaviors—a credible power need only wield coercive force. As long as states are rational and self-interested actors under anarchy, power politics will do the order-producing trick. Because power politics wield force, order is automatic (Rapoport 1999). In this way, power politics are thought to be a source of order.

But the attribution of "sourceness" to power politics is misplaced. Consider again the logic that moves this story: Power politics are inevitable among states, and because they are forceful, they trap states into predictable responses that are understood and expected by all states involved. But are power politics really inevitable among states? As "critical"[12] theorists of many stripes have persuasively argued, there is no natural "logic of anarchy." In turn, there is no particular reason why power politics should be inevitable among states. While there are different versions of this argument, they all point out the fact that states respond to anarchy in a manner commensurable with what anarchy has come to mean to them rather than with some assumed, exogenous, or natural meaning. Thus, whereas realists begin with an assumption about the pregiven meaning of anarchy and the pregiven interests of state actors, critical approaches treat the meaning of anarchy and the content of state interests as social knowledge. Both are products of collective learning among states and what they learn can vary over time. Anarchy and state interests are both evolving, changing cultures (Bukovansky 2002).

What follows from this critique is that as states learn and assign different social meanings to anarchy, the content of their interests change, as do the behaviors appropriate in response to different material stimuli—such as power politics. Take the contemporary era as an example. The meaning of anarchy to states in world politics today can hardly be described as singular and universally shared by all states. Rather, a more apt description is of multiple anarchies, the meanings of which are defined by the different subsets of states that populate them. The culture of some of those anarchies is rightly described in terms of Waltzian relentless competition. India and Pakistan may experience this kind of anarchy. But among some states, the meaning of anarchy has been constructed as downright friendly. In this category is the anarchy that the United States and Britain experience in relation to each other, or the members of the European Union, or the U.S. and Canada, and so on. Certainly under a Waltzian type of anarchy, the material stimulus presented by forceful power politics may be inevitable and may indeed force rational states to engage in mutually expected balancing or compliance behaviors. In such a case, where there is a competitive culture of anarchy, power politics may well be sufficient for international order. But in the latter case, where anarchy is prosocial, or even if it were just neutral, power politics may seem irrational.

Instructive in this regard was the reaction of British Prime Minister Anthony Eden, during discussions before the British invasion of Suez, about the possibility that the U.S. might react against Britain with a military retaliation. Eden reportedly "snorted" at the possibility that the U.S. would do anything but "lie doggo" (Shaw 1996, 171). That the U.S. might turn on the British to the point of threatening or using force against them was not even conceivable.[13] In such an instance, the force of power politics lacks credibility. The shared meaning of the Anglo-American anarchy as peaceful made any potential American power politics toward Britain unreliable as a source of order.

That different meanings of anarchy constitute different types of interests and provoke different responses to material stimuli deals an irreparable blow to the claim that power politics, as conceived by realists, are a source of order. Again, "sourceness" demands sufficiency, which means that wherever power politics exist, order must also exist. But if power politics are "forceless" to compel order against the backdrop of at least a prosocial anarchy, the criteria of sourceness are unfulfilled. Indeed, it appears that using power politics against the backdrop of an anarchy that is not hostile, competitive, and fearful is more likely sufficient for *disorder* than order; it is more likely to lead to confusion and uncertainty. Thus, whereas realists argue that the effects of power politics to force order are automatic, it seems rather that the effectiveness of power politics to force order are indebted to a *prior* international order of shared knowledge about the significance of those material, physical stimuli.

Finally, and significantly, implied in this discussion is the suggestion that power politics would be insufficient to impose order upon disorder. Disorder reflects a relationship among states in which shared understandings of expectations and behaviors are nonexistent or unreliable. If constructing a threat that is credible demands a stable and larger social context or culture in which states can reliably know what kinds of threat systems would incite fear, the problem is that during disorder this is precisely what is lacking. That material power politics could automatically engender order from within a context of disorder is a leap of faith rather than a logical claim of sufficiency. It seems clear that power politics are better understood as contributing factors and that the sources of order are to be found somewhere else.

Common Interests

The same critique—that contributing factors have been mistaken for sources—also applies to common interests. The common-interests approach to international order comes in a variety of formulations, but all variations share a commitment to the idea that one way for states to develop shared understandings of expectations and behaviors (order) is through issue-specific cooperative arrangements intended to achieve particular, substantive, joint goals. Students exploring this avenue point to the order-engendering effects of international law (Bull 1977; Slaughter 1997), free trade (Mattli 1999), environmental regulation (Young 1989), and cooperative security orders such as concerts (Kupchan 1998). All of these domains of order, it is argued, are indebted to the willingness of states to collaborate on common goals. John Ikenberry and Robert Jervis have even argued in separate works that some of the international security orders—such as hegemonies—that are commonly assumed to be indebted to power politics may be more accurately understood as functions of common interests (Jervis 1985; Ikenberry 1998–9). Regardless of the specific order and the issue area it governs, the animating and unifying notion among these perspectives is that without reference to common interests among states, the emergence of certain regimes of international order do not make sense.

And yet, Kenneth Boulding's characterization notwithstanding, the claim that common interests are a source of order has not acquired the same status of certainty that realists claim for power politics, even among scholars dedicated to studying the connection between common interests and order. In this regard, it makes sense to think in terms of two genres of common-interest-based approaches to international order—the rational institutionalist approach and the English School approach. Each genre advances (implicitly or explicitly) a different claim about the sufficiency or sourceness of common interests for international order. The rational institutional approach, which includes work informed, for instance, by neoliberal institutionalism and regime theory, overtly contends that common interests are *not* sufficient for order. The English School approach, which includes work informed primarily by Hedley Bull, maintains that they are. In this sense, only the English School is subject to the critique of having mistaken common interests for a source of order. But since rational institutionalism ultimately rests upon the realist focus on power politics and, like realism, mistakes power politics for a source of order, it too is worth attention. I turn first to rational institutionalism.

Robert Keohane's neoliberal institutionalism (NLI) is undoubtedly the most popular variant of rational institutionalism. The NLI story about international order begins with the same (untenable) understanding of anarchy as realism does; that it is an environment of unmitigated competition and fear about survival. Moreover, Keohane, like realists, recognizes how important it is for states, as rational actors, to maximize power. However, as Keohane argues, precisely because states are rational and interested in their own power, they can recognize that one way to achieve power gains (and, if lucky, security) is through cooperation (1984). In this regard, NLI posits that states continuously make cost-benefit calculations about how to cope with anarchy, and that when absolute gains are adequate states will prefer to collaborate rather than compete (Grieco 1988). When iterated over time, the theory posits regimes of international order will emerge (Krasner 1982; Oye 1985). As states cooperate, they will come to share understandings about the benefits of that cooperation and the costs of defection. They come to understand that they can reliably expect one another to comply.

However, there is an important caveat to this logic—one that Keohane embraces. Since NLI shares with realism a view of anarchy as a self-help environment, relative gains seeking trumps absolute gains seeking, except under very constrained circumstances. More specifically, circumstances conducive to absolute gains seeking exist only when the international environment is *already stabilized* through the practices of power politics among states. As Robert Powell (1993, 228) puts it, the threat of force is only one step removed from cooperation and the international order it produces. In this way, it is the power politics that make the difference between order and disorder; common interests amount only to contributing factors that specify the practices through which states will enact their order.

It is worth noting, however, that as contributing factors to order the difference made by rational institutions is rather significant. Indeed, the durable power-politics-based orders that enable states to focus on absolute gains are visibly different from the realist hegemonies or balance of power thought to be based solely on power politics. For one, the former may be more normatively appealing as a vision of the "good life" (though Keohane carefully distances himself from such a conclusion). Moreover, cooperative regimes may arguably be more stable since they involve multiple layers of order. In this way, rational institutionalism may not make much of a case for common interests as sources of order, but it can show just how important contributing factors can be in shaping the specific expectations and behaviors states use to enact their shared understandings. The key, however, is that NLI does not see common interests as something that can make the difference between order and disorder. That function is reserved for power politics. Of course, given that power politics are actually *not* sufficient for order, rational institutionalism falls the way of realism. It confuses power politics for a source of order when, after all, it can be no more than a contributing factor.

In contrast, the English School (an appellation that refers primarily to the works of Hedley Bull and his contemporary followers (e.g., Buzan 1993, Dunne 1998, Jackson 2000, and Hurrell 2001)) pins much more on common interests than does rational institutionalism. Whereas in NLI the role of common interests and regime building is as an enactment of a prior order allegedly rooted in power politics, in the English School account, common interests are seen as sufficient for order. They are held up as a source. It is true that, in some senses, the logic of Hedley Bull's approach to common interests converges with Keohane's: Both focus on the emergence of cooperative international orders under anarchy. But for Bull (and his followers), the logic of anarchy and its competitive self-serving demands do not trump all other logics. On the contrary, Bull makes what he calls a Grotian claim that common interests are the fundamental organizing mechanism for all international interaction—even orders that ultimately entail power politics.

States, Bull argues, have three natural, pregiven common interests and values: They all value independence, they all have an interest in keeping treaty agreements, and they all have an interest in limiting the use of force. States recognize their common interests and values and so they cooperate to build institutions, such as sovereignty and international law, in mutual service of preserving their interests. The result is international order, which Bull refers to as *international society*. In an international society, states share understandings that the particular rules and norms they have developed are for their mutual benefit, and because they are, states can reliably expect one another to behave in keeping with them. In this respect, common interests are sufficient for international order because, as the argument goes, in a state of disorder the recognition of common interests is what allows states to develop institutions and stabilize expectations and behaviors. Indeed, Bull resists assigning any order-producing capacity to power politics. He argues that unless power politics are practiced within the confines of the rules of international society, they will have no order-relevant effects at all. It is clear that for Bull, power politics are not a source of order—common interests are (1977, 13).

But Bull's account of common interests as a source of order, like the power politics account, confuses a factor for a source. Bull argues that states' common interests are extant, natural, and pregiven. They are, in a sense, immutable material truths that states should just naturally know to be uniformly held by all. And yet, as Bull himself acknowledges, not all states seem to know about their common interests. International society forms primarily among states of similar cultures and seldom seems to transcend cultures. Additionally, in different international societies the contents of the constitutive rules vary, in some cases not adhering completely to the three basic common interests and values. Assuming, then, that Bull is right that states share particular universal interests, there is a serious question about how this empirical variation could make sense. Even more puzzling is that if, as Bull contends, states just naturally share interests, how could there ever be international disorder? Logically, states should naturally recognize the benefits of maintaining an international society. That states have not always done so suggests that even though common interests may matter a lot, they are not sufficient for order. Something apart from them or in addition to them turns common interests from mere "material facts" to active components in the production of order.

It is true that Bull was sufficiently disturbed by the awkward ellipses in his own Grotian logic to borrow from his intellectual mentor, Martin Wight, the notion that shared cultural identities might explain these empirical variations in the constitution of international society (Bull 1976). However, Bull never fully followed through on the implications of this intellectual appropriation, which would have led him away from the claim that common interests are sources of order. Rather, he awkwardly maintained his uncertain stance that in the end, the rationalism of common interests was source of international law and the other institutions that constituted international society (Bull 1977, 38). But regardless of how exactly one characterizes Bull's position, what is clear is that Bull himself bumped up against the limitations of common interests when it comes to thinking about the sources of order. Because common interests do not, in the end, appear to be "material truths," extant and naturally obvious to states, alone they cannot impose order upon disorder. They must, like power politics, be contributing factors rather than sources. And because IR scholars and policymakers have yet to recognize this distinction between factors and sources, they have toiled repetitively on ill-directed investigations about whether power politics or common interests provides the most reliable source of order.

Identity

If neither power politics nor common interests can account for the difference between order and disorder, what can? Dennis Wrong offers a useful suggestion when he writes that, precisely because order rests upon shared understandings, the problem of order becomes a problem of epistemology (Wrong 1994, 5). What this means is that locating the sources of order requires some command of how states acquire shared categories of understanding,* how that shared knowledge is maintained, and how it constitutes the organizing principles by which those states conduct their social interactions under anarchy.

It is in this regard that international identity is imminently useful. Broadly conceived as the mutual, cognitive, sociological, or emotional ties through which states understand themselves, especially in relation to others, identity is an *embodiment* of shared categories of Self-other understanding. Identity as such is one crystallization of precisely the kind of webs of shared understandings that characterize international order. In this way, zeroing in on the process through which identity is formed and maintained may be tantamount to zeroing in on one process through which stable, shared understanding emerge and thus, through which order is imposed on disorder. The very process of identity formation and maintenance, that is, may be a source of order.

Tapping into the process by which identity is formed and maintained, however, is a complex endeavor. For one, there is a multiplicity of identity theories, at least three of which have been introduced into IR literature and each of which models international identity differently. Primordial theories, for instance, treat international identities as natural facts, whereas social identity theories treat them as demarcating psychological and emotional structures. Social constructivist theories, in contrast to both, treat identity as a sociological and political structure. Inasmuch as each theory characterizes identity differently, each tells a different story about how

---

*The idea that states have Selves that can acquire and hold shared understandings is ontologically problematic. I address this issue in Chapter 3.

identity is formed and maintained and so, in turn, a different story about its relationship to international order. But which, if any, identity theory captures the process through which shared understandings are formed and maintained? And to what extent do any of those theories provide a model of identity that speaks to its potential as a source of international order?

One useful way to answer to these questions is to consider how the different accounts of international identity—primordial, social identity theory, and social constructivist theories—model the emergence of specific international orders. Below, I do so focusing on the security community international order because there is now a broad consensus among scholars that international identity is crucial in these regimes of order. When Karl Deutsch first coined the phrase "security community" as a part of his effort to understand how reliable expectations for nonviolent conflict resolution emerged in the North Atlantic region, international identity was not part of the explanatory mix (Deutsch et al. 1957). But Deutsch never did satisfactorily address the question of how security communities emerged. His emphasis on quantity of interactions drew criticism for failing to capture any compelling causal mechanism. As a result, for some time this finding that there were groups of states who could stably expect each other not to threaten or use violence floundered. More recently however, Emanuel Adler and Michael Barnett picked up the security community project where Deutsch left off, persuasively arguing that security communities are significantly implicated with a type of collective identification among states that they call "we-ness." Understood as a particularly robust form of pro-social identity—a thick, interstate friendship characterized by shared values, trust, and common fate—we-ness is thought to be intimately connected to the emergence of the organizing principle of nonviolent expectations and behaviors among states. We-ness as such provides a kind of causal mechanism through which security communities emerge.

Empirical corroboration of Adler and Barnett's suggestion is rich. For instance, cumulative historical and analytical research demonstrates that the nonviolent orders enjoyed by the U.S. and U.K., the U.S. and Canada, NATO, and the states in the E.U. cannot be adequately understood through a power-political or common-interests lens. They require reference to we-ness (Williams and Neumann 2000; Bially Mattern 2003). Moreover, most scholars now accept that the democratic peace is the result of we-ness identification among democracies, reflecting a security community among democratic states (Kahl 1998; Russett 1998). Finally, as new security communities, such as MERCOSUR and ASEAN, emerge and old ones like NATO expand, scholars are finding it increasingly difficult to understand the construction and maintenance of these regimes without reference to we-ness identity (Schimmelfennig 1998; Acharya 2001; Kuhonta 2002). In short, security communities cannot be understood simply as nonviolent groups of states; they must be understood as nonviolent groups of states whose expectations for that nonviolence is rooted in we-ness.

It is the weight of this consensus that we-ness identity is integral to security communities that makes the security community a useful foil for evaluating different identity theories. After all, if we-ness identity is implicated in security communities, then *any* identity theory worth its salt should be able to help specify the manner in which it is, why it is, and how. And in some degree, I argue, they all do. However, only the social constructivist account can do so in a way that capitalizes on the opportunity to probe the boundary between order and disorder. Only social constructivism addresses the issue of how social knowledge emerges and it is, thus, the only one that really examines the role of we-ness in specifying the nonviolent organizing principles of the security community international order. In this way, it is also the only one that surpasses either power politics or common interests in terms of zeroing in on the epistemological dynamics sufficient for international order.

Primordial Identity

Consider a primordialist account of the emergence of security community. As an approach to understanding identity, primordialism is a commitment to the idea "that certain social categories are natural, inevitable, and unchanging facts about the social world . . . . Particular social categories are fixed by human nature rather than by social convention and practice" (Fearon and Laitin 2000, 848). As applied to the international domain, primordialism suggests that states' identities in relation to one another are pregiven. What this says exactly about how a security community order is formed is difficult to extrapolate, especially because (to my knowledge) there are no primordialist accounts of security communities that were intended by their authors to be so. Indeed, the most renowned application of primordialism to international politics, Samuel Huntington's *Clash of Civilizations* (1996), uses that logic to advance the exact opposite vision of order. On Huntington's view primordial identities will engender an international order of inevitable conflict among states that will erupt along the fault lines of different cultures or civilizations.

However, it is possible to piece together an account of primordialist security communities from within the logic that animates Huntington's *Clash* argument (though Huntington surely did not have such a function in mind). Huntington argues that in the absence of the muting effect of bipolar nuclear rivalry, conflict between civilizations will naturally emerge. What makes this so natural and inevitable is that identities bear innate hostility toward difference and so, *ceteris paribus*, conflicts between civilizations will surge forth unfettered (Huntington 1993). In addition, Huntington predicts that violent conflict in the contemporary era will only significantly occur at the boundaries between "us" and "them." In other words, even though intercivilizational conflict might besiege the international system as a whole, *intracivilizational* peace is theoretically consistent. It is thus *within* civilizations that the emergence of we-ness and a security community becomes possible. In fact, given the inevitability of us-them violence, incivilizationality appears as a *necessary* condition for we-ness and a security community.[14] In this way, one can extract from the *Clash* argument that primordial identities are causal components, not just of a clash of civilizations order, but also in security community orders.

While there is some intuitive appeal to the argument that we-ness is more likely to develop among states that already share civilizational culture, as an explanation of the emergence of a security community order this (admittedly cobbled together) primordialist identity account is both empirically untenable and theoretically incomplete. First, on empirical grounds it seems clear that shared civilizationality is not at all necessary for the emergence of security communities. Transcivilizational security communities are just as feasible. For instance, the ASEAN security community is constituted of member states that cannot accurately be understood to have previously been members of some single civilization.[15] Even more poignantly, the NATO security community, allegedly the perfect embodiment of Western civilization, includes Turkey, which is hardly Western by most accounts, and has recently integrated Russia as a junior partner into its regime of nonviolence.

But even bracketing these empirical exceptions, there is a big problem with the primordial approach: primordial identity is not theoretically sufficient for the emergence of a security community. In fact, the logic of primordial identity offers nothing in terms of illuminating when and how a security community emerges. Simply put, primordialism naturalizes and reifies self-other knowledge among states as timeless and unchanging. This means we-ness among states, to the extent it exists, must be timeless and unchanging as well. So identity drops out as anything other than a background, environmental condition, a contributing factor, in the emergence of international orders. Indeed, many security communities are only now evolving, so the explanation for why, cannot lie with this unvarying "variable" that has always existed as such. In this way, primordial identity cannot be something that makes the difference between the existence of that order and its absence, and so it gets us no closer to understanding the sufficient conditions for security communities. It also gets us no closer to understanding the sufficient conditions for international order more generally. After all, even on Huntington's account the when, why, and how of the clash of civilization were indebted to something other than primordial identity.

Social Identity Theory

At first blush, Social Identity Theory (SIT) appears more insightful on the question of how states acquire shared categories of we-ness, and how we-ness constitutes a security community. But ultimately it too disappoints. SIT draws on cognitive and social psychology to explore how group identity shapes group behavior (Tajfel 1978; Robinson and Tajfel 1996). Unlike primordialism, SIT begins with a view of group identity not as natural or extant, but as constructed through its individual members' "self-concept."[16] Each group, that is, is constituted of individual actors, each of whom attains a self-concept in reference to a set of social categories to which he *feels* he belongs (for example, nationality, political affiliation, or civilization). It is significant, then, that self-concept, which is the building block of group identity, is a product of subjective individuals' beliefs.

Individuals are theorized to acquire their self-concept through the dual processes of categorization and self-enhancement. *Categorization* refers to a cognitive reaction through which individuals "sharpen inter-group boundaries by producing group-distinctive stereotypical and normative perceptions," while *self-enhancement* is an assumption about human nature which holds that individuals have a "very basic need to see themselves in a positive light in relation to others" (Hogg and Terry 2001, 4). These two processes work together. As individuals categorize themselves into in- and outgroups, they also necessarily ignite competitive behaviors with outgroups.

When it comes to international order, Jon Mercer has argued that SIT sketches a picture in which individuals categorize themselves into nations and, in the process, translate their self-enhancing egocentrism as a group into ethnocentrism (Mercer 1995). Identity on this read is sufficient for international order because the process of "categorization, comparison, and a need for a positive social identity" will mean that wherever there are two states, they "will compete against the other regardless of the other's behavior" (Mercer 1995). Because states recognize the necessity of each other's ethnocentrism, they will reliably expect competitive hostility.

But what does this say about security communities, which of course rule out physical violence between states? In this regard, Mercer is careful to highlight, through the SIT lens, that the boundaries around in- and outgroups are constructions of individuals' subjective self-concept, and thus they are mutable. "My argument," he writes "is not that group boundaries are fixed but that a group—however constituted—will be egoistic" (249).

As such, when individuals' self-concepts expand, so can ingroups expand to include states that were previously considered in outgroups. Moreover, because being a part of the same ingroup requires that individuals abstain from pursuing self-enhancement at one another's expense, "ingroupness" functions, on Mercer's implied view, as a sufficient condition for a security community.[17] Thus, while the shared understandings of inevitable ingroup/outgroup competition are the source of balances of power, shared understandings that self-enhancement is normatively prohibited renders ingroupness the source of security community orders.

There is much to be said for the SIT account, especially that it does not naturalize membership in any given identity. It explicitly provides an account of group identity formation, maintenance, and evolution rooted in the mutability individuals' self-concept. However, the view that ingroupness is sufficient for security communities is unsustainable. After all, if this were the case, one could expect as many security communities in world politics as there are ingroups, which is clearly not the case. Something more than ingroupness must be at work. It is useful here to recall that not just any old prosocial identity among states is enough for a security community; the identity has to be robust to the level of we-ness. But SIT lacks the theoretic resources to differentiate the content or quality of different ingroup identities or different degrees of pro-sociality among individuals within ingroups. Because it is interested in the *subjective* (private) basis for group identity formation, SIT treats identity as nothing more than the coincidental collision of numerous individuals' self-perceptions that they each belong in some category. Group identity is thus simply a demarcating structure between selves and others, so the possibility of exploring the specific content of the *intersubjective* meanings forged among members of the ingroup is lost. There is simply no way to talk about the emergence of we-ness as a specific form of ingroupness, much less to offer a compelling account of how and why this identity gives rise to security communities. In fact, because SIT fixates on subjective rather than intersubjective aspects of identity, it also offers no means of differentiating among the variations in outgroup identities. The only possible understanding an ingroup can have of an outgroup is enmity. SIT posits that as natural. In any case, SIT does not conceive of identity in a way that illuminates how states come to share the particular categories of understanding about each other. In this way, it fails to get us closer to the sources of order—to the stuff that produces *shared* understandings among states for expectations and behaviors.

Social Constructivist

The third approach to identity, social constructivism, does what neither primordialism nor SIT does—it focuses explicitly on how intersubjective knowledge of Self and other emerges. Because it does, it offers a much clearer account of where, when, and why we-ness develops among certain groups of states and how it engenders a nonviolent organizing principle for international order. However, there is no one single social constructivist account of identity, which makes any exposition of the basic logic something of a challenge. The problem is that the phrase "constructivism" properly applies to an extraordinary range of theoretical arguments about the role of knowledge in the structures of human association. To name just a few, the appellation variously refers to accounts of identity born of economic rational-choice theories (Fearon and Laitin 2000), sociological theories of structuration and symbolic interactionism (Wendt 1992), poststructuralist philosophy (Campbell 1992), feminism (Sylvester 2002), and Habermasian critical theory (Kratochwil 1989) —each of which have found their way into IR. Moreover, as Ronen Palan notes, the ontological and epistemological assumptions of many of these constructivisms are incommensurable with one other, making some kind of overarching synthesis dubious (Palan 2000). Finally, even among forms of constructivism that share meta-theoretical commitments, there is disagreement over whether identity is even a useful or interesting lens for thinking about shared knowledge (Onuf 2003). Even among those who accept identity as useful, there is concern that it may be becoming an overused and catch-all phrase (Legro and Kowert 1996; Brubaker and Cooper 2000).

In seeking a way to summarize a constructivist account of identity, then, it is helpful that something of a consensus has emerged, at least among U.S. IR scholars, regarding the legitimate referent for the phrase "constructivism." Through a communicative process that is interestingly consistent with the very constructivist theory being discussed, IR scholars have winnowed down the multiplicity of meanings of the phrase, collectively producing knowledge such that it now, by convention, signifies only certain variants of the logic. In the U.S. academy, in particular, constructivism chiefly refers to variants that couple an ontologically "almost all the way," or "weak," constructivist position with an epistemologically positivist stance on issues of research method and truth claims (Price and Reus-Smit 1998). In this vein, the most visible example is Alexander Wendt's *tour de* theoretical *force Social Theory of International Politics* (1999), which blends sociology's structuration and symbolic interactionist theories to produce a positivist, constructivist account of the role of identity in producing the international system. Also included in this category are a variety of scholars whose substantive focuses differ from each other significantly, but whose work either explicitly or implicitly abides by the requisite criteria (Katzenstein 1996; Barnett 1998; Finnemore and

Sikkink 1998; Hall 1999; Checkel 2001).** What is useful about this convention for the current purpose is that it focuses the analysis of constructivist accounts of identity away from other variants toward "Wendt's
world"[18] and its associated strains.

At issue then is how this constructivist account of identity models the
emergence of the security community. Wendt sees identity (1999) as an
actor's self-understanding. However, that self-understanding derives from
neither objective conditions (like primordialism) nor subjective ideas (privately held, like SIT). Instead, identity comes almost[19] entirely from social
relationships with others. Thus, identities are intersubjective in the important sense of ideas shared among at least two actors, self and other. Because
it is intersubjective, identity provides a collective reference point from
which the actors involved can understand one another's interests and likely
behaviors. In the case of states, then, intersubjective self-other knowledge
enables them to recognize each other, and so constitutes stability in their
expectations for each other's behavior. Identity enables states to expect
"symmetry of response" from each other (Mead, cited in MacKinnon 1994;
Weber 1995).

This idea—that identity, as an intersubjective structure, shapes interests
and structures behaviors—is the key to a constructivist model of the emergence of international order, whether that order is a security community,
balance of power, or other. For instance, when states intersubjectively hold
knowledge of self-other as hostile, they acquire a collective reference point
of enmity. Playing out roles as enemies requires egoist self-protection, ultimately rendering power politics an expected behavior among them. It follows that something akin to a balance-of-power order will emerge. In
contrast, when states develop intersubjective self-other knowledge of each
other as friends who trust each other and share values, they develop we-
ness. In turn, they have an interest in each other's welfare and so share an
understanding that they can reliably expect each other to refrain from

---

**Most notably and definitively excluded from this construction of the term "constructivism" are
the rational-choice and post-structuralist accounts, the former because it brackets its ontology and
the latter because it embraces post-positivist epistemological assumptions. (For instance, Bleiker
2000, Fearon and Wendt 2002). There are also a variety of scholars informed by starting points other
than those so far discussed who use the term "constructivism" (such as Kubalkova, Onuf and Kowert
1998 and Kratochwil 1989) but since they have largely resisted the notion that identity is a useful
concept for thinking about international politics their relevance to this portion of the discussion is
limited. It is interesting to note in this regard that this last group of scholars have been called to task
for refusing to integrate with Wendt's world of constructivism (Peceny 2000).

ing violence. Either way, the claim is that identity, via the
it embodies, is sufficient to produce order.

primordialism and SIT, it largely appears that construc-
onceptualize identity in a way that encapsulates the vari-
...ied shared understandings on actors and, similarly, on
international order. This is particularly noticeable in regard to the issue of
how actors come to share particular intersubjective self-other meanings
(identities) in the first place, which is one of the issues on which both SIT
and primordialism flounder. Neither of the latter provides a dynamic view
of the content of identity, and so they put restrictive theoretical limits on
the realm of possible orders, leaving awkward gaps in their ability to account for various empirical facts. On this score constructivism fairs much
better. Because it treats identity as an embodiment of intersubjective
knowledge, the only limit on the types of identities that can form (and orders to which they can give rise) is the types of knowledge that states can
collectively produce. More specifically, Wendt argues that as particular
states interact with each other, they collectively forge and learn a set of representations that define categories for understanding themselves in relation
to one another. The precise content of those categories will depend on the
representations that states collectively constitute, but, within the limits of
the larger systemic constraints and the demands of their corporate needs,
it is up to the states as to how they project themselves to one another. Over
time and with repetition, states internalize or learn the categories of self-
other understanding that they have collectively forged so that the identity
becomes stable and naturalized. They become mutually constituted by it
(Wendt 1999, 324–36). It is at such a point that an identity is stable enough
to engender "symmetry of response," and so international order among its
member states.

Importantly, though, what makes this a constructivist account is that
identities are not permanent once they are formed. For the identity to remain meaningful or legitimate, and so for the order it engenders to persist,
member states need to continue to relearn and internalize the same representations through their interactions. As Wendt puts it, "identities and interests are not only learned in interaction . . . but sustained by it" (331).
The identity and its order are theoretically only as stable as the process that
produces them. So, for states to learn we-ness and develop and maintain a
security community, they must continually forge positive, reinforcing representations of shared values, trust, and so forth. The same process goes for
a balance-of-power order, except that in this case, the representations re-
produced and continually learned would need to be hostile and antagonistic. The underlying logic of identity formation and maintenance (and so

order formation and maintenance) then, says Wendt, is a self-fulfilling prophecy (331).

This is significant since, as Wendt presents it, an identity is always sensitive to the categories of shared understanding that give rise to it in the first place. Identity is an identification process, not an identity condition. Identity is, allegedly, never reified. On the constructivist view, identity amounts not to some substantive, unchanging set of relationships between states as in primordialism, or some inevitable psychological relationship between protean ingroups and outgroups, as in SIT. Identity is a container for shared understandings among states, which gives them directions about who they are in relation to each other and how to behave toward each other. In this way, the constructivist approach to identity can model the relationship between identity and the emergence of any variety of international orders as one of sufficiency. When identity, at least as modeled through the constructivist theoretic apparatus, emerges then, no matter what its content, it can impose order upon disorder. No account of power politics or common interests could manage such a claim. In this way, the identity formation and maintenance process—at least on the constructivist rendering —appears as a source of order.

The stakes of an "uncovery"[20] of this sort are considerable, even momentous. It counsels an identity turn or transformation in the whole course of study along any number of dimensions. For instance, in the domain of theory, an identity-as-source approach to order requires an ideas-first approach, or an idealist view of international politics. This requires designating more intellectual legitimacy to interpretative methodological frameworks. In the domain of history an identity turn requires a radical rereading of past international orders. For instance, it would mean rethinking the underlying dynamics of the Cold War and its end in terms of Soviet/U.S. knowledge structures instead of only in terms of the distribution of power. On an applied dimension, an identity turn means significant revisions in the advice that scholars pass on to statesmen and other practitioners involved in trying to convert their fantasies about international order into realities. It means highlighting strategies for ordering international politics that promote the desired identities rather than strategies of power balancing or cooperative regime building, per se. In fact, an identity turn implies that the long-standing preoccupation with those factors may well be part of the reason why the passage from fantasy to reality has been so hard to implement. Practical reorientation toward identity might facilitate some forward motion.

Order in Crisis

But it also might not. In spite of its persuasiveness compared to primordialism and SIT, a deeper and more subtle reading of the constructivist account reveals that ultimately it cannot sustain the logic that identity is a source of order. In a nutshell, the problem is that while the constructivist theoretic apparatus appears to support a sufficient relationship between identity and order during *settled times*, in which foundational, shared basic truths among states are not challenged, that same theoretic apparatus can say nothing about identity during *unsettled times*, or times of disorder, such as international crises. Hence, there are simply no grounds upon which to sustain the claim that identity is sufficient to impose order upon disorder.

To see this, reconsider the constructivist account of identity formation and maintenance. Identity is formed and maintained through an ongoing process of interaction and social learning. Once states collectively recognize the shared meanings they have learned, their new knowledge constitutes the parameters of the international order among them. It structures their expectations and behavior. But this basic description of mutual constitution through symbolic exchange is really just the tip of the constructivist theoretical iceberg. As Lars-Erik Cederman notes, more detailed theorizing is required to flesh out the processes by which states learn the meanings of the symbols they exchange, and through which they sustain those shared meanings (Cederman 2001, 28). Anarchy may be, as Wendt has famously put it, "what states make of it," but beyond simply noting this, the theoretical challenge is to figure out how states come to make one thing of it rather than another. Thus, the real heart of the constructivist model of identity is its theory of how states learn through interactions. But that theory of learning, as it turns out, undermines the notion that identity is a source of order.

In *Security Communities* (1998), Adler and Barnett offer one of the most well-developed constructivist accounts of how states learn international identities. In particular, they are interested in how states learn we-ness, but their model also travels across the spectrum of international identities more generally. Adler and Barnett's burden is to demonstrate why and how states construct, internalize, and continuously heed the knowledge that they share we-ness (which is characterized by shared values, intertwined security fate, and trust). They begin by positing "a positive dynamic process" among states, facilitated by such external factors as technology, economics, and external threats. Like Wendt, they emphasize that those external factors and facilitative conditions will only produce we-ness when states interactively communicate with each other in ways that lead them to collectively interpret those events in a positive, trust-promoting manner (Adler and Barnett 1998). But, of course, interaction and communication can produce very different interpretations among actors about their self-other relations

—actors, that is, can learn different lessons from the same experience. Thus, in order for actors to come to *share the same* knowledge about their particular self-other relationships, some authority (sometimes called an identity entrepreneur (Keck and Sikkink 1998) or cultural virtuoso (Montgomery 2002)) needs to offer up and disseminate an interpretation to which all involved ascribe. In this regard, Adler and Barnett argue that within any given group of states, certain core states will hold "the authority to determine the shared meanings that constitutes the 'we-[ness].'" Those authorities define the meanings of events for the group and so "teach" the states in the group how to interpret their interactions (Adler and Barnett 1998). In this way, learning to share we-ness is a process that is shot through with the power of the authoritative states.

As it turns out, so is the process by which the sharing of we-ness is sustained. Like any identity, we-ness is an ongoing process and so the learned self-other knowledge of shared values, trust, and common fate continually need to be relearned in the context of new events, external actors, and novel interpretations of the meaning of the relationship among the states. The core authoritative states are central to this function as well because they act as gatekeepers of any new intersubjective knowledge that emerges over time. They confer, defer, or deny the relevance of emergent knowledge for the community, thus deciding on an on-going basis what to include and exclude from the we (Adler and Barnett 1998, 39). When new knowledge is admitted, authorities frame it, organizing its meaning in reference to those intelligible, familiar "truths" about who we are (Barnett 1999; Cruz 2000; Payne 2001). In this way, we-ness formation and maintenance rest on the twin processes of learning and framing,[21] both of which, in turn, depend upon the authoritative power of core states, because their power is what constructs intersubjectivity. Authoritative power enables certain states to teach and protect the very sharedness of meaning.

Importantly, this can be extended to less prosocial identities. Although the content of the intersubjective meanings that core states disseminate, teach, frame, and maintain differ across the spectrum of possible international identities, it is nevertheless the case that regardless of the content *something* is required to glue together the sharedness of the meanings produced through the interactions. This is so even among states that end up learning hostile identities. Even though most IR scholarship assumes those identities come naturally, the key logic of constructivism indicates that even hostility is a social construct. Thus, in order for it to take hold as a shared meaning, core states with the authority to teach and frame the relationship must project that image and cultivate its continued relevance.[22] In this sense, it is fair to apply Adler and Barnett's model across the spectrum of identities.

Adler and Barnett's model of learning is persuasive in that it recognizes that interaction and symbolic exchange do not lead naturally to the construction of some single interpretation among participants. Moreover, and importantly, it recognizes that power—in the form of core authorities— plays a fundamental role in the production of intersubjectivity, or sharing. However, when it comes to thinking about identities that have been constructed in this way as a source of international order, the trouble starts. If authoritative power is necessary to teach the sharing that in turn constitutes identity, one must then ask where states get their authority in the first place. Asking this question begs further questions because authority is an embodiment of legitimacy, and legitimacy is nothing if not a product of shared beliefs—the very phenomenon that Adler and Barnett are trying to explain in the first place.[23] Where, then, do *those* shared beliefs come from? What exactly is it at base that allows states to learn identities?

One way to react to this now somewhat tiresome search for the foundations of shared self-other meanings is to simply begin looking for ways to model the emergence of legitimacy and in turn authority. Not surprisingly, there are many possibilities. For instance, Thomas Schelling suggests that states collectively legitimize particular states to wield authority because those states are prestigious; that is, because those states inspire an awed fear on the basis of their military or economic power (Schelling 1966). Rodney Bruce Hall, in contrast, suggests that states bestow legitimacy, and so authority, on the grounds of moral persuasiveness (Hall 1997). For their part, Adler and Barnett argue that states bestow legitimacy to the core states in light of a "magnetic attraction" to the appealing lifestyle and values of the latter (Adler and Barnett 1998). And there are others (Wrong 1994). But all of these—including prestige, moral clout, magnetic attraction, and so on— are socially constructed beliefs in themselves. Each indicates that states' authority depends on some already-established sharing among states about what is awe-inspiring, what is morally compelling, and what is attractive. In this way, identity formation and maintenance is not just dependent on appointing an authority, but also on a prior epistemological order of shared values, culture, and self-other relations that makes the appointment of that authority possible. Identity, and so international order it seems, depends on an ever-receding horizon of pre-existing shared meanings and international identities.

So what does this mean for the constructivist model of identity as a source of international order? For one, it could mean that identity is not a source of order, but a factor. On this view, the source instead must be authority, or perhaps the underlying self-other relations (magnetic attraction, prestige, moral clout, etc.) that constitute the authority in the first place. But this is perhaps a misplaced conclusion. While authority, and the self-other relations that legitimate it, are certainly prior to identity, none speak for themselves in terms of what they mean for state expectations and behaviors. For instance, magnetism may be resisted, and authorities can neglect their responsibilities as teachers and framers. In either case, no shared meanings are constructed among states, so no specific directions are given to states about how to behave and what to expect, and so no international order emerges. It is only when magnetism designates authority and when authority is deployed on behalf of identity formation and maintenance that sufficient conditions for international order emerge. In this way, these preconditions may be contributing factors—even necessary ones— for order, but they are not sufficient for it. Only when they congeal into identity do they provide states with the shared meanings and understandings for what to expect from each other. In this way, identity remains sufficient for order, even though the manner in which states learn identity remains elusive.

Thus, the second way to come to terms with the apparently inapprehensible foundations of sharing is to accept that international identities are born of an ever-receding horizon of other international identities. (Weness, for example, is born of a prior positive identity that makes the epistemological order of magnetic attraction possible, and that prior positive identity is made possible by some other prior identity, *ad infinitum*.) In this case, international order—indeed, international politics in general—must be identity formation and maintenance *all the way down*. Locating the sources of any given international order would amount to tracing the formation and maintenance of the particular identity under girding it, beginning with the prior epistemological order that legitimated the authority of the core teaching and framing states. It may be infinitely regressive, but it is amenable to study.

But there is a significant glitch to this solution. As Ann Swidler (1986) notes, there are frequent moments in history during which relevant prior epistemological orders either do not exist or dissipate to the point of being incapacitated as foundations upon which to build other social structures. In particular, Swidler makes a distinction between settled and unsettled times. Settled times, which are perhaps better described as settled issue domains, exist when groups of people can take for granted certain implicit, unarticulated identities and cultural truths (prior epistemological orders), using them as knowledge resources to orient themselves to new circumstances and form or maintain identities.[24] For instance, in the domain of international politics, one might argue that it is a deeply and implicitly assumed truth that states will prosper through free trade. In another instance, it is a settled truth between the U.S. and Britain that the two are the world's most committed freedom-loving democracies.

Such settled truths help define what counts as materially prestigious, morally compelling, magnetically attractive, and so on. In this way, settledness provides the prior epistemological resources necessary to form and maintain an international identity (at least in the manner sketched by the constructivist model). For instance, because states revere free trade, they can marshal a consensus based on magnetism, prestige or so on, to assign legitimate authority to certain core actors (like the U.S.), who they believe best embody free trade. By appointing those states as teachers and framers of the capitalist identity, the process of learning shared self-other meanings is set in motion, as is the development of particular expectations and behaviors, or an international order, that follows from that sharing. In this way, as long as there are relevant, settled basic truths from whence an identity might be formed and maintained, the appeal to the ever-receding horizon of prior epistemological orders works as a basis for the argument that identity is sufficient for international order.

However, during unsettled times, the appeal to the ever-receding horizon of epistemological orders counsels that this identity is *not* sufficient for international order after all. As Swidler explains, unsettled times (usually periods of social transformation) are moments in which taken for granted shared-knowledge resources are either unavailable or "jettisoned" so that relevant basic truths are up for grabs and open to question (Swidler 1986, 278–80). The ever-receding horizon of epistemological orders, upon which to build and sustain identities, dissolves or disappears. To be clear, unsettledness does not mean that *all* shared basic truths and epistemological orders among states dissolve; the ever-receding horizons of truths through which states orient themselves toward each other exist along a multiplicity of issue axes at once. In this way, unsettledness can occur in one issue area without necessarily occurring in another; the absence of shared prior truths within one issue-specific domain does not necessitate it in all domains. Certainly various issue domains or axes may be so interconnected with each other that unsettledness in one creates unsettledness in other, even in extreme cases, generating a domino effect across *all* aspects of self-other knowledge (to the point that states cannot even recognize each other as states any longer). However, in other cases, issue domains are relatively discrete, connected to a few, but not all, of the other shared understandings through which states orient themselves toward each other. But regardless of the breadth of the unsettledness, the obscurity of shared basic truths in given issue areas means that there is no foundation to fuel the identity process in that domain.

In the context of international relations, first encounters are one instance of unsettled times. When actors meet each other for the first time they may or may not have pre-interaction beliefs about each other. Even if they do have them, though, they are not shared, and so there is no prior shared epistemological order from which to forge (no less sustain) a shared understanding of stable expectations and behaviors (Wendt 1999, 56). In this way, first encounters are moments of disorder, and hypothetically, even moments of disorder across *all* issue areas.

Another example of an unsettled time in international relations—and more appropriate in the contemporary world, where there are few first encounters among states—is international crises. Crises are moments during which statesmen, diplomats, politicians, and other key leaders on the frontlines of an international event come to view that event as so divisive that it demands a complete reassessment of the status-quo relationship among the states involved with respect to the issues at hand (Guthrie 1935; Barkin and Cronin 1994, 114–15). In contrast, for instance, to arguments among states, which are characterized by a dispute coupled with a shared goal of achieving a productive resolution (Risse 2000), crises are instances of discord during which actors become so alienated from each other that they reject the prevailing shared knowledge among them.[25] Generally (though not necessarily) crises are less encompassing as unsettled times than first encounters. Nevertheless, within their relevant domains crises deprive actors of the shared basic stock of knowledge from which to intersubjectively fathom self in relation to other.

This was the case between the U.S. and Britain during the Suez Crisis. They were each so infuriated with the other by the way each handled the events of that crisis that both sides questioned and ultimately rejected the long-ossified, settled truths about each other as freedom-loving democrats (Chapter 5). The result was that the very epistemological order through which it had become possible to learn and maintain the specific sharing necessary for Anglo-American we-ness identity was dismantled. The Suez Crises created epistemological *dis*order between the U.S. and Britain.

This is where the glitch for constructivism occurs. Where there is epistemological disorder—like in first encounters or crises—an identity process cannot be initiated (formed) or be sustained. After all, on the constructivist model when shared basic truths among states do not exist (first encounters) or when they are dislodged to the point of being obscured (crises), there are no resources with which to designate core authorities or, to teach and frame the content of an identity on an ongoing basis. Reconsider weness. As Adler and Barnett argue, we-ness is learned by states via the instruction of a magnetically-legitimated authoritative teacher-state that is attractive to others because of the lifestyle it provides its people. So in this case, the settled basic truths or prior epistemological order is one of shared knowledge among states that particular ways of life are admirable. Thus, magnetic attraction (to the states that best embody those ways of life) animates we-ness. However, as Nicholas Rescher argues, magnetic attraction is fickle. It is a social process, the continuation of which requires a particular type of stable, "magnetic-friendly" environment; a settled time in which bodies know what is attractive to them and so can recognize each other. When the magnetic environment becomes unsettled, such as during an international crisis, the bodies within it become *demagnetized*. They cannot recognize what is attractive to them, much less find attractiveness in each other (Rescher 1996).[26] In the current context, demagnetization upends settled truths about what is admirable as a lifestyle and so de-authorizes the core state as interpreter and framer of the we. When that occurs, states stop learning themselves as a we. Instead, they interpret their interactions in multiple, possibly incommensurable ways.

The result is that we-ness, at least in the theoretic model, must break down. Furthermore, given the logic of the constructivist identity-order connection, once we-ness breaks down, the stability of the expectations and behaviors engendered by we-ness—the security community order—also breaks down. So what begins as epistemological disorder wrought by the unsettling of taken-for-granted ossified truths ends as international political disorder. From the constructivist view, then, identity during unsettled times is a source of international *disorder,* not of international *order.*

This point, by the way, travels beyond just magnetism and we-ness. International identity in general, on the constructivist view, simply cannot exist during unsettled crises times. Replace magnetism with prestige or moral clout—and the security community with a balance of power, hegemony, or cooperative regime—and one still faces the breakdown of learning and framing, and therefore the sharing of identity, during crises and other unsettled times. There is still the upending of that necessary prior epistemological order that enables states to arrive at some consensus about who they are or, at least, about who should teach them who they are. There is thus still the problem that constructivism, no matter the identity or order, cannot theorize an international identity or, for that matter, an international order, that survives a crisis.

Perhaps one might overlook the glitch in the constructivist model, chalking it up to an unfortunate, incidental empirical claim. As I argue later, though, it is actually not so empirically unlikely that identities and orders are constantly breaking down (Chapters 4 and 5). The glitch with constructivism is not really with the empirical indication that the identity process breaks down during crises, but rather, with the logical implication that therefore identity cannot be a source of order. Of course, the theoretic logic of constructivism makes this conclusion impossible to avoid; after all, if identity requires a settled foundation to form and persist, it cannot be repaired or form anew in the midst of a crisis, and so cannot be sufficient to impose order upon disorder. During crises, identity simply disappears. In this way, the biggest problem with constructivism is that it can say absolutely nothing about the relationship between international identity and international order during times of disorder. Not only does that counsel against an identity turn, but it also makes for an incomplete theory.

It is worth noting that some theorists have tried to make the theory more complete by offering suggestions from within a constructivist framework about what becomes of identity during crises. Interestingly, all those of which I am aware actually resist their own theoretical logic by looking for ways to theorize the *persistence* of identity and order during crises. Some have appealed to mechanisms like cultural lags (Swidler 1986, 281), momentum (Adler 1981), natural instinct (Wendt 1999, 331), or they have simply observed that identities can survive crises without explaining why or how (Risse-Kappen 1995). Whatever their differences, all of these approaches have in common the willingness to embrace implicitly or explicitly a particular ontological move—the "almost all the way down" move. This move, which as I suggested earlier is characteristic of the constructivist approach (as I use the phrase here), was formalized by Wendt in an effort to combine an appreciation for the social construction of state's identities and interests with some commitment to the idea that those identities and interests can have an ontological status apart from the processes through which they are constructed (Wendt 1996; Wendt 1999, Chapter 5). For Wendt, the purpose of this move is to allow for constructivist theorizing about interstate relations without having to worry about continually investigating the construction of the state itself. But in this context, the "almost" move also has the benefit (or cost) of implying that state identities can take on a life of their own—that they can stick around, lag, have momentum, or what have you during crises even when their underlying foundations are unsettled. In this way, and on a more subtle read of constructivism, the idea that identity is actually just a container for shared understandings among states must be qualified. The "almost" move means that it is *more* than just a container; identity is not always sensitive to the processes that give rise to it. Identity also has *real* material, or, as Wendt calls it, corporal components.

If this "almost" move provides theoretic leverage for resisting the conclusion that identities must break down in crisis, it is, unfortunately, not very persuasive. For one, there is an awkward tension between the very idea of constructivism itself and the concept of corporality. While construction implies an ongoing process, corporality implies a condition entity, or substance. This difference raises more than just questions about the right imagery for describing identity; it raises questions about how to study it. In fact, that little bit of corporality ends up working like a get-out-of-jail-free card for scholars who wish to bracket various processes entailed in the formation of international identity. More specifically, the idea that some identities and interests are permanent allows researchers to assume some elements of identity to be analytically independent of the actions by which they are produced. But exactly which elements those are and why the line is drawn where it is seems to depend more on the researcher and his degree of tenacity for tackling difficult questions than it does on reasoned logic (Maynard and Wilson 1980, 287). In short, the almost move allows for the very reification of identity that Wendt sought to avoid with constructivism in the first place.

In the end, in fact, the "almost" move slips an unexplained primordial nugget into the constructivist theoretic framework, which brings with it many of the same the problems that plagued primordialism and SIT. Just like those models, constructivism replaces self-other understandings at the source of order with natural facts or givens, ultimately obfuscating more than illuminating the origins of identity while simultaneously obviating the need to think seriously about an identity turn (Zehfuss 2001). Finally, this move has the tendency to reify not just the identities and interests of states but states themselves as well (Doty 1997). While there is nothing objectionable about state-centric analyses of international politics and order per se, the idea that one can do so without radically interrogating the question of who states are, what they want, and who speaks for them implies a status quo bias, one unlikely to be attentive to change in international order. In other words, the almost move pushes constructivism from a position in which order cannot last because identities cannot withstand crises to one in which it is impossible to imagine disorder. There is always a settled Self to each state, irrespective of others. Thus, there are always resources for sustaining order, no matter what kinds of crises befall it. In either case, identity drops out as a compelling component in the quest for understanding international order.

In light of this, it seems that the best result that can be obtained through a constructivist lens is that identity may be crucial for order during socially settled times, but that because it disappears during crises, it is not sufficient for order. Thus, identity is not a source of order and the sources of order remain mysterious. Taking an identity turn makes no more sense than continuing to labor at the familiar impasse between power politics and common interests. However, as I argue empirically in Chapter 3 and theoretically in Chapter 4, the answer is not to retreat from identity, but to forge ahead by thinking beyond constructivism. This means abandoning the requirement of settledness and limitations on process.

CHAPTER 3
The Suez Puzzle

As conceptualized through a constructivist lens, identity is not a source of order. So where does this leave the study of international order? In this chapter, I argue that in spite of the limitations of constructivist theory to coherently explain how, there is still empirical reason to suspect identity as a source of order. Consider "the Suez Puzzle."[1] In 1956, Egyptian President Abdel Gamal Nasser nationalized the Suez Canal. Britain, acting in cooperation with France and Israel, used force to reverse the nationalization. Against expressed American preferences and in secrecy, the three colluded to invade Egypt. In the context of the Cold War and the East-West struggle for the allegiance of the Middle East, the Americans were deeply concerned about the implications of this act. Beyond that they were aghast at the duplicity of their allies, especially the British, with whom the Americans had long shared a well-known "Special Relationship" based on trust and mutual consultation. So given the high stakes of this situation—both in terms of the Cold War and the wounded American ego vis-à-vis its allies—the American response to the situation was curious. They demanded that the British and French withdraw immediately from the Canal Zone, but they never threatened their fallen allies with their considerable military might. Instead, the U.S. relied on sanctions and diplomatic pressure. Indeed, military force was never even discussed as an option. The puzzle of the Suez Crisis lies in understanding why.

For an identity theorist, it is tempting to chalk up American nonviolence toward its allies to the Anglo-American security community international order. Prior to the Suez Crisis, the U.S. and Britain had enjoyed at least ten uninterrupted years as a security community, replete with we-ness identity and shared stable expectations for nonviolent conflict resolution. It therefore seemed logical that expectations for nonviolent behavior engendered by Anglo-American we-ness made it unthinkable for the U.S. to use or even threaten force with the British. In the Suez context, according to such an argument, Anglo-American we-ness also protected the French and Israelis from American military threats. In this way, the nonviolent resolution of the Suez Crisis among the Western allies might be understood as an extension of the effects of Anglo-American nonviolent international order.

But empirically, an appeal to the Anglo-American security community does not hold up. Just as the constructivist model of identity would expect, the Suez Crisis unsettled the shared basic understandings between the U.S. and Britain, demagnetized their relationship, and in the end, produced a full crisis of Anglo-American we-ness. We-ness broke down. So deep was the disaffection of the British and American allies with one other that both sides repudiated the idea of shared values, trust, and a common security fate. This left both sides with subjectively held, unshared constructs of antagonism, and a practical environment of confusion rather than stability of expectations. In short then, because we-ness was inoperative, the idea that a security-community order could have had anything to do with American nonviolence makes no sense.

And yet there are also no compelling *nonidentity*-based explanations of the nonviolent resolution of that conflict either. Traditional theorists often try to explain the nonviolent resolution of the Suez Crisis in reference to either the material facts of alliance politics in the Cold War context or the American ability to leverage compliance from its allies nonviolently via selective incentives. On these views, the nonviolent resolution of the Suez incident was a continuation of the effects of either international orders rooted in power politics or in common interests, respectively. To the extent that either of these accounts are compelling, they explain away anything puzzling about the Suez crisis resolution, not to mention repudiate the idea that power politics and common interests are merely contributing factors in international order. Indeed, to the extent that either is compelling, they counsel the irrelevance of identity for getting access to the sources of order and so the imprudence of an identity turn.

As it turns out, though, neither of these nonidentity explanations holds up. In fact, both implicitly (though unwittingly) end up appealing to none other than we-ness for the purpose of absorbing the slack in their own models. In this way, all roads, as it were, awkwardly point back to we-ness identity as the source of the sustained nonviolent order during the Suez Crisis. That we-ness identity is so unavoidable case suggests that the real imprudence would be to abandon the notion of identity as the source without further investigation. Indeed, above all the Suez Puzzle counsels that there is probably something about the relationship between international order and international identity, at least during crises, that has escaped identity theory and empirical research alike. What is called for is deeper theoretical and empirical engagement with identity and its relationship to order, especially during crises.

I illustrate the ineluctability of Anglo-American we-ness identity to the nonviolent resolution of the Suez Crisis in four steps. In the first section, I propose empirical guidelines, informed by constructivist identity theory, for recognizing the existence of we-ness identity and hence a security community among states. I then use those guidelines to sketch the process by which the U.S. and Britain developed into a security community. However, in the third section, I use the same guidelines to sketch (briefly for now, and more fully in Chapter 5) how we-ness and so the Anglo-American security community broke down during the Suez Crisis. Finally, in the fourth section, I seek to solve the Suez Puzzle by investigating alternative explanations for the nonviolent resolution of that crisis and also for the persistence of nonviolent international order. Finding no solution that does not refer to we-ness (now broken down), I propose retrenchment of identity theory.

Recognizing We-ness

Britain and the U.S. have a unique relationship; they enjoy an unusual propensity for effective cooperation and an extraordinary history of non-violence. But the prolonged peace between the two countries is more than just a pleasant historical accident. Anglo-American cooperation and non-violence is a reflection of the particular type of international order that has formed between the two countries—a security community. The validity of this contention, of course, calls for some discussion, particularly since it rides almost entirely on the empirical existence of we-ness identity between the two states. Security communities, after all, are not just characterized by stable, shared understandings for expectations of nonviolence among states. By definition, they exist only where those shared understandings are rooted in a shared identity of we-ness (Adler and Barnett 1996). In this way, if we-ness does not exist among states, even if they are behaviorally nonviolent with each other, there is no security community order.[2] Historically, it is clear that the U.S. and Britain are nonviolent toward each other. But do they share we-ness?

Getting empirical access to the nature of an international identity shared among states poses something of a challenge. Identity, because it is "just" an intersubjectively held idea, is not easily captured through the kinds of tangible, easily recognizable research indicators upon which social scientists like to rely. To be sure, many analysts of Anglo-American relations have tried to tell the story of the emergence of Anglo-American we-ness identity in reference to such tangible indicators—for instance, common language, family ties, and the common experience of history (Gelber 1938; Allen 1955; Gelber 1961; Ovendale 1985; Hitchens 1990; Bartlett 1992; Danchev 1996; Baylis 1997). However, most of these have been unpersuasive because there is hardly perfect correlation between these variables and the development of Anglo-American we-ness or nonviolence. For instance, shared common language has often been more a point of division rather than cohesion between the U.S. and Britain and has certainly never militated against Anglo-American violence (Jones 1997). The same is true of the common historical experience of American rebellion and revolution (Dobson 1995). The problem is that the self-other Anglo-American understandings and the two countries' propensity for nonviolence has evolved over time, while these factors have remained constant. Recognizing we-ness and linking it to nonviolence as such demands more socially, intersubjectively situated, empirical indicators.

With this in mind, one way to empirically discern we-ness and security communities among behaviorally nonviolent states is to take to heart Adler and Barnett's emphasis on learning. From their view, states come to share an identity of we-ness through interactions in which magnetically-attracted states authorize other states to teach them the nature of their relationship. Only when those authorities teach, when those "students" learn, and when all acknowledge their shared values, trust, and common fate in the domain of security, can states be said to experience we-ness. Moreover, the very content of we-ness (particularly its emphasis on trust and a belief in a common security fate) constitutes the states' self-other understandings in such a way that necessarily implies nonviolent behaviors. Thus, where states learn these components of we-ness, their nonviolence can be chalked up to a security community. Empirically, the question is whether the U.S. and Britain have been collectively learning shared values, trust, and common fate in the domain of security over time through their interactions.

It is possible to answer this question because collective learning implies intersubjectivity; actors must publicly convey to each other the lessons they have internalized (else they remain private, subjective knowledge). As a result, the character of states' identities is empirically accessible in the way states publicly *represent* the nature of their relationship—domestically, internationally, in policy formulation, and through other communicative venues. More specifically, inasmuch as the U.S. and Britain represent themselves as bound up in a cooperative security relationship based on shared values, trust, and common security fate, then we-ness and a security community can be considered a shared, lived experience between the U.S. and Britain.

There are, however, a variety of standard objections to relying on representations as data for supporting empirical claims. Most common is the concern about how to distinguish earnest or real representations of friendship and trust from mere political rhetoric. Representations might be read as a "mask covering up deeper material interests" (Cronin 1999,16). But such objections miss the point of social construction: Just because a representation has strategic purposes does not rule out its constitutive effects for identity and behavior. Rhetoric is just as real as an alleged earnest representation. A more serious objection relates to what it means in practical terms for a *state* to represent and acquire an identity. Despite common heuristic assumptions, states are not unitary, intelligent beings. So who within the state represents we-ness? Because there are surely multiple possible actors involved, how often, or how robustly, must it be represented in order for we-ness to count? This question is another way of wondering about state ontology—about where exactly identity is inscribed within a state, and how it gets translated into a force that shapes political behavior.

In his reflections on the Anglo-American identity, Peter Jones advances a *multilevel, issue-specific* conception of states' "identity locus," which serves well as a methodological touchstone for empirically locating we-ness within states, and also for exploring the evolution of Anglo-American security community over time. Consider the multilevel criterion first. Shared self-other knowledge, Jones suggests, is cultivated and represented within each state on at least three levels, each with varying degrees of intensity. The first and most powerful is that of individual leaders. At the leadership level, personalities and personal ties are prominent, and therefore magnetic attraction, when it exists, is direct and strong. As Christopher Hitchens (1990) suggests, magnetism among leaders is often activated by socially settled or deeply ingrained social ties of "blood, class, and nostalgia" as well as of settled political ideals and commitments. For instance, this has been true among a number of British and American leaders including British Prime Minister Churchill and U.S. President Roosevelt; Prime Minister Thatcher and President Reagan; U.S. Secretary of State Dean Acheson and U.K. Ambassador to the U.S. Oliver Franks; and more (Macmillan 1971; Smith 1990; Danchev 1998; Stafford 2000).[3] These relationships facilitate the conditions for teaching and learning the various components of we-ness, both to each other as well as to the administrations and publics they lead. Just which leader in any given relationship is authorized to teach and which is to learn depends on the particular source of magnetism and the particular point in time. As Hitchens puts it, at certain times the British act as teachers and Americans as students, and at other times, the reverse. But either way, the leadership level is often rich with magnetic attraction and as such makes for a robust site for representations of we-ness. Moreover, as Henry Kissinger notes, in the Anglo-American case, the representations of friendship and trust that have emerged out of those leadership relationships have often provided the foundation for cooperation and unified security policies between the two states (quoted in Jones 1997, 3–4).

Yet leaders change with each administration, and so do the magnetic personal relationships that facilitate the construction of we-ness representations. But as Jones argues, a second, often autonomous, site of identity representation exists within states—the bureaucracy. In fact, as Inis Claude has put it, "the identity of every organization—be it an industrial corporation, a community welfare agency, a national government, or an international organization—tends to become lodged in its professional staff" (Claude 1984, 191).

Indeed, when personal relationships, such as Roosevelt and Churchill's or Acheson and Franks', generated pressure to develop unified Anglo-American security policies, they also generated collaboration at the level of the states' security bureaucracy in ways that promoted representations of we-ness. The Anglo-American story is rich with such examples, especially among the military, diplomatic, and intelligence services. As Hitchens describes the intelligence relationship, for instance, the connections between those British and American bureaucracies were shot through with organizational magnetic attraction; that is, with certain "bonds between certain addresses in and around Curzon Street in London and certain floors of a complex in Langley, Virginia" (319). In the first half of the century, it was the British intelligence machine that guided and taught the United States, while later the magnetic flow reversed (320). But in both periods, bureaucrats taught their counterparts a sense of organizational common fate or we-ness, even to the point that intelligence functionaries on both sides of the Atlantic have represented their partnership with pride, trust, and a sort of clubbiness as the "hub of the Western intelligence wheel" (337). What is more, as a site of we-ness representation, the bureaucratic level often becomes distinct from the leadership level, even independent of the fluctuations in magnetism that plague the latter from administration to administration. Indeed, Anglo-American bureaucracies have frequently remained in contact and maintained we-ness during periods when the personal relationships between leaders were under strain (Jones 1997, 4).

The third locus of identity cultivation and representation that Jones discusses is the level of the public. At this popular level, shared values, trust, and common-security fate develop through a variety of channels but, as Jones notes, the most prominent are the news and other mass media, which are poised to play on shared, settled truths in the U.S. and British publics, respectively. For instance, D.L. LeMahieu (2000, 262) writes that "in the late twentieth century, scores of cinema and television productions represented the British past to a mass American audience" in ways that highlighted the common American and British "principled character." By highlighting such common ground, mass media facilitates the kind of environment in which each could teach the other specific aspects of we-ness. As Tony Shaw (1996) notes, the British and American public-information services have worked hard at this, teaching each other's publics a sense of unity and common fate in the global domain. It has often resulted in representations of we-ness at the mass level, especially as articulated through editorials, fiction, or other literature (for instance, see Lader 1998).

The public level of we-ness is important because public perceptions affect electoral politics. In fact, this popular-level identity can affect policy expectations and behavior, influencing the decisions of leadership and bureaucracy. However, the public, as a level of the state, is itself multilevel. This makes it hard to gauge as a locus of we-ness. Moreover, precisely because popular sentiment is frequently beholden to sources like the media, which are in turn frequently influenced by the leadership, Jones suggests that the public should be de-emphasized as an empirical indicator of state identity. On the one hand, this may seem convenient since it is often the case that "perception of the mass public does not accord with the nuances of political policy and is at odds with official opinion." Indeed, public attitudes on either side of the Atlantic have been fickle, swinging dramatically from friendship to hostility over the course of a given incident. But on the other hand, the lack of mass public support has never been sufficient to undermine the we-ness experienced and practiced by the Anglo-American political leadership and bureaucracies (Jones 1997, 5; Dumbrell 2001). Nor has a strong sense of public we-ness ever renewed magnetism and we-ness among leadership where it has been absent (Seib 1998). In this way, it is unclear to what degree popular-level we-ness is autonomous from other levels. What is clear is that where mass public representations of we-ness exists, it provides an additional source of strength to representations of we-ness articulated at other levels.

What is gained by Jones' multilevel conception of the location of international identities is certainly greater empirical sensitivity. But this scheme also pronounces, seemingly counterproductively, the complexity involved in ascertaining when identity exists to a point of political significance. After all, representations of identity forged at each level do not always align with one another (for example, the leadership may not share we-ness while the bureaucracies do). What can such dispersion of representation mean in terms of the self-other meanings that state actors learn and share?

It is in this regard that the issue-specific criterion of Jones' method becomes relevant. As Jones notes, disparate representations of identity across levels does not necessarily negate the intersubjectivity and political relevance of a given representation. It is not necessary for all three levels of identification to cohere in order for identity to have sociopolitical import. Rather, international identity is, empirically speaking, issue specific. What is important is not that there be perfect uniformity at all levels of representation, but just that the actors at the levels most relevant to the issue at hand represent identity. For recognizing we-ness, this means that the most relevant actors are usually leaders and bureaucrats. After all, we-ness is defined by representations of shared values, trust, and common fate in the *domain of security*, which, more than any other national or political issue, is managed at the elite level. In other words, in the domain of security the public's lack of autonomous effect on we-ness is particularly salient (see also Dumbrell 2001, 38). In light of this, it is empirically sound to maintain that we-ness, and so a security community, exists to the extent that both the political leadership and representatives of the state bureaucracies forge and sustain representations of shared values, trust, and common security fate with each other. This, I argue, has been the case between the U.S. and Britain since World War II.

The Special Relationship

Anglo-American we-ness became real on March 5, 1946. On that day British Prime Minister Winston Churchill stood next to U.S. President Harry Truman in Fulton, Missouri, and proclaimed in a now famous speech that Britain and the United States had a "special relationship." Compared to the usual relationships between sovereign states, this was hardly debatable. After all, the U.S. and Britain had enjoyed an extraordinarily enduring, nonviolent, and resilient alliance. But by "special relationship" Churchill meant something deeper; for him specialness denoted we-ness. Churchill was unambiguous about this. He openly called up shared Anglo-American values and the fraternal, intimate trust between the two countries and linked these unique gifts to their common security fate. In fact, Churchill was frank that it was his intention to represent we-ness into existence. "It is," he announced, "the crux of what I have traveled here to say."

And yet, Churchill did not invent the representation of the Anglo-American Special Relationship (and the we-ness it reflected) from scratch. Rather, he grounded his representation on a prior longstanding, taken for granted, settled Anglo-American truth; the truth that the only acceptable society was one that revered freedom and democracy, and that when it came to these qualities, the U.S. and Britain stood together, apart from the rest of the world.

The people of any country have the right, and should have the power by constitutional action, by free unfettered elections, with secret ballot, to choose or change the character or form of government under which they dwell; that freedom of speech and thought should reign; that courts of justice, independent of the executive, unbiased by any party, should administer laws which have received the broad assent of large majorities or are consecrated by time and custom. Here are the title deeds of freedom which should lie in every cottage home. Here is the message of the British and American peoples to mankind. Let us preach what we practise—let us practise what we preach.... (Churchill 1974)

By speaking in reference to these settled truths Churchill mobilized, or triggered, a magnetic attraction between the two countries. He activated a mutual respect for each other's way of life and so set in motion the self-other learning process of being a we.

As the authorized teacher of the time, Churchill also defined the specific course of action demanded by being the Anglo-American we. What he taught other leaders and bureaucrats was that, as freedom-loving democracies, the U.S. and Britain needed to collaborate for each others' protection.

Fraternal association requires not only the growing friendship and mutual understanding between our two vast but kindred societies, but the continuance of intimate relationships between our military advisers, leading to common study of potential dangers, the similarity of weapons and manuals of instructions, and to the interchange of officers and cadets at technical colleges.... (Churchill 1974)

In this way, Anglo-American we-ness was not just an epistemological order of self-other knowledge held in the minds of the two states (at various loci). It demanded deeds in the form of security cooperation. In fact, it demanded it to such a degree—to the point of deep military cooperation—that we-ness also implied nonviolence between the two countries. In this way, the Special Relationship was not Churchill's only legacy that day. He also represented the Anglo-American security community order into existence. He ordered Anglo-American international politics.

While Churchill was the first to successfully teach we-ness and the security community, he was not the first to try, nor was he the last authoritative framer or gatekeeper of the Anglo-American identity and order. In fact, representations of shared values, trust, and common security fate were articulated among political leaders on both sides of the Atlantic almost immediately following the War of Independence. George III, for instance, appealed to the American elite on the grounds of shared political culture. He pondered a relationship in which "religion, language, interest, and affections may, and I hope will, yet prove a bond of permanent union between the two countries" so that "past conflict . . . would not foster future animosity." In service of his vision for transatlantic peace, he invoked fidelity to democratic institutions, individual liberty, rule of law, human rights, economic progress, and social justice. These collective values, he suggested, rooted a common fate and fed mutual security (Nicholas 1975, 8). At the time, though, such representations were the aberration, and perhaps because the idea of a shared Anglo-American political culture was not a settled or magnetically-attractive image at the time, George III was never an effective teacher of we-ness. But as a step toward the eventual settling of such a culture, these early representations helped lay the foundations that eventually made Anglo-American we-ness possible.

Representations of any sort of collective Anglo-American identity continued to be the aberration during the nineteenth century, which was predominantly a time of transatlantic criticism and bitter disagreements over both the history of British colonialism and the practice of American slavery. Yet alongside these disagreements grew an increasingly robust Anglo-Saxon cult among the elite (Hitchens 1990; Dumbrell 2001). The cult of the elite started to develop around the time that the American frontier expanded. As the interior territories of the North American continent were settled, the American elite began to understand the logic of imperialism and began looking abroad for territory. This volte face struck a familiar chord with the British elite, who viewed this as confirmation of their own ways, not to mention an overdue sign of American deference to the authority of the British model for world affairs. In turn, many of the American elite themselves even invoked a parent-child analogy to acknowledge that the "American-child in world politics" now looked to the British for direction (Dumbrell 2001, 23). The moneyed class in the U.S., at least, was increasingly drawn to the images of power and success projected by the British Empire.

By the end of the century, the cultural and political elite on both sides of the Atlantic began to represent, for the first time, the idea of an Anglo-American relation. For a few reasons, this idea was a watershed on the path toward settling the notion of the U.S. and Britain as the premiere freedom-loving democrats, upon which Churchill ultimately built the Special Relationship. First, the representation of an Anglo-American relation referred not merely to some complex of bilateral foreign policies between the U.S. and Britain. It referred to a domain of Anglo-American experience distinct from that which could be experienced in relations with other countries. In this way, it was a significant step toward the specialness of the

American-British tie. Moreover, the concept of an Anglo-American relation was represented as a communal notion, in the sense that the elite taught it to both the American and British publics; the idea became common knowledge and was disseminated across a variety of socioeconomic circles. But most significant of all, among the political leadership the concept of an Anglo-American relation was eventually rerepresented and internalized instead as "Anglo-America" (Roberts 1997). In this representational move, the U.S. and Britain became what anthropologists refer to as a cultural area; not only was the relationship unique from other international relationships, but in this image, Anglo-America actually existed in its own right by bounding out others who did not cohere with their traits (Said 1978). As the British political elite constructed it, the English-speaking peoples were distinct from others, most importantly on the grounds of reverence for political choice and trade (Turner 1971, 50–2; Nicholas 1975, 31). Freedom of choice for governance and goods was, as historian James Cronin (2000) has called it, the "Anglo-American model."

As the idea of an Anglo-America area and model became increasingly settled, it in turn provided a solid basis of shared knowledge from which British and American leaders could forge further collective representations. Among these was the now infamous representations of shared Anglo-American moral duties to enlighten the uncivilized by opening their markets and promoting democratic ideals. Of course, for British at all levels of the state (leaders, bureaucrats, and the public), this responsibility was nothing new. Britain had traditionally seen itself as in charge of, or custodian of and champion for, Europe, advocating government through constitution and liberty. But now, Britain and the U.S. (which had its own unique messianic vision of a new nation, founded on principles of justice) together saw their job as that of a guide helping lesser states to find their way out of a "contaminated condition" (Dobson 1995, 7). In this light, it is possible to understand the nineteenth-century imperial expansion as a bonding experience (Ovendale 1998, 8). Whereas the British had empire, the Americans had the doctrine of Manifest Destiny (Bartlett 1992, 3). In an interesting way, then, in the nineteenth-century Britain and the U.S. shared an Anglo-American paternalistic fantasy about ordering international politics.

One effect of this symmetry of goals was to provide the opportunity for constructing further representations of shared values, especially of common fate. The view that the two were responsible for civilizing the uncivilized world provided reason and opportunity for the elite to represent and live the experience of Anglo-American superiority, and it encouraged the beginnings of a sense of common fate in a domain of international policy that converged with national security interest. Moreover, this course of ideas about Anglo-Americanism increasingly rendered the prospect of war between the two countries as "sheer folly" (Turner 1971, 56–7). The various components that would ultimately nourish we-ness—and its attendant expectations for behavioral nonviolence—were beginning to develop.

It is, to be sure, unusual to suggest that imperialism helped provide the foundations upon which Anglo-American we-ness was built. Against the backdrop of twentieth-century history, during which Americans were quite vocal about their disapproval of colonialism, it seems an unlikely argument.[4] It is certainly true that by the twentieth century, the tension between the principles of political choice, enshrined in the shared values of the Anglo-American model on the one hand and British imperialism on the other, had moved to the forefront of the minds of American leaders and bureaucrats. It created an increasing source of strain between the U.S. and Britain. By the same token, though, the British found American isolationism hypocritical. It seemed, in their view, inexplicably at odds with the responsibility to spread democratic civilization, which was much more than rhetoric in the British rationale for colonialism. It became their real reason for colonialism. Indeed, as historian Gordon Martel (2000) has persuasively argued, the only compelling reason the British sustained colonialism for as long as they did is because they had come to truly believe in its civilizing, democracy-promoting function.

Yet each of these behaviors during the twentieth century (British imperialism and American isolationism), however abhorrent to the other as a specific policy, were based on, and justified in reference to, a shared ideal of freedom to choose governments and goods. Both were represented in reference to the Anglo-American model; they were simply different ways of revering the shared values enshrined by it. In this important way, tensions during that time were balanced by *trust* in each other—the ability to believe, in spite of uncertainty and incomplete information, that even if through different means, both countries were pursuing the same ideals (Nicholas 1975, 4; Adler and Barnett 1998, 46). Up until at least the 1956 Suez Crisis, trust enabled each government to believe that in spite of discord over strategy and tactics, the other really did mean to honor Anglo-American principles of freedom-loving democracy, even as it served its own interests.

The question is just how the U.S. and Britain came to trust each other in the first place, at least at the level of political leadership and bureaucracy. One answer to this question lies with the course of events and representational opportunities that occurred in the interim between the early expression of shared values in nineteenth-century cult of the Anglo-American elite and the twentieth-century tolerance of each others' misguided policies of colonialism and isolationism, respectively. For one, during that interim period, the shared representation of the U.S. and Britain as the world's premier freedom-loving democrats had settled into the status of granted knowledge between the two. It had become an episte order, providing the prior foundations upon which new repres could be constructed, taught, and learned. The more prosocial kn   ge that accumulated and settled, the more possible it became for particular leaders, such as President Roosevelt and Prime Minister Churchill, to teach the bureaucracy and even publics of the U.S. and Britain to trust. That trust learning moved the two countries ever-closer to the defining intersubjective elements of we-ness.

But even before the pivotal Roosevelt-Churchill relationship, there were particular events that provided powerful representational moments for trust. Foremost among these was the Venezuela border dispute of 1895. As the gravest Anglo-American conflict of the nineteenth century, the border dispute challenged two decades of remarkably untroubled diplomacy between the two states. In that incident, the Americans insisted that Britain submit to arbitration their dispute with Venezuela over the boundaries of British Guiana. The U.S. supported its insistence by citing the type of shared freedom-loving democratic values now enshrined in the Anglo-American model: reverence for rule of law, self-determination, and social justice (Nicholas 1975). In fact, the U.S. would use just this sort of logic in its resistance to a first-resort use of force during the Suez Crisis. For reasons I discuss in Chapter 5, this appeal to shared values did not sway Britain in 1956; but in 1895, the British were compelled. While they were anxious to secure their interests through whatever means necessary, including force, they nevertheless submitted to American demands for arbitration, specifically representing their concession in terms of a commitment to the great cause of democracy and the maintenance of law and order in international society. This incident was thus simultaneously an opportunity for both countries to reinforce shared democratic and freedom-loving Anglo-American values, and for American leaders in particular to publicly recognize trust in their British friends, who had acted on principle even against what they perceived as their own national interest (Gelber 1938, 12). The Venezuela border dispute gave the U.S. reason to trust—to believe, in spite of uncertainty—in Britain's loyalty.

Unfortunately, during World War I, the prosocial self-other knowledge and trust that had steadily been developing stalled, especially among the leadership of the two countries. The war had raised serious questions about the U.S. as a long-term friend, and clashes in personalities and national moods were plentiful. The interwar period, was marked by the notorious American isolationism and while, as I have suggested, isolationism did not undermine the burgeoning Anglo-American friendship,[5] it did severely hamper opportunities to further bolster representations of shared values, trust, and common-security fate. While the Atlanticist movement in the U.S. during this time tried to create such opportunities specifically by seeking to distinguish the fact of American isolationism from American feelings about Britain, these efforts merely prevented the unsettling of existing Anglo-American identity (Roberts 1997). They did nothing to further develop prosocial collective identity—no less to further cultivate we-ness.

There was, however, one locus of continued development for collective Anglo-American identity during the interwar years—the public. In literary, religious, and business circles, public men such as Andrew Carnegie and John Dos Passos called for a "common Anglo-American citizenship" and for the two nations to become one "if it were geographically possible" (Allen 1955, 127; Roberts 1997, 349). In a subtler vein, the 1930s witnessed a curious confluence in the styles of British and American journalism, theater, and fashion, and this provided opportunities to perpetuate representations of shared culture and understandings (Allen 1955). In these ways, the promise, or at least the memory, of shared values and an emerging trust were kept alive.

When the U.S. was ready to exit its political isolationism in 1939, American political leaders and bureaucrats were quick to resume intimacy with their British counterparts and eager to cultivate further trust. Surely this was driven by wartime concerns and interests, but nevertheless the representations that American statesmen and functionaries relied upon to court their British equivalents as accomplices was increasingly shot through with references to democracy, common-security fate, and a desire to cultivate international order in the Anglo-American image (Nicholas 1975, 77). The vocabulary was contagious. When the British finally switched their policy of appeasement toward Hitler, they justified it in terms of their desire to accord a higher priority to the Anglo-American value system. The Americans responded with "sweeping acceptance" of the about face and welcomed the British King and Queen for a visit in June 1939, in order to symbolize their ideological solidarity with the British. As the first visit of any reigning British sovereignty to American shores, the visit was a loaded representational moment for shared values, common-security fate, and especially trust (Nicholas 1975, 88).

But perhaps most important of all to the cultivation of the ever-strengthening Anglo-American collective identity was the mythical and magnetic personal rapport shared between President Roosevelt and Prime Minister Churchill. Whatever the source of the magnetism between the two, it energized their relationship and enabled them to work together to teach the various aspects of Anglo-American we-ness—most importantly and most difficult of all, trust—to all levels of their respective states. Relying on their personal touch and warm, informal relationship, they first wooed British and American citizens, setting them at ease and ultimately teaching them what it meant to be an Anglo-American we. They frequently disseminated their representations through radio, the popularization of which did a lot to advance a sense of common fate. For the first time, Americans could hear the voices of their British counterparts, and listening to the British experiences surrounding the blitz elicited deep sympathy and response by the American public. When the U.S. finally made the decision to join their British compatriots in their struggle, it was represented by both sides in terms of shared values, common-security fate, and the requirement of helping friends (Nicholas 1975, 91). It was a representation that taught the British people to trust in the Americans.

Roosevelt and Churchill's relationship also provided the platform from which we-ness was eventually formed at the organizational level, since it was on the initiative of these two men that secret cooperative defense and intelligence programs were designed and implemented. Put into motion between 1940 and 1941 (and continued to this day), these practices of information and military sharing institutionalized opportunities to promote and perpetuate an autonomous organizational community. As Hitchens describes the relationships that formed among the members of the intelligence community at that time, American "rising stars in the intelligence world *magnetized*" other British intelligence officers, creating "full-scale dual loyalty" (Hitchens 1990, 337, emphasis added). The intertwining of these bureaucracies—the epicenters of national security—marked a qualitative shift in the character of Anglo-American representations of shared values, trust, and common fate. In the context of a world war and in such close proximity—nine thousand British military, diplomatic, and intelligence officials were based out of the British embassy in Washington— anything less than believing in each other would have been difficult to imagine (Ovendale 1998, 48). They were partners and friends in saving the West (Lash 1971). Moreover, because the intelligence community is not in the same public spotlight that so frequently shines on the political leadership, and because the intelligence community has a decentralized structure, it has often been sustained as a rather robust and enduring site of Anglo-American identity, even during disputes among the leadership (Aldrich 1998, 337).

And yet, even as Anglo-American we-ness began to coalesce across all three levels of the state during the Roosevelt/Churchill years, it was also during those years that great-power status began irrevocably shifting from Britain to the U.S.. This changing of the guard significantly complicated the dynamics entailed in the development of the Anglo-American identity. At the same time that representations of common values and trust in the domain of security were expressed with frequency and familiarity, they also became more bound up with representations of each country's national interest (Woods 1990). It became harder to tell what was Anglo-American we-ness and what was national interest. At the extreme, such developments make it tempting to dismiss the Anglo-American union as a mere pax anti-Germanica or a pax anti-Soveitica. In that case, the British should be seen as simply one among many allies to the powerful Americans, while the Americans were necessary protection for the declining British (Hathaway 1981; Reynolds 1982; Rogers 1986). But the burgeoning we-ness and national interests were not either/or components of the Anglo-American relationship. On the contrary, they pulled in the same direction; national interest and collective identity promoted a double-bond. Anglo-American identity shaped the way that each understood and pursued their national interests (Dimbleby and Reynolds 1988, 355; Hahn 2000, 277).

The effects of this double-bond were particularly pronounced in aspects of American behavior during the wartime alliance. If anything, after the power shift, the U.S. sought to further intertwine itself with the British, even trusting the British in domains that were not strictly necessary, or even prudent from the perspective of national interest. For instance, in 1942, FDR proposed the Combined Chiefs of Staff (CCS), a joint American and British committee with general jurisdiction over grand strategy and the allocation of materiel. Headquartered in Washington but staffed equally by Americans and British, CCS broke new ground in strategic cooperation. It required the two countries to entrust one another with their troops and strategies in the fight to defeat Hitler (Ovendale 1998, 16). In spite of the fact that he held the power to control the committee, Roosevelt worked with the British as an equal rather than junior partner (Danchev 1998). Even the process of settling the British-U.S. disagreement over Stalin's intentions in Russia was marked less by American strong-arming than by a high degree of American tolerance. Ultimately, American political leaders became concerned about "British needs in terms of *how the British* saw those needs" rather than in terms of how they suited U.S. interests (Dobson 1995, 92; Kirby 2000, 387, emphasis added). Thus, while each sought to use the other to promote its own national interests, shared Anglo-American knowledge of Self and other as the world's premiere freedom-loving democrats, who were bound together by common-security fate and able to trust one another, still had unique ordering effects on Anglo-American international relations.

Finally, in 1946, after more than a century of interrupted but progressive settling of shared basic truths, of magnetic appeal and authoritative teachings, and of the translation of those lessons into bureaucratic organizational identity and security practices, that intersubjective knowledge that the two countries shared we-ness was taught, learned, and collectively recognized. When Winston Churchill coined the phrase "the Special Relationship," he signified it in reference to the development of shared values of freedom-loving democracies and the trust and common-security fate of the U.S. and U.K., and indeed of the whole West. In no uncertain terms, he put the Anglo-American bond at the core of Western salvation. At that point, when the Special Relationship was signified as the crystallization of we-ness, the Anglo-American security-community international order became a collective reality.

Since then, with the exception of the breakdown during the Suez Crisis, Anglo-American we-ness and the security community has been maintained at varying degrees of intensity.[6] In the immediate postwar years, the Special Relationship (we-ness) and the security community was perhaps at its strongest ever. At first, Churchill carried the primary authoritative responsibility for sustaining we-ness representations, and he did so vigilantly, framing new knowledge for his magnetically captivated "students" in the leadership and bureaucracy of both countries. However, a good many others —including Roosevelt, and (especially between 1949 and 1952) Dean Acheson and Oliver Franks—eventually joined him and took over for him (Danchev 1998, 119).

As we-ness became increasingly settled, so too the effects of the security community became more pronounced for Anglo-American interactions. For instance, shared expectations of mutuality and openness in information exchange became, along with nonviolence, part of the complex of normative expectations that derived from we-ness (Jones 2003). Even when there was quarrelling and irritation between the American and British political and military leadership over how to implement shared security goals (for instance, how to manage China, Korea, or oil interests in the Middle East), most of these conflicts were resolved through a process of mutual open consultation. In this way, conflicts were not allowed to vitiate the special cultural closeness that pervaded political, diplomatic, and military discourse and practice. In fact, they tended to do the reverse, providing an opportunity for augmented sensitivity and further representation of shared values, trust, and common-security fate (Dumbrell 2001, 39). This was especially true for Americans who, given their disproportionate power, were on guard about listening carefully to what Britain had to say. "London was back-seat driving and Washington was relying upon it" to do so (Jones 1997, 12). And therefore, Anglo-American we-ness not only produced a security community order, but one in which asymmetry of power was tempered by cultural preferences.[7]

By the mid-1950s the U.S. would tolerate "no receptive audience for anti-British rhetoric." Indeed, it was considered downright *un*-American not to consult and include the British in American security policy (Hahn

.es 2003). It was an extension of Self to other of one of the
,orts for states. Indeed, it was virtually on the eve of the Suez
President Eisenhower represented his relationship with
; "a homecoming" (Hahn 2000, 279), and Secretary of State
Joɪɪ. Dulles reflected on the "indispensable harmony" of the Anglo-
American relationship, which he viewed as rooted in "personalized" and
"intimate" bonds. And at that time, the U.S. Department of State issued an
official position that "US-UK relations are not based only on a power calculus but also on a deep community . . . intimate relations . . . The 'Special
Relationship' . . . (is) Anglo-American reality" (Ovendale 1998, 131).

The Suez Crisis

But the Suez Crisis changed all of that—for a while, anyway. Unlike previous disagreements, conflicts of interests, or disputes that the British and
Americans had faced up to that point, the Suez Crisis did not provide an
opportunity to reinforce representations of we-ness. Rather, the Suez Crisis
unsettled the very shared knowledge base upon which we-ness had been
represented in the first place—the truth that, together, U.S. and Britain
were the world's premiere freedom-loving democracies. Once this settled,
social truth was put to scrutiny the magnetic attraction among American
leaders and bureaucrats was as well until it became *demagnetized*. There
was no longer a legitimate authority to frame the events of the Suez incident in a way that reinforced representations of we-ness. In fact, so obstructed was any prior epistemological order of positive self-other
Anglo-American understandings that no one on either side was willing to
do so anyway. As a result, we-ness broke down and, along with it, the stability of shared expectations. Thus emerges the Suez Puzzle, in which a
nonviolent resolution between the U.S. and Britain prevailed in spite of the
breakdown of the normative order between them that required it. While
the details of this puzzle are explored in much more detail in Chapter 5, a
simple, broad-brush picture here illuminates its parameters.

The trouble over Suez began when the British, French, and Israelis,
working in a concealed alliance, colluded to reverse Nasser's nationalization of the Suez Canal by forceful invasion of Egypt. On October 29, following the protocol of their prior secret arrangements, Israel invaded Egypt
across the Sinai Desert. Per their plan, Britain and France then issued an ultimatum to Israel and Egypt to withdraw to ten miles from the canal (but,
still a hundred miles inside Egyptian territory; an unacceptable arrangement from the perspective of the Egyptians). Egypt predictably refused the
ultimatum. In response, and on the pretext of separating the warring Israeli
and Egyptian parties, the British and French bombed Egyptian airfields,
dropped paratroopers in Egypt, and invaded Port Said with a seaborne force.

From the very outset, the Americans had strongly opposed using force, citing concerns about Cold War strategy and preservation of the Western image. As compared to the Soviets, the West had positioned itself on the moral high ground as law-abiding international citizens committed to self-determination. Since Nasser's nationalization of the canal was legal, it would be overtly hypocritical and self-defeating for the West to try to retake the canal through force. The disincentive to use force was further compounded by the fact that the Suez Crisis coincided with the Soviet repression of rebellion in Hungary. For the West, and *especially* for a former colonial power, to use force in Egypt could only indicate that the West was as oppressive as the Soviets. Finally, the U.S. had strategic concerns about not alienating Nasser, who as far as they could see, was still unaligned in the Cold War. All considered, from the perspective of American policymakers, the stakes of Suez were way too high to engage in force as a first resort—or even as a second. With the Cold War, the future of the Western reputation, and control of the Middle East at stake, the U.S. wanted to take no chances (Gorst and Johnman 1997).

As the plan unfolded—the Israeli invasion followed by the British and French occupation of the Canal Zone—the Americans became increasingly enraged with their allies for disrupting the delicate Cold War balance and sabotaging the West in the process. While blame was directed at all three allies, the Americans were particularly angry with the British. The British were guilty of something much more egregious than strategic disagreement and bad policy choice; they were guilty of violating the trust entailed in the Special Relationship. More precisely, as I have argued, in addition to the norm of nonviolence, the Special Relationship had given rise to a number of commonly recognized norms to which each trusted the other to conform. At issue for the Americans was that the British collusion with the French and Israelis violated one of those—the norm of open, mutual consultation with regard to security issues.

The Americans reacted strongly, especially by proclaiming alienation from the British. They felt that British actions had revealed a British character that was distinctly bellicose and unfamiliar. In other words, the Americans were disturbed not just because the norm violation resulted in a use of force that they viewed as a strategic mistake, but also because that normative digression revealed a British personality that, in the Americans' eyes, was in stark contrast to the long taken-for-granted values that they thought were the very basis of the Anglo-American friendship. To the Americans, being a freedom-loving democracy implied restraint, law-fulfulness, and self-determination among nations (Danchev 1998). The British decision to use force against a legal nationalization—not to mention their collusion to do it—indicated that the British did not share those values. Instead, they were aggressive, bellicose, and deceitful.

Just as the American leaders and bureaucrats had come to learn we-ness, many of them now began to speak of something that approximated its opposite. Eisenhower for instance, totally distanced himself from the British, saying "I just don't know what got into *those people*." No longer emotionally part of a we, Eisenhower continued on to describe the British "as the bully" who used to be "our best friend"(Kingseed 1995, my emphasis). Speaking for the American intelligence community, American intelligence operative Donald Downes, long known as an Anglophile and avid admirer of the British intelligence agency (M15), pronounced the British character as "depressing" and "scheming" (Hitchens 1990, 334). Therefore, the British violation of the Anglo-American norm of open consultation ultimately revealed to the Americans a grave disjuncture in their allegedly shared values with the British. At that point, for the American leadership and bureaucrats, the foundations upon which trust, the Special Relationship, and we-ness identity rested, dissolved. Once those constructs had broken down, so did the security community. The U.S. no longer believed, despite uncertainty, that it knew the values that motivated the British or how the British would behave. All the American leaders and bureaucrats knew for sure at the time was that the British were bellicose.

The Americans, however, were not the only ones for whom faith in the Special Relationship and stability of expectations had dissolved. In fact, repudiation of Anglo-American collective identity went both ways across the Atlantic. As the British interpreted the events of the Suez Crisis, it was the Americans whose duplicitous and fickle character had been revealed. To the British, Nasser appeared an aggressive dictator who posed security and economic threats of Hitler-like proportions to Europe, but the U.S. refused to take Nasser seriously enough to contemplate force. The British viewed this refusal as a revelation about American indifference toward the freedom of Europe (Lucas 1996). This shocked and angered the British, whose view of freedom-loving democracy emphasized freedom, especially in their own back yard. From this perspective, then, it was the Americans who had betrayed the Special Relationship, and so betrayal became a key theme of the reaction of both British leaders and bureaucrats. British Prime Minister Anthony Eden was infuriated at how the Americans could "take the lead against us" (Greenwood 1999, 138) while British intelligence functionaries lamented that the U.S. had "betrayed the West" by "conspiring against . . . the resuscitation of a "British sphere" (Hitchens 1990, 334). Thus, Eden, who had earlier thought it absurd that the Eisenhower administration would do anything but "lie doggo" in response to the British action in Suez, was now shocked into realizing that he did not know *what* the U.S. might be capable of doing (Shaw 1996, 171).

By mid-October, 1956, relations between Washington and London were so bad that the two administrations hardly seemed to be speaking to one another, and when they did, it was only to disparage and delegitimize the other (Dumbrell 2001). Leaders and bureaucrats on both sides of the Atlantic continued to publicly repudiate their trust and engaged in diplomatic behaviors to signal their uncertainty and distance themselves from one another, particularly in the international forum of the United Nations. In these ways, what occurred during the Suez Crisis was not a mere argument between friends, but an identity crisis for U.S. and Britain (Risse-Kappen 1995). It was a major demagnetizing event—a revelation that shared values were not shared after all, that attractions were false, and that we-ness was a lie, as was trust and reliable expectations that the other would conform to norms, including the norms of nonviolence. Indeed, mistrust and bewilderment was expressed on both sides of the Atlantic as both states sought to redefine their relationship without specialness or the normative and behavioral burdens that followed from it (Rosenberg 1987; Calhoun 1991).

It was in this complicated context of Cold War concerns, political and economic interests, and the collapse of the Anglo-American Special Relationship that the U.S. had to formulate its reaction to the British and French occupation of the Canal. The dissolution of Anglo-American friendship, coupled with the larger international order of competitive anarchy and the primacy of force as a political strategy in other international relationships, makes it curious that, so far as available evidence indicates, the U.S. did not even consider using force to compel its allies to cease their occupation. So what did happen? How was the Suez Crisis resolved among the Western allies without violence or even threats of it?

(Not) Understanding Nonviolence

Given the robustness and durability of the Anglo-American security community prior to the Suez Crisis, it would be tempting to appeal, as constructivists do, to some unexplained stickiness or persistence of we-ness and its attending normative environment. The idea here might be that, in spite of the cessation of the underlying processes of representation from whence the identity was formed and maintained, something about we-ness still rung true for the Americans—probably something wrought by Soviet otherness—and that this made an appeal to force unthinkable. Thomas Risse-Kappen suggests such an explanation when he argues that both the U.S. and Britain knew that they had violated some of the rules of the game, but both also knew that their shared values of democracy were too important to breach with force (Risse-Kappen 1995, 103–4).

But, as convenient as such an account might be, it is empirically awkward, to say the least. After all, to say that shared democratic values, highlighted against the backdrop of Soviet otherness, prevented the U.S. from threatening force against the British, is to turn a blind eye to the fact that the whole crisis of the Suez incident, at least as it applies to the U.S. and Britain, began with the unsettling of shared understandings of each being true democracies. What is more, at various times, each side likened the other to the Soviets (see Chapters 5 through 7). How could shared democratic values in the context of anti-Sovietism have been what prevented force when the very idea each had of the other as democratic and other-than-Soviet was up for question?[8] Thus, inasmuch as nonviolence was the product of some international order of stable expectations between the U.S. and Britain, those expectations must have been nourished from some source other than we-ness. It must have been some order other than a security community.

There are, of course, alternative explanations about where expectations and behaviors of nonviolence might have come from during the Suez Crisis. By and large there are two genres: alliance accounts that focus on the material distribution of power in the international system and institutional accounts that focus on the role of common-interest-based institutions in structuring behavioral incentives and disincentives. Whereas the former explain states' behaviors and expectations in relation to material power politics, the latter explains them in relation to common interests. To the extent that either successfully explains American nonviolent behavior toward its Western allies during the Suez Crisis, the need to think about identity at all in understanding international order—no less to take an identity-first turn—is obviated. In this way, if either of these conventional accounts were able to solve the Suez Puzzle, then there would be no remaining dispute to be had regarding the sources of international order. But neither of these nonidentity alternatives is successful. In a most ironic twist, neither is able explain that persistent nonviolent order without smuggling in an appeal precisely to we-ness. Each, that is, depends upon identity in order to explain American nonviolent behavior.

Alliance-based accounts of nonviolence begin with neorealist assumptions about the importance of the distribution of material power in international politics. Given relentlessly competitive anarchy, states must seek to balance power against external threats. One way to do so is to form alliances. Alliances are temporary cooperative responses to the overriding threat of a greater power, which, in the case of the Western alliance during the Cold War, was the Soviet Union. This account of nonviolence, then, should explain U.S. restraint from threatening or using force on allies in reference to their collaboration against the more potent Soviet threat. In short, stable expectations for nonviolence between the U.S. and Britain, as well as its other Western allies can, on this view, be chalked up not to some dissolved security community, but to the quite intact Cold War international order of bipolarity, which necessitated continued unity within the West.

Yet it is not quite so simple because, in its classic form, alliance theory is strict about the idea that within alliances, today's friend is tomorrow's enemy (Mearsheimer 2001). Thus, once the British, French, and Israelis betrayed the U.S. through their secretive Suez collusion, it should have been considered too dangerous for the U.S. to continue to cooperate with those allies against the Soviet Union. On this view then, the only circumstance under which the U.S. should have been willing to continue aligning with those countries would be if it could forcefully subdue its errant allies into a subordinate and compliant position. In this sense, classic alliance theory would have expected the U.S. to react to the Suez debacle with military posturing intended to remind its weaker allies of their precarious position (Risse-Kappen 1995; Richardson 1996).

Of course, the puzzle of the Suez Crisis is precisely that this is not what happened. The order persisted nonviolently; there was never any military posturing, nor were there even threats of it. In response to this fact, other scholars sympathetic to the alliance explanation for nonviolence have been vocal in their reminder that the *distribution of power* is what dictates alliance necessity. An overriding external threat would be expected to trump the U.S. desire to teach its smaller allies a lesson through military posturing. On this view, then, the bipolar structure of the international system during the Cold War context was unforgiving. A strong Western alliance was critical for effective balancing so that the United States could not afford to alienate its Western allies by threatening or using force (Neustadt 1970). The magnitude of the external threat posed by the Soviet Union meant that the smaller allies had a degree of power and freedom within the alliance that was disproportionate to their real material power. The U.S. could not risk Western fragmentation, thus, threatening to use force on the British, French, and Israelis was out of the question.

But this is still an unpersuasive account of why the U.S. stayed in the bounds of the nonviolent international order. While there is no doubt that the very real material and security threats posed by the Cold War were critical in the Suez Crisis and in the American calculations about how to handle their fallen allies, this exclusive focus on bipolarity offers an under-determined account for the nonviolent policy choices made by the U.S. The neorealist argument rests on the overriding necessity caused by the distribution of material power—a Western alliance was necessary. Yet if this material logic offered such a determinate rational incentive for bipolar alliances, then there would have been no reason for the U.S. to fear that threatening force with its allies would ultimately break up the Western alliance. Presumably, the British and French quest for security under the bipolar structure would have led them to rekindle the Western alliance, even if the U.S. had humiliated them with threats or use of force (Risse-Kappen 1995). What is more, the policy choices the U.S. ultimately made were arguably more humiliating or alienating (to the British in particular) than a carefully articulated threat of force would have been. Indeed, one of the most astounding things about the combination of sanctions and United Nations diplomacy that the Americans finally used to compel British and French withdrawal from the canal is just how much they were designed to humiliate and alienate the British. In this sense, concerns about the durability of the Western alliance alone are not compelling. Finally, if the Cold War international order was so unforgiving of disunity within the Western alliance, why did the British and French risk the invasion of the Suez Canal in the first place? All in all, bipolarity had more relaxed implications for state behavior than the focus on the distribution of power indicates. Something else, beyond bipolarity, must have made the U.S. abide by the nonviolent expectations of the Anglo-American international order.

The fact that there is logical slack in the material structural approach has actually been implicitly recognized by some neorealists. Joseph Grieco (1988), for example, suggests that in moments of conflict, long-standing allies will get the benefit of the doubt, meaning that states will refrain from using force against their allies. This proposition would explain the U.S. nonviolence toward its allies during the Suez Crisis. But it is also unsatisfying, because it is an extra-theoretical argument; there is nothing in the material distribution of power under anarchy that makes giving the benefit of the doubt a rational choice. After all, today's friend is tomorrow's enemy. Indeed, willingness to give the benefit of the doubt implies the antithesis of material focus: It relies upon *trust* among the parties. In order for the alliance account to work, the U.S. needed to believe without certainty that its allies deserved the benefit of the doubt, while its allies needed to believe without certainty that the materially powerful U.S. would indulge them with the benefit of the doubt. Interestingly, then, this allegedly materialist alliance explanation for the persistence of nonviolent order during the Suez Crisis turns into a story about how prosocial self-other knowledge, accumulated over a long-standing relationship among states, generated trust and behavioral constraints on violence even during this moment of conflict. In this way, it is an account that rests most fundamentally upon we-ness.[9] It implies that a security community was responsible for the nonviolent order-nourishing work.

The same is true of institutional accounts of American nonviolence during the Suez Crisis. Most closely related to neoliberal institutionalism in IR theory, this genre of explanation is generally articulated in two primary variants. Both variants accept the materialist premises that the distribution of power will largely determine state behavior and so international order, but they also acknowledge that slack exists in that connection. Instead of taking an identity-turn to tighten the slack (as Grieco accidentally does), both variants of institutionalism seek to supplement power-politics accounts with some kind of common-interests account.

The first variant of institutionalism does so by developing the view that nonviolence was the result of institutionalized habits of cooperation among the Americans and its allies. On this view, the Western alliance should be seen as an institution based on Western common interests, an institution embedded, in turn, within the larger institution of bipolarity. Despite the slack in the demands of the latter, and of the British, French, and Israeli violation of the former, the U.S. behaviors had become so habituated by these regimes that it failed to consider force as an option. Thus, even as the alliance institution was disrupted, its behavioral implications persisted. As Arthur Stein (1993) describes this, the U.S. failed to recognize that it no longer had common interests with its allies and simply had not readjusted to the new context before it had to make a policy choice. So it fell back on old habits.

While this is instinctively compelling (we have all failed to detect the subtleties of situations because we are so entrenched in our habits), such habituated mechanical behavior is anathema to crisis situations. Crises erase familiar routines and in this way disallow institutionalized habits; they eliminate the comfortable institutions that promote mechanized reactions by states. The Suez Crisis was a crisis in precisely this sense, *especially* when it came to the Western alliance. The U.S. simply did not know what to expect from its allies. Under these crisis conditions, and with the stakes as high as the U.S. perceived them to be, it is unpersuasive to think that the U.S. would have drawn up its nonviolent policy unthinkingly. It makes more sense to think that the U.S. made a conscious policy choice in which it decided that it was not in its interest to use force against Britain and France; that it was better to preserve the nonviolent order. But how they calculated that interest remains inadequately explained: The material distribution of power left slack in that choice, and the habitual, institutionalized rationality was disrupted by the crisis. The result is that the habituated common-interests account of the persistence of nonviolent order is logically precarious.

The second institutionalist account of persistent order is slightly different, but not incommensurable. This view relies not on the habits associated with institutions to explain nonviolence, but on the costs that can be ex-acted through institutions. It does not assume that the U.S. never consid-ered force (on this view it may have), or that it just gave its allies the benefit of the doubt. Instead, it suggests that the U.S. realized that it could achieve the desired effect of British and French withdrawal from the Canal most cheaply and efficiently by using international institutions to generate selec-tive incentives. The U.S. could alter the payoff structure of the Suez occu-pation such that its allies realized that it was in their own best interest to withdraw. On this view, the U.S. realized that Britain, in particular, would be vulnerable to cost-based incentives that the U.S. could architect through the IMF, the UN, and oil trade. The U.S. blocked British IMF withdrawals and used economic and oil sanctions to deplete British resources, plus it en-listed the UN in a diplomatic process designed to humiliate Britain before the international community. The result was a price too high for the British to endure, both in economic and prestige terms. The sum effect was to leave Britain with no hope of success, and with the Tory government facing a vote of no-confidence at home, the British realized that it was in their own interest to give in. As soon as the British folded, the French had to as well. Thus, they acceded to American demands for withdrawal without the U.S. ever having to use force. The sustained nonviolent order thus appears as a by-product of cost-benefit calculations put into action through institu-tions.

This explanation is compelling in a variety of ways. It is clear, for in-stance, that the American strategy was to use institutions to tighten the noose on the British, in turn bringing down the French. In doing so, ra-tionality and institutions mattered in producing the nonviolent outcome of the Suez Crisis. Moreover, deprivation of resources is a rather compelling reason why the British gave in without threatening some kind of force or violence themselves. They were simply too sapped to fight back.

However, even this account leaves explanatory gaps in why Americans abided by the nonviolent order. In particular, left unexplained is just how the U.S. arrived at the conclusion that it would be cheaper and more effi-cient to exact surrender through selective incentives than through force. To begin with, the process of arriving at this rational calculation would have required statesmen to have a discussion about the costs and benefits of using force. However, there is no evidence in any of the archives that the Americans ever entertained that possibility, even behind closed doors. Of course, scholars have imperfect access to documents, and the documenta-tion process is itself imperfect. So, such a conversation may have taken place. But even if it had, the costs and benefits of force versus sanctions seem unlikely to tilt in the direction of sanctions on the basis of substantive

rationality alone. A simple threat of force (not even its actual u
have accomplished the job of compelling a British and French wi
from the canal a lot faster and more cheaply (and as I argued above
not necessarily have disrupted the Western alliance or bipolar ba .nce).
Indeed, the costs of sanctions seem particularly obvious in light of the
diplomatic energy the U.S. had to expend coddling the British during the
process of withdrawal. Eden famously demanded a "fig leaf," which
Eisenhower and U.S. Secretary of Treasury Humphrey bent over backward
to provide in spite of the high costs to the U.S. (Cooper 1978).

So why did the Americans choose not to use force? Were they acting ir-
rationally without considering the costs? That seems unlikely. In order to
account for the willingness to endure the relatively high cost of sanctions
and fig leaves over threats of force, one must, as David Dessler (1999)
argues, acknowledge the myth of substantive rationality. Rationality is not
objective and material. It is socially constructed. What counts as a cost and
benefit must be considered against the backdrop of the social contexts
within which choices are made. The American calculus not to use violence
does indeed become more intelligible when one considers that what
counted as a cost or benefit to the Americans was not strictly material, but
conditioned and shaped by the Anglo-American normative prohibition on
violence. International structural constraints of the bipolar system and ma-
terial-power inequities notwithstanding, the Americans had choices about
how to deal with the Western alliance in the context of the Suez Crisis. They
opted for a strategy that would not rouse violence. But in order to get full
purchase on why and how they made that choice, some allusion to Anglo-
American we-ness and the behavioral constraints it imposed for nonviolence is unavoidable. In this way, like the alliance account, the
institutionalist accounts must either collapse under the weight of their own
logical lacunae, or they must appeal implicitly to identity as the source of
that sustained nonviolent order. They end up deferring nonviolent resolution to some version of a security community account of order. In short,
each depends upon identity to fill crucial logical gaps in their accounts.
Because they appeal to the very identity described by the security community account, they are hardly alternatives to that account; they are better
understood as addenda to it.

In sum, then, on the one hand, any logically compelling account of the
sustained nonviolent order during the Suez crisis appears to invoke a security community. On the other hand, the security community was inoperative at the time. We-ness and stable expectations had broken down. The
puzzle, as such, persists. Given this empirical and theoretical conundrum,
the best course of action cannot be to abandon the prospect of identity as

a source of that order or, for that matter, to dismiss the identity turn. Indeed, the surreptitious appeal of alliance and institutional accounts to we-ness reinforces the intuition that identity is somehow a source of international order. The best response is a deeper investigation into what becomes of identity during crises.

CHAPTER 4

Forcing Order

International identity appears simultaneously impossible and ineluctable as a source of international order. On the one (theoretical) hand, its socially constructed nature implies that international identity breaks down during unsettled times—like international crises—and so it is logically impossible to contend that identity could impose order upon disorder. Identity, that is, could not engender stable expectations and behaviors among states in contexts where they are otherwise absent (Chapter 2). And yet, on the other (empirical) hand, it appears that identity *must be* a source of international order. Against the foil of the historical puzzle of sustained nonviolent order among the Western allies during the Suez Crisis, it appears that there is no explanation for that outcome that *does not* depend on identity. Indeed, the traditional power-politics and common-interest accounts both invoke Anglo-American we-ness identity to absorb the slack in their explanations of that event (Chapter 3). What, then, should be made of this theoretical and empirical disjuncture? The answer I pursue is that something is amiss with the constructivist theoretical rendering of identity; something which has led to misapprehension of how identities function during unsettled times. By reconceptualizing identity along postconstructivist lines, it is possible to reconcile the empirical and theoretical disjuncture in a way that makes sense of the international identity–international order connection.

The postconstructivist model, like the conventional constructivist variant, begins with a theoretical apparatus that implies that international identities break down during crises. However, unlike the conventional variant, the postconstructivist model also recognizes that identities can be produced or re-produced (produced anew but with the same content) by states from within that unsettled context. The difference is that whereas the conventional account sees identity as a relatively un-owned by-product of interactions and social learning, the "post" variant treats identity as an agent-driven process, made possible through the power of actors' words. By thinking of identity this way, it becomes clear that during unsettled times, when the social learning mechanisms that instantiate identities (like teaching and framing) are ineffective or delegitimated, states nevertheless have the power to *do something* about the condition of their Self-other relations. They have *language-power*, which they can use to produce or reproduce sharing (of truths, knowledge, values, etc.) among actors; sharing that is needed to repair a broken-down identity, or to produce an altogether new one.

During crises, however, one form of language-power in particular will be the most effective at re-producing sharing—representational force. Like all language-power, representational force is expressed through the structure of the language that an author uses to articulate a vision or representation to others. However, unlike other forms of language-power, when effectively deployed, representational force leaves those at whom the force-laden representation is directed with no real choice but to agree with or "share" the knowledge it presents. So in circumstances where an identity has broken down, states can *fasten*, fix, or cement the identity back together via representational force. When they do, the identity becomes shared again among states as a lived experience and a behavior-shaping structure. It works as though it had never broken down at all. In this way, fastening identity through representational force *forces order* back upon disorder.

The fastening effects of representational force for international identities are significant for a variety of reasons. For one, fastening provides the theoretical logic from which to allow that international identity can exist in unsettled times, and so can be a source of order. Moreover it provides new empirical research tools for investigating that theoretical possibility. By applying theoretic insights about representational force to, for instance, the Suez Puzzle, new directions of inquiry into that historical moment become possible. Finally, because it provides theoretical logic and an empirical research tool for examining identity as a source of order, the postconstructivist account confirms the call for an identity turn in the study, history, and practice of international order. However, given the importance of states as agents and of representational force for animating this postconstructivist approach, an identity turn predicated on this framework would demand considerable rethinking about the types and extent of power dynamics entailed in ordering international politics.

In this chapter, I offer an overview of a postconstructivist approach to identity, beginning with an introduction to the idea of language-power, and then, to representational force, as one particular form of language-power. I focus specifically on the capacity of representational force to fasten, or forcefully impose, identity, and so order, back upon states during crises. While other nonforceful forms of language-power, especially persuasion and manipulation, also find expression in communicative practices among states (especially through bargaining and arguing), these, I argue, are inadequate tools for re-producing and fastening identities during crises or other unsettled times. But why and how does an author choose to re-produce a broken-down identity with representational force? To answer these questions, I draw on Jean François Lyotard's narrative theory of "reality" to develop a contextual method for seeing representational force within the structure of representations of international identity. Finally, I take up issues of agency and rational choice, which course through the whole discussion. By making explicit the logic of how it is possible for a being to choose among forms of language-power, I am also able to explore the question of when and why an actor might choose to represent with the other, unforceful forms of language-power, even though these do not fasten.

Language-Power

Constructivist approaches to identity cannot envision that identity could be formed or maintained during crises. A postconstructivist conception can. In a nutshell, the difference has to do with the way each understands power and its modes of expression in the identity process. On the constructivist model, international identity is understood as ongoing shared self-other knowledge that can only be formed and maintained when states somehow bestow authority on other states to teach and frame the content of their shared understandings. Authoritative power, as such, factors prominently into the constructivist identity process. Yet authority is a form of power that depends on legitimacy while legitimacy, in turn, depends upon some form of consensus among states about who should be legitimated. As a result, the constructivist account indicates that identity can only form and persist against the backdrop of some previously settled, shared truths (an epistemological order) about who is attractive (Chapter 2). Power as such is, at best, a secondary resource in the construction of identity. What really matters for the formation and maintenance of shared self-other knowledge are interactions among states that occur against a settled backdrop. Only under such conditions can states appoint an authority and so collectively learn the same lessons about who they are in relation to each other.

The postconstructivist conception of identity puts power, rather than settled truths, at the core of its model. More specifically, instead of viewing identity as a social construction, formed and maintained through interaction and learning that occurs within a prior order, this approach views identity as more fundamentally formed and maintained through *language*. As the fundamental act of social life, language is not just words that mirror some True Reality; rather, language is a practice through which people *perform* "reality" into existence (Wittgenstein 1958). Put more boldly, the world is not real in any socially meaningful sense unless actors find ways to communicate about it. To do so they must create collective sign systems (languages)[1] for signifying and representing what they perceive. As they do, they create the very world they observe. Actors produce language and language produces "reality." Thus, when applied to the question of how international identities are formed and maintained, the linguistic approach holds that they are represented or performed into existence by states (or more exactly, the people in whom states are embodied—Chapter 3) as they produce collective sign systems for signifying each other. Identities as such are not merely *social* constructs, they are *sociolinguistic* constructs.

Treating identity as a sociolinguistic construct marks a key departure from constructivism, which, as Karin Fierke (2002) notes, has for the most part refused to think seriously about language.* Indeed, in this emphasis on language, the postconstructivist model follows poststructuralist thought, which treats all international "structures," political spaces, and lived experiences as contingent products of linguistic dichotomies (Ashley 1988; Der Derian 1988; Shapiro 1989; Campbell 1992; Weber 1995). For instance, RBJ Walker has famously argued that the linguistic dichotomy of "inside" (political community, ethics, and identity) and "outside" (anarchy, self-interest, and difference) legitimates the notion of state sovereignty and produces the lived experience of domestic and international political realms (1992). What is gained by this kind of language-centrism is greater clarity about the centrality and ubiquitousness of power in the production and re-production of international identity. After all, on this view, language produces the worlds in which we live, from our political spaces (domestic or international) to our identities (us or them), and so it shapes who we are, the choices we make, and the lives we lead. In this sense, language is weighty; it has productive or performative features that make it a political action and expression of power in itself (Lyotard 1988). Language, that is, may be better understood as *language-power* and, on a postconstructivist view, identity is both a product and encapsulation of language-power.[2]

---

*This refusal can be linked to the "almost all the way" move, discussed in Chapter 1. Among the few self-identified constructivists who do focus on language, there is a resistance to thinking about identity as a relevant component of international politics in general, no less international order. See Onuf (1989) and Kratochwil (1989) who prefer to focus on the sociolinguistic construction of norms and rules.

In addition to facilitating an appreciation for the pivotal, constitutive role of power to the process of identity, the language-centrism of a postconstructivist approach facilitates an appreciation of the importance of agents. More specifically, any time an actor speaks, writes, utters, narrates, or otherwise calls upon a system of signs to communicate about the world, he necessarily wields the power of language and so participates in the forging of "reality." He becomes an *author* (Lyotard and Thébaud 1985); an agent of the action of representation. Hence, in the context of forging shared self-other knowledge among states, all states that speak up (or, more exactly, all the people in whom the state is embodied that speak up) are agents involved in the production of the "reality" of that relationship. In this way, its not just that international identity is fundamentally constituted of power; it is also that states are the agents of that constitution.

Notable about this is that, while the postconstructivist emphasis on language-power is informed by poststructuralism, its emphasis on agency marks a departure from it. After all, most poststructuralist frameworks view agency as wholly dispersed, lurking in intangible ways within social networks. For instance, Foucault sees power as something not wielded by people, but rather, as something that "happens" through the ritual practices of society (Foucault 1983). But, as Roland Bleiker (2000) has recognized, the idea of human agency (to wield power, among other activities) is not actually theoretically incommensurable with the kind of sociolinguistic framework that poststructuralists adopt.[3] Of course, Foucault and others knew this,[4] but they purposely neglected the sources and character of that agency because of normative anxieties about participating the production of the theoretical edifices would then become power-laden ritual practices of society (Connolly 1991). The postconstructivist approach follows Bleiker's lead; it recognizes the ability of people to purposively wield their language-power and so places agency front and center in its framework (regardless of the normative implications).[5] The result is a model that can provide what a poststructuralist model cannot (or will not) —a sociolinguistic framework that can still account for *who* wields the power that produces and re-produces international identity and how they do so.

Yet a postconstructivist model of the identity process still faces an important issue: with so many agents (any one who can relevantly speak on the topic at hand—Chapter 3) and so much language-power being expressed (in everything that is spoken), there is an obvious question about how one particular representation of states' self-other relationship ever becomes the dominant, real, or legitimate one. This question of how particular sharing or social knowledge wins out over other possibilities is precisely the question in response to which Adler and Barnett propose magnetic attractions and authorized core teacher states. But when identity is treated as

·d linguistic construct, the answer need not lie with some
-owned and ephemeral magnetic authorization; it lies with
ιage-power that an author—purposive agent that he is—
ρ..ιιυy or explicitly) to wield through his representation. In
ʋιιort, authors can express language-power in various forms in their utterances. They do so depending on how they structure those representations.
But some forms of language-power are more vigorous or compelling than
others in different contexts. Thus, while all representations wield some
power of language, in the face of multiple, competing representations,
some will express that power more effectively than others. Those representations that wield their power most effectively are the ones most likely to
become stable, shared knowledge and to produce lived "realities." Critically,
however, what determines their effectiveness, or success-potential, is not
the substantive content of the representations, but the manner in which
they are *structured*; the manner in which the author chooses to express
language-power through his representation (Lyotard 1988).

This last point goes to the very crux of the postconstructivist conception
of identity: it is not just that identity is produced and maintained through
language, or that language is a form of power, or that authors wield that
power when they signify the world "out there." It is that language-power
can be expressed in different ways and that authors can choose which ways
to express it. So when a British diplomat, for instance, wishes to signify the
character of the Anglo-American relationship as a we, he makes a choice
about the *kind*, or *form*, of power he wants to express in the course of making that representation. He may for instance, seek to structure the content
of his representation in a way that *persuades* his audience into agreeing with
his view. Persuasion is a form of language-power that is expressed through
argument, and so the diplomat would need to organize his language in a
way that reflects that genre of speech, rather than, for instance, the genre of
command, interrogative, or so on. Alternatively he may seek to structure his
representation in a way that *manipulates* his audience into sharing the
knowledge of Anglo-American we-ness. Although it is not clear which
genre of speech wields this form of language-power (perhaps metaphor or
analogy?), it is clear that manipulation entails persuasion but with purposefully omitted information, intended to sway the audience's reaction
(Wrong 1988). In this way, the diplomat would need to organize the language of his message in a way that it conceals certain ideas. Theoretically,
any form of power—authority, magnetism, moral clout, and even (and
most interestingly), force—can be expressed as language-power. All that is
required is that its author expresses it via the linguistic structure of representation rather than via physical act.

Just why an actor chooses to use one form of language-power over another, not to mention why he chooses to represent some particular knowledge over others in the first place, is another story entirely (and one I take up later). For now, suffice it to say that representing particular knowledge is one way to situate oneself in the world, and that in constructing a representation, one must make a choice (implicit or explicit) about the type of language-power that will be used. The choice is important because in different contexts, different forms of language-power will have different degrees of efficacy for compelling an audience to share a particular representation. The type of language-power, that is, makes a difference in how widely accepted, shared, or internalized an author's representation becomes to those at whom it is directed. My suggestion (which I also discuss over the course of this chapter) is that during settled times, when states already share some basic truths and agree on some particular tenets of who they are in relation to one another, representations of knowledge that deploy persuasive, authoritative, or manipulative forms of language-power can be quite effective at producing the sharedness or intersubjectivity required for a particular representation of a self-other relationship to become a social reality.[6] However, during unsettled times, or crises, in which those shared basic truths are disrupted, these forms of language-power are unlikely to successfully engender sharing. During unsettled times, I propose there is only one expression of language-power that can do the sharing-producing trick—representational force.

Representational Force

Representational force is an expression of force like any other: It is a form of power wielded in a blunt manner so as to radically limit the options of the subjects at whom it is directed (Chapter 2). But rather than being mediated through material or physical expressions, representational force is wielded through the structure of the language that an author chooses to use in forming representations.

To see how the structure of language can be forceful, it is useful to call to mind some of the distinctions that Thomas Schelling makes about forceful power. Force, he points out, can be wielded in either brute or coercive style. Brute force limits the options of its subject through conquest—by overcoming the victim's strength. Coercive force limits the options of its target by making the victim so afraid of some pain or loss that he succumbs in order to avoid it. Coercion thus works like a trap. It generates a credible threat to hurt and inflict damage, leaving the victim with a choice between compliance and suffering or even death. In this way, coercive force confronts its victims with a nonchoice: Either do what is demanded or suffer gravely, perhaps even die. As Schelling notes, it is just this nonchoice or trapping quality that makes coercion an effective tool for exacting submission (1966, 3–4).

As an expression of power, representational force most closely resembles coercive force. In fact, it has the same logical structure. An author presents it bluntly, nonnegotiably, and with self-interested intentions in order to radically limit the options of his victims. When he does so successfully he generates a credible threat that traps his victims into nonchoices between suffering and compliance. However, the kind of threat posed through representational force derives its credibility from a different source than that associated with coercive force. Generally speaking, when an actor wields coercive force he traps victims with the credible threat emanating from potential physical violence, such as assault with guns. When states engage in deterrence, for instance, they are relying on the credible threats that emanate from their guns to trap their adversaries into submission. Representational force, in contrast, traps victims with the credible threat emanating from potential violence to their *subjectivity*.

By subjectivity I mean an encompassing sense of Self, or more exactly Self-consciousness, above and beyond a being's particular identities or roles (self-other). For instance, beyond my identities (each intersubjectively constituted in relation to specific others) as professor, wife, mother, and so on, I have an overriding sense of my Self—my character—as simultaneously playful, strong-willed, serious, concerned about politics, and so on. Likewise, beyond its (intersubjectively constituted) identity as special friend to Britain, the U.S. (or at least the political leaders and bureaucrats in whom the U.S. is most directly embodied) understands its Self to be powerful, savvy, morally righteous, wealthy, and so on. These beliefs about our Selves, or our subjectivity, position us in the world, and so are precious.

And yet subjectivity is not just something one has innately, truthfully, or naturally. It does not actually just exist beyond, above, or outside of our situated, specific identities, but rather, subjectivity is the product of those identities in the first place. It is the product of the complex of a being's prior multiple and interrelated identities. In this way, subjectivity is intersubjectively constituted through shared self-other relationships and the sociolinguistic constructs through which *they* are constituted (Van Pelt 2000). The implication is that my overriding sense of my Self as playful, for instance, is not actually *overriding*, but instead, *underwritten*. It is made "real" by the social (and so linguistic) relationships through which I have come to know my self in the world in relation to others. In turn, the content and integrity of my subjectivity depends upon the content and integrity of the sociolinguistic environments in which those component relationships are constituted. In this way, subjectivity means having a concept of Self and a place in the world, but it also means being *subject to*, even at the mercy of, the world that produces that Self (Foucault 1978; Butler 1997).

This is important when it comes to understanding how threats of violence can be directed at subjectivity: A being's subjectivity is subject to (contingent upon) the persistence of the particular configuration of sociolinguistic identity constructs upon which it is based and from whence it is constituted. So, for instance, the U.S. can only sustain its sense of Self as, say, morally righteous so long as the sociolinguistic environment permits it. If the identities that constitute the American subjectivity are renarrated in some manner that they come to contradict the logic upon which that "reality" of moral righteousness is predicated, then that aspect of the U.S. subjectivity will cease to be "real." The key then is that aspects of a being's subjectivity can "die" when the configurations of the self-other relationships that constitute it change. Representational force, plays upon this vulnerability. When an author wields representational force the credibility of his threat derives from his ability to "kill" important or precious aspects of his victim's subjectivity by shifting the sociolinguistic grounds upon which those aspects rest. He traps his victims not with material guns pointed at their heads, but with linguistic "guns" pointed at the delicate constitution of their Self.

So how does one point a linguistic "gun" at a Self? That is, through what representational maneuvers can an aspiring force-wielding author credibly threaten to undo some sociolinguistic "reality" precious to a being's subjectivity? One way is through a forceful speech act. Speech acts are a genre of language in which the utterance performs the action as it is spoken, such as, "I promise" or the wedding vows, "I do" (Austin 1961; in IR Onuf, 1989; Fierke 2002). Speech acts can be forceful. For instance, when an employer tells an employee "you're fired," he is bluntly, nonnegotiably, and self-interestedly performing the firing of the employee. Assuming that this employee understands some aspect of his very Self as somehow wrapped up with this particular job, this utterance surely kills off some treasured aspect of his subjectivity. It reconfigures the sociolinguistic world from whence that aspect of his subjectivity was constituted because he can longer identify himself as an employee at that firm. (Of course, if this is an employee who *does not* understand his Self to be implicated with his work in this particular firm, this speech act would not affect his subjectivity at all.)

But while the linguistic force of this speech act is undeniable, it does not wield representational force as I mean it here. Representational force is coercive, not brute. It is *not* an attack or an assault, it is a *credible threat* to attack or assault. Saying, "you're fired" offers the victim no unsavory nonchoice with which he can comply in order to save his subjectivity.

One might fathom instead a speech act in which an employer gives his employee a nonchoice between doing something that he desperately does not want to do and being fired.[7] However, this does not wield the linguistic "gun" of representational force either, because the threat is structured such that it would not be threatening were it not for prior settled knowledge between the interlocutors. More exactly, in order for the employee to experience this threat as a blunt, nonnegotiable and self-interested trap, he must share an understanding with the employer about what it means to be an employee, what it means to be fired, what life is like if one gets fired, the conditions under which the employer has the right to fire a worker, and so on. In other words, the structure of forceful speech acts fall the way of other expressions of language-power (such as authority and, as I argue below, persuasion): They only work to produce sharing during *settled* times. During unsettled times, when the nature of self-other knowledge (employee-employer) is contested, the credibility of the threat and so the fear of violence and the trap is gutted.

In contrast, the defining feature of representational force is that it is structured in such a way that its trap does not lose its potency during unsettled times. Indeed, as Lyotard argues in *Le Differend*, force is not only possible but common during unsettled times.[8] It works like this: Whereas during settled times, a force-wielder may exploit shared self-other knowledge (for example, of the employer/employee relationship) to construct a trap that threatens his victim's subjectivity (for example, do "X" or you will be fired), in unsettled times, when the "reality" of that knowledge dissolves the force-wielder can instead create a credible threat by structuring the language of his utterance in a way that exploits the various *other* "realities" that constitute his victim's subjectivity. Representational force, more exactly, works by highlighting the intolerable incongruities and inconsistencies among the multiple, often overlapping identities that make up the rest of the victim's subjectivity. By teasing out the victim's various component identities and exposing their incommensurability, representational force turns the components of the victim's Self against his very Self.[9] In this way, representational force derives its threat from *intra*subjective sources rather than *inter*subjective ones.

For the victim, representational force amounts to a nonchoice between doing what the force-wielder wants or, essentially, becoming his own "killer." To refuse to comply would be to sanction the killing off of aspects of his Self by allowing the various, contradictory sociolinguistic realities upon his subjectivity rests to be exposed and challenged. The linguistic "gun" of representational force, then, is a way of trapping victims into a situation in which they face a nonchoice between compliance with force-wielder's demands and the exposure of intolerable incongruities within their own subjectivity.

For an aspiring force-wielder, acquiring the wherewithal to deploy representational force is not difficult. Since subjectivity is constituted by the complex of a being's multiple identities, and since most of us harbor inconsistencies among those identities, our subjectivity or Selves are vulnerable to exploitation (Weissman 2000). I am, for instance, both playful and serious—a contradiction that, when exploited by others, can be unsettling to my sense of Self.** The same goes, as I argue later, for the U.S. and Britain during the 1950s. Each had subjectivities that were constituted of many conflicting identities, and these became fodder for each to wield representational force over the other. Of course, not all aspects of our subjectivity are equally as important to us, and so there are times that representational force may fail to make its victims feel trapped. Victims may, that is, be willing to allow some aspect of their subjectivity to be "killed off." The same logic applies to physically coercive force—it always carries the possibility of failure. Regardless of whether or not the forceful effort turns out to be successful, locating the leverage for at least attempting to wield representational force is not hard for a would-be forcing agent to do.

Of course, representational force does require that the aspiring force-wielding author have the voice to communicate his forceful nonchoice to his victim. It also requires that he be able to discern the content of and incongruities in a would-be victim's Self concept. But neither of these are problematic requirements, even during crises or other unsettled times. In fact, in terms of the capacity of an author to speak, crises may be the best times since voices that may otherwise be suppressed are liberated when the institutions of a "reality" are disrupted. Similarly, the requirement that an aspiring force-wielder know the content of his victim's Self is easily accommodated. Actors publicly reveal the constitutive identities that configure their Selves all the time as they engage in the ongoing narrative process of maintaining those identities. Thus, it is not difficult for an aspiring force-wielder to acquire knowledge of his victims Self, or to find leverage internal to the victim's subjectivity for threatening to disrupt it. In this way, representational force remains viable during unsettled times when other forms of language-power fail.

**Of course some contradictions within our subjectivity are irrelevant in the sense that they do not disrupt our subjectivity at all. Whether some specific contradiction matters to some subject will depend on the broader configuration of "realities" within which he is embedded. Indeed, the failure of representational force is likely related to the failure of the force-wielder to recognize the relative unimportance of some intra-subjective contradiction to his targeted victim.

In sum, representational force is a threat of violence directed at a victim's subjectivity in which the threat comes not from the force wielder's relationship to the victim (not from intersubjectivity), but from the force-wielder's capacity as a speaker and his ability to hone in on the contradictions among the constitutive identities of his victim's Self (intrasubjectivity). When articulated, successfully representational force poses a blunt, non-negotiable, and self-interested threat that traps its victims with no choice but to comply, even during unsettled times. Actors can use it even during crises to get others to share the knowledge that they want.

Understood this way, representational force offers significant analytic gains for thinking about international identity during crisis times. During international crises, when the sharing of self-other knowledge that animates a given international identity breaks down, states can appeal to representational force to either form a new identity or re-produce the old one.[10] Statesmen and bureaucrats relevant to a particular crisis—those who speak on behalf of concerned states—can wield linguistic "guns" of representational force to trap the spokespersons of states who have authored representations that they find unacceptable, conflicting, or dissident. If they can wield their "guns" effectively the force-wielders can bring nonconforming authors into the fold of the particular self-other knowledge they wish to produce or re-produce. They thus force specific sharing upon their victims. As I argue, this is exactly what happed to Anglo-American we-ness during the Suez Crisis. Statesmen and bureaucrats on both sides of the Atlantic, though for different, incommensurable reasons, appealed to representational force to force we-ness back upon the other. They constructed representations of shared values, trust, and common-security fate (the tenets of we-ness), but they structured those representations using the linguistic "gun" of threats that preyed upon the inconsistencies within the subjectivities of those they targeted.

There is more. Successful campaigns of representational force like this do not just produce or re-produce the representations of an identity. They force dissidents (by now, victims) to *live the experience* of the identity into which they have been coerced. More exactly, the process of acquiescing, through which a victim avoids killing off his own subjectivity, demands that he articulate the force-wielder's preferred representation exactly as the force-wielder wants him to. This amounts to publicly concurring on the terms of the knowledge, making it shared or intersubjective. Of course, this process of acquiescing—of speaking the representation—may not change the victim's internal mental state, at least not right away. He may still wish to dissent from sharing the self-other knowledge being forced upon him. But lest he continue to subject himself to threats of force, he must behaviorally abide the demands of what he has uttered. He must demonstrate a significant degree of consistency between what he represents and *how he behaves* (Cruz 2000, 283). In this way, representational force actually *fastens* or affixes the identity so that it becomes (or as in the Anglo-American case, becomes once again) the "reality": the dominant, "natural," "right," or "true" characterization of the relationship, and so an expectation and behavior-shaping structure.

It is in this passage, from the wielding of representational force to the fastening of identity as a "reality", that representational force resolves questions about how international identity can impose international order upon disorder. During moments of disorder, state-authors can forcefully produce or re-produce sharing and so fasten an international identity that imposes particular stable expectations and behaviors on states. Identity as such can be a source of order during crises.[11] Indeed, the effect of forceful identity-fastening suggests how Anglo-American we-ness could have broken down and yet still have been the source of the nonviolent Suez resolution. As I illustrate, the U.S. and Britain forced each other into compliance with the terms of we-ness, and as they did, they also fastened the expectations for nonviolent behavior demanded by that particular shared self-other knowledge. In this way, recognizing representational force as a part of identity renders identity fathomable as a source of order. In turn, it provides the theoretical tools for solving the Suez Puzzle.

There is one final analytic point about representational force and its fastening effects worth pointing out. This is that wherever representational force is the form of language-power used to produce or re-produce identity, the model of international order that follows from it looks significantly different than that theorized by the constructivist model. In the latter case identity, and thus international order, forms through some unowned, relatively power-free process of interaction and learning. In contrast, when representational force enters into the picture, identity and international order are actually products of threats of violence (to subjectivity). International identity, and so international order, are essentially *forced* upon states by one another. Because of this, the postconstructivist model of identity-and-order production (at least during crises when representational force is called upon) starts to look rather more like a traditional realist model of order than it does like any other identity-based model. Order is produced or re-produced through a form of power politics, only in the postconstructivist case, it is a *power politics of identity*. Whereas traditional power politics wield coercive threats of physical force to trap physical adversaries into behavioral acquiescence, the power politics of identity wield coercive threats of representational force to trap the authors of adversarial representations into representational (and so behavioral) acquiescence.[12] While one operates at a physical level and the other at the level of identity, the logical and structural similarities between the two forms of power politics are undeniable. It suggests that a possible postconstructivist identity turn in the study of international order may, in some respects, merge more neatly with traditional realist imagery about international order than with conventional constructivism. Indeed, it suggests a possible future for a "realist constructivism" (Barkin 2003).

Bargaining and Arguing

One critique likely to emerge from the preceding discussion is that representational force cannot be the only sociopolitical practice or form of language-power that can do the identity-producing or re-producing trick during crises. After all, with all the possible ways of eliciting rhetorical compliance from others, why should this kind of forceful linguistic maneuver be the only effective course of action? The answer has to do with the character of crises as unsettled times. Without belaboring the notion of unsettledness any further, recall simply that crises are times in which specific taken-for-granted, shared-interpretative frameworks either do not exist or are so challenged that they no longer provide a compass for dealing with each other (Chapter 2). For instance, during the Suez Crisis, the U.S. and Britain lacked the shared interpretative framework of "freedom-loving democracies," which had been the indispensable basis upon which Anglo-American we-ness identity was built. As such, in place of shared understandings of we-ness and the behavioral norms they had implied there were now two separate, subjectively held beliefs about who the other was, who one's self was in relation to that other, and so, how to behave toward each other (Chapters 3 and 5). The question is how, in such instances, concerned actors can seize control of the collective field of imaginable possibilities about who they "really" are in relation to each other (Cruz 2000, 277). It is a problem about how to create a shared sense about "reality" without a common ground from which to operate (Duportail 2000; Schedler 2000).

So aside from representational force, what else might produce (or re-produce) shared understanding during crises? One obvious possibility is physical violence. Here the idea is that states produce or re-produce shared Self-other knowledge through coercive or brute physical violence. Of course if they can (and do) do this, then a postconstructivist model of identity would be moot because postconstructivism roots the identity process in language-power, not physical power. But as it turns out, physical violence alone cannot produce shared intersubjective knowledge. Just as material stimuli do not speak for themselves as sources of international order, they also do not speak for themselves as sources of international identity. Consider, for instance, Alexander Wendt's (1999) popular example of the unsettled first encounter between the Spanish explorers and the Aztecs.

While the former sought to use physical violence to force the latter into shared Self-other understandings of conquistador and vanquished, the Aztecs did not learn that particular knowledge from the violence. Instead, they interpreted that violence in a way that reinforced their own subjectively held "reality" of the Spaniards as gods and themselves as worshipers. Surely that interpretation got the Aztecs killed, but this only makes the point that nothing in the violence itself required them to acquiesce and so share the Spaniard's version of "reality." If they had, perhaps they would have better known what to expect and so how to behave to defend themselves. That nothing in the physical violence forced the Aztecs to view the Spanish as dangerous illustrates that physical violence does not by itself produce intersubjectivity. Rather, the production of social "reality" must be performed through communicative exchange—that is, through language. The tools for producing or re-producing intersubjectivity must be found in language-power rather than physical power.

But why should representational force be the only effective form of language-power for producing or re-producing identities during crises? Since there are as many forms of language-power as there are of material or physical power, an unqualified claim that representational force is the *only* effective one is impossible. Yet it is possible to probe, on a general level, the way that nonforceful language-power works to produce "realities," in this case shared Self-other understandings. In service of this it is crucial to note that whatever the other characteristics exhibited by an nonforceful expression of language-power, by definition of its nonforcefulness it must necessarily leave its targets *room for refusal*. So, for instance, when an author uses manipulation (a nonforceful expression of language-power), he may try to trick targets into accepting some desired outcome by concealing information, but since manipulation by definition entails no threat of punishment, the target can always back out of his agreement. In some way or another, this kind of ability to refuse is present in all nonforceful forms of language-power. The implication is that any nonforceful form of language-power will be a poor bet for an author seeking to produce or re-produce identity during unsettled times.

Consider two examples, bargaining and arguing. Not only are these common communicative practices among states in international politics, but they are, strictly understood, forms of communicative exchange that entail only nonforceful expressions of power. When it comes to producing or re-producing shared understandings among states during crises, however, neither is compelling—that is, unless they degenerate into coercive (i.e., representationally forceful) variants of their own format.

Take bargaining. Bargaining is a form of communicative exchange among states in which actors accomplish their goals by exchanging demands. Settlement is reached when bargainers instrumentally calculate that they have reached a deadlock in their iterative exchanges and that further deadlock is too costly to abide (Drezner 2000). What makes bargaining interesting as a form of communicative exchange is that one can imagine a situation in which states "bargain over beliefs"—that is, in which they exchange demands about who they ought to be in relation to one another, eventually settling on some shared epistemological framework (Goodin and Brennan 2001). Even more interesting is that a demand—which is the linguistic genre of exchange at the heart of bargaining—is taken to be a nonforceful form of language-power. While it is difficult to interpolate from the literature on bargaining just exactly what kind of nonforceful linguistic structure demand takes, it is clear that it is not thought of as something that wields blunt, Self-interested, and nonnegotiable threats. There are, to be sure, classes of alleged bargaining situations in which demands degenerate into threats. But scholars have been careful to conceptually cordon off such situations as a distinct form of communicative exchange called *coercive* bargaining (Raiffa 1982). Coercive bargaining occurs very much "in the shadow of power" and so sheds little light on how nonforceful forms of language-power can produce shared understandings among states (Powell 1999). But regular bargaining, based on the exchange of nonforceful demands, does not. In this way, regular bargaining is useful as foil for thinking about whether nonforceful language-power can give states the tools to produce or re-produce intersubjectivity in crises.

But the logic of nonforceful bargaining as a path to shared knowledge does not hold up in unsettled contexts. Because agreement is achieved only when actors have determined that they have reached a prohibitively costly deadlock in their demand-exchange process, successfully negotiating an outcome means knowing a lot about what the other parties' interests are and how committed they are to them. In order for an actor to know that he has pushed to the point of deadlock, he requires a fairly clear picture of the threshold or resolve of the others that are involved in the demand exchange. And yet, as Leonard Schoppa points out, the ability to acquire knowledge about other actors' resolve presupposes, at the very least, the kind of taken-for-granted stable social context of shared norms and even trust that is absent during unsettled times. It requires that bargainers understand each other's reputations (Schoppa 1999, 5). Because this is precisely the kind of shared self-other knowledge that comes under fire during crises, it renders the prospect of successfully bringing negotiations to a close during unsettled times unreliable at best. Bargainers may get lucky, of course, and decide just to give up and settle the exchange at an appropriate time. But that kind of a success cannot be chalked up to the bargaining exchange or the nonforceful language-power it entails. Rather, it must either be an accident of chance or a product of some other communicative process that produces sharing. In the case of the latter, representational force looks suspiciously convenient.

Even more damaging to the prospects of bargaining for producing sharing during crises is the very idea that bargaining requires its participants to *want* to reach a settlement. They have to want to hear each other's demands so that they can settle their relationship and get on with the business of some desired collective action (Goodin and Brennan 2001, 258 fn. 4). But during crises, states can become so disenfranchised from each other that, as Anthony Eden famously contended during the Suez Crisis, "going it alone"[13] carries far more appeal than bargaining to re-establish the conditions of cooperation. In this way, it seems that bargaining over beliefs is not even likely to occur in the first place in crisis contexts—not unless someone *forces* it. That would be no testament to the capacity of nonforceful forms of language-power to produce or re-produce shared knowledge among states during unsettled times.

Arguing, as another nonforceful form of communicative exchange, suffers similar problems during unsettled times. Also referred to as dialogue, deliberation, or communicative engagement, arguing in international politics is a process of public reasoning among states (Risse 2000; Crawford 2002; Lynch 2002). Its purpose is to establish or re-establish common expectations and understandings. In this way, arguing seems perfectly suited for constructing the kind of shared understandings upon which international identity and order are constructed. It is also promising because it works quite differently (in theory) than either representational force or bargaining. Whereas the procedure for representational force centers on blunt, Self-interested, and nonnegotiable threats to subjectivity, and the procedure for bargaining rests on the exchange of nonforceful demands, the procedure for arguing depends upon persuasion. Persuasion is a form of language-power in which an author structures his representation so that proof, evidence, or reasons are as clear as possible to the listener. It is a form of language-power through which authors seek to change the minds of their listeners via logic and competence (Habermas 1990). So, whereas with representational force, settlement on shared understandings is reached when victims are trapped into compliance; and in bargaining, settlement is reached when states deadlock over demands; in argument, settlement is reached when states are persuaded by the truth-value or "unforced force" of the better argument (Habermas 2000, 40).

But for all its sophistication and normative appeal as a means to produce sharing, arguing is by definition impossible during unsettled times. The hitch is that because persuasion wins over its listeners by an appeal to evidence and truths, some prior settled epistemological order is necessary for participants to be able to recognize the meaning and truth of the evidence or proof that is presented to them (Richardson 2001, 145). In fact, argument theorists, especially those following in the tradition of Habermas, are overt and unequivocal about this: In order for a communicative exchange to count as an argument at all, a common "lifeworld"—some basic stock of unquestioned knowledge that allows the listener to perceive the talker as legitimate—is a necessary precondition (Risse 2000, 10). Even those not informed by Habermas's teachings still overtly associate argument with persuasion and persuasion with settled times. For instance, many consider framing to be a form of persuasion and this is precisely why framing is thought only to work against the backdrop of prior, familiar, public truths (Keck and Sikkink 1998; Cruz 2000; Payne 2001).

The upshot is that arguing, via persuasion, *may* work to produce shared understandings among states during settled times,[14] but during unsettled times, honest, evidence-based, truth-seeking persuasion is likely to fall on the deaf ears of an audience who has no grounds upon which to accept the speaker as legitimate. Indeed, in the absence of a settled common lifeworld or familiar public truths, arguers eager to achieve agreement are likely to rely instead on coercive persuasion (Elster 1996). Surely such tactics can be used to manufacture sharing, but then, as in coercive bargaining, it is not a nonforceful form of language-power that is doing the stabilizing work. It is representational force.

Unreliability during unsettled times is a difficulty common to all nonforceful forms of language-power because, by definition, they all entail room to refuse. The implication is that while nonforceful language-power can provide useful tools for producing sharing in a settled context in which states already have some harmony of interests, goals, ideas, or visions and so are not as inclined to refuse, during crises when states do not know what to think of each other nonforceful language-power amounts to cheap talk. It may work to produce sharing on a lark or by dint of luck, but during crises, more costly forms of talk, like representational force, are the best bet for an author who desires to produce or re-produce identity. It is the most vigorous, effective form of language-power.

Terror and Exile

The efficacy of representational force for producing or re-producing identity depends upon an author's ability to threaten his victim into compliance by playing on his victim's intrasubjective contradictions. But how does one structure the language of a representation in such a way? What exactly does representational force *look like* in a communicative exchange among actors? Knowing something about this is crucial to evaluating the alleged fastening effects of representational force on identity and international order, and so to recovering the demand for an identity turn from the conceptual oversights of the constructivist model. It is useful, then, to further mine Lyotard's various works[15] for more specific information about the logic and linguistic structure of representational force (and by extension, nonforceful forms of language-power).

Narrative

The first step for "seeing" representational force in practice is knowing where to look. Like all forms of language-power, representational force is expressed when actors represent their knowledge of the world to others. Hence, seeing representational force (or any language-power for that matter) requires looking at those representations. But *which* representations should an analyst look at? There are numerous communicative forms through which actors can represent knowledge to each other—gestures, drawings, metaphor, etc.—all of which rely upon languages of different sorts and so any of which can harbor representational force. Lyotard, however, focuses his attention on one particular genre of representation —narrative. As he and others argue (Hayden White 1987a; Paul Cobley 2001; Homi Bhabha 1990), narrative is *the most fundamental* form of linguistic communication. Narrative can be understood as a manner of speaking and writing that is used to signify Real (physically, materially existing) events, people, behaviors, and other phenomena by charging them with meaning and imbuing them with coherence. Through this process, narrative makes things "real" in the sense of socially meaningful (White 1987a, ix). It takes the world "out there" and brings it "in here;" turning the unintelligible Real into the intelligible "real."

In fact, no other form of representation can do this. As White has shown empirically, when putatively Real events are offered in a nonnarrative form or without a narrative to support them, that which the speaker wishes to communicate is meaningless to others (White 1987b, 4). For this reason narrative is prior to and necessary for all other forms of communicative exchange.[16] Because narrative is the most fundamental type of "reality"-creating representation, it offers the most fertile point of investigation into the expression of language-power in its various forms. In other words, seeing whether and toward what ends states use representational force in the production and re-production of identity is best accomplished through a focus on the narratives relevant to the identity in question.[17] So, in the case of the U.S. and Britain during the Suez Crisis, an inquiry into the role of representational force for re-producing we-ness, and so for fastening the security community international order, would have to center on the narratives that each of those two states constructed over the course of the crisis to represent their respective versions of the "reality" of their self-other relationship.

Analyzing those narratives, however, must be more than a simple comparison and contrast of their substantive content as they changed and evolved over the course of the crisis. The analysis must be sensitive to the kind of language-power that was being exercised by the authors as they inscribed the narratives. In this regard, Lyotard provides some guidelines, which I use as a jumping-off point to develop what David Herman (2001) calls a "science of text"—a contextualized method for analyzing the textual problem at hand. In this case that means a method for accessing the forms of language-power expressed in the narratives of an international identity. Over the course of developing this method, I introduce a number of unfamiliar phrases, which are summarized below.

Fastening—The practice of using representational force to fix an identity so that it works as a behavior-shaping structure as if it had never been interrupted. When fastening is successful, it forces victims not only to represent the forced identity, but also to live the experience of it. This fastening effect of representational force is what makes it such a potent form of language-power and such a valuable resource for imposing order upon disorder.

Phrase—Word or word sequences defined by an author in a way that supports his "reality."

Link—The logical connections an author makes between phrases. Links give a narrative meaning and, in turn, reinforce the significance of its constitutive phrases. Linking is an act of power because it fundamentally gives meaning to "reality."

Phrase-in-dispute—Word or words defined by an author in a way that dissents from any particular "reality."

Tolerance—A nonforceful link, which an author can use to perpetuate his narrative in the face of a phrase-in-dispute. Tolerance is not a forceful expression of power and therefore does not have fastening power.

Terror—A forceful link, which an author uses to force the dissident to succumb to a redefinition of a phrase-in-dispute so that it becomes supportive of the dominant narrative.

Exile—A forceful link, which an author uses to force the dissident to exclude a particular phrase-in-dispute from entering into the dominant narrative.

Phrases and links

To see language-power (especially representational force) in the narratives of international identity, Lyotard directs attention first to the composition of the narrative form. Narrative has two components: phrases and links. Phrases are words or sequences of words that designate something (a concept, an idea, a person, etc.). Phrases, that is, are signifiers that can take a variety of forms—from complete sentences, to single words, to descriptive paragraphs—but they always construct, assign, and define a referent or a signified. Links are the mechanisms authors use to connect phrases. Linking is a linguistic act that unites the various referents into a larger context. For instance, currently the phrase 'U.S. President' conjures up such other phrases as 'George W. Bush,' 'U.S. Administration,' and 'Republican.'

The phrase 'Special Relationship' conjures up phrases such as 'U.S.,' 'Britain,' and 'Trust.' None of these phrases are necessarily or naturally related to the others. Rather, they evoke each other because they have been linked into a larger context; a narrative which gives them each meaning in relation to one another. (For clarity, all phrases under examination are capitalized and in single quotes.)

The manner in which phrases are linked together inscribes particular knowledge, or a "reality." For instance, depending on how the links between 'U.S. Administration' and 'Republican' are formed, very different "realities" are forged. We may know through these links that the Administration is dominated by a Republican policy agenda, or we may know that given the divided American polity the Administration is too constrained in practice to implement the Republican agenda. Each version suggests not only very different "realities" about the relationship of the current administration to Republican interests but also, by extension, very different "realities" about the U.S. President—one as an effective advocate of the Republican policy agenda and the other as the compromise produced by the divided American polity. Similarly, disparate or divergent "realities" can be constructed with the phrases 'U.S.,' 'Britain,' 'Trust,' and 'Special Relationship' depending on how the links among them are formed. Whatever the example, the version of the narrative that becomes more "real" (more shared as "true" knowledge, more socially internalized, legitimated, or settled) is also the version that constitutes the shared understandings for expectations and behavior. It is the narrative that constitutes order. And which version of a narrative becomes more "real," as I have argued, depends on the type of language-power expressed through it.

Language-power—of whatever type—is expressed through the links. When authors link, they imbue phrases with meaning and coherence in relation to each other, and so it is only after linking is accomplished that a narrative becomes intelligible. In this way, linking is the fundamental "reality"-creating practice: Links enable narratives, narratives inscribe representations, and representations create "realities." Finding the form of language-power that an author uses to construct his "reality" thus requires an analysis of the links in narratives. Just as there are different kinds of language-power, there are also different kinds of links. As Lyotard (1988, 80) puts it, authors have no choice but to link if they wish to be understood, but they do have a choice about *how* to link. It is possible to conceive of (at least) three kinds of links that an author can use to narrate international identity—two that exert representational force and one that does not (Lyotard 1988, 3–31). "Tolerance" is the nonforceful link. When an author uses Tolerance to represent an identity, it means that he constructs his narrative of that self-other relationship in such a way that the connections between phrases are open ended or negotiable. Thus, as the name suggests, when an author uses Tolerance he allows room within that narrative for listeners to refuse his logic. While Lyotard never designates one particular form of language-power as appropriate to fashioning links of Tolerance,[18] it is clear that the forms of language-power that it expresses must necessarily be nonforceful (for example, authority, persuasion). It follows that Tolerance is not an effective choice for an author who wishes to fasten the knowledge communicated in his narrative as the shared, true "reality," or, in this case, international identity.

In contrast, "Terror" and "Exile" are excellent choices.[19] As expressions of representational force, the whole purpose of Terror and Exile is to craft, disseminate, produce, and fix some particular narrative of a self-other relationship against alternative possibilities. Rather than Tolerant openness to alternative perspectives on "reality," Terror and Exile aim for settledness or closure. Toward that end, both of these types of links (though, as I explain below, in different ways) structure the phrases of their stories in such a way that listeners become victims; they are given a nonchoice about complying with the terms of "reality" inscribed by the narrative. But precisely because Terror and Exile are methods for squelching alternative "realities" they are, by their nature, context-specific and defensive. An author wields them in reaction to some particular challenge to his preferred narrative posed by some particular other actor. They are, that is, directed at a *specific* listener. To empirically see Terror and Exile at work, therefore, and especially to understand how they pose credible threats that prey on their victim's intrasubjective contradictions, one must first locate the challenges in response to which they are deployed.

Phrases-in-Dispute

Challenges to an author's narrative "reality" are wrought by other actors and can be manifested in many forms—physical, material, symbolic, or otherwise. However, as with anything socially meaningful, challenges are always communicated first via narrative. The challenger does this by authoring a narrative component that Lyotard calls a phrase-in-dispute. Just like regular phrases, phrases-in-dispute are articulated as words or strings of words. However, when phrases-in-dispute are linked into a narrative, they do not imbue it with coherence—as regular phrases do—rather, they disrupt its coherence. They disturb that status quo "reality" by introducing a contradictory phrase into the logic of its representation. For instance, the "reality" of the Anglo-American Special Relationship (and so the behavioral practice of the security community order) rests on a narrative that links together phrases that designate trust, shared values, and common-security fate (since those constitute we-ness). A phrase-in-dispute of that Anglo-American "reality" and international order is any word or word group whose meaning in a particular context challenges the logic of those links. For instance, in the context of the Suez Crisis, one of the many phrases-in-dispute of Anglo-American we-ness that U.S. statesmen and diplomats authored was 'Collusion' (referring to the British secretive collaboration with the French and Israelis). The logic of 'Collusion' conjured up a "reality" of the British not as trusted friends but as bellicose rascals.

At the very least, phrases-in-dispute shed doubt on the truth value of a "reality." After all, how can the British be at once both trusted friends and bellicose rascals? In this way, 'Collusion' shed doubt on the status quo "reality." But even more, phrases-in-dispute can be fatal for a "reality." Particularly during crises or other unsettled times when the opportunities for dissent from settled truths flourish, multiple phrases-in-dispute can be authored to the extent that they can *dissolve* the links that connect the phrases of their target narrative altogether. For instance, the many other phrases-in-dispute that the U.S. authored during the Suez Crisis magnified the effects of 'Collusion' so that it became impossible to ignore just how much 'Collusion' contradicted the logic of important Anglo-American phrases like 'Trust.' The result was that more than just *challenging* the links that constituted the narrative of the Special Relationship, 'Collusion' rendered it *completely* illogical. In the end, one could no longer reasonably link phrases like 'Trust' to the phrases 'U.S.' and 'Britain,' and so the "reality" of we-ness and the security community dissolved.

When one "reality" dissolves like this, the dangers for other realities are heightened: The dissolution of one narrative "reality" can create a domino effect, putting dissolutionary pressure on associated "realities" and, ultimately, even on authors' subjectivities. Put differently, phrases-in-dispute can reconfigure the sociolinguistic foundations upon which an actor's subjectivity is predicated. Again, think of collusion. What made this a phrase-in-dispute of the Special Relationship in the first place was that American authors had signified 'Collusion' as a reflection of British bellicosity. Indeed, the Americans had authored a number of other phrases-in-dispute as well, all of which supported the idea of British bellicosity to the point that bellicosity was inscribed as a "reality." And yet, that "reality" of bellicosity also functioned as a phrase-in-dispute of an important identity in the larger complex of narratives that constituted the British Self or subjectivity. Specifically, Britain still viewed its Self in some overriding way as the great and powerful Lion, but that "reality" of the Lion depended on the British having continued moral authority and military prowess in the eyes of other states in the international system. The phrase-in-dispute 'Bellicosity' challenged that authority and prowess by depicting the British as haphazard. Thus, if 'Collusion' were to fester, not only would the Special Relationship remain dissolved, but 'Bellicosity' would be reinforced in ways that put the

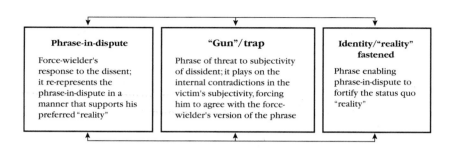

Phrase-in-dispute	"Gun"/trap	Identity/"reality" fastened
Force-wielder's response to the dissent; it re-represents the phrase-in-dispute in a manner that supports his preferred "reality"	Phrase of threat to subjectivity of dissident; it plays on the internal contradictions in the victim's subjectivity, forcing him to agree with the force-wielder's version of the phrase	Phrase enabling phrase-in-dispute to fortify the status quo "reality"

———▶ = Link. Phrases can be linked together in the narrative in any order

Figure 4–1 Terror

"reality" of the Lion, and so the British Self, in danger. In this way, the domino effect between phrases-in-dispute and "realities" can cascade in ways that threaten other aspects of a states' subjectivity.

When states experience the possibility of such a domino effect as high stakes (that is, they are unwilling to allow some reconfiguration in their subjectivity), they can choose to author a narrative that squelches the offending phrases-in-dispute. This is the function of Terror and Exile; they are narrative forms of Self-defense. When effectively deployed, both provide linguistic "guns" that bluntly, nonnegotiably, and for Self-interested (or more exactly, subjectivity-interested) reasons trap the author of the phrase-in-dispute so that he abandons his dissent and complies with the force-wielder's version of "reality." Indeed, as expressions of representational force, each accomplishes this by organizing the relationships among the phrases in the narrative so as to trap its victims within their own intrasubjective contradictions. However, when it comes to the particular narrative configuration by which the link accomplishes this nonchoice between subjective death or acquiescence, Terror and Exile work somewhat differently.

Terror
Terror, which can be empirically recognized in the narrative structure depicted in Figure 4–1, is the preferred strategy for an author seeking to defend his Self through representational force. Terror constructs a trap in

which the victim must not only abandon his dissent, but also na
self as a supporter of the "reality" preferred by the force-wielder.]
Terror turns a phrase-in-dispute into a phrase-in-support of the ﹍﹍﹍ ﹍
that is under attack. It forcefully incorporates the dissident author into the
force-wielder's status quo narrative (Lyotard 1979; Lyotard and Thébaud
1985). In narrative terms, an author accomplishes Terror by linking together three kinds of phrases: one which reiterates the particular "reality"
he seeks to preserve (the status quo or dominant "reality"); another which
redefines the dissident's articulated phrase-in-dispute in such a way that it
supports rather than contests his status quo "reality"; and one that poses
the threat and so points the linguistic "gun." As I have argued, this last type
of phrase plays into the vulnerabilities within the victim's own subjectivity,
threatening to exploit them unless he complies. The construction of such
logic leaves the victim no palatable out; his subjective survival becomes logically linked to the survival of the force wielder's status quo "reality."

During the Suez Crisis, the British used Terror to redefine the significance of the phrase 'Nasser,' which the Americans had narrated as an indicator of British overreaction to the Egyptian president. For the British, this
American version of the phrase 'Nasser' was a problem because it (along
with 'Collusion') supported that unacceptable "reality" of British bellicosity. So the British constructed a trap: The Americans either had to endorse
a definition of 'Nasser' that supported Anglo-American we-ness (instead of
British bellicosity) or admit that they were indifferent toward the security
of Europe. This was intolerable for the U.S. because to admit to indifference toward Europe would be to "kill off" a crucial aspect of its *own* subjectivity; the U.S. sense of its Self as the responsible protector of the West,
which was crystallized in the identity of the Eagle. Instead of risking that
aspect of their Self as Eagle, the U.S. succumbed to British Terror of
'Nasser.' It did so as all victims of representational force do—by mimicking
the logic of the status quo representation exactly as the force-wielder
wished. The victim thus becomes incorporated into (he *shares*) the force-
wielder's "reality." In this case, that "reality" was that Britain's reaction to
Nasser had not been bellicose but on the contrary, just the type of courageous valor that one could expect from Anglo-America. 'Nasser' became a
phrase-in-support of we-ness.

Of course, the use of the word Terror to describe this narrative linking
process is provocative by most standards—especially recently, given the rise
of terrorist attacks around the world. It is true that traditionally this word,
terror, has been reserved to signify the utter fear wrought upon people
through physical means. So using it to depict a linking strategy—a mere
arrangement of phrases into a narrative—is something of an irreverent

challenge. And yet this is precisely why Lyotard selects this graphic phrase: He means his use of the word Terror to be a phrase-in-dispute of the dominant contemporary "reality," in which terror is taken only to be something that is experienced via physical threat. His point is precisely that the narrative act and the physical act evoke emotionally similar reactions in their victims. Terror, he writes of this particular link, is a language game in which "a victim consents not because he has been refuted in a discussion but because his ability to participate has been threatened. . . . (Terror) says 'adapt your aspirations to our ends—or else!'" (Lyotard 1979, 64). In this regard narrative Terror, just like physical terror, works through utter fear of the consequences. One need not be the victim of physical terrorism to feel terror (Byford 2002, 35).

Obviously terror that is practiced on the body through physical means is more urgent, perhaps experienced more intensely (though that probably depends on the physical act), and, for most people, is more normatively troubling. Lyotard does not mean to trivialize this, nor do I by adopting his phraseology. On the contrary, the message is that what trivializes the experience of feeling terror is the contemporary representation of it as something which only counts if it is physically provoked.[20] The experience of terror is a psychological one; the means through which it is wrought—physical, narrative, or otherwise—should not detract from its political relevance. This becomes particularly poignant for thinking about representational force as a strategy by which statesmen might force international identity (like spreading the democratic peace) in an effort to order international politics.

Exile

When it is effective, Terror compellingly re-produces the status-quo "reality," which, in the case of the "reality" of an international identity, amounts to the sharing of particular self-other understandings. However, as an expression of representational force, Terror does not always work. Sometimes it is impossible for the force-wielder to generate a sufficiently compelling or credible threat to a dissident's subjectivity to the degree that the dissident will feel trapped (this happens with physical coercive force as well). In that case, a dissident will refuse to completely relinquish his dissent.

In such an instance an author can resort to Exile, the second type of forceful strategy for responding to phrases-in-dispute. Whereas Terror works by trapping authors of nonconforming perspectives into a nonchoice situation where they must support the status quo identity, Exile traps dissidents into a nonchoice situation where they must accept silence. In this way, Exile renders phrases-in-dispute inconsequential for the status-quo "reality" that the force-wielder wishes to protect by reducing their message (that is, their version of "reality") to an external, apolitical status. During the Suez crisis, British authors linked the phrase 'United Nations' to a narrative "reality" of American betrayal by telling a story of the various humiliations they had suffered at the UN at the hands of the U.S. Of course, to the Americans, 'Betrayal' was a phrase-in-dispute of that aspect of their Self as the Eagle, the responsible Western leader. In response, the American authors waged a campaign of Exile over 'United Nations' such that definitions of that phrase which supported the "reality" of betrayal would no longer be admissible in the discourse. American authors forcefully silenced these pejorative versions of the phrase 'United Nations' from Suez-related discussion so that it could not conjure up 'Betrayal,' or for that matter, dispute the Special Relationship.

Exile, however, is not the first-choice strategy, because the ammunition is not as powerful as that of Terror. Terror wins the language game by subsuming the dissident, incorporating him back into the status quo "reality," while Exile settles for banishing or excluding that dissident's particular phrase-in-dispute so that it no longer affects that "reality." Exile is less preferable for an author concerned to stabilize his subjectivity because it does not directly reinforce the "reality" under attack. In fact, in order for Exile to work, the force-wielder must make a compromise of his own: He must forgo the opportunity to renarrate the phrase-in-dispute. Whereas with Terror, the phrase-in-dispute is resignified as a phrase-in-support ('Nasser' became evidence of Anglo-American we-ness), with Exile the phrase-in-dispute is just excluded from the game altogether. No one can enlist it. Yet it is precisely because of this compromise that Exile works where Terror fails. Since the force-wielder using Exile no longer expects the victim to support his "reality" (but rather just to get out of his way), when faced with the nonchoice between subjective death and silence, the victim will be less willing to "die" for his cause. This makes it easier for the force-wielder to trap the dissident.

To use Exile successfully, a force-wielding author must logically connect four types of phrases (as sketched in Figure 4–2): a phrase that signifies the status-quo or dominant "reality" that the author wishes to protect; a phrase of compromise in which the author accepts some fundamental aspect of the dissident's phrase-in-dispute; a phrase that makes the disruptive phrase actually seem irrelevant, alienated, or unimportant to the logic of the narrative "reality" under attack, thus rendering it a phrase which can be silenced; and, finally, the trap to the dissident's subjectivity, threatening to expose some contradiction in that Self unless he complies with the banishment of the dispute. Once the compromise is made, alienation from relevance is proclaimed, and the terms of its trap are set, Exile is equally as forceful as Terror. It gives the victim the nonchoice of accepting the compromise of banishment or narrating death to some important aspect of

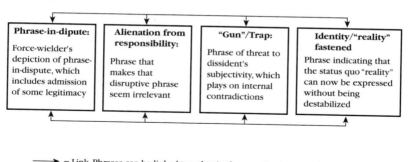

Figure 4–2 Exile

their own Self. In this way, like Terror, Exile bluntly, nonnegotiably, and Self-interestedly stops the domino effect between phrases-in-dispute and precious "realities."

When state-authors use Terror or Exile, or a combination of the two, to systematically squash the phrases-in-dispute that unsettle the narrative "reality" of an international identity, the overall effect is to fasten that identity so that it works once again as a source of shared understandings for stable expectations and behaviors. In this way, as representational force re-produces identity, it also forces order through a power politics of identity.

Tolerance

But what of Tolerance? When might an author respond to the challenges of phrases-in-dispute with this type of link? Can it play any role at all in the production or re-production of sharing during unsettled times? Logically, this link makes no effort to fasten, and so empirically, it should follow that Tolerance in narratives appears as descriptive phrases linked one after another in support of some proposed "reality" but without any trap to force its adoption (see Figure 4–3). In this way, Tolerance appears to be powerless to squelch phrases-in-dispute. Because of this, Lyotard literally writes Tolerance off as relevant to the concerted production or re-production of sharing. Indeed, he takes comfort in the fact that Tolerance cannot produce sharing because it offers hope for living without committing wrongs

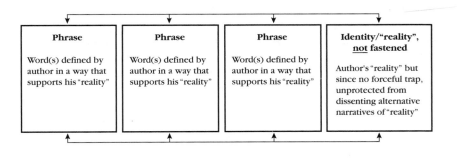

Figure 4–3 Tolerance

against heterogeneity (Lyotard 1988, xii, 69, 76). Notwithstanding Lyotard's ethical aspirations for this mode of linking, it does seem unlikely that an author would even choose to narrate with Tolerance if his interest were in stabilizing his subjectivity. However, Tolerance can be central to narrative in other contexts. To see why and how an author would choose Tolerance one final theoretical foray—this time into how a subject is able to know his interests and choose his links in the first place—is helpful.

Agency, Rationality, and the Uses of Tolerance

Terror, Exile, and Tolerance are a matter of choice. Lyotard is unequivocal about this (Lyotard 1988, 80). States (or at least those in whom states are embodied) make reasoned choices about how they want to narrate the world in which they live and so by extension about how they want to narrate themselves. They can try to "choose identity" (Chai 2001). But this claim is somewhat uncomfortable for social, political, and even linguistic theory because it conjures up two persistently intractable ideas: agency and rationality. Whereas the former refers to the notion that states are actors in the sense of being motivated, willful, or purposive, the latter refers to the idea that they are capable of assessing possible options in terms of their logic and acceptability as means to a desired end (Elster 1989; Emirbayer and Mische 1998). What makes these ideas intractable is they are unavoidable for thinking about any social, political, or linguistic action—in this case, the action of constructing some particular narrative and so rationally choosing the links to do so. And yet there is little consensus among scholars (little shared knowledge, as it were) on just how beings acquire their actorship and the interests from which to rationally deduce the best way of acting.

In fact, this "how?" problem of agency and rationality is even more pronounced in Lyotard's thought, and so by extension, the postconstructivist model of identity that it informs. It is hard to fathom how a being's very Self and so his ideas, beliefs, wants, needs, and choices, can be relentlessly rooted in ever-shifting sociolinguistic constructs, and yet how he can still have the will or resources to act, no less to know what his interests are or the best narrative link for constructing a "reality" that serves them. This tension between the radically socially constructed being and his capacity to know his own interests and make choices about how best to achieve them is so ubiquitous in poststructuralist philosophy (like Lyotard's) that it has typically led to the conclusion (very nearly embraced by Foucault, as I argued above) that there must be no agency at all. The author, proclaimed Roland Barthes (1977), is dead. Of course, as Lyotard would note, Barthes' proclamation is one of authorship. Indeed, Lyotard makes the claim, unusual among his intellectual cohorts, that the author is far from dead. The question is how Lyotard gets around what Barthes and others have not. In finding an answer, it becomes possible to think more clearly about when and why a state-author might choose to link with Tolerance.

Agency and Rationality

How do beings become actors? Moreover, when they act, how do they know what they want and so the best way to achieve it? Traditionally, these big questions have been formulated into debates about the relative weight of agency and structure in shaping human behavior. The agent-structure debate is common in some form across all disciplines of social thought—from IR theorists, who are interested in figuring out whether statesmen can order international politics or whether the structures of international politics order the behavior and interests of statesmen; to linguists, who wonder whether individuals pick their own narrative forms or whether the ambient communicative community (structure) does it for them. However, so far neither agent-based approaches nor structure-based approaches to human behavior have prevailed.

Consider the structural end of the spectrum. Among IR theorists, this kind of account is most readily associated with neorealism in which state action and choice are reducible to the determinative qualities of the anarchic structure of the international system (Waltz 1979). State rationality (means-ends calculations) is derived from the demands of the environment. The same logic informs the structuralist views of narrative choice. On this view, the choice a person makes (as an embodiment of state in the current context) about how to construct his narratives is thought to be defined by "the grammar of [his] speech community;" the logic of his constitutive social groups (for example, East as opposed to West, small state as opposed to large, etc.) (Labov 1989). But just as Waltz has been criticized for "smuggling" agency into state behavior, so has the social-structures approach to narrative behavior been criticized (Wendt 1987; Myers-Scotton and Bolonyai 2001, 3). The critique in both cases is that the rationality of the choice made by the statesmen/author cannot logically be deduced from the structures in which they are embedded. Some independent will and interest is implicitly assigned to the actor.

Yet the other end of the spectrum, in which agency is overtly emphasized, fares no better. Most common here are rational-choice models, which assume that beings are innately capable of action; they are innately actors. This means that they have certain exogenously given interests, that they know what those interests are, and that they have the will or wherewithal to make choices about how to best pursue them. In IR these approaches seek to explain state behavior through the microeconomic logic of game theory, in which cost-benefit calculations about expected payoffs are used to model state choice (Axelrod 1984). The same logic has been introduced to understand narrative construction: Authors are motivated to select certain communicative forms that best serve their preferences and intentions under a particular set of perceived opportunities (Myers-Scotton and Bolonyai 2001). Yet these rational-choice perspectives have been criticized for their neglect of structure. Rational choosers are unacceptably taken to be unencumbered by meaning, as if their rationality were presocial or reactive to structural conditions rather than endogenous and recursive with them (Cruz 2000, 281). Although some rational-choice models attempt to take structure seriously, when they do so they lose their "distinctive profile and logico-deductive elegance" (Mouzelis 1993, 683).

In light of the problems at either end of the agent-structure spectrum, a middle position has emerged—a position which seeks to conceptualize agency (actors, their interests, and their rationality) as a product of structure and structure as a product agency. The two are mutually constitutive. In IR this is best captured by the constructivist account, which, aside from a theory of identity, also provides a theory of state action. On the one hand, states' interests are constructed by the social relationships within which states find themselves, but on the other hand, since states are not constructed "all the way down," they also have some innate agency that enables them to construct those social relationships in the first place (Wendt 1999, especially Chapter 5). In this way, a states' rationality or reason for choosing one behavior over others is endogenous to structures (Dessler 1999), but since states are also agents prior to those structures, they can make choices that change those structures (Wendt 1999, 337). The same logic operates in middle-position theories of narrative behavior; On this view author choices are based on a rationality that is contextualized by communicative structures (for example, conversation, argument, and letter writing), but those choices can also alter communicative structures (for example, can switch an argument to a conversation). Habermas, for instance, understands the process by which actors select narrative actions in this way (Warren 1995).[21]

But for all of their sophistication, neither of these middle positions really stays the middle course. In both IR and narrative studies, agency is privileged over structure. For instance, Habermas undermines the significance of structure through the presumption of a prediscursive Self whose motivations can be completely transparent prior to discursive exchange (Garvey 2000). Similarly, Wendt privileges innate or corporate interests of the state by focusing on them as the units of international political action rather than on the political action of the system itself (Behnke 2001, 127–8). In other words, in spite of their apparent attention to structure, these middle ways are no more divorced from the micrologic of rationalist and exogenous interests than rational choice (Doty 1997; Emirbayer and Mische 1998).

So where does this leave us? Even this middle approach ends up pointing back to agency, and yet the question still remains about where agency comes from and so how states become actors with interests and the need to make choices in pursuit of those interests. In light of this, it is perhaps more promising than problematic that Lyotard approaches agency and rationality from a different angle. To be clear, his view bears similarities to the (attempted) middle course charted by Habermas (or Wendt), in which beings are taken to be both socially constructed by structures and, at the same time, actors who can author (act) in ways that suit their interests. However unlike those middle-course formulations—in which the tension between the effects of structure and the will of a person is resolved by assuming that beings have some natural, innate agency—Lyotard maintains that beings have absolutely no Real ontological status. They are only epistemological manifestations; they do not exist apart form the narratives that inscribe them as real. Thus, for Lyotard, a being's agency and rationality are both rooted more fundamentally in the narratives—the sociolinguistic constructs —that construct his Self. Roland Bleiker expresses a similar idea when he notes that there is an axis connecting narrative to agency (Bleiker 2000, 11). For instance, currently the subjectivity of the U.S. is constituted by a complex of narrative identities that includes Anglo-American we-ness, American Eagle as leader of the West, Freedom-Loving Democrat, and so on. On this approach, then, the ability of the U.S. to act or author (its agency) and the content of what it authors (the substance and links it chooses to author) can be derived from that complex of narratives. In this way, the author is not dead. Rather, he becomes capable of authoring in light of that which authors him.[22]

Importantly, this means that for Lyotard, agency and rationality are contingent experiences. Just as the Self is contingent upon the sociolinguistic structures that produce and sustain its constitutive identities, agency and rationality are contingent on those as well. So during unsettled times like crises, or when phrases-in-dispute dissolve the links that narrate some particular identity, the agency and rationality derived from that identity break down as well. For instance, once the Special Relationship dissolved under the weight of phrases-in-dispute, neither the U.S. nor Britain drew any capacity for action from it, nor did they sustain any interests derived from or related to it. The capacity to act as Anglo-American and in Anglo-American interests dissolved along with the narrative of Anglo-American we-ness.

So how do people and states have the agency to act/author and the rationality to know how to best do so during crises? More to the example, where did American and British political leaders and bureaucrats find the will to bother reproducing the Special Relationship? Why did they care? The answer refers back to the multiplicity of Self-sources; subjectivity, and so agency and rationality, are not singularly located in one identity or one narrative "reality." So when one narrative "reality" is disrupted or dissolved (for example, the Special Relationship) actors have other narrative-agent axes from which they derive their identity, agency, interests, and rational perspective. As I argue, the Americans for instance, drew on that aspect of Self as Eagle, while British drew on that aspect of Self as Lion. Phrases in each of those narratives overlapped significantly with phrases in the narrative of the Special Relationship, so when the latter dissolved, the former were threatened. Drawing on the agency, and in service of the interests of the Lion and Eagle respectively, Britain and the U.S. each set out to do something to stabilize the other sources of Self, to prevent their very existence from cascading away. The idea in this is that agency and rationality are contingent on subjectivity, but since subjectivity is not singular in its sources, understanding how an author acts/narrates requires a well-rounded picture of his Self and the overlaps in its constitutive identities.

Finally, though, there is the question about how an author chooses his particular links. Just because it is rational to do something (i.e., that is, to narrate a "reality"/identity) does not necessarily mean that it is more rational to choose Terror and Exile over Tolerance. Certainly it seems that the greater the overlap of phrases in an actor's multiple identity narratives, the greater the potential for subjective death when one of those narratives dissolves. Inasmuch as an actor cares about the survival of his Self, narrating with representational force and so fastening to prevent the domino cascade seems rational. However, there are, even during crisis times, some instances during which people and states might find that fastening the dissolved identity (and so forcing order) is not the most rational (important, desirable, interest-serving) practice. It is in these moments that Tolerance becomes useful to authors/agents.

Tolerance

Tolerance, by definition, has no trap to compel a unity of perspective or shared knowledge. It constructs a narrative "reality," putting it out there for evaluation, but it does not demand that it become truth. For instance, Lyotard (1985) characterizes his book, *L'Économie Libidnale,* as a narrative structured by Tolerance: It is a message in a bottle intended to produce ongoing thought and coummunicative exchange, not effects. Because Tolerance is supposed to engender a process rather than a specific outcome, it necessarily follows that using Tolerance to re-produce shared knowledge is a fruitless prospect. Of course, sharing via Tolerance may occur as an accident or a matter of luck,[23] but since the question is when is it *rational* for an author to narrate with Tolerance, it seems clear that any reasoning agent looking for logical and acceptable means to specific ends would recognize the disutility of Tolerance for such a goal.

But when the goal is not to produce or re-produce the shared self-other knowledge of a particular identity there are a variety of instances—indeed, infinite instances—in which Tolerance is the most rational linking strategy for an author. One such instance is during a dialogue or discussion among actors who are embedded in very highly institutionalized, settled contexts, exchanging narratives without a focus on the outcome. For instance, Tolerance might be the rational choice among couples who enjoy a well-functioning marriage—one in which the terms of self and other have already been worked out and fastened. In the domain of international politics, one might find this among state representatives in an entrenched bureaucracy, the rules and relationships of which are already established and naturalized. Although there are not many of these situations, there are some: the United Nations General Assembly, the European Central Bank, and so on. What makes these contexts amenable to Tolerance is that shared knowledge is already fastened and so certain kinds of disputes are ruled out or impossible. It becomes a safe environment for a subject to just talk. Of course, this is exactly what Habermas had in mind when he envisioned discursive democracy. This kind of narrative exchange is undertaken within a very rigid (settled) set of communicative rules in which the participants understand that consensus need not be achieved. Thus, if somehow consensus were reached, it would be through the truth or resonance of the better argument (Habermas 1996).

It is worth noting, however, as Lyotard does in reaction to Habermas, that institutionalized situations get institutionalized somehow. Settledness is not an accident of luck. Once such environments exist they may indeed provide fertile opportunities for Tolerance, but one ought still be aware that the process by which the rules of that discursive environment are settled require forceful incorporation and exclusions of its own (Poster 1998). In this way, Tolerance can become rational during settled times, but the question remains of just how the terms of settledness were narrated as "real" and "true" in the first place. It may be that the decision to use tolerance rests upon the prior fastening effects of terror and exile.

Other instances are perhaps more interesting for current purposes because they do not necessarily require a settled context to render Tolerance a rational choice. What they do require is that an actor not have, as his end goal, a concern to create shared self-other knowledge. One such imaginable situation is where the unsettledness and phrases-in-dispute do not touch upon or so threaten the actor's subjectivity or "realities." In that case, he can exert his narrative capability from a position of neutrality or indifference. He constructs narrative "realities," but just as possibilities; he puts them out there to be considered without concern about which, if any, become "real." In international politics one can imagine that a third party in a conflict mediation situation *might* adopt this position. I emphasize the *might* because it is not clear that in practice there has ever been a mediator whose subjectivity is unaffected by the outcome of the discussion he mediates. Indeed, Lyotard would likely argue that the moment an author speaks in a conversation his subjectivity becomes implicated in it. Nevertheless, the degree of his implication of his Self with that outcome may be minimal enough that Tolerance remains a rational way for him to fulfill his role.

In yet another case, the author is also disinterested in producing sharing, but not because his Self is unthreatened by the phrases-in-dispute. Rather, in this case his Self is very much at risk, but his particular sense of Self is Self-destructive and so he welcomes the reconfiguration of the constitutive sociolinguistic foundations of his subjectivity. He is besieged by unsettledness, but he wants to "die" for some or another reason. At the level of individual people, one might find this among people who are (physically) suicidal. Inasmuch as one does not care about their physical existence, it would be hard to imagine that they care about their subjective existence. I would note about this suggestion though that Tolerance is decidedly not a rational form of narrative for suicide bombers who understand their Selves as martyrs. For them, physical death is a reaffirmation of their subjectivity and so one would expect that their rational narrative strategies in the face of phrases-in-dispute would very much entail representational force to fasten their subjectivity. It is a bit hard to envision suicidal subjects in contemporary international politics (perhaps a state that is imploding or failing), but the theoretic possibility of this rationale for Tolerance does exist.

Finally, Tolerance becomes a rational-choice linking strategy for authors with a particular ethical stance. On this view, the Self is constituted very strongly by some identity that attunes him to concerns about oppression and force, and so he seeks to live without a unified subjectivity and without imposing shared knowledge on himself or others. This ethical aspiration is what makes Tolerance a rational linking strategy for Lyotard. He is not alone in this aspiration, for there are a variety of thinkers working on such postmodern ethics—ethics intended to promote global societies in which actors narrate only fluid, force-free identities. Those who aspire to live postmodern ethics aim to narrate social relationships that are without closure or unity, to be subjects without subjection (Corlett 1989; Connolly 1991; Campbell 1994; Meyers 1994). In such visions it is not just that Tolerance is a rational choice; it is the *only* choice.[24]

Each of these uses of Tolerance are interesting and politically significant. However, in the current context, where the concern is to model the re-production and fastening of international identity and order during crises times, a focus on subjects who are uninterested in narrating sharing is not particularly illuminating. Tolerance may be rational for some actors during crises, but it is Terror and Exile—the power politics of identity—that do the international identity and international order-producing work.

Forcing Anglo-American Order

In theory, representational force accomplishes a great deal. It provides the cornerstone for a postconstructivist model of identity that is capable of doing what the conventional variant cannot—support the logic that international identities can exist during international crises and so can be a source of international order, sufficient for imposing order upon disorder. Among the various possible implications of this theoretic "uncovery" is that statesmen who are interested in ordering international politics to their advantage might do well to put identity—or more exactly, forceful narrative realities of particular desired identities—at the center of their practical agenda. But how well does the theoretic uncovery of representational force, as part of an identity and an order-producing tool, gel with empirical practice? Can and do state-authors really use representational force to produce or re-produce preferred international identities? If so, do such forceful practices really have fastening effects on international orders?

In the next three chapters, I illustrate that they can, and they do. I demonstrate how, during the Suez Crisis when Anglo-American we-ness broke down, the British and American authors relied upon Terror and Exile to re-produce it. They did so by forcefully refashioning the links of the dissolved narrative "reality" of the Special Relationship against the phrases-in-dispute that had destroyed them. As they re-produced that collective narrative "reality" of shared values, trust, and common security fate, the British and American authors also fastened the nonviolent behavioral expectations that characterized the Anglo-American security community order. They relied upon a power politics of identity to force order back upon themselves. Beyond the obvious payoff of confirming that states can and do use representational force to order international politics, this post-constructivist analysis of the events of the Suez Crisis between the U.S. and Britain breaks new explanatory ground in the previously inscrutable Suez Puzzle. It demonstrates how, after all is said and done, Anglo-American we-ness *was* viable—in spite of its breakdown—as the normative and behavioral structure that shaped U.S. restraint from even threatening force against its allies. The postconstructivist analysis makes sense of the tendency of all compelling explanations of that outcome to refer back to we-ness.

Illustrating the forceful fastening of Anglo-American we-ness during the Suez Crisis, and so the solution to the Suez Puzzle, is a three-phase endeavor. Each phase, taken up in separate chapters, illustrates how key theoretical claims associated with the postconstructivist model are empirically actualized in the dynamics of the narrative of the Anglo-American we-ness identity (Special Relationship) during the Suez Crisis. The first phase (Chapter 5) focuses on the historical processes, through which the settled magnetic attraction that made the ongoing teaching, framing, and learning of Anglo-American we-ness possible broke down into an unsettled demagnetized environment. It is an exercise in understanding why and how dissent from the narrative of the Special Relationship became a collective possibility and desire among author-members. The second phase (Chapter 6) builds on the first. I trace out historically the particular manifestations of dissent articulated during the Suez Crisis, especially focusing on how the relevant political leaders and bureaucrats parlayed the events of the Suez Crisis into various antagonistic and hostile alternative interpretations of the Anglo-American association. The result, I argue, was to entirely dissolve the demagnetized we. In theoretical terms, this is an exercise in isolating the particular phrases-in-dispute authored during the crisis and illustrating how they were linked into dissident narrative realities that broke down we-ness. Finally, in the last phase (Chapter 7) I empirically examine the theoretical claim that relevant authors used representational force to squelch that dissent, with the effect of fastening Anglo-American identity and reproducing it as a source of international order. This requires a historical understanding of why the disputants felt the stakes bound up with eradicating the various phrases-in-dispute were so high as to require Terror and Exile, how they carried out those campaigns of force, and what their effects were for narrative, expectations, and behavior.

There are, however, two analytic qualifications worth highlighting. First, it is, unfortunately, artificial to conceptualize the identity rupture and repair process during the Suez Crisis as if it fell into three distinct, consecutive chronological periods. It did not. The schedule on which each demagnetizing event emerged was articulated as a dissolution-producing phrase-in-dispute of the Special Relationship, and was then squelched through Terror and Exile, was different. Indeed, some of the events that were parlayed into dissent were Terrorized or Exiled before others even developed (though there were always multiple pressures at once on the narrative of the Special Relationship). However, this kind of phase-oriented, chronological organization is useful both for helping situate the historical context of the crisis and for clarifying the interplay of identity, agency, and rationality in the practice of fastening. I urge readers, however, to keep in mind that at any given time, authors were engaged in and constituted by overlapping and sometimes interactive narratives that were at different phases of the process of rupture and repair.

This is particularly important in Chapter 7, where I demonstrate the practice of fastening through representational force. Authors deployed Terror and Exile to force phrases-in-dispute out of the realm of admissible discourse just as soon as they became high-stakes threats to other aspects of their subjectivity. Thus, each phrase-in-dispute was removed and replaced through a separate campaign of representational force. In this way, just as the dissolution of we-ness occurred piecemeal, so too did its re-production. But it did not occur ad seriatim, as implied by the way the information is organized here. It occurred in the messy, interactive way that life does.[1]

A second analytic issue to bear in mind is that the kind of narrative analysis I undertake here is a meticulous, microlevel enterprise. It involves focusing on the structure of linguistic formations and interpreting their meaning in a given context. This raises the theoretical problem of demonstrating how the micropractices of Terror and Exile shape macrohistory. Theoretically, this would require an exhaustive analysis of every relevant author's demagnetization from the we, their dissent from the we, and their forceful re-incorporation back into it. The problem is demonstrating with adequate certainty that dissent was squelched on a *collective* level, even though the practice of its squelching occurred on an *individual* level. Even accepting limitations on which actors count as the relevant embodiment of a state (Chapter 3), it is too ambitious to think that one could account for *all* the relevant speakers. Besides, not all texts are available for perusal, making some of the narratives unavailable for consideration. For these reasons, I have made choices proceeding on the assumption that a critical mass of systematically gathered evidence on most of the relevant authors can offer an adequate basis from which to rule out a coincidence between representational force and the re-production of Anglo-American identity and international order.[2] Even keeping the limitations of research in mind, the role that representational force played in re-producing weness—and so fastening the Anglo-American security community order —is undeniable. It counsels taking the international identity-order connection seriously.

CHAPTER **5**

Demagnetization

Anglo-American we-ness broke down through a narrative process. Dissidents on both the American and British sides authored phrases-in-dispute of the Special Relationship, and those dissolved the links constituting that narrative "reality." But the process began even before those phrases-in-dispute were authored. It began when the idea of dissent occurred to British and American authors in the first place; when the events of the Suez Crisis were interpreted by each the British and the Americans in ways that demagnetized their attraction to each other and so halted the ongoing process of learning and teaching we-ness (Chapter 2). In this way, the Suez Crisis provoked the conditions that made it possible for the U.S. and Britain to conceive of dissolving their special friendship. In fact, this was precisely what set the Suez incident apart from the many disagreements the two countries had endured previously over the years. Whereas others never penetrated the settled magnetic attraction upon which the Special Relationship was built, the Suez incident did. But how did it accomplish this effect? What exactly happened during the Suez Crisis to unsettle the magnetic attraction that underwrote Anglo-American we-ness?

Nasser's Unsettling

We-ness, which took narrative form as the story about an Anglo-American Special Relationship, had been formed and maintained on the basis of the settled shared conviction that British and Americans were kindred spirits. They were the apex of the West; the world's most committed and sophisticated freedom-loving democracies (Chapter 3). So naturalized had this narrative become that it functioned as a fundamental truth, a prior episte-mological order that drew the two countries together. As long as that order remained settled, and so the two countries shared an understanding of each other as freedom-loving democracies, they—or at least the specific British and American statesmen and bureaucrats who spoke for the two countries —had no problem legitimating and authorizing each other to teach and maintain the content of their we-ness (shared values, trust, and common security fate). In this way, the "reality" of freedom-loving democracy made possible the "reality" of the Special Relationship and the expectations and behaviors of nonviolence that followed on that.

But Nasser's nationalization of the Suez Canal unsettled the narrative "reality" of freedom-loving democracy. It created a crystallizing opportu-nity for a long-smoldering, latent conflict of identity between an important aspect of the British Self and an important aspect of the American Self. The Special Relationship, after all, was only one of many constitutive identities of each country's subjectivity (Chapter 4). Britain's Self, for instance, was also largely constituted by the identity of the great and powerful Lion, a leader in the West. Even though by the time of the Suez Crisis Britain's de-cline was relatively clear in material terms, no substantive event had actu-ally occurred to solidify Britain's diminished postwar status, or therefore, to dissolve the "reality" of that narrative in the international system. It was in recognition of this point that Dean Acheson made his famous quip that Britain had lost an empire but had not yet found a role.[3] The Suez Crisis of-fered Britain an opportunity to narrate such a role.

At the same time, however, the generally isolationist and unreliable U.S. had, at long last, begun to internalize the idea that its Self was bound up with being the leader of the West. Of course, in material terms, the U.S. had been the leader of the West for some time, but as Alan Dobson notes, the American Eagle—the identity that signified the U.S. as a proud and capa-ble leader—was, up until this time, an identity inscribed in the American Self predominantly through the narratives of domestic politics. Indeed, be-cause the Eagle as an international presence had not been incorporated in the configuration of identities that constituted the American Self, the U.S. had shunned international responsibilities acting unpredictably on the in-ternational stage. Since the end of World War II, though, this had begun to change—the Eagle as an international presence had been narrated so re-lentlessly by other states and by a smattering of new-thinking American au-thors that it had finally become the dominant narrative "reality" to the U.S. In this sense, the American Self conception was beginning to catch up with the material reality (Dobson 1995, 10). The result was that, although the U.S. and Britain shared a narrative "reality" as friends (the Special Relationship), the claims engendered by their respective narratives as Eagle and Lion also poised them for an identity competition over the "reality" of who, in "fact," was the leader of the West.

For a time, the rivalry was averted as the awkward tension between the respective claims of the Lion and the Eagle and were funneled into a narrative "reality" that supported positive, collaborative behaviors. More precisely, the conviction that the two countries shared an incontestable kindred freedom-loving democratic nature enabled the key authors to accept narrative "realities" about the Eagle and Lion as equal partners in the protection of the free world (Kunz 1991, 25). Put in Lyotard's terms, prior to the Suez Crisis, 'the Eagle' and 'the Lion' were not phrases that disputed each other within a larger narrative context; rather, they were commensurable. But during the Suez Crisis the complex confluence of Cold War politics, changing international norms surrounding colonialism and nationalism, and the idiosyncrasies of individual leaders and bureaucrats on both sides of the Atlantic ignited conflicts that even Nasser understood would disrupt the enfeebled "reality" of unity between the Lion and the Eagle. He boldly pointed out that the U.S. was "the coming" and Britain was "the going," and that although the U.S. was increasingly eager to take on its leadership role, the British were unwilling to let go of theirs. Nasser accurately anticipated what would occur if he nationalized the Suez Canal: a zero-sum competition for credibility between the Lion and the Eagle, and so between the British Self and American Self (Reynolds 1981, 26, 3). Nasser, it seems, was prescient. The Suez Crisis turned out as a competition for the right to claim leadership. The 'Eagle' and 'Lion,' rather than commensurable phrases in a larger narrative "reality" about freedom and democracy-loving partners in protecting the West, became competitive narrative "realities" in their own right.

Of course, that Nasser's nationalization engendered a conflict of strategy and policy between the U.S. and Britain is obvious from the historical record on simple behavioral terms. One need not delve into the underlying identities and subjectivity of the two states to see this. And yet, only by doing so is it possible to make sense of why the divergence in their policies and strategies became so unsettling for Anglo-American we-ness. In behavioral terms, the divergence between the two countries was over whether or not to react to Nasser's nationalization with (physical) force. Britain believed force was called for but the U.S. did not. Although there were also material reasons for this divergence, it was the Lion/Eagle conflict that made the divergence so divisive for the Anglo-American relationship. Whereas the British narrative "reality" of the Lion as leader of the freedom- and democracy-loving West hinged on the successful use of force to reverse Nasser's nationalization, the American narrative "reality" of the Eagle as leader of the freedom and democracy-loving West hinged on avoiding the use of force in dealing with Nasser's nationalization. Thus, for the British, 'Use of Force' was a phrase that was logically supportive of the Western ideal of freedom-loving democracy, whereas for the Americans 'Use of Force' was a phrase-in-dispute of that same "reality." These diametrically opposed interpretations of force unsettled the taken-for-granted truth that the two countries were kindred freedom-loving democracies—it revealed how the Lion and the Eagle had differing interpretations of what that meant in the first place. The prior epistemological order, which had made the Special Relationship between the U.S. and Britain possible, thus collapsed into uncertainty, or disorder.

But why did the narrative of the Lion require the use of force in the Suez context while the narrative of the Eagle could not tolerate it? The answer lies within the history of the Suez Canal conflict, in particular in the way that British and American identities developed conflicting interpretations of their interests in that region. When Nasser nationalized the Suez Canal he (possibly knowingly) ignited a complicated network of interests and conflicts between the West and the Middle East (Murray 1999). Nasser had come to power in 1950 in the wake of the coup against King Farouk, and in 1954 he replaced General Neguib as president. Nasser's aims were to ensure the economic development of Egypt; to assume leadership of the pan-Arab movement; and to consolidate Egyptian independence, which he planned to achieve by reorganizing the army and ensuring the evacuation of British forces from Egypt. Since 1882, Britain had been the dominant colonial power in Egypt. In accordance with the terms of the 1936 Anglo-Egyptian Treaty of Alliance, there were still 75,000 British troops in the Suez Canal in 1953. In 1954, British Prime Minister Anthony Eden, encouraged by the American government but over the opposition of many members of his own Conservative Party, concluded the Anglo-Egyptian Treaty and agreed to the withdrawal of all British forces from their base in Egypt within 20 months. The base would be maintained by up to 1,200 British civilians for seven years, during which time Britain reserved the right to reoccupy the base in the event of an emergency.

In an effort to encourage the Egyptian government to focus its attention and resources on economic development, and in the hope of keeping Egypt in the West's camp, the United States and Britain, together with the World Bank, offered to help finance the construction of a high dam at Aswan. Nasser was willing to accept the offer, but he was not willing to halt his anti-West rhetoric, which received widespread support domestically and which he used as a means of asserting his leadership in the Arab world. Nor was he willing to concentrate on economic development to the exclusion of military spending. He felt that his assertion of national identity and Arab leadership required a strong military as well as a growing economy (Neff

1981). When the United States equivocated over Egypt's request for military assistance, Nasser turned to the Soviet Union, concluding an arms agreement with them in September 1955 via Czechoslovakia. In May 1956, in an assertion of independence from both superpowers, and in a bid for leadership of the nonaligned movement, Nasser became the first head of state to recognize the People's Republic of China.

In response to Nasser's behavior, pressure mounted in the United States against funding for the dam. Because the offer of aid was not evoking the compliant behavior that American leaders had hoped for, allies complained that the lesson to be drawn from financing the dam would be that noncooperation was more highly valued than cooperation. Congressional critics, particularly those from cotton-producing states who feared competition from Egyptian cotton, threatened to oppose any foreign aid for so undeserving an ally. Advocates of Israeli interests argued that the aid should be blocked as long as the Egyptian military buildup continued. Meanwhile, the treasury secretary, George Humphrey, warned that the Egyptian economy was not sufficiently strong to service both the debts incurred by the dams and the arms deal. Thus, when Egyptian ambassador to the U.S. Ahmed Hussein arranged a meeting with U.S. Secretary of State John Foster Dulles on July 19, 1956, to accept unconditionally the Western offer to finance the Aswan High Dam, U.S. Secretary of State John Foster Dulles took the opportunity instead to rescind the U.S. offer. Britain and the World Bank followed suit shortly thereafter. Nasser's response was startling. On July 26, he announced the nationalization of the Suez Canal Company and declared that profits from the canal would be used to finance the building of the dam.

The implications of this for Britain were critical. The canal had opened in 1869 and operated under the Constantinople Convention of 1888, an agreement that guaranteed freedom of passage through the canal for ships of all countries. By 1956, the canal had become a vital artery for the transit of goods throughout the world. It was heavily used for the import of oil from the Middle East to Europe. Between 1952 and 1955, the total oil tonnage passing through the canal rose almost 50 percent, and by 1955 it had exceeded 207 million tons. Of this, 67 million tons were Middle East oil headed for Europe, and that comprised half of Europe's total oil imports. The United Kingdom received 20.5 million of those tons, which amounted to two thirds of its crude oil needs. In comparison, France received only 12.1 million tons of oil, and the United States only 8.6 million tons. In fact, British tonnage comprised 28.3 percent of total canal traffic, making Britain by far the largest user of the canal. Because Britain relied so heavily on oil transported through the Suez Canal, it was critical to the health of the British economy. Moreover, the British government, with three-eighths

, of the canal's total stock, was the largest single shareholder in the Suez Canal Company (Richardson 1996, 14).

It is probably not surprising, then, that as soon as word of the nationalization reached London, the British cabinet met for an emergency meeting. Immediately the British government decided that given their dependence on the canal, the nationalization would have to be reversed, by force if necessary. The French government, also concerned about their oil interests, agreed. But beyond these material concerns, both countries were also concerned about the incommensurability between an increasingly potent Egyptian nationalism and British and French leadership in related regions. It was no secret that Nasser's nationalization had "deeply moved the Arabs' hearts" (Love 1969, 364). In fact, the narrative that Nasser had constructed to explain his action was intended to do just that. In his speech announcing the nationalization, Nasser said:

> After the past four years, and as we celebrate the fifth year of the revolution, we feel . . . *that we are stronger and more resolute in our determination, power, and faith* . . . . At this moment as I talk to you, some of your Egyptian brethren are proceeding to administer the canal company and to run its affairs. They are taking over the canal company at this very moment—the Egyptian canal company, not the foreign canal company. . . . They are now carrying out this task so that *we can make up for the past and build new edifices of grandeur and dignity.* (Lucas 1991, 46, my emphasis)

In other words, for Nasser, this was an act of rebellion and independence. This alarmed both the British and French. The French were concerned, for instance, about their control in Algeria. At the time, French dominance there was being challenged by Algerian rebels whom Nasser was assisting. As such, French Prime Minister Guy Mollett was convinced that as long as Nasser was in power, the French problems in that region would be impossible to resolve (Connelly 2002). The British had similar apprehensions. U.K. Prime Minister Anthony Eden was certain that Nasser would seek to spread his power across the Middle East, depriving not only that region of its freedom but the British of their one last domain of international control. To the British, then, the nationalization was very grave, and if they didn't manage to check Nasser they would be finished.[4] In this sense, beyond just losing their ease of access to oil, they stood to lose their grasp on the region, creating a greater loss and one much harder to replace. A loss of the Middle East to a dictator would make any narrative of Britain as a great defender of freedom, democracy, and so of the West logically untenable. The Lion would be crushed by a third-world dictator.

The British and French governments thus agreed that the reversal of the nationalization could not just be about reclaiming control of the canal. It would also have to provoke the downfall of President Nasser—at any cost. To buttress their stance, the British fixated on a representation of Nasser as a criminal, as a Hitlerlike character that had to be broken lest he encroach further, not only on the economic and political freedom of surrounding nations, but also on the political freedom of Europe. After all, when Nasser vowed to "make up for the past" and spoke of Egyptian "grandeur" the British were sure they detected expansionist intentions. After the Arab world, they argued, the next stop was Europe—the West. For instance, British Foreign Secretary Selwyn Lloyd argued that Nasser was a paranoiac, like Hitler, and was so threatening that the British people felt they "could not let Nasser get away with his action on the Suez Canal."[5] Lloyd cautioned the Americans against being duped by Nasser who, like Hitler, was surely adopting a strategy in which "after a coup he was sweetly reasonable for a time" (Lloyd 1978, 109–10). Sir Ivone Kirkpatrick, permanent undersecretary of the British Foreign Office, carried on in this vein as well, comparing Nasser in Suez to Hitler and the Rhineland. His conclusion was that "we will have to have a row with Nasser. . . . It's just a question of how long all of us would have to go along appeasing Nasser before we had the inevitable row."[6] British Ambassador to the U.S. Roger Makins also goaded the Americans over the issue of appeasement. He reminded Dulles that Nasser could be a "blow" to the West unless an "immediate statement of clear and decisive Western policy" was made. It was the freedom and the democratic way of the West that was at stake, he argued, and to ignore that grave threat would be perilous.[7]

Alongside these public narratives directed at the U.S. and the international community, British officials also privately articulated to each other their concern that Nasser's nationalization was an event urgently shot through with implications for British international identity and prestige (Nutting 1967). Indeed, the extraordinary degree to which concerns about the integrity of the Lion shaped the British stance on force is made transparent in the British deliberations about just how to handle Nasser. They well knew that force was not their only option to secure their oil interests, which is why the British, unlike their hawkish French collaborators, hemmed and hawed for a long time before ultimately committing to the secretive use of force. For instance, the British considered the possibility of supporting a coup.[8] But ultimately the desire to preserve the Lion won out; as Kirkpatrick later explained, Her Majesty's Government refused to watch its great power status "perish gracefully," and that meant clearly and decisively showing her force (Kunz 1991, 4; Lucas 1991, 306). As Prime Minister Eden and Chancellor of the Exchequer Harold Macmillan—both strong-minded people thoroughly imbued with the tradition of British greatness—argued at the time, the British should "go down fighting." One forceful blow against Nasser in the Middle East would demonstrate the Lion's strength and shore up British glory.[9]

When the British officials finally decided to collude with their French allies, the decision was narrated (or, more accurately, was admitted in after-the-fact memoirs to have been narrated) in terms of the desire to preserve the freedom and democracy of the West, for which the British Lion stood.[10] As the British government saw it, "Suez was a test" of Western resolve, "which could only be met by the use of force." Playing into "the wider questions" that would be raised if Nasser's encroachment on "freedom of navigation . . . and other rights" were allowed to go unchecked, Eden argued that using force would teach dictators about the power of freedom against oppression (Love 1969, 368–9, 374). On August 2, with the phrase 'Use of Force' now linked both to the narratives that signified the phrase "Lion" and the narratives that signified the phrases 'Freedom' and 'Democracy' (especially against dictators), the British joined the French in secret military planning for the invasion of Egypt. In the British "reality," use of force was a testament to their commitment as a freedom-loving democracy.

Statesmen in the U.S. government saw things very differently. They were not just opposed to using force. They were, at best, ambivalent about precipitating the demise of Nasser. For one, they feared that deposing Nasser would create a long-term threat to the successful containment of the Soviet Union by opening the way for some new, unknown, and potentially even more belligerent, freedom-threatening leader (Nicholas 1975, 155). In terms of the Suez Crisis policy, this meant that, quite contrary to the British approach, all that a protector of the West should do is make sure the canal remained open and functional (Nutting 1967, 60–2). It should not cause any further provocation. Rather than force, then, President Eisenhower's preference was to gradually "isolate Nasser and gain a victory which would not only be bloodless, but would be more far reaching in its ultimate consequence than could be anything brought about by force of arms."[11] Implicit in this stance was that, on balance, the Americans saw Nasser as nothing more than a nuisance—a "two-bit dictator."[12] He could be managed by manipulative coddling and surely did not require all-out effort. Moreover, the American view was that Nasser's interests were *not necessarily* anti-Western (meaning they did not need to remain so), so there was no reason why the U.S. could not win at least his tacit support in the Cold War context. Dulles, one of the most vocal advocates of this "reality" about Nasser, quickly convinced other American statesmen that the best way to deal with the Egyptian president was to provide him with opportunities that would promote his nationalistic goals but that would also shift the weight of his power, prestige, and policies in favor of Western goals. It was not long before the American narrative about the Suez incident and its implications for Western-Egyptian relations was "quite hopeful [that it] might be possible to get things unstuck (Neff 1981, 254)."

But there was more to the U.S. position on Nasser's nationalization than just the belief that Nasser could be manipulated to the West's Cold War advantage. The U.S. also recognized another dimension that especially Eden refused to acknowledge: Nasser's nationalization was technically legal, and as such, democratic, law-abiding nations should recognize that there was no just cause for force. Eisenhower and Dulles were especially alarmed by Eden's disregard for this fact because "in setting himself above the law, Eden crossed the alleged British attachment to the ideal of a rule of law in international affairs (Love 1969, 365)."

In fact, for the Eagle aspect of American subjectivity, this issue about rule of law and the responsibility to observe it had special importance. As a key author of the "reality" of the Eagle in the 1950s, Eisenhower's vision was to use peace—not force—as a leadership tool. In keeping with his own personal identity as the Peace President, Eisenhower signified 'the Eagle' such that its capacity to lead was indistinguishable from its democratic and capitalistic stature, which, he argued, would promote peace if adopted around the world. In particular, the American Eagle, reverent as it was toward the freedom to choose government and goods, could lead the world by power of example toward a wealthy, free, and benevolent international system. The idea was that as an "open hegemony," the U.S. would advocate abroad that which it advocated as a democracy at home: respect for law and Self-determination (Kingseed 1995). By respecting international law, the U.S. could demonstrate to less powerful states that they would not be exploited; that they could rely upon fair procedures; and that they could be collaborators in the quest for greater economic well-being, rather than competitors for military power. In this way, playing by the international rules was the path to peace and greater prosperity (Murray 1999).

In light of this construction of the Eagle, to use force without just cause or considered process would be anathema. It would not only flout democracy by flouting rule of law, but by extension it would set a bad example and upset the international march down the path to prosperity. As Eisenhower put it, "if any large nation should attempt to settle by force an argument with a small one, without first having exhausted all of the peaceful avenues open to it," it would weaken and possibly destroy these "prospects for peace and wealth."[13] From the Eagle's view, then, use of force, especially in the

Suez case, was more than just a strategic mistake; it contradicted the very fiber of what it meant to be a freedom-loving democracy.

Beyond this logical contradiction between the phrase 'Use of Force' and the phrase 'Freedom-Loving Democracy' on the grounds of rule of law, Dulles highlighted another reason that 'Use of Force,' 'Eagle,' and 'Freedom-Loving Democracy' were incommensurable. For him, the issue was the Cold War. As was Dulles's wont, his perspective on international politics focused almost exclusively on the Cold War. But rather than a mere focus on the material parity (or lack thereof) between East and West, Dulles seemed to understand that the Cold War logic rested more fundamentally on ideological distinctions; on drawing and maintaining an identity/difference (self/other as opposed to self-other) boundary between the East and West. The Eagle, as leader of the West, had a responsibility to police that boundary. In this way, leading the West meant preventing the East not just from physically expanding into the West, but from muddying up the logic of what it meant to be Western in the first place. A moralistic and religious man, Dulles consistently maintained that the way to do this was to adopt a moral high ground that the East could not emulate or attain. Whereas the East was morally depraved—especially because of Soviet communist expansion and quasi-colonialism—the West revered self-determination and political freedom. It was the job of the Eagle, if it were to provide leadership for the West, to highlight this distinction. In practice, this meant informing foreign policy with a commitment to God and, as Eisenhower had emphasized, democratic values, especially anti-colonialism (which Dulles took to be a moral truth) (Kunz 1991, 27; Kirby 2000).[14]

But this narrative of the Eagle meant that during the Suez Crisis, *especially* force by any Western country, could not be tolerated. The problem was that the Suez Crisis unfortunately coincided with the Hungarian revolt of October 1956, during which the Soviets were bloodily repressing protesters. In this way, the Soviets were at that very moment demonstrating their disregard for the freedom, democracy, and the moral high-ground that defined Dulles's West. It was a perfect moment for the Eagle to protect the West by juxtaposition of the two worlds. Such a strategy, though, called for utter restraint, especially by the British, who as a former colonial power in Egypt had to avoid the appearance of Soviet-style imperialism at all costs. The West could not be at once "napping and doing nothing" about the Soviet suppression in Hungary and engaging in pseudo-imperialism in Egypt and still expect to maintain its moral high ground (Kunz 1991, 115).

In fact, Dulles also realized that if the West were to use force in Suez, it would not merely put the West on moral par with the Soviets, it would make them look *worse* or less moral than the East. The deep hypocrisy between the Western rhetoric of self-determination on the one hand and use of force to quash a legal, self-determining action on the other would not be lost on the Soviets, who would surely exploit the opportunity to upset what little trust the West had managed to earn among the unaligned states in the Middle East, Southeast Asia, and Africa. A moral slip-up in Suez could provide an opportunity for Soviet expansion into those regions. Any Western use of force in Suez would not just put the moral stature of the West at stake, but the freedom of the rest of the world as well (Kunz 1991, 115). Any freedom-loving democracy should recognize this. For the Eagle, whose narrative logic depended upon the ability to protect that freedom and democracy, it was a matter of subjective life and death that force be avoided.

In these various ways, Nasser's nationalization rendered 'Use of Force' a phrase-in-dispute of the taken-for-granted "reality" of freedom-loving democracy shared between the U.S. and Britain. Deciding what to do about the nationalization pit the "reality" of the Lion against the "reality" of the Eagle in a competition that centered on the phrase 'Use of Force.' For the Lion, force supported the logic of freedom-loving democracy—a leader who would protect the freedom and the political values of the West at all costs. For the Eagle, force disputed freedom-loving democracy—it would undermine the democratic commitment to rule-of-law and self-determination and so any leader who condoned it would be lowering the West to the moral and political level of the East. The upshot was the revelation that there was no longer a shared truth about what it meant to be a freedom-loving democracy. The very meaning of the phrase 'Freedom-Loving Democracy' had become unsettled, and so the "reality" upon which mutual Anglo-American attraction was predicated had as well. The relationship had been "demagnetized."

Getting to Force

Because Nasser's nationalization unsettled the meaning of 'Freedom-Loving Democracy' in a way that demagnetized the British and American attraction to each other, the Special Relationship was left vulnerable. Now there were no legitimate knowledge gatekeepers to sustain the sharing that constituted the we. Indeed, political leaders and bureaucrats on each side of the Atlantic experienced the unfolding events of the Suez Crisis in rather varied and often incommensurable ways. In this way, once Nasser's nationalization unsettled the foundation of magnetic attraction, the entire unfolding of the Suez events became fuel for the logic of dissent.

Once the initial shock of Nasser's nationalization had been digested and the British and Americans had each made clear their position on force, each swung into action. The British began open discussions with the French about joint military operations in Egypt as early as July 29 (three days after Nasser's nationalization). In reaction, Secretary of State Dulles set out on a lengthy diplomatic mission through which he hoped to promote a more cautious course of action. Ultimately Dulles's diplomatic efforts would become a major point of contention between the British and U.S., prompting one of the most potent dissolutionary phrases that British authors would narrate in dispute of the Special Relationship. The potency of the British reaction to Dulles is unsurprising because, as a powerful international figure and negotiator, Dulles held the key to legitimizing British action in the Middle East. As Britain saw it, if Dulles would just legitimize its actions, then American and British versions of 'Freedom-Loving Democracy' could be reconciled, and the Lion and Eagle might be able to renegotiate some kind of productive relationship.

And the British had reason to think that Dulles just might pull through for them. After all, Dulles was cagey at first, never directly rejecting force even though the Eisenhower administration had come out against it. This gave the British hope and so they played along with Dulles's diplomacy. Their thinking was that once all diplomatic avenues were exhausted, Dulles might back a deployment of force. This is why it took the British until October to agree to secretly collude with the French, taking underground what had originally been open planning. But Dulles never seemed to reach this threshold of diplomatic exhaustion, and all the while the stakes for the Lion were rising. Eventually, the British began to realize that Dulles had no intention of sanctioning force. As historian Alistair Horne put it, Dulles "infuriated all his British interlocutors . . . by his ambivalence and apparent duplicity—and not without reason. By appearing to blow hot and cold, he did a great disservice to the Special Relationship" (Horne 1988, 424).

And blow hot and cold, he did. Dulles's first diplomatic attempt was a conference of 22 maritime powers in London on August 16. By August 23, 18 members of the conference had agreed upon a set of proposals to create an international agency to operate the canal. Yet when it was time to present to Nasser the 18 Power Proposal produced by that conference, Dulles refused to go. This gave the unfortunate appearance that Dulles did not necessarily support the proposal. In September, the proposal was instead presented to Nasser by the Egypt Committee, which was headed by Australian Prime Minister Menzies. In the absence of Dulles's support, Nasser predictably rejected it. The British understandably felt that Dulles had undermined the product of his own conference and were frustrated that they had been waylaid by his manipulative antics—especially because

by this point it was early September and the Suez situation was heating up.*
The British were beginning to feel that unless they took action soon, the
credibility of their threats would be lost.

But Dulles did not relent. His second diplomatic effort was to create a
Suez Canal Users' Association, which became known as SCUA. The plan
was to have Britain, France, the United States, and as many of the other
London Conference powers as possible join together as users of the canal.
They would form a cooperative, which would enable them to exercise their
rights under the Constantinople convention. These rights included hiring
pilots, organizing convoys, collecting dues, paying Egypt, and representing
the group in dealings with the Egyptian authority. As Dulles described it:

> From the moneys received Nasser would be paid the share that
> [SCUA] felt Egypt ought justly to have. They would seek Egyptian co-
> operation. If it were forthcoming, good; if not, they would pass
> through the canal with the aid of their own pilots. (Finer 1964, 207–8)

At first, Eden was astonished by this incredible proposal, and asked if
Dulles was really serious. However, the more he thought about it, the more
he was attracted to it, in particular to the fact that the canal dues would go
not to Nasser, but to the User's Association. If the United States were to participate fully—and it was, after all, an American plan—not only would
Nasser's revenue be reduced so drastically from the canal as to be minimal,
but the reality of control would be removed from Egyptian hands. In effect,
if Nasser accepted SCUA, it would have enabled the British to make a mockery of nationalization. That kind of result would work for the Lion by enti-
tling the British to retain de facto control in the region. Moreover, as Harold
Macmillan noted, even if Nasser did not accept SCUA, his refusal would
"serve to bring the issue to a head," justifying use of force (James 1986, 511).

---

*Why did Dulles adopt such manipulative tactics in his effort to prevent the British from using
force? After all, Dulles might just have easily sought to promote a diplomatic solution without relying on such maneuvers to coax British participation in negotiations. But precisely because 'Use
of Force' had unsettled the shared foundations of 'Freedom-Loving Democracy,' Dulles did not
know how to orient himself toward the British, particularly when it came to how much cooperation to expect from them in terms of operating within the parameters of international law. Shrewd
strategist that he was, Dulles calculated that manipulating the British into cooperating with diplomacy would be more prudent than expecting them to do so on the merits of a possible diplomatic
solutions alone. For an interesting discussion of Dulles's strategic disposition see Immerman
(1998). As Dulles represented his behavior to the British later, he had manipulated them for their
own good, to save them from apparently inevitable mistakes (see Chapter 7).

Lloyd concurred: "We decided to support the SCUA plan . . . if we tried SCUA without success, use of force would be the policy" (Lloyd 1978, 134).

Thus, by the time the Menzies mission had failed on September 11, Eden, Lloyd, and Macmillan were all eager to push SCUA. From September 19 to 22, a second London conference was convened to discuss this proposal. During the conference, participants agreed that if the Egyptian government should seek to interfere with the operation of the association or refuse to cooperate with SCUA, then it would be a breach of the Convention of 1888. In that event *any member of SCUA* would be free to take the steps they deemed required to assert their rights (James 1986, 513). In other words, if Nasser failed to comply, Britain would be justified in using force. It sounded perfect to the British. But once this agreed-upon statement was released Dulles did an about-face, effectively gutting the plan. He announced in a press conference that the U.S. did "not intend to shoot our way through [the canal]. It may be that we have the right to do it, but we don't intend to do it as far as the United States is concerned." In this sense, no sooner had the ink dried on the agreement than Dulles seemed to deliberately undermine any threat value it had.

Eden was furious. Dulles had ardently advocated the adoption of the SCUA plans by his allies knowing that the readiness of those allies to accept the proposals rested heavily on the supposition that the United States was a serious party. Yet Dulles showed no hesitancy at backing away after his allies were publicly committed. Dulles had used his clout in duplicitous and double-crossing ways. It was in this context that the British began in earnest to brew their own duplicitous plans with the French and Israelis. They decided they would continue to play along with SCUA, but at the same time they would begin planning their invasion. This way, they could continue to garner credit with Dulles and keep him at bay while still making their own contingency plans. Moreover, even though SCUA no longer held promise for justifying force, it could still be used to deprive Nasser of his dues. As Lloyd explained to British Cabinet members, members of SCUA could have to get tough on the issue of payments; that is, as little as possible should be paid to Nasser (Lloyd 1978, 126). Thus, continued participation in SCUA, and the rights to withhold dues that it entailed, would offer Britain de facto control over the situation and the image of power while they surreptitiously hatched a plan to use force.

But Dulles foiled even this potential dues-withholding benefit of SCUA. On October 12, when Lloyd went to discuss with Dulles the pressures that could be brought to bear upon Egypt through SCUA dues, he discovered that Dulles's idea was that "the dues should be paid to SCUA and then 90 percent of them handed on to Nasser. That would mean that Nasser would be getting a larger proportion than he was already receiving" (Lloyd 1978,

162). The effect was that Dulles had entirely refashioned SCUA; in fact, he had mutated it so that the user's association had developed into a completely different institution from the one to which the British had initially signed on. Lloyd "was horrified" (Lloyd 1978, 62). He was not the only one; Eden and Macmillan were mortified, particularly because French Prime Minister Guy Mollet, who had been skeptical of Dulles's plan from the start, had been proven right that Dulles was not to be trusted. Indeed, for Eden the stakes were even higher than just embarrassment in front of Mollet. He had presented SCUA to the British Parliament as a failsafe plan because it would both legitimate force and, in the absence of that, provide a mechanism for withholding dues; to his political embarrassment, neither turned out to be true. SCUA had not only been gutted of its force-legitimating function, but instead of a mechanism for withholding dues, it had perversely been turned into a means of financial support for Nasser. In light of all of this, it is not surprising that the British experienced Dulles's diplomatic efforts as antithetical to the stuff of trust, which was so central to we-ness and the Special Relationship.

It is significant, however, that although the SCUA debacle did not come to a head until mid-October, the British realized long before that they could not afford to rely on Dulles for legitimation of force—there would always be another conference, another diplomatic effort, and another promise. Convinced as they were by the lessons of Nazi Germany that dictators must not be appeased, the British political leadership agreed that saving Western freedom (and along with it, their identity as the Lion) would require taking precautionary steps of their own, even if it meant going against Dulles and taking their military operations underground.[15] From late July, when Britain and France had struck up open (non-secretive) planning for an Egyptian invasion, they had been patiently, though anxiously, awaiting, some provocation by Nasser that would provide a legitimate pretext for force. However, Nasser carefully avoided all provocation. He proved that his people could operate the canal at least as efficiently as their predecessors and he permitted free passage through the canal. Britain and France nevertheless continued to be convinced that Nasser posed a grave threat to their position in the Middle East. Finally, the British became more aggressive about pushing their agenda.

On September 12, Britain and France took their first controversial (and for Anglo-American relations, divisive) steps by bringing their case to the UN Security Council in the hopes of gaining support for the use of force. After all, if Dulles were not going to give them the backing they needed, the moral backing of the international community would suffice. Certainly, if the British could introduce a resolution for force that was internationally condoned, their Self as a decisive, righteous power would be reinforced.[16]

The U.S. staunchly opposed this move, and Dulles was characteristically vocal in arguing against it. Of course, the U.S. had its own Self-interested reasons for adopting this oppositional stance. For the Eagle, the Suez Crisis was an opportunity to demonstrate its ability to enhance global stability via peaceful means. The idea was for Eisenhower, the Peace President, to wage peace rather than war during this election year. Waging peace was also important for shoring up that moral boundary between the depraved East and the morally conscientious and free West. To involve the UN would be to let management of the Suez Crisis become bogged down in an East/West conflict, one that would inevitably steal the show away from the image of the U.S. as the capable leader. For these reasons, Eisenhower pleaded with Eden to hold off on UN involvement.[17]

But Eden was uncompelled. As he would write later, "The repercussions in the Middle East showed that if we waited longer our position would slip. Therefore, even though the United States still favored delay, we could no longer hold our hand" (Eden 1960, 550). In light of this, the British appeal to the Security Council on September 12 was internalized by the Americans as nothing less than a blatant challenge by the Lion, of the Eagle. In this sense, it was not just that there was a divergence in their conceptions of what it meant to be a freedom-loving democracy. It was that the divergence prompted the British to take actions that Eisenhower experienced as hostile and antagonizing. What is more, when the British did take their case to the UN, they did so without consulting the U.S. —a blatant violation of the norms of mutual, open security-policy consultation that characterized the Special Relationship (Chapter 3). This kind of deception would not be the last, but as the first it made the British distinctly unattractive to the Americans. It was an event upon which American dissent from the Special Relationship would seize.

Once the British had filed their appeal to the Security Council, Egypt immediately filed a counterprotest against Anglo-French military threats. But by now it did not matter. Anglo-French military preparations for an invasion of Egypt had continued throughout the process, and the British and French had every intention of using those plans regardless of the outcome of their UN appeal. Extensive public and private meetings were held among the various UN contingents charged with drafting a resolution of force. When they presented their case in the Security Council on September 23, the Americans stood firm against it. Henry Cabot Lodge, U.S. ambassador to the UN, characterized the Anglo-French resolution as "a device aimed at placating world opinion. . . . It indicates willingness to have a showdown" (Neff 1981, 321). It was a position that did not bode well for American trust in their British allies. Finally, after ten days of discussion at the United Nations, a vote was taken in the Security Council. Although Lloyd had disingenuously defended the British, saying that "we have no idea of using the Security Council as a cover for military operations," the original U.K.-French resolution against Egypt was shelved.[18] In its place, six principles were voted in that dictated the terms of a Suez settlement. The British took only partial satisfaction in this October 13 outcome; they "were left with six principles, and principles are aimless unless translated into action." But action would not be forthcoming. The Soviets had vetoed the part of the resolution that demanded action. Although further negotiations were scheduled to resume on October 29, the British were astonished to see that the Americans had appeared *relieved* by the Soviet veto (Eden 1960, 564).

In the midst of all of this, Britain and France got even more serious about force, finally agreeing that they would have to pursue their agenda secretively. In mid-October, Acting Foreign Minister of France Albert Gazier and General Maurice Challe approached Eden with a proposal from French Prime Minister Guy Mollet that they work together to set the Suez situation right. They presented a "possible plan of action . . . to gain physical control of the canal," which contrived that Israel would attack Egypt across the Sinai Peninsula so that France and Britain could then order both sides to withdraw their forces from the Suez Canal (Nutting 1967, 93). What was in it for Israel was that its troops could seize Sinai.[19] What was in it for France and Britain was a pretext for forcefully intervening and occupying the canal. The guise was that the France and Britain would be saving the canal from the damage that would certainly result from Israeli-Egyptian fighting. In this way, the two powers could enter the region under the pretense of separating the combatants and preventing conflict. Britain and France could then seize control of the entire waterway and its terminal ports, returning the canal operation to Anglo-French management. Once in control, the two countries could increase the benefits for the Israelis because they would be in a position to break the shipping blockade in place against their partner. In short, all parties stood to reap significant gain.

Apparently, Eden could hardly conceal his delight at this proposal (Lucas 1991, 227). But he could not accept it immediately. He was befuddled because Britain, France, and the U.S. had signed the 1950 Tripartite Declaration, in which they agreed to oppose any aggression across Arab-Israeli frontiers. Eden promised Challe and Gazier that he would answer them shortly and then set about looking for loopholes in that Declaration. His British compatriots realized that he must have found one when Eden averted his gaze as the French secretly delivered more than 60 Mystère IV fighters to Israel and then dismissively made light of his protégé Anthony Nutting's request to question this delivery (Nutting 1967, 90fn). It was obvious that Eden was in. On October 16, he made his complicity official during a secret meeting held in Sevrés, France. The secrecy surrounding these talks was such that most senior British government officials, not to mention American allies, were unaware they were taking place. Again, this kind of secrecy and flouting of the norms of open consultation would become a fuel for the Americans to construct dissenting narratives about their shared identity with the British.

During the course of this process, Dulles decided that it was time to switch the American position on the UN. Originally the reason the U.S. opposed going to the UN was because the UN was a tool to *legitimize* the use of force. However, it was also possible to treat the UN as a tool to *prevent* force. American leaders resisted doing this at first because it would pit the U.S. and Britain against each other in the public eye of the international community. The Americans knew this would be both humiliating to the British Lion and divisive of the West, something unacceptable to the Eagle. But as the British resistance to Dulles's other diplomatic efforts perceptibly increased, Dulles decided to take that risk. He turned to U.S. Ambassador to the UN, Henry Cabot Lodge, to help him deploy the UN on behalf of the American anti-force stance.

Although this strategy of using the UN to manage the parties to the Suez Crisis became more central to the U.S. after the Anglo-French-Israeli operation, at this point prior to the invasion there was nevertheless one effort in particular which fueled British disaffection with the U.S. and so their ability to imagine dissent. In late October, the Americans used the UN to pressure the British by involving the Security Council in the enforcement of the Tripartite Agreement. That agreement guaranteed that the U.S. and Britain would come to the defense of any Middle Eastern country that was a victim of aggression. By raising the specter of the Tripartite Agreement in the UN, the U.S. essentially shamed Britain, issuing a public reminder that they were legally bound to abstain from using force in the Middle East. Even more interesting, perhaps, was that the terms of the Tripartite Agreement also legally bound the signatories to use force against any country that *did* aggress on the Middle East. Strictly speaking, in other words, if the British attacked Egypt, the U.S. would have to use force against the British. In these senses, invoking the Tripartite Agreement under the auspices of the UN was a way of openly warning the British about the legal and military trouble they could face if they became even tangentially involved with a country that used force against Egypt. Also notable—and something of which the British certainly took note—was that in raising the specter of the Tripartite Agreement, the Americans came perilously close to threatening violence; a violation of Special Relationship norms and a near-breach of the security community to be sure. In the absence of the settled truths of shared commitments to freedom and democracy, the magnetic draw which might otherwise encourage the British to laugh and think that "Ike would just lie doggo" failed (Shaw

1996, 171). In British eyes, the Americans had lost their legitimacy as a part of the we; the British did not know what to expect anymore.

Although the British were irritated, they were not cowed into changing their plans. When U.S. Ambassador to the UN Henry Cabot Lodge spoke to U.K. Ambassador to the UN, Sir Pierson Dixon, about living up to the Tripartite Declaration, Dixon responded, "Don't be silly and moralistic. We have got to be practical." The British backed up their logic with the further argument that the treaty was antiquated and that Nasser had already repudiated it with his own declaration that "the Tripartite Declaration did not apply to Egypt." Eden apparently excitedly exclaimed, "So that lets us off the hook. We have no obligation, it seems, to stop the Israelis [from] attacking the Egyptians" (Nutting 1967, 92). Before the U.S. could put the British to the test by raising the Tripartite issue in the Security Council, Israel invaded Egypt, attacking positions in the Sinai desert.

Using Force

On October 29, 1956, Israeli defense forces entered Egypt, engaged *fedayeen* units, and seized positions in the vicinity of the Suez Canal. A statement issued by Israeli Minister of Defense David Ben Gurion claimed that the action was in response to Egyptian military assaults on Israeli land and sea transport. In fact, there had been no aggressive action by Egyptian troops, but the assertion served as a face-saving excuse (Neff 1981, 361). The first victims of the war were the innocent. Arabs living within Israel were put under curfew, and by 6 P.M. on the first day of the invasion, 47 men, women, and children had been slaughtered. The Israelis also took advantage of the confusion to grab hold of a small village in the demilitarized zone on the Syrian border (Neff 1981, 375).

The contrived Israeli acts of war, combined with British and French long-standing and widely vocalized concern about Egyptian inability to run the canal, gave the two all the credibility they felt they needed to issue the ultimatum that both sides withdraw. On the morning of October 30, Mollet and his foreign minister, Christian Pineau, flew to London to play out the charade. The Anglo-French leaders went through the motions of conferring on what they would do, and by that afternoon had declared their solution. Eden announced the ultimatum to the otherwise uninformed House of Commons. "Knowing what these people [Egyptians] are," he stated, "we felt it essential to have some kind of physical guarantees in order to secure the safety of the canal." He added disingenuously that haste was necessary in the intervention because "the Israelis appear to be very near to Suez" (Neff 1981, 375).

Eden informed Eisenhower separately in a cable in which he argued, "Egypt has to a large extent brought this attack on herself." The last line of the letter held out the possibility of Anglo-American cooperation. "We feel that decisive action should be taken at once to stop the hostilities. [But we will] go with you to the Security Council" (Lucas 1991, 260). This token gesture was probably intended to soothe the shock, but it did not mollify Eisenhower, who was astounded. When he heard about the ultimatum, he remarked to Dulles that he just could "not believe Britain would be dragged into this" (Horne 1988, 438). Dulles was less surprised. He had not been so unsuspicious of the British that the (fabricated) ultimatum caught him off-guard (indeed, he suspected collusion right away), but by the same token he also was not as quick as Eisenhower to reject them as "unworthy and unreliable" allies (Neff 1981, 372). Dulles mused over how to give our allies "a reasonable time" in spite of their brash response to the Israeli invasion of Egypt.[20] But as evidence of the British involvement in those misdeeds accumulated, even Dulles's predilection to remain measured in his reaction waned.

First among the indicators that something was not right with Britain's story was that Eden's decision to work with France was too sudden to be credible. Anyone familiar with military operations would have understood that the risks entailed in undertaking an intricate collaborative effort on such short notice should have been prohibitive. Most military planners would not have been willing to take on such gambles.[21] Complex maneuvers would be required for the British and French to work under a joint command and to successfully separate the combatants. Plans for that operation would have to be devised quickly and under trying circumstances. It was curious to the Americans that the British would have committed themselves to such a challenging mission on such short notice and without preparation.[22] As it turned out, of course, the British had not undertaken the mission without planning; the Americans simply were not aware of the full story yet. Indeed, there was not only prior planning, but also a third party: Israel. With three parties, military logistics would have been even more difficult and harder to carry out, even with the benefit of the collusive planning.

It was not too long before telling glitches in the operation developed, and with each one, American political leadership gathered more intelligence and became more suspicious about the collusion behind it.[23] The first phase of the attack, for example, which had been designed to appear as a retaliatory raid, was to be unleashed by the Israelis once the British Royal Air Force planes had delivered an attack against Egyptian airfields. The latter attack was necessary because it would help decrease the risk to Israeli forces, and the Israelis would not have cooperated without such protection. Once they were on the ground however, Ben Gurion and General Moshe Dayan refused to move their troops into the fray of war until the promised attacks by their British allies had already taken place (Neff 1981, 263). But the Royal

Air Force was paralyzed by internal coordination problems, which sprang from the fact that not everyone in the British military command structure was apprised of the truth about British involvement with the Israelis. As a result, the entire operation stalled (Neff 1981, 383; Lucas 1991, 238). In the meantime, the Israeli troops frittered away the time waiting for the British. They moved slowly and purposelessly on the ground, attacking only "rag-tag" Egyptian units (Neff 1981, 367).

In the midst of all of this, the Americans could not help but notice that the Israelis were squandering time, nor could they ignore the accumulating intelligence of the RAF's mobilization. If they were under the impression that none of this military activity was coordinated, this war stoppage was more than just a little curious. Indeed, before too long the CIA had gathered enough evidence to suspect links between the Israeli and British behaviors (Lucas 1991, 268). In fact, once the British sorted out the military problems, delivered their raid, and the mission started moving again, those connections between Israeli and British behavior seemed even more obvious. The coordination of the two country's movements continued. Although there was no official reason to expect the Israelis and British would collaborate, the fact that Israeli movements seemed to depend on British ones, raised eyebrows.

As information trickled in, American tempers rose. Coupled with British duplicity prior to the invasion, the Americans were not predisposed toward giving their "friends" the benefit of the doubt. But the Americans hesitated to draw any firm or publicized conclusions. Eisenhower was up for re-election in a matter of days. At the same time that the American administration was furious with the British for getting involved in such a stunt on the eve of this important event, the president sought to have his administration present a calm and united front to the American public. Although taking a strong stance against Israeli aggression "may have cost Eisenhower some votes," stirring up the pot with the British would have cost him the election. It would have made Eisenhower look the way that his Democratic opponent, Adlai Stevenson, portrayed him: as "getting in bed with Communist Russia and the dictator of Egypt" instead of with our British allies (Kingseed 1995, 98).

But there were other reasons not to jump to conclusions. A pairing of Israel and Britain, however imagined and however mediated by other partners, was just too unlikely. Traditionally, the British had been not only pro-Arab but also, given their interests in Palestine, none-too-subtly anti-Semitic (Neff 1981, 181; Henderson 1999). Eden had studied Arabic at Oxford and as a foreign secretary in the 1930s, had worked for closer British ties with Arab states, including the negotiation of the 1936 Anglo-Egyptian Treaty. During the Second World War, he had proposed the formation of the

Arab League and rejected Cabinet proposals for the creation of a Jewish state. In fact, as it turns out in the early days of the crisis, Eden and Lloyd did not want to work with the Israelis. At first, they rejected any connection with Israel in the Suez Crisis, resisting Pineau's proposals for collaboration with Tel Aviv (Lucas 1991, 228).

In light of this history, cooperation between the two states hardly seemed fathomable. However, all appearances suggested the contrary. The Americans could either ignore the coincidence of activities or analyze the situation with flexible ideas about what was possible. The latter approach won out when CIA head Allen Dulles finally stated frankly to his brother Foster that he suspected "our allies are guilty of . . . acts of aggression" (Mosely 1978, 420). Once these words were spoken, it did not take long for them to take root among the American leadership as the most credible narrative about what had happened in Suez. Quickly the story behind the Israeli attack and the supposed British reason for intervention into the Canal Zone lost credibility and the Americans began to come to terms with the idea that their three closest allies had colluded. It was a difficult story to swallow at first, but in light of British eagerness to use force and backhandedness at the UN, it had begun to seem straightforward.

The first challenge was to understand what had prompted Eden to reverse his policy toward Israel. As it turns out, the French had shrewdly managed to change Eden's mind by pointing out a variety of Middle Eastern tensions that were going to explode against the British unless they took action now, in cooperation with the Israelis. In particular, Gazier and Challe pointed out that given British sponsorship of the Iraqi-Jordanian axis and the Franco-Israeli alliance, rising tension on the Israeli-Jordanian border could lead to an Anglo-Israeli war. Gazier speculated that if Israel attacked Jordan, Britain would have to stand by the Iraqi-Jordanian axis and provide air and naval support to Amman. If Britain did not, it would face the possible dissolution of the Iraqi-Jordanian axis. Gazier appealed to Eden to prevent the Iraqis from provoking the Israelis further by helping to stop the Iraqi deployment. In developing this narrative about the risks Britain would run if it did not cooperate with Israel, the French took advantage of a complex set of conditions to persuade Eden to reverse his traditional stance toward the Jewish state (Lucas 1991, 228–36).

Thus, in order to ensure that British primacy in the Middle East would remain unchallenged after reclaiming the Suez Canal, which was obviously what Eden wanted, it was best to include Israel now, thus deflecting future animus. As complex (and possibly uncompelling) as this logic was, it was probably not that hard a sell. Eden just *wanted* to take military action in Suez. He knew that if Britain could manage the Middle East situation well, it would lend enormous credibility to the narrative "reality" of the Lion. But he was constrained from taking action on his own because Britain had an inadequate military presence in the Middle East. Teaming up with the Israelis would solve the military logistical problem (Horne 1988, 400–1). By going along with the French proposition, including the collaboration with Israel, Eden stood to fortify Britain's prowess and image as a decisive international force. From Eden's perspective, it was simply a good political decision.

Of course it still puzzles analysts why the British and French thought that their pretext for sending forces would fool anyone. Their alleged reason for entering the canal was flimsy, at best. Eden pronounced that Britain's only goals were to end the fighting and "guarantee freedom of transit through the canal." Israel and Egypt had exactly 12 hours in which to acquiesce. At that point, barring favorable responses from both sides, Britain and France would intervene militarily "in whatever strength may be necessary to secure compliance" (Calhoun 1991, 374). But it was not clear on what grounds Britain and France proposed to act as world policemen. The UN Charter made no provisions for any such role and there was no compelling reason why Britain and France could not postpone any action until the UN spoke. So wanting was this pretext that no more than 40 minutes after the invasion did Dulles turn to U.S. Senator William Knowland and say: "My guess is that the Israeli attack has been worked out with the French at least, and possibly with the British" (Neff 1981, 365). When the U.S., understandably disturbed, finally confronted Eden about the collusion, Eden seemed to show no remorse. The U.S. was careful not to reprimand Eden for trying to shore up the Lion, but it did point out that collusion was an unacceptable way to go about demonstrating prowess. But Eden was neither conciliatory nor repentant. He continued to deny his involvement and to stand by his coy, deceptive behavior.

In one instance of his belligerence that greatly irked the U.S., Eden never apologized for a scheme he authorized just prior to the invasion in which the British planted intelligence expressly intended to lead the United States astray. The British had actually fabricated reports, which made it seem that Israel was going to invade Jordan. By the morning of October 29, and just in time for the attack, the British and French appeared to have successfully thrown the Americans off track. At eight in the morning, Dulles telephoned the president saying that there was nothing new on Israel's mobilization. Eisenhower reportedly sighed with relief and concluded that "things . . . seem a little better this morning than last evening" (Neff 1981, 361). At virtually the same moment, half-way across the world, Israeli Army Chief of Staff Moshe Dayan was "snickering with delight" at the extent to which Eisenhower had been misled. "It is apparent," he said, "that Eisenhower thinks the imminent conflict is likely to erupt between Israel and Jordan and that Britain and France will cooperate with him in preventing this. How uninformed he is of the situation!" (Neff 1981, 262).

In this similar belligerent, unapologetic vein was Eden's calculated rudeness toward the Americans regarding the delivery of the ultimatum to Egypt and Israel. After the invasion occurred, Eisenhower expressed to Eden his desire to be kept informed. But Eden ignored this request. He further humiliated the Americans by taking matters into his own hands and issuing the ultimatum without properly notifying Washington in advance. On the morning of October 30, when U.S. Ambassador to the U.K. Winthrop Aldrich questioned Lloyd about British plans, he was repeatedly put off. It was not until late that afternoon that Aldrich found out about the ultimatum, and only then because Eden was already announcing it to the Commons. About that same time of day, Eden also officially informed Eisenhower via telegram about the ultimatum and the putative reasons behind it. Upon reading the telegram Eisenhower apparently turned to Dulles and remarked, "We should have read this message yesterday." Dulles responded that they had not had the message yesterday. The oversight must have been intended, Dulles pointed out, because "if we had had it yesterday, we might have stopped them." Eden later admitted that indeed he had not sent the message earlier because "I didn't want to give time for Ike to ring up and say, 'Dulles is on his way again'" (Neff 1981, 375). The British did not want the U.S. stopping them.

After Force

Once the rage provoked by the initial shock passed, Eisenhower in particular felt a bitter sense of the British perfidiousness. In a personal letter to his friend Swede Hazlett, he wrote, "this is something of a sad blow because "Britain . . . has been our best friend" (Horne 1988, 438). But Eisenhower and his administration did not waste time when it came to formulating a reaction. The U.S. took a two-pronged approach, involving diplomatic action through the UN on the one hand and direct economic pressures on the other. By December 3, the combination of these strategies drove the British and French to a complete and humiliating withdrawal from Egypt.

If initially Dulles had been concerned that stepping up the efforts to use the UN as a means for pressuring the French and Israelis would undermine the unity of the West, in light of the recent events, he now thought the unity of the West was best defended by dissociation from the British. The UN could be used to protect the Eagle from guilt by association with the Lion (as well as with France and Israel), who for all purposes now seemed more rogue than West. Of course to the British, this decision to use the UN, and the diplomacy, negotiations, and resolutions to which it gave rise, could be understood as nothing less than abandonment.

When the Security Council met on October 30, the day after the Israeli attack, the American delegate, Henry Cabot Lodge pressed for an immediate
vote on a new resolution that demanded an Israeli withdrawal. He did so
against pleas for time made by his British colleague, U.K. Ambassador to
the UN Pierson Dixon (Nutting 1967, 113). The resolution, which provided
that no support be given to Israel by other nations, was issued prior to the
Anglo-French ultimatum but after the British had already publicly announced their intention to issue an ultimatum. And so when the Americans
proffered the complete reverse suggestion—that no country should aid
Israel—it demonstrated to the international community how far apart the
British and Americans stood. In fact, the American proposal gutted the
British plan. Of course this was precisely Dulles's intention (because the integrity of the West depended on distancing the Eagle from the Lion). But
for the British, this maneuver was humiliating. As soon as the U.S. introduced their suggestion, they turned the Anglo-French ultimatum from a
fait accompli into a mere suggestion open to be debate in the UN.[24] This
move by the U.S., not coincidentally, had the effect of appropriating the
British ultimatum to serve American interests. It demonstrated the commitment of the Eagle to relentlessly waging peace even under such adverse
conditions; it demonstrated how the U.S. could creatively rely upon debate
in international organizations rather than force to control even a dictator.

Unsurprisingly, the British and French defeated the U.S. resolution with
their vetoes. It was the first time that Britain had ever used its UN veto
rights. Eden justified this practice, for which the British had so many times
rebuffed the Soviets, on the grounds that:

> Two standards of conduct are being evolved. One for the free na-
> tions who wish to be law-abiding; The other for . . . powers who see
> no incongruity in denying the authority of the United Nations to in-
> fluence their own actions, while noisily demanding sanctions
> against others. Satan rebuking sin is a modest moralist beside them.
> (Eden 1960, 553)

But to the U.S., Eden's appeal to law-abiding nations was just ironic, and
so the U.S. continued to use the UN against the British even after the veto.

In a second incident, the Americans encouraged other United Nations
member-states to introduce the previously written Uniting for Peace resolution (UfP), under which deliberations on the Suez Crisis could be shifted
to the General Assembly within 24 hours if the UN Security Council was
inhibited from action because of a veto. The UfP, a U.S. initiative that was
adopted by the UN in 1950, was originally intended to circumvent the
Soviet veto of UN action in Korea. Importantly, it was an initiative that was
strongly advocated and backed by the British. But, if in 1950 the UfP

reflected the efficacy of the Anglo-American partnership, in 1956, when the U.S. turned it against the British during the Suez Crisis, it became a testament to the partnership's failure. In fact, a UfP meeting of the General Assembly was called for five o'clock on the afternoon of November 1. Although the U.S. did not go so far as to initiate this move themselves, they encouraged it and voted in its favor. The Americans made no secret of the fact that they hoped that moving the talks to the General Assembly might keep hostilities from spreading, even if ultimately it would be unlikely to deter British and French from action.

The General Assembly, of course, was one aspect of the United Nations that the British and French had been desperately trying to avoid. Eden had feared it from the outset as "a backwater at the United Nations" and "a quagmire" into which the British case could become counterproductively "submerged" (Eden 1960, 553). What scared Eden was the effective dominance in the General Assembly of newly independent states with anti-British and anti-French biases. Moving deliberations to the General Assembly via the Uniting for Peace proposal thus put the resolution of the Suez Crisis into the hands of interests eager to undermine the Lion. Significantly, as the British interpreted it, it was the United States who had led them into that quagmire. And, as if that was not bad enough, during the debates in the General Assembly, U.S. Ambassador Lodge continued to maintain a stance of righteous indignation toward the British delegation, ignoring all British requests for compromise and publicly establishing the distance between the U.S. and U.K. (Nutting 1967, 113).

The first item taken up by the General Assembly was a resolution for a cease-fire. Once again, the Americans took the initiative against the British operation. Dulles moved for a resolution that urged all parties now involved in hostilities in the Suez area to agree to an immediate cease-fire and to halt the movement of military forces and arms. It also called on all member-states of the UN to refrain from introducing military goods into the area of hostilities. The resolution was voted into acceptance on November 2. But fueled by the now-common British sentiment that the U.S. was leading the charge against them and the French, Eden rejected it the next day. The UN had become a battleground among the Western countries.

After taking stock of the damage that the Americans had wrought for his plans, and of the increasingly dire economic situation facing Britain (more on this below), Eden asked Dixon to offer a counterproposal that would better serve the Anglo-French mission. Dixon proposed that UN forces occupy the area once French and British forces had been installed. This plan had the potential to construct the image that the British and French forces were clearing ground for an international operation. In this way, the Lion would still appear as an effective leader and still sustain the appearance of some control in the region. But in keeping with its concern not to appear as though they had joined hands with the British, the U.S. initially rejected the plan. This move humiliated the British once again, and the Americans knew it.[25] Eventually, however, Dulles recognized the potential for deal-making in the British proposal and agreed to lobby for a UN force to replace the Anglo-French forces. But he suggested this only in exchange for an Anglo-French acceptance of an unconditional cease-fire. Over the initial objections of both the French government and its officers in the field, Eden and Mollett agreed to a cease-fire before the polls closed in the United States on November 6. Eisenhower, of course, was re-elected.

The mandate of the cease-fire agreement included the establishment of a UN command for an emergency international force that would secure and supervise the cessation of hostilities. According to the UN deal, the cease-fire was to be unconditional and no forces from any of the Great Five powers would be part of the UN emergency force. The French in particular did not like this aspect of the agreement and put pressure on the British to resist.[26] Eden, still not convinced that the deal with the UN put the best possible face on the Anglo-French debacle, tended to agree with French Prime Minister Mollet. The two were tired of the U.S. and the political antics they were playing at the UN, and together needed little encouragement from each other to break ranks with the agreement. Finally, Eden proclaimed that in spite of the cease-fire, British and French troops would not withdraw until UN forces had arrived.[27] The reason, Eden claimed, was to prevent a power vacuum in the Middle East.

Eisenhower recognized Eden's claim as an excuse and calculated that Eden was procrastinating withdrawal to make it appear that Britain had helped create stability in the Middle East. It was a face-saving device that Eisenhower did not like, but one that he politically understood and was willing to indulge. So, in a pragmatic move designed to convince the British to withdraw their troops, the president offered a different ploy to take the heat off. He invited Mollet and Eden to come to the U.S. to iron out questions about the Soviet Union and NATO, which were unrelated to Suez. The meeting would provide an opportunity to paper over for the benefit of the press what he now referred to as the Anglo-American "family spat," but it also provided Eden with the appearance of collaborating with the U.S. on "some spectacular act at this time" related to "the Bear" (referring to the Soviet Union). At least this way, even if the Lion could not be saved as the leader of the West, especially in the Middle East, Britain could still appear as a player in East/West politics. The idea was that in all of the commotion surrounding the visit to the U.S., the British and French could withdraw from Suez quietly and without attracting too much attention. As they were no longer in a position to be choosy, Eden and Mollet readily accepted. The three heads of government agreed to make the meeting a media event and planned a simultaneous announcement in all three capitals.[28]

Just as impulsively as he had issued the invitation, however, Eisenhower postponed the visit. The president's advisers had cautioned him that appearing too chummy with the British so shortly after their aggressive act might upset the precarious balance and trust the U.S. had achieved with Arab countries since the cease-fire. After all, the British and French would want some communiqué to reaffirm their solidarity once the conference had ended, which would be out of the question if the Eagle were to preserve its standing as moral example and to keep the law-abiding West cordoned off from the rogue British and French. But even beyond such a communiqué, the very fact that the talks had occurred would imply American sympathy for Anglo-French Middle Eastern objectives. Neither the Arabs nor the North Africans would understand or accept the strategic political dealmaking that really motivated the meetings. It would, as Dulles understood, make the U.S. guilty-by-association with these unlawful nations, rendering the moral boundary between the East and West too porous.[29]

Although Eden professed to understand, his humiliation was apparent. Still, he knuckled down yet again to try to salvage the wreckage, this time by asking for a definitive date for the postponed visit that he could announce to the public. But Eisenhower turned down even this meager request by making the announcement of a definitive new date contingent upon the withdrawal of Anglo-French troops from Egypt.[30] But this bribe had no upside for the British and French because the visit was supposed to *deflect* attention from withdrawal of the troops. By making withdrawal a precondition for the visit, Eisenhower in effect highlighted the British and French failure. The U.S. had again insensitively humiliated the British through UN channels.

The British responded to this last humiliation with defiance. Knowing full well that the U.S. had by now exhausted the various pressure mechanisms available to them through the UN, the British made one last effort to save face through one last effort to define the terms of the withdrawal. This time they proposed that the withdrawal come at the end of a four-week period in which the United Nations Emergency Force (UNEF) could be implemented. In the meantime, Britain and France would immediately begin overseeing the clearing of the Canal Zone. Lloyd told UN Secretary General Dag Hammarskjold that the British would set a definitive date on withdrawal when he was satisfied that arrangements for the clearing operation were in order. This proposal was another attempt to represent the Anglo-French intervention as the necessary preliminary work for introducing an international force to the Middle East.

But the U.S. would have none of it. The Americans wanted the British and French troops out right away. However, the avenues of leverage available to the U.S. through the UN were now exhausted, and so to ensure immediate withdrawal, the U.S. turned to economic pressures. Throughout the Suez Crisis, the British had been vulnerable to economic pressures. Indeed, one of the first things the British realized when they started considering a military mission was how important American economic support would be to its success. The reasons were twofold. First, there was the question of confidence in the British pound. As Chancellor of the Exchequer Harold Macmillan had pointed out, "there was bound to be a sense of anxiety. Yet so long as America was firmly on our side on the main issue there would be no flight from the pound." The second reason why American support was so crucial was the potential "interruption of oil supplies." Macmillan pronounced this "far more serious" than the stability of the pound, but pointed out that "assuming that . . . the Americans cooperated to the full, it should be possible to meet the full needs of Europe." Macmillan concluded, "if action had to be taken it must be short and successful" but "for immediate needs we could no doubt expect American aid" (Macmillan 1971, 109–110). As chancellor of the exchequer, Macmillan's opinion on these economic issues was the final word.

Although during that early phase Macmillan presumed the Americans would offer assistance, evidence suggests that he was also realistically aware that the combination of the tenuous balance of Middle East politics and the impending presidential election put the Americans in a somewhat sticky position. His expectations for support were accordingly qualified by the realization that complete and overt American endorsement of the British might not be politically possible. However, the British felt that the Anglo-American friendship, combined with allied interests, ensured that the U.S. at least would remain publicly neutral but privately supply a "helping hand." In the worst case scenario, the U.S. would simply lie low and provide background assistance while Britain carried out its mission. Perhaps this was Macmillan's calculus behind his hawkish urging to push forward with force. Certainly it was Eden's, who even outlined for Dulles his idea of an appropriate plan for quiet assistance:

> We would like to have the United States' . . . moral and economic support in terms of petroleum products diverted from our side, and would want U.S. to neutralize any open participation by the Soviet Union. . . . We and the French could take care of the rest.[31]

But from the start, the Americans had been uncomfortable with such an arrangement. As permanent U.S. Representative at the UN, Herbert Hoover, Jr. pointed out, "no amount of planning" could make the "pie" available to the British any bigger without putting the Americans in an unacceptable political position.[32] During a White House conference, Hoover, Dulles, and Eisenhower wondered whether the French and British were trying to force the Americans into a choice between themselves and the Arabs. Hoover observed that "they may in fact have felt that they have forced us into a position where we must go against the Arabs." The president speculated, "if oil is cut off and American ships take the route around the Cape, the oil supplies to Europe will be greatly cut down. The British may be estimating that we would have no choice but to take extraordinary means to get oil to them." Dulles concurred with both men, stating plainly that the British and French were thinking that "they will confront us with a *de facto* situation in which they might acknowledge that they have been rash, but would say that the U.S. could not sit by and let them go under economically."[33]

Much to British surprise, not only did the Americans "let them go under economically," but they actually hastened the economic decline of the British mission. Through a series of events and economic policy decisions, the Americans constructed a response to the unpleasant choice between their Western allies and the Arab world that seemed to the British decidedly in favor of the Arabs. The U.S. did not sit by, neutrally waiting for the economic situation of the two countries to degenerate on their own. Rather, the supposed best friend of Britain took an active role in precipitating its economic deterioration.

The economic strain began almost immediately with increasing speculation against the pound. Sterling had come under pressure as early as September when British reserves fell by $57 million. In October the losses had reached $84 million, a loss that Macmillan still described as tolerable. A treasury official warned him on October 31, however, that the pound was coming under such pressure, in New York particularly, that the drop could reach a dangerous $100 million within the first week of November. It might even climb as high as a ruinous $200 million, the memorandum suggested.[34] In fact, by Macmillan's own figures, the losses in just the first six days of the month approached some $280 million. By this point, Macmillan had assumed (wrongly, as it turns out) that the U.S. Federal Reserve Bank was speculating against the pound, selling "far above what was necessary as a precaution to protect the value of its holdings" (Macmillan 1971, 164).[35] The market quickly went wild with as many as a million pounds or more put up for sale in single blocks. As speculation on the pound wreaked havoc on the British economy, the British became convinced that the Americans, fickle and double-crossing as they had been throughout the crisis, had masterminded it (Kunz 1991).

The instability of financial markets in Britain was a serious problem. But Macmillan was certain they could get through it if Britain could withdraw some of the capital it had on deposit with the International Monetary Fund. The British had every right to reclaim that money, some $130 million, which would have been more than enough to shore up sterling and drive away the speculators. But all the withdrawals had to be approved by the IMF board of directors, in which the votes were weighted according to the amount of each nation's deposit. The American director therefore had the biggest voice in the IMF's counsels, and although he could not have blocked Britain's access to its money indefinitely, he could slow down the process in the short-term. With reserves plummeting, the next few days were to be decisive. Britain needed either a loan from the United States or American cooperation in expediting procedures in the IMF (Calhoun 1991, 491).

Those were matters for Eisenhower's secretary of the treasury, George Humphrey, to decide, and Macmillan had been "begging the Secretary to go easy on the pound" ever since the beginning of the Suez Crisis (Calhoun 1991, 492). Humphrey's response was stern and unrelenting. America would be generous with its British ally only if London acceded to the UN's demands for a cease-fire. The IMF application would be expedited and a direct U.S. loan approved, but both depended on Britain's prior agreement to the cease-fire agreement. Macmillan telephoned Humphrey early in the morning, November 6, to make a last plea for help. The answer was the same. America would cooperate only if Britain agreed to an immediate cease-fire. Humphrey was quite specific about what was considered immediate; the U.S. demanded that the fighting end by midnight. Despite the French encouragement to rally forth anyway, Eden finally gave in.

But it was in actually getting the British to withdraw that the U.S. became most proactive about its economic leverage. The whole process of withdrawal had all along been muddied by the fact that the cast of characters dealing with the crisis had almost completely changed by late November. Dulles had been hospitalized and Hoover had been appointed as acting secretary of state in his place. Eden, who had been in ill health throughout the fall, had collapsed. Although he returned for some time in late December 1956, in the interim there was ambiguity about whether Macmillan or House of Commons Leader Rab Butler was the man in power (ultimately Macmillan became prime minister). Eisenhower, unsure about how to proceed, did not want to make assumptions that would play favorites and so, confusingly, both Macmillan and Butler were having daily contacts, discussions, and negotiations with Aldrich, U.S. ambassador to the U.K., who was brokering communication about the withdrawal (Kunz 1991, 144). In case all of this was not complicated enough, Eisenhower too was adjusting to new arrangements because there was a new U.K. ambassador to the U.S.; Roger Makins had been replaced by Harold Caccia immediately following the November 7 cease-fire.

In light of all the personnel chaos, and recognizing that, in economic sanctions, they had hit upon a formula for extracting British compliance, Humphrey and Eisenhower did the only sure-fire thing to get through to the British. They blackmailed them. As the UN politics surrounding the negotiation of withdrawal dragged on and Macmillan began looking to the U.S. for oil supplies to sustain Britain until the crisis was settled, the U.S. decided simply to refuse the British unless they complied. Exasperated, Macmillan exclaimed: "Oil Sanctions! Good god. . . ." (Kunz 1991, 137–50). On December 3, 1956, thoroughly humiliated and spent, British troops withdrew from the Suez Canal.

For whatever else had (or had not) been achieved through the British and American divergent reactions to Nasser's nationalization, one thing was for sure: Between the demagnetized Anglo-American attraction and the proliferation of vast material from which either side could draw to craft dissenting narratives from the Special Relationship, dissolution of the we, and so the security community order, was imminent.

CHAPTER **6**
Dissolution

So just how did dissolution happen? Once 'Use of Force' had unsettled the shared "reality" of kindred, freedom-loving democracies and had demagnetized the attraction between the United States and Britain, dissent from the Anglo-American Special Relationship became *thinkable*. It became a collective possibility. That possibility was seized upon by leaders and bureaucrats on both sides of the Atlantic and, in fact, broke down more or less along national lines. British state leaders and bureaucrats tended to identify with the Lion and its interests, so they authored with other Britons against the Americans, and vice versa. Because authorship broke down more or less along national lines, I refer to the authors discussed in this analysis as either British or American. However, this signification is a simplification justified by the empirical condition of the Suez Crisis, rather than a theoretical claim about the unity of state actors and their capacity to speak with a single voice. In fact, the dissolution of the Special Relationship was not carried out like a coordinated onslaught enacted by a unified group of single-minded dissidents—on either the British or the American side. While each political leader and bureaucrat involved was purposeful about what he narrated and certainly each took cues about what to say from each other, my theoretical claim is that each dissented for reasons related the configuration of his own subjectivity, identity, and therefore, interests. This is precisely why most authorship of dissenting phrases broke down along national lines —most people working for the U.S. government formed identities and subjectivities that reflected some interest in sustaining the Eagle, while most in the British government acquired some interest preserving in the Lion.

There were exceptions, of course. For instance, the American Joint Chiefs of Staff (JCS) participated in narrating some of the phrases-in-dispute that produced the "reality" of Americans as untrustworthy and unreliable, while Anthony Nutting, who resigned as Prime Minister Eden's assistant during the crisis, helped narrate some of the phrases-in-dispute and constructed his own countrymen as untrustworthy and unreliable. But such exceptions actually underscore the subjectivity-based motivation of authorship. For example, it was central to the subjectivity of the JCS to keep the military complex at the center of American foreign policy. Waging peace, as Dulles and Eisenhower proposed to do, did not help advance that JCS Self. As a result, the demands of maintaining the integrity of JCS subjectivity congealed more with the demands of maintaining the British identity of Lion than with the American identity of Eagle. After all, the Lion put use of force and military operations at the forefront of reinscribing its prowess. In this sense, the JCS had "British" interests. In the context of this study, thus, one may prefer to think of the appellations *British* and *American* less as signifying less an author's formal nationality than as reflecting the sociolinguistic content of his subjectivity.

In the context of the unsettled foundation of their we identity, these various British and American authors narrated their frustration, anger, and alienation from each other by seizing on the key divisive moments during the Suez crisis, which for them crystallized the failure of the other to *be* Anglo-American. The British became fixated on the events surrounding John Foster Dulles's diplomatic antics, on the American strategy at the United Nations, and on the American use of economic sanctions; the Americans fixated on the British reaction to the nationalization of the Suez Canal, on Britain's perspective on Nasser, and, of course, on the collusion of the British with French and Israeli officials. One by one, authors on both sides narrated all those events in ways that challenged the logic of the links between the phrases that constituted the "reality" of the Special Relationship (shared values, trust, and common-security fate). Furthermore, they did so in a way that blamed the other for the damage. Through this process 'Dulles,' 'United Nations,' 'Economic Sanctions,' 'Nationalization,' 'Nasser,' and 'Collusion' all became phrases-in-dispute of the Special Relationship.

And yet, while each of these six phrases-in-dispute expressed language-power and so had the potential to threaten the Special Relationship, none stood alone as dissolutionary pressure on that "reality." Rather, their power as disintegrative forces resulted from the fact that each side authored its phrases-in-dispute to the point that, beyond mere stand-alone disputes, each also became components of a different "reality"—a "reality" that was simply incommensurable with that of the Special Relationship. The British authored their phrases-in-dispute so that their logic also functioned as phrases-in-support of a dissident "reality" of the Americans as betrayers, while the Americans authored theirs so that they also functioned as phrases-in-support of a dissident "reality" of the British as bellicose. These alternative "realities" ultimately brandished the coup de grace to Anglo-American we-ness. Neither of them could be reconciled with the logic of shared values, trust, and a common security fate. They were simply irreconcilable. With such dissident visions issuing forth from both sides of the Atlantic, something had to give way. That something was the "reality" of the Special Relationship—and all of the shared understandings, normative and behavioral burdens, and international order that flowed from it.

Narrating American Betrayal

Just after Nasser nationalized the Suez Canal Company, President Eisenhower and his administration came down firmly against the use of military force as an appropriate response. For the British, that was bad news. In addition to making it more difficult to advance the identity and interests of the Lion, the American stance against using force revealed something curious to the British about their American friends: They were remote from British concerns about freedom. The Americans seemed questionable, at best, as freedom-loving democrats (Chapter 5). That discovery was jarring and unsettling for the British on its own (it demagnetized their attraction to the U.S.). As the crisis unfolded, however, things only got worse. The Americans held tight to their wayward path of disrespect for freedom in ways that directly antagonized the British. To the British, the Americans seemed to be going out of their way to humiliate them, and in the process violated any pretense of the shared values, trust, and common-security fate that constituted the supposedly special friendship the countries shared. It was not just that the United States did not share with Britain the same view of what it meant to be a freedom-loving democracy. Rather, everything the U.S. did demonstrated its indifference toward the British; Americans were fickle, untrustworthy, backstabbing, and double-crossing. They had betrayed their friends.

Over the course of the Suez events, three American maneuvers in particular fueled the British transition from caution about their American friends to utter disbelief in the friendship, and so subsequent dissent from it. Using the language-power resources, to which all with voices have access, British authors represented each of the three events as direct challenges to the Special Relationship and as narrative evidence for the dissident "reality" of American betrayal.[1]

Dulles

The "reality" of American betrayal first began to gain legitimacy against the Special Relationship when the British narrated the phrase 'Dulles' in a way that represented the U.S. Secretary of State as a crystallization of American untrustworthiness. The logic of this representation centered on two things: the way that Dulles was conducting his campaign of diplomacy during the Suez Crisis; and Dulles's very personality. As to the campaign of diplomacy, it is important to remember that the British did not view diplomacy itself as a problem. In fact, after their first failed move to legitimate the use of force through the UN, they were thankful for it; they had hoped that diplomatic efforts would fail quickly and on purpose in order to provide a cover for approving the use of force. Dulles, at first, gave the British every reason to believe that his diplomatic efforts *would* ultimately result in the U.S. condoning force. As Dulles said:

> I do not care how many words are written into the Charter of the United Nations about not using force; if in fact there is not a substitute for force, and some way of getting just solutions of some of these problems, inevitably the world will fall back again into anarchy and chaos. (James 1986, 517)

In the context of such promises, playing along with diplomacy seemed to the British like a good investment of their time. But it turned out to be a hoax. Dulles, as the British saw him, used diplomacy to deceive them, to buy precious time from them, and ultimately to con them. He accomplished this through duplicity, repeated backstabbing, and by taking advantage of British good will. He capitalized on British trust only to turn it against them.

There was no shortage of incidents upon which the British could draw evidence for attaching this logic to 'Dulles.' The 18 Power Proposal and the agreement that arose out of the August 16 London conference were Dulles's brainchild. He had suggested it, convened it, and pushed the agreement that arose from it. Yet when it was time to present it to Nasser, Dulles refused to attend the meeting. He had duped the British into supporting a proposal that did not reflect their own interests and, as it turned out, he himself did not support. But it bought time against a British use of force and that is all that mattered to him. Dulles behaved in a similarly untoward manner over SCUA. He led the British to believe that the organization could be used to help advance their interests and that it could even be constructed in a way that would legitimate the use of force. Dulles seduced them into negotiations, which the British then undertook in good faith. But then, just as SCUA was shaping into something the British felt they could rally behind, Dulles pulled the rug out, again withdrawing his support. He was even blunter this second time than he had been with the 18 Power Proposal; he came right out and said that the U.S. did not see SCUA as a way to legitimate force. When asked whether this kind of a pronouncement had pulled SCUA's teeth, Dulles replied, "I know of no teeth; there were no teeth in it so far as I am aware, if that means use of force" (Neff 1981, 320). In fact, Dulles then turned around and characterized SCUA as an organization created to finance Nasser's activities—that is, to help him! Finally, as if this were not enough, during the course of events Dulles decided that it was time to switch the American position regarding the UN. Indeed, he was the mastermind behind using the UN against the British.

Beyond all the diplomatic hoodwinking lay the problem of Dulles's persona. It, too, fueled the logic that turned 'Dulles' into a phrase-in-dispute of the Special Relationship and in support of the "reality" of betrayal. This was because Dulles was simply an unlikable character. Dulles was a power-monger with an arcane speaking style, and, worst of all, he overshadowed President Eisenhower, a far more likable individual.[2] As Chancellor of the Exchequer Harold Macmillan described him, Dulles had "strange uncertainty of character" that was exceptionally vexing, particularly in circumstances where clarity was of the essence (Macmillan 1971, 91–5). He was on the one hand a moralistic, legalistic, and self-righteous man—a diplomat among warriors—yet on the other, he was a schemer whose willingness to step outside the bounds of the law in different circumstances appeared unbridled (Murphy 1964). As historian Herman Finer has written, "if Dulles had been the most crafty and conscienceless of Machiavellians, and not a devout Christian, he could not have contrived a more enticing and deadly trap" than the diplomatic ones in which he ensnared the British (Finer 1964, 214). Perhaps worst of all was Dulles's pedantic comportment, which made him difficult to understand and which most people took as purposeful obfuscation. Unnamed British observers at the SCUA conferences are recorded as describing Dulles as "highly disingenuous," especially in relying to a great degree on the subtleties of legal interpretation without spelling something out. The whole performance created the impression of "hypocrisy and even prevarication" (Joynt 1967, 245 n. 50).

Given this dual-pronged and ever-growing "evidence," it was not much of a stretch for the British political leadership and bureaucrats—including Prime Minister Eden, British foreign secretary Lloyd, Macmillan, and British ambassador to the U.S. Roger Makins—to narrate 'Dulles' as a phrase that signified duplicity and temporizing deceit. Furthermore, given Dulles's central role in the U.S. administration, such a representation referred to more than just Dulles as a man or Dulles's diplomatic antics; it was about the untrustworthy character of the U.S. on the whole. The phrase evoked American betrayal and directly negated of the notion of trust that was central to the Special Relationship.

The repercussions from the combined effect of 'Dulles' as treacherous, the logic of American betrayal, and the dispute of the Special Relationship are highlighted, for instance, in one of U.K. Foreign Secretary Selwyn Lloyd's narratives of 'Dulles.' In a letter to Dulles himself on October 15, 1956 Lloyd wrote:

> My Dear Foster: . . .
>
> I have been deeply disappointed to find how far apart our con-
> ceptions of the purpose of the User's Association now are I
> think you will agree that the original idea was that SCUA should . . .
> play a practical part . . . . This conception of SCUA has been aban-
> doned . . . . SCUA was intended to strengthen our hand, not to
> weaken it . . . . I cannot believe that this is what you really intend.
>
> We are both very conscious of the fact that this is a testing time
> for Anglo-American relations. I have done my utmost to prevent ex-
> aggeration of our difference of approach to the Suez Canal problem
> in recent weeks . . . But we must face the fact of so grave a diver-
> gence between us.[3]

In this narrative, Lloyd represents Dulles—even to Dulles himself—as a problem for the Special Relationship through key links between three key phrases: "this conception of SCUA has been abandoned," "SCUA was in-tended to strengthen our hand, not to weaken it," and "I cannot believe that this is what you really intend." In forging links between these phrases, Lloyd at once calls to mind Dulles's cunning over SCUA (where he pulled its "teeth" and left the British with a useless organization) and implies that Dulles intended to achieve this effect. Of course, Lloyd pretends that "he cannot believe" that such a consequence was what Dulles had intended, but his remark (probably intentionally) had the opposite effect of highlighting the degree of British mistrust for Dulles. After all, the phrase implies that the British had actually considered whether or not Dulles intended to weaken the British position. If the statement evokes some breach of trust, Lloyd makes that idea perfectly overt when he links the debacle over SCUA with the "testing time for Anglo-American relations" and "so grave a diver-gence between us." The total effect is a narrative that rendered Dulles re-sponsible for duping the British into considering SCUA and which thus naturalized a connection between 'Dulles' and a "reality" of betrayal of trust. It is a connection that by definition disputed the logic and credibility of the "reality" Special Relationship.

If Lloyd minced a few words in narrating 'Dulles' as a phrase-in-dispute of the we and in support of betrayal, Prime Minister Eden minced even fewer. In reference to SCUA, for instance, he said:

> The United States had put its whole authority behind the scheme. We had been strung along over many months of negotiation from pretext to pretext, from device to device, and from contrivance to contrivance. At each state in this weary pilgrimage we had seen our position weakened. (Eden 1960, 563–4)

Then, in references to Dulles's comment that SCUA had "no teeth" to begin with, Eden pointed out that Foster Dulles's words were "an advertisement to Nasser that he could reject the project with impunity. . . . Such cynicism toward allies destroys true partnership. It leaves only the choice of parting . . ." (Horne 1988, 425; Lucas 1991, 202).

Like Lloyd—though with less delicacy—Eden depicted Dulles as having tricked the British into participating in disingenuous diplomatic efforts. In fact, he depicted those efforts as actual "contrivances" designed to "weaken" the British position. Combining the idea that the British had been "strung along" as unsuspecting dupes with the idea that Dulles's whole goal was precisely to undermine the British, gives ample force to a logic that linked 'Dulles' to betrayal. That this betrayal was a betrayal of the Anglo-American friendship is made clearer in Eden's remark—in response to Dulles's "no teeth" comment—that such "cynicism destroys true partnership."

This narrative undoubtedly constructed 'Dulles' as a phrase-in-dispute of the Special Relationship and it came through loud and clear to the Americans. 'Dulles,' associated as the phrase was with SCUA, had become "ground zero" for the "reality" of American betrayal and for the dissolution of the Special Relationship. On December 5, W. Park Armstrong, Dulles's special assistant for intelligence, filed a record of events report in which he emphasized the extent to which the British felt Dulles had betrayed them.

> They were persuaded—practically bludgeoned, in their eyes—into discussion of the Suez situation. Although the British and French governments accepted the SCUA principle and expressed a willingness to cooperate in its implementation, . . . Eden was as determined as [French Premier Guy] Mollet not to accept a situation of diplomatic drift and inaction which he apparently believed by early October had been largely confirmed by events . . . . The first week of October did not open well for Anglo-American relations. The British and French, it may again be noted, seemed not to have fully accepted the SCUA arrangements as more than a temporary U.S.-sponsored device.[4]

United Nations

But 'Dulles' was not the only phrase-in-dispute of the Special Relationship and in support of betrayal. British authors narrated 'United Nations' as such a phrase as well. In this case, the reason was that the British could find no other way to understand the American actions at the UN than as a calculated strategy to humiliate and ridicule the British in front of the international community. Indeed, a number of interrelated incidents at the UN provided the fodder from which the British represented the phrase in such a way. The first occurred in late October, when the Americans used the UN Security Council to pressure the British with the Tripartite Agreement. The agreement required Britain and the U.S. to defend any Middle Eastern country that was a victim of aggression. Using the UN to remind the British of the Tripartite was a way for the U.S. to warn the British that they were legally bound to abstain from using force in the Middle East, and that the U.S. would be legally entitled to use force against the British if the British attacked Egypt. While some reference to the Tripartite was to be expected (at least the British expected it), the British did not expect it to surface through the Security Council, nor did they expect the Americans to be the ones to plant it there. By airing the Tripartite issue in such a public setting as the Security Council, the United States alerted the whole international community to the legal bind Britain had backed itself into. Even worse, because the U.S. was the one that raised the issue, the entire world also knew that the Anglo-American team was now at internal loggerheads. The public announcement to the world of the United States' disagreements with Britain was more than just humiliating to Britain, it was a completely unexpected blindside.

It was not the last such blindside to be reckoned with, either. On October 30, when the U.S. introduced to the UN a resolution for Israeli withdrawal from Egypt, it did so in spite of British entreaties to keep that issue off of the UN table. In fact, the U.S. introduced a resolution, the terms of which amounted to an unconcealed effort to neutralize the Anglo-French intention of using an ultimatum to justify a Suez occupation (the U.S. resolution ruled out aid to all combatants). Moreover, since the U.S. also knew that the British and French would surely veto its proposal straightaway, the British reasoned that the only purpose for introducing the motion at all must have been to signal once again to the international community just how disassociated the U.S. and Britain had become. For the British—now feeling the strain of being cast out—the maneuver was not merely humiliating, it was a blow for the basic logic of the Lion who intended to lead the very West from which it had just been cast out.

But the U.S. did not stop there. It further humiliated Britain at the UN by backing the Uniting for Peace resolution. This backing shifted Suez

Crisis deliberations from the Security Council to the General Assembly. The Americans knew how counterproductive such a move would be to Britain's goals because it would put the question of the legitimization of force in the hands of ex-colonies, who would surely refuse it. Indeed, Eisenhower even made a point of acknowledging that this was precisely why the U.S. had backed the move.[5] Finally, as if all of this were not enough, the Americans overtly took charge of the hunt against the British and the French. Just as soon as Uniting for Peace was in place and the discussion over Suez had been moved to the General Assembly, none other than Dulles moved a resolution for a cease-fire. Relying on the support of U.S. ambassador to the UN Henry Cabot Lodge, the U.S. pushed the cease-fire through with all the weight of its prestige and power.

In light of these various events, British political leaders and bureaucrats constructed the phrase, 'United Nations,' to signify a concerted American effort to disgrace the British and thus another element that contributed to the reality of betrayal. This version of 'United Nations' also sat entirely uncomfortably with the notions of trust and shared values essential to weness and so functioned as a phrase-in-dispute of the Special Relationship. Among the authors who narrated this particular dissent were the obvious (Eden, Lloyd, and Chancellor of the Exchequer Harold Macmillan), but also many lower-level bureaucrats such as U.K. ambassador to the UN Pierson Dixon, and House of Commons leader Rab Butler (who, in light of Eden's worsening health, was alongside Macmillan in stepping up to fill Eden's shoes). Macmillan's narrative (one of his many) exemplifies the type of logic these authors constructed in their representations of 'United Nations:'

> Dulles would not pledge himself to give us full support in the Security Council . . . with my American background and experience of the Americans . . . . [I] was baffled by this fog of contradictions . . .
>
> We were now forced [into] long and slow retreat on almost every point, accompanied by humiliations almost vindictively inflicted upon us at the instance of the United States Government. . . . The Americans, not content with the cease-fire, were now demanding an immediate evacuation. (Macmillan 1971, 119–67)

Here Macmillan was reflecting on the whole gamut of American behaviors at the United Nations, from the American reaction to the British initial appeal to the United Nations just after the nationalization (when the British sought to justify force and the Americans refused to support them), to the late stages of the crisis when the Americans took the lead in bullying the British and French into a cease-fire and withdrawal. Interestingly, in order to imbue these events with continuity and intelligibility, Macmillan constructed a set of links that pictured the U.S. as having pursued some grand plan that amounted to betrayal. As Macmillan described it, from the beginning the U.S. (and especially the already controversial Dulles) had purposely shrouded their behavior in a confusing "fog of contradictions" which later resonated as "humiliations" that were "almost vindictively inflicted upon us at the instance of the United States government." These humiliations became fuel for the "reality" of betrayal because nothing in Macmillan's "American background and experience" had prepared him for any of it. The U.S. was behaving in ways that were simply incommensurable with the kind of shared norms and ideas to which Macmillan had become accustomed. In fact, by the very same logic—that is, the departure from shared norms—Macmillan positioned 'United Nations' also as a direct phrase-in-dispute of the Special Relationship.

In another example, Sir Pierson Dixon narrated a representation very similar to Macmillan's in its disputatious effects for the Special Relationship, but in some ways, Dixon's pugnacious narrative went even further. In his report on the October 30 UN resolutions sponsored by the U.S., Dixon linked United Nations to a "reality" of American betrayal, not only using the logic of humiliation, but also using the logic of American association with the Soviets. In this way, he signified 'United Nations' as even more potent evidence of that alternative, dissident "reality."

> Our action was in the general interests of security and peace. . . .
> There were three meetings of the Security Council on October 30th
> . . . . At the after-dinner session there were two Resolutions—Soviet
> and U.S.. We and the French vetoed both of them. I explained our
> position on the grounds that the urgency of the situation compelled
> us to take drastic preventive action. . . . We were opposed by the
> Americans on every point. I urged Mr. Lodge not to submit his res-
> olution until he had reconsidered presentations being made in
> London. He not only tabled [sic] it forthwith but included an extra
> paragraph clearly directed against the Anglo-French action. . . .
>
> The PM asked me how things were going in NY. I said that we had
> just finished an emergency session of the Security Council called at
> an hour's notice by the Russians. The Russian proposal amounted to
> a Russia-U.S. action against France and Britain. . . . The Americans
> . . . were leading the pack. . . .
>
> It is astonishing that the arrangements for the international force
> should be made without consulting us. . . . The Americans seemed
> to be completely behind the Secretary General. (Dixon 1968, 264,
> 272, 275)

Dixon linked "the general interests of security and peace" (supposedly a shared value of the U.S. and the U.K.) to something that the U.S. "opposed on every point," and then linked that opposition to his sense of having been humiliated. In this regard Dixon believed that simple opposition was not enough for the Americans; they were after blood. They drew that blood by way of Ambassador Lodge's determined condemnation of the Anglo-French action with "an extra paragraph clearly directed against the Anglo-French action." But it is in the next link, in which Dixon characterized the resolution as a "Russia-U.S. action," that humiliation of the British and its connection to American betrayal is most powerful. As Dixon constructed it, the Americans had done the unforgivable: They had teamed up with the East (the enemy) in order to lead the pack against Britain. In fact, the whole complex of American actions was "astonishing"—both that the U.S. would adopt such a quarrelsome position toward the British without at least first trying to consult with them, and then, that on top of it, that they would do so in concert with the Russians. Insult (the humiliation of public opposition without prior consultation) and injury (the effort to prevent the British ultimatum) were compounded by the fickle American character that could be the only explanation for a joint action with the Russians. Through these potent links, Dixon rendered the 'United Nations' evidence of American betrayal and a phrase-in-dispute of the Special Relationship.

It was not long before British dissent began to register with American political leaders and bureaucrats. In November, the head of the CIA, Allen Dulles, reported to the National Security Council (NSC) the anxiety in Britain over the evident decline of their prestige and their disapprobation of American policies and the Americans more generally, both of which had risen consistently with the perception of the British demise.[6] U.S. ambassador to Britain, Roger Makins, reported that Her Majesty's Government was displeased with proceedings at the United Nations, and that its representatives felt they could not count on the United States.[7] Both men communicated in no uncertain terms the heart of the British representation: The U.S. was responsible for humiliating Britain. The Americans had betrayed their friends in the context of the United Nations and, as a result, the very friendship had lost its meaning to the British.

Economic Sanctions

A final event—or, more precisely, a final group of events—that British authors produced in dispute of the Special Relationship and in support of betrayal was 'Economic Sanctions.' In this instance, fewer British authors were involved—only Macmillan, Lloyd, and Dixon—because by this late time in the crisis, Eden was incapacitated, and others simply remained silent.[8] Nevertheless, the phrase 'Economic Sanctions' reverberated powerfully. For the British it represented one of the most condemning aspects of American behavior during the Suez Crisis. British authors used the phrase to refer to the various economic pressures that the U.S. had applied to its allies in seeking to leverage their compliance with a cease-fire and withdrawal from the canal. But that phrase was more than descriptive; the British formed certain ineluctable narrative links between 'Economic Sanctions' and invidious American plans of sabotage, blackmail, and the ever-mounting, apparently intentional, humiliations of the British.

The British interpretation of 'Economic Sanctions' was fueled most fundamentally by what the U.S. later claimed was Macmillan's misconception that the U.S. would provide financial support to Britain during the months of the Suez occupation. Macmillan did indeed assume that Britain could "no doubt expect American aid" to stabilize confidence in the British pound during the British operation (Macmillan 1971, 109–10). But, instead of providing financial support, the U.S. did the complete reverse: It deployed a variety of strategies to exacerbate the unstable conditions of British commerce and the severe pressures being put on British monetary reserves as a result of their operation in Egypt. The United States refused to grant a loan to ease this pressure (without, of course, Britain's agreement to a cease-fire), and it further refused to support a British request for the release of funds from the IMF (which Britain intended to use to stem the run on the pound). The effect was a financial situation that the British perceived to be so precarious that they could see no alternative but to agree to a cease-fire. The British had been, in their view, fooled into expecting American financial support, only to find that their financial dependence on the U.S. had been used against them. It was nothing short of sabotage.

Worse yet, sabotage turned to blackmail and blackmail to a humiliating second round of sabotage. After the British and French agreed to the cease-fire, the U.S. focused its attention on bullying the British into setting a withdrawal date. This time the leverage was oil. Given that the Canal was now blocked and the Syrian pipeline was severed, a U.S. refusal of oil aid had grave implications. As Macmillan explained to the British cabinet, such punitive measures would surely drive the economy into the ground. The only thing Britain could do to prevent that catastrophe would be to withdraw.[9] In this way, oil sanctions were nothing less than economic blackmail, and the British succumbed. British leaders were so demoralized that they withstood the blackmail with the bit of consolation accompanying its offer: Eisenhower's invitation to Eden to visit the U.S. The visit, they hoped, would soften the blow of withdrawal a bit, and take the spotlight off of the retreat from Suez. Given that domestic support for the Tory government had waned significantly and left it vulnerable to a vote of no-confidence, Eden's administration was desperate to find ways to retain some image of international prestige in the hope that it would lend some domestic legitimacy to his party.

However, for fear of seeming too cozy with his wayward allies, at the last minute Eisenhower postponed the visit. In fact, he made a date for the visit contingent upon the withdrawal of Anglo-French troops from Egypt. Eden, who was edgy, desperate, and about to fall ill, was humiliated into suffering this further sabotage. The U.S. had first undermined the British international mission with economic sanctions and then had done the same to the Tory party's bid to sustain domestic legitimacy. The whole incident ended up calling greater attention to the failure of the mission rather than deflecting attention from it.

Above all, the British found it hard to believe that the whole affair was not an intentional act. Although the historical record in the U.S. suggests that this second round of sabotage was not planned, and while Eisenhower later admitted to deeply regretting the entire incident, such sentiments did not help at the time (Cooper 1978). The British experienced it as yet another calculated deceit made possible by U.S. economic sanctions. Given such a narrative context, 'Economic Sanctions' became an inexorable phrase-in-dispute of the trust and common fate constitutive of the Special Relationship. Interpreted in this manner as sabotage, blackmail, and humiliation, 'Economic Sanctions' were linked far more easily to the "reality" of betrayal. As Macmillan constructed it in one of his more subtle narratives,

> One of our difficulties at this time was how to present the full case for "making Nasser disgorge" without endangering confidence in sterling, all the more so because the Americans were blocking neither private Egyptian accounts nor fresh dollar accruals to the Egyptian government. This decision was neither logical nor helpful. If the Americans had agreed to block new accruals in dollars, we would have had little difficulty in persuading the Germans and other European countries to do the same. Until this could be affected it was hard to persuade others to follow. (Macmillan 1971, 111)

Macmillan constructed a logic of sabotage by potent reference to an utterance made by Dulles early on in the crisis. In one of his first responses to the Suez nationalization, the secretary of state had pronounced that some way would need to be found "to make Nasser disgorge what he has seized. . . . Nasser must be made to disgorge his theft."[10] This "disgorging" comment quickly became infamous among the British, especially as one of Dulles's statements that led the allies astray about the degree to which the U.S. could be expected to back the British. To Macmillan—and to everyone else, for that matter—Dulles's words encouraged the notion that the United States was "solidly behind Britain and France" (Nutting 1967, 52).

Given the history of the phrase "making Nasser disgorge," Macmillan's link between it and American economic policies that were "neither logical nor helpful" set the stage for interpreting the American unanticipated reversal of its economic support as, at the very least, a nuisance. But clearly those policies were more than just an irritant for Macmillan. In light of his further link between American economic decisions and the difficulty the British would thus have in "persuading the Germans and other European countries" to follow the British lead, Macmillan viewed those economic policies as an American attempt to sabotage the British mission by interrupting the political-economic power of the Sterling area. With this link, Macmillan constructed a picture in which American refusal to economically penalize Nasser (by blocking dollar accruals) undercut the value of Sterling, thus making it politically impossible for the British to rally support from other countries. The U.S., by its economic policies, had pulled the rug of legitimacy out from under the British. They had implied support and then, without warning or notice, had done exactly the opposite of what was necessary to give that support. It was not a narrative that boded well for trust and the Special Relationship, and it was surely one that provided logical support to betrayal.

Whereas Macmillan's narrative illustrated a connection between the logic of sabotage and economic sanctions, Lloyd constructed one linking the logic of blackmail surrounding oil sanctions to that phrase. In mid-November he realized that,

> Eisenhower was determined not to have the United States used as a cat's paw to protect the British oil interests. That was the attitude which distressed us . . . Perhaps we had exposed our realization of our weakness too frankly to Eisenhower and Dulles in Washington the previous January. They knew that we knew that economically we were very poorly placed. That was not a strong bargaining position. (Lloyd 1978, 214)

In the links between the phrases "British oil interests," "exposed our . . . weakness too frankly," "economically . . . poorly placed," and "not a strong bargaining position," Lloyd authors a story about how the British trusted the Americans, confiding in them and exposing their vulnerabilities, only to have that trust turned against them. The American friends exploited the knowledge of British weakness to their advantage, particularly in the context of negotiating over oil. It is a narrative of American blackmail. Furthermore, Lloyd's story is quite evocative of all kinds of violations of the Special Relationship—from the American exploitation of the norm of

mutual consultation and openness (which prompted the B
their weaknesses in the first place), to a violation of trust and
an Anglo-American common fate that should have made
with, rather than against, the British. In its emphasis on how
tantly took advantage of Britain's guileless adherence to
Relationship, Lloyd's narrative constitutes 'Economic Sanctions' not just as
a phrase-in-dispute of the Special Relationship, but also as a phrase-in-support of the "reality" of betrayal.

The Americans were made quite aware of this disputatious signification
of 'Economic Sanctions.' Beyond the communication of this message via
day-to-day exchanges between Dulles and Eisenhower and their counterparts in the U.K., stories also quickly filtered back to the U.S. informally
about the British feelings. In one famed scene described to the American
leaders, when Macmillan heard of the oil sanctions he threw his arms in the
air and cried contemptuously, "That finishes it (Lloyd 1978, 206)!" Between
'Dulles,' 'United Nations,' and 'Economic Sanctions' it seems, betrayal had
simply just won out over specialness as the British version of the "reality" of
Anglo-American relations. The logic of the narrative "reality" of betrayal—
and of its connection to the narrative "reality" of the Special Relationship
—is sketched in Figure 6–1.

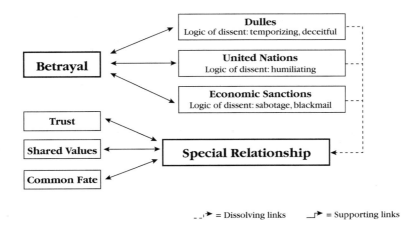

Figure 6–1 Interplay between "Realities" of American Betrayal and Special Relationship

Narrating British Bellicosity

The British were not the only ones authoring the disputes that fueled dissi-dent "realities" and dissolved the Special Relationship. The Americans told their own version of the Suez story. Once the phrase 'Use of Force' had de-magnetized Anglo-American attraction by unsettling the "reality" of kin-dred freedom-loving democrats, the Americans became attentive to aspects of their British so-called friends that they had previously overlooked. In particular, the events of the Suez Crisis developed in such a way that led American authors to believe that the British, far from being peoples consti-tuted by the fabric of virtue, were intrinsically bellicose, aggressive, and de-ceitful by nature. On top of that, the Americans began to believe that the British had been hiding their true character and true values all along sim-ply to manipulate the Americans.

Three events in particular led the Americans to these conclusions: the British reflexive reaction to Nasser's nationalization; the analogy the British drew between Nasser and Hitler; and the British deception of the U.S. over their participation in the covert invasion of Egypt. To the Americans, these events signified that the British had never given up colonialism, they had never understood nor revered rule of law, and even worse, that they had never intended to honor that principle. Instead, the Americans believed that the British had purposely deceived them in order to reap what benefits they could from an Anglo-American alliance. The "reality" was that the British were bellicose and that the Special Relationship had been a farce. The shared values, trust, and norms of mutual, open consultation on mat-ters of common security, which had characterized the Special Relationship, had all been lies.

Nationalization

American political leaders and bureaucrats narrated 'Nationalization' as a phrase-in-support of the "reality" of British bellicosity, and as a phrase-in-dispute of the "reality" of Special Relationship, because Britain's thought-less call for force in response to Nasser's action seemed to be an overreaction, rooted, above all, in their intentions to pursue imperial inter-ests. Of course this did not mean that the Americans supported Nasser's claim to the waterway. Rather, they agreed with the British that Nasser's move was drastic, and required a firm response. Yet, the immediacy and in-tensity with which the British opted for force, especially without seriously considering other options, smacked of British colonial interests. By the late 1950s, most Americans believed that colonialism was out of line with Western sensibilities. To the extent that the British were acting on colonial impulses, they were violating the very logic of Westernness. Even worse, however, was how the British had openly and publicly professed to have abandoned their colonial interests in order to represent themselves in a way that appeared to cohere with the contemporary demands of Westernness. Thus, insofar as the British reaction to nationalization reflected an imperialist urge, the Americans could not help but view the event as a moment of revelation in which false pretensions of reform were uncovered as a mask for a more bellicose and, apparently, more deceptive, British character—a character that the U.S. did not understand and could not trust.

This American version of 'Nationalization' rested on two crucial interpretative moves by American authors: an interpretation of the immediacy and intensity of the British reaction to nationalization with a call to arms as indicative of colonialist intentions, and the discovery of British colonial interest in the Suez context as some kind of revelatory experience or crystallizing moment of the true nature of who the British were as a people. American authors associated the rapidity and doggedness of the British reaction with colonial aspirations primarily because the British refused to consider any alternative proposal before taking up their battle cry. No sooner had Nasser made his announcement then the British responded with the claim of the necessity of force, and then they had taken their claim, almost immediately and against American expressed preferences, to the United Nations. The British goal, stated clearly to all, was to legitimate the use of force to secure the functioning of the Canal. But as British leadership also made clear in private discussions with the American leaders, the other goal was to depose Nasser.[11] Their very quick move to the UN, and the seeming urgency in deposing Nasser, immediately stirred American suspicion. Both the U.S. and Britain knew that if Nasser was deposed immediately, there would be no viable leader to rise up and take his place in the short term, leaving a convenient vacuum of power, which, as the Americans quickly deduced, the British hoped they might fill. As Dulles concluded, "the goal of the British could only be a return to the situation in the Canal Zone that existed a few years ago . . . with nearly 90,000 troops there."[12] In this way, Nasser's nationalization offered a handy opportunity for the British to reassert rule of Egypt.

Of course, the British defended their reaction to nationalization by invoking oil interests, economic control, and European security. As Dulles noted, however, any one of those might have been beneficially secured through diplomacy—in fact, diplomacy was likely the most effective way to secure many of those interests. For the Americans the question then became: why the British so quickly decided that diplomacy was pointless? The only credible answer pointed to colonialism: They believed that the real British interest was in securing an outcome that they never could achieve through diplomatic processes (Martel 2000). To American political leaders and bureaucrats, the phrase 'Nationalization' thus became logically associated for the U.S. with notions of British imperialism.

From there, American authors made their second interpretative move in deducing what they believed was the true British nature. The significance of nationalization, in other words, was not only about British imperial interests. It also was about the Americans emerging from a cloud of deception about the nature of the British character. The British were not *real* Western democrats, nor had they *ever* been. Rather, they were an aggressive people, and they had been hiding it from the United States all along. At this point 'Nationalization' became a phrase-in-dispute of the shared values, trust, and common security fate that constituted the Special Relationship, providing evidence in support of British bellicosity.

So just how did American authors move from narrating 'Nationalization' as a British colonial interest to narrating it as evidence that the British were truly deceptive and aggressive, and had been concealing a bellicose temperament? The answer had to do with the American concern for waging peace. Waging peace—which was Dulles's and Eisenhower's preferred Cold War policy—was partly a way to maintain the moral and political distinction between the East and West, and partly, as Eisenhower and Dulles hoped, a way to promote a harmonious international system on the whole. Regardless of which way one sliced it, waging peace had a moral foundation. It was, for both men, the practical implementation of the Judeo-Christian religious imperative to lead the world by example. Waging peace was linked to the universal striving toward the salvation of humankind (Marks 1993; Murray 1999; Kirby 2000). In practice, this meant that any God-fearing democracy worth its salt must do everything in its power to demonstrate by example, the contrast between an empty, repressive, atheistic Soviet-style life, and a life in which liberty and justice were supported and protected. Most important, this meant allowing peoples' self-rule (Drummond and Coblentz 1960, 228).[13] Of course, self-rule meant the eradication of imperialism and yet, as the Suez incident demonstrated to the U.S., the British were not interested in giving up colonialism. This situation raised more than a few eyebrows among the Americans—about whether the British were truly God-fearing, whether they valued self-rule, whether they cared about justice, and so on. In short, it raised questions about the British character and especially about whether or not Britain was truly Western in any compelling way.

To be sure, British imperialism was nothing new. Yet the U.S. had never questioned Britain's character before because, for some time prior to the Suez Crisis, Britain had seemed to acknowledge the moral and strategic importance of giving up its far-flung empire. In the context of the struggle to maintain an East/West boundary and in the effort to build a better post-war world, imperialist practices, even British ones, were outdated. Indeed, Britain had begun granting independence to former colonies, such as Egypt, and also had actively participated in the design and day-to-day affairs of the United Nations (an institution the very fiber of which embodied anticolonial commitments and sentiments). In light of such moves, the Americans had comfortably believed that the British were committed to making the transition to a fully Westernized democracy, and that they were committed to the Judeo-Christian values embodied in that. Significantly then, it was not just that the colonialism was no longer acceptable to the international community, it was that the U.S. no longer expected it from the British.

The British reaction to nationalization with what the U.S. interpreted as colonialist conduct seemed to belie all that supposed progress. It shook the Americans because above all it suggested that the British had intentionally planned to deceive the Americans about who they really were and about what they really valued. On the one hand, the British had taken active pains to convey to the Americans that they shared the same beliefs about the importance of self-rule for maintaining the integrity of the West, and for leading the world by moral example. Yet on the other hand, just when it mattered the most, the British reversed their stance by advocating a policy that looked like a throwback to colonialism in the Middle East (not to mention to a Soviet-style atheistic disregard for Judeo-Christian moral imperatives, as Eisenhower and Dulles understood them). It was perhaps unfortunate for the British that their apparent imperial interests in Suez coincided with the Soviet oppression of the Hungarian revolt, because it was hard not to draw parallels. Just as the Soviets were demonstrating their moral depravity by oppressing the Hungarians, the British were proposing to act out a parallel story in Egypt. The British knew that such parallels would be drawn, yet they still decided that the integrity of the West and moral-religious imperatives were less important than the larger goals they had in mind (Kecskés 2001, 52).

In light of the British imperialist intentions and their evident disregard for context and timing, it was easy for the Americans to narrate the British as charlatans: They were not who they said they were and, even worse, they had sought to deceive the U.S. about it. While the British had made every effort to make it look as though they were concerned for the good of the West and the overall betterment of humanity, they were instead mere opportunists unbounded by concerns for the collective good. As American authors interpreted it, Britain had played the U.S., biding its time until the occasion to pursue its real interests arose—interests that relied on aggressively and irresponsibly wielding power, and that were defined only in terms of reasserting control at all costs, even in an outdated fashion (Neff 1981, 373).[14] The British, as it turned out, were more bellicose than special, for they surely could not be trusted.

When American authors—especially Eisenhower, Dulles, and Vice President Nixon—began to narrate 'Nationalization' as a phrase-in-support of bellicosity and as a phrase-in-dispute of the Special Relationship, it seems quite clear that in part, their narrative was motivated by a goal of salvaging the moral mission of the Eagle—that aspect of U.S. subjectivity in which it identified itself as leader of the West charged with protecting the West from the East (Chapter 5). The idea was to cordon off the West from the British (and French). As Dulles frankly put it in a meeting with Eisenhower and Nixon, it was important to put some moral and social distance between the U.S. and those "countries pursuing colonial policies." The president and vice president readily agreed.[15] Consider, for instance, a narrative spoken by Dulles on November 1, when he recapped to the National Security Council his feelings upon hearing about the British impulsive reaction and call to arms in response to Nasser's nationalization. He says that when he heard the news it struck him that.

> The United States would survive or go down on the basis of the fate of colonialism if the United States supports the French and British on the colonial issue . . . . It is nothing less than tragic that at this very time when we are on the point of winning an immense and long hoped-for victory over Soviet colonialism in Eastern Europe, we should be forced to choose between following in the footsteps of Anglo-French colonialism in Asia and Africa, or splitting our course away from their course . . . what the British and French have done was nothing but the straight old-fashioned variety of colonialism of the most obvious sort.[16]

By linking phrases describing the "British and French colonial issue" with those invoking the specter of "Soviet colonialism," Dulles effectively drew a parallel between the Soviet East and Britain and France in the West. Through these links the British (and French) reaction to nationalization became obviously un-Western, and their imperialist intentions were depraved enough to warrant comparison to the Soviets. In turn, the law-abiding Eagle and so, by implication, the West it sought to protect, "would survive or go done on the basis of the fate of colonialism." In other words, this imperialist-aspiring reaction to nationalization was sure to pollute the reverence for self-determination embodied by the U.S. and the West and, as Dulles's narrative implied, if the West were to survive the moral degradation of such colonialism, the U.S. would be forced into "splitting our course away from their course." Bellicosity needed to be pried away from Westernness; the U.S. needed to be pried away from Britain. Through the set of links that narrated Britain's imperialist-seeking reaction to nationalization as un-Western and Soviet-style, 'Nationalization' fueled the logic of bellicosity and disputed the "reality" of a Special Relationship.

Dulles's narrative went further yet. It implied that beyond engaging in Soviet-style behavior, the British (and French) also were Soviet-like in their *character* as well. They were shady. They had been hiding or concealing their naturally belligerent temperament. After all, while the U.S. had been struggling to win "an immense and long hoped for victory over colonialism," the French and British were reversing course, investing their energies *against* that struggle. Although the British especially had seemed to be with the Americans on their quest, instead they were revealing their desire to engage in "the straight old-fashioned variety of colonialism." That the British were capable of thinking in that "old-fashioned" way suggested to Dulles that they had never had any intention of moving away from their colonial policy, as if they had never been anything but "old-fashioned." Meanwhile, they had led the U.S. to believe otherwise. The duplicity that Dulles's narrative highlighted further reinforced the logic of the British as a power-mongering, bellicose people, one that the U.S.—or, for that matter, the entire West—could not trust.

Vice President Richard Nixon authored similar narratives, in which 'Nationalization,' via the logic of imperialism, became a phrase that simultaneously cast Britain out of the West and out of the Special Relationship. During a campaign speech in which he addressed the unfolding situation in Suez, and how the U.S. would respond to Nasser's nationalization, Nixon said:

> In the past, the nations of Asia and Africa have always felt we would, when the pressure was on, side with the policies of the British and French governments in relation to the once colonial areas ... We have to show independence from the Anglo-French policies which seems to us to reflect the colonialist tradition. That declaration of independence will have an electrifying effect. (Lloyd 1978, 201)

Crucial to the logic of this dissenting narrative were Nixon's references to Asia and Africa, most of which were or had been British and French colonies. Nixon pointed out that assuming that the U.S. would back Britain and France in their forceful reaction to the Suez nationalization was incorrect. Rather, Britain and France had colonial intentions from which the U.S. was independent. Interestingly, Nixon did not blame the British and French for deluding the U.S. about their intentions to fully move beyond colonialism (as Dulles had done), but he nevertheless managed to represent colonialism as bellicose and barbaric in ways that the U.S. could not tolerate. In particular, he pointed out that the U.S. needed to "show independence" from such policies, which, by implication of the need for such independence, one must take to be wrong morally and politically. Moreover, Nixon's statement called up the "electrifying" effect that such a show of independence would have; it would draw a line between good and evil in a place that put colonial powers, including France and Britain, on the evil side. In this way, Nixon constructed his narratives such that Britain's imperialistic responses to Nasser's nationalization fed the logic that Britain was involved in unacceptable, bellicose activities—activities that had to be delineated from the U.S. and could not be squared with the principles of the Special Relationship.

Given British sensitivity to the Americans on the issue of colonialism and their own anxieties about being cast out of the very West they sought to lead and protect, these dissenting American narratives of 'Nationalization' resounded among British political leaders and bureaucrats. The question on the minds of the British was how the Americans could so regularly misconstrue—almost to the point of maliciousness—British activities as a legacy of outdated colonialism.[17] 'Nationalization' thus became a phrase caught up in a vicious cycle of accusations that contributed significantly to the dissolution of Anglo-American we-ness.

Nasser

In addition to the narrative fracas they had fomented over 'Nationalization,' American authors drummed up another point of contention over the phrase 'Nasser.' The Americans believed the British were strategically and disingenuously making Nasser out to be a bigger menace than he really was. Indeed, one way the British had been seeking to deflect international criticism about the coincidence between their Suez policy and colonialism was by calling attention to what they believed was the grave threat Nasser posed to the security of Europe. As Gordon Martel (2000, 406) put it, British leaders believed that the Americans had failed to perceive the very real dangers posed by what they referred to as "Nasserism," but also had been mesmerized by their own prejudice against what they mistakenly referred to as "colonialism."

Eden, Macmillan, and Lloyd, along with various British ambassadors to the UN and U.S., sought to set the U.S. straight. They repeatedly invoked the specter of Nasser as the next Hitler or Mussolini to justify their call to arms. No policy, they argued, was too pro-active to stave off such a threat; 'Nasser' was evidence *against* the view that the British were bellicose throwbacks to old-fashioned colonial ways. But the Americans did not buy it. A wide-ranging sentiment existed among American political leaders and bureaucrats that Nasser was, in the final analysis, not a big deal. Surely he was a smart opportunist who needed to be "cut down to size,"[18] but essentially he amounted to nothing more than a "two-bit dictator."[19] In addition, Egypt remained more or less unaligned in the Cold War struggle, and to American analysts, it seemed counter-productive to automatically treat him as an antagonist. Working with him rather than against him, they reasoned, might pay dividends in wooing the Arab Middle East more firmly onto the West side of the East/West struggle.

But neither of these reasons is why Britain's characterization of Nasser as a greedy Hitler-like dictator became fodder for the American dissenting narrative. What prompted American authors to narrate 'Nasser' as a phrase-in-support of bellicosity and as a phrase-in-dispute of the Special Relationship was that Nasser's nationalization was legal. Indeed, under international law, Nasser had every right under to nationalize the Canal Company and "was careful to the point of fastidiousness in acting legally" when he did so. This was precisely because "he wanted by all means to avoid giving the West an excuse to accuse him of violating the 1888 Convention of Constantinople that guaranteed free passage through the Canal" (Neff 1981, 283). Thus, even though the U.S. had agreed that Nasser's nationalization was a nuisance that created serious problems, it was preposterous to characterize this careful legal act as the act of an aggressive, expansionist dictator. Had Nasser actually harbored expansionist intentions, the Americans reasoned, he would more likely have expropriated the Canal Company than nationalized it. Given that there existed, technically, little ground for the British numerous complaints and battle cries, the Americans concluded that the British were the ones with expansionist intentions. The British were suggesting force (and, ultimately, used it) to respond to a legal activity. Not only was the British policy unjustifiable in the moral terms that defined the West, but, because it was, it made Britain look bellicose—like a greedy power looking for a pretext to seize territory. To the Americans, the British view of Nasser was the problem, not Nasser himself.

To be certain, their was no necessary reason that the British and American differences of opinion over the degree of Nasser's rascality needed to prompt American authors into narrating 'Nasser' as a phrase-in-dispute of the Special Relationship. Certainly, American leaders could have been more reserved in their interpretation of British intentions. For instance, they might have more generously concluded that the British rendition of 'Nasser' was just a panic reaction, or an isolated incident, rather than a real reflection of some belligerent streak endemic to British character. Only in the case of a belligerent British character would the phrase 'Nasser' feed the logic of bellicosity in a way that made it incommensurable with the logic of shared values, trust, and common fate that characterized the

Special Relationship. But the Americans did not adopt the "isolated incident," more generous interpretation. In the context of an already demagnetized we, the ever-cumulating stock of mystifying British proclamations and decisions puzzled the U.S. to the point of alienation from their alleged friends. The British simply refused to let go of their hostile view of Nasser even as the Egyptian president demonstrated daily his benign, nonexpansionist intentions. That the British never adjusted their view of Nasser to the facts of his actual behavior nourished the idea brewing in American minds that the British had some preset mission—that they were pursuing some indefensible goal, which they were trying to hide from the U.S.

What finally led U.S. leaders to the conclusion that the British were defaming Nasser in order to justify some nefarious purpose of their own, was the discovery, through midlevel meetings, that the British fully acknowledged the legality of Nasser's action, and fully recognized the hypocrisy of their logic to use force to reclaim the Canal.[20] In fact, the U.S. learned that Eden was so deliberate about the ruse that when he realized his intentions had become too transparent to others, he decided to shift tacks. Once it became impossible to deny the legality of the nationalization, Eden altered his justification for the use of force: Instead of claiming Nasser's expansionist intentions he shifted the focus to how Nasser would run the Canal. Eden argued that because Nasser was an unpredictable dictator, there were no grounds to trust Nasser's commitment to and respect of Egypt's international obligations to keep the Canal running smoothly. Given that the Canal was an "international asset of the highest importance," and given Nasser's dictatorial nature, such uncertainty was intolerable and justified using force to reclaim it (Neff 1981, 283–84).

Unfortunately for the British, Nasser proved this logic to be unfounded as well. He quickly demonstrated in no uncertain terms that he would not only keep the Suez Canal open, but that Egyptian operators were capable of managing it as efficiently and without bias as the previous international organization had been (Neff 1981, 283). Still, Eden and Macmillan pushed on, going so far as to pressure other key British actors—including Lloyd and Nutting—into publicly agreeing with their now-exposed justificatory logic. Indeed, dissenting British voices became louder; Nasser's control over the Canal, they cried, was putting a knife to the economic neck of Europe (James 1986, 459). In this context, the British leaders again invoked images of Hitler and their dubious fears of expansionism.

These alarmist messages coming from the British, however, had provoked a different fear among the Americans: The irascible persistence of Britain's reaction to Nasser, no matter what he did or how he acted, ultimately led the U.S. to believe that the British were not experiencing real panic over real threats. Rather, the U.S. began to fear that Britain simply did not care about legality or rights or about respecting the freedom of nations. By persisting to demonize Nasser even as he acted within his rights, and by attempting to use an (inaccurate) demon-status to justify force, the British were themselves edging toward an unjustifiably aggressive stance toward the Egyptian leader. For Dulles and Eisenhower—both of whom had been forced to think deeply about the relationship between legality, aggression, and freedom in formulating their policy on waging peace—any nation that truly believed in freedom would ipso facto rule out unjust or illegal aggression because it was, by definition, impossible to simultaneously revere freedom and be unjustifiably aggressive. Indeed, only communists—the embodiment of oppression over freedom—could justify an illegal aggression (Drummond and Coblentz 1960, 188; Marks 1993, 24). In light of Britain's unwarranted, aggressive stance toward Nasser, the British were starting to look an awful lot like communists; they were trying to justify an act that violated the very freedom they were claiming to preserve. To the Americans, the discovery echoed a discovery they had made in relation to the phrase 'Nationalization': The British were not fully on the Western side of the East/West, Good/Evil demarcation line. The British had been concealing their bellicosity. The whole Special Relationship—the shared values, trust, and common fate—was predicated on fraudulence about who the British really were.

A great number of American authors narrated 'Nasser' as evidence of Britain's bellicosity and as a phrase-in-dispute of the Special Relationship, including both Eisenhower and Dulles. But some of the most interesting, first-hand representations were authored by midlevel U.S. diplomats. U.S. ambassador to Egypt, Henry Byorade, for instance, had been talking with Britain's ambassador to Egypt, Humphrey Trevelyan, and those conversations profoundly shaped his conviction that the British were demonizing Nasser for their own opportunistic reasons. In a series of August communiqués to U.S. deputy undersecretary of state Robert Murphy, Byorade relayed the message that he conveyed to Trevelyan.

> Would it not be wise to let things calm down while preparing the way for action if and when Egypt violates these international commitments? This is a time of high emotion and if a move is made now involving force . . . it would merely be moving against the sovereign right and pledged word of Egypt rather than [against a] proven act (such as stoppage of shipping), detrimental to our vital interests. Under these circumstances, I fear Nasser would have the masses behind him and certainly would further consolidate his emotional hold over Middle East. . . . While there are no forces here which it is not in Western power to overthrow we would, I fear in this day and age, live with the after effects for many years to come . . . it

seems to us that possibly we should *only* plan for future moves if and when Nasser violates Egypt's international commitments.[21]

A few days later, Byorade followed up on this communiqué, adding that he had told Trevelyan that it seemed unlikely that Nasser would ever violate his international commitments (as laid out in the Constantinople Convention). Nasser, he pointed out, was rational, fair, had a calm temperament, and had been consistently "relaxed and friendly."[22]

Through this series of narratives, Byorade indicated that British were disregarding international law in order to stir up the pot with Nasser, forging a number of links that produced 'Nasser' as a phrase-in-support of bellicosity and as a phrase-in-dispute of the Special Relationship. In a first step, Byorade emphasized Egypt's "sovereign rights" and Britain's implied lack of wisdom in moving ahead with force before "things calm down," which he then followed with a representation of Nasser not as maniacal or Hitlerlike, but rather as "relaxed and friendly." He implied that the British conception of Nasser was not only wrong, but as a foundation for policy decision, it was dangerous. It would likely lead to poor—even illegal—judgment and action. Moreover, Byorade's narrative took on the tone of accusation of British bellicosity. As he put it, "if a move is made now involving force" against Nasser, it would "put masses behind him" and "would lead to effects for many years to come" all for "no proven act . . . detrimental to our interests." In other words, Byorade carefully scolded that Britain's willingness to violate Nasser's legal rights to self-determination and independence, and to risk the dangers of a mass movement as retaliation for a nationalization that would not necessarily hurt Western interests over the long run, suggested that Britain was on a witch-hunt. Byorade's narrative conjured up a picture of an aggressive and undiscerning Britain whose bellicosity had been revealed to the U.S., and who therefore was unfit for American trust and a Special Relationship. Trevelyan directly received Byorade's message, and thus, so did the British leadership.

Another mid-level statesmen who played a central role in narrating Nasser as a reflection of British bellicosity (and so as phrase-in-dispute of the Special Relationship) was Loy Henderson, a U.S. deputy undersecretary of state. Like Byorade, Henderson had spent time in Egypt with Nasser, in particular, as a participant in the Menzies mission (led by Australian prime minister Sir Robert Menzies). Though it failed, that mission had sought to persuade Nasser to accept the SCUA plan. Through his experience, Henderson reached the conclusion that while Egyptian nationalism was increasingly anti-Western, Nasser himself was not the problem. He was a determined but not hot-tempered or unreasonable man. On the contrary, it was the British who Henderson found to be that way.

We deeply regret failure of mission . . . Nasser nevertheless has sufficient respect for collective power and influence . . . not to assume toward us attitude calculated to give offense. . . . Nasser personally exercised extreme care in showing us every courtesy, consideration and facility. . . . Have studied British suggestions for situation . . . seems a tireless campaign for military measures.[23]

While Nasser showered "respect" and "every courtesy, consideration, and facility," the British were unreasonably on a tireless campaign for military measures. The weight of responsibility fell to the British. They were bellicose, a character trait incompatible with the "reality" of the Anglo-American Special Relationship.

Even as the British heard this dissent, they dug in their heels and pursued their goals in ways that only made them seem more bellicose. As John Hamilton, long-time political adviser to Eden, maintained after Trevelyan communicated American concerns to the prime minister, it would have been foolish to let American apprehension and the constraints entailed in quelling them get in the way of the "real plan."[24]

Collusion

From the American perspective, the phrase 'Collusion' dealt the final blows to the Special Relationship. For one, 'Collusion' posed a threat to the "reality" of the Eagle. The deliberate secret plot among Britain, France, and Israel to invade Egypt made a public mockery of the idea that the U.S. was the leader of the West, and illustrated how easy it would be to deny crucial information to the U.S. about a high-stakes international situation. Even more, 'Collusion' signified the sheer treacherousness and disloyalty of the British, and presented powerful evidence for British bellicosity and against the Special Relationship. Britain, of course, was not the only American ally involved in the duplicity—France and Israel were likely the event's instigators. Yet, as the Americans constructed the narrative, Britain was the worst of the duplicitous partners. While France and Israel were just as guilty of subterfuge as the British, the Americans had higher expectations for their Anglo friends.

To configure 'Collusion' as a phrase-in-dispute of the Special Relationship and in support of bellicosity, the Americans focused on the manner in which the plot depended upon a continual, sustained, and conscious British pattern of lying to the Americans. As the Americans saw it, the British had at least two other options. First, they could have simply abstained from use of force—the policy which the U.S. preferred. As an alternative second option, had they not abstained, the Americans claimed that the British could have at least honored the trust and norm of openness they shared with the U.S. by being frank about their plans. Such openness was not something the Americans expected from Israel or France, but they counted on receiving it from Britain. Thus, jarring as it was that the British did not bother to consult with the Americans or even to warn them, it was downright disturbing that they instead had sneakily concocted a scheme to prevent their friends from discovering their plans. It went to the heart of a violation of the Special Relationship.

Even worse, as the Americans saw it, was that among the three colluding allies, the British had led the pack in dreaming up the lies. The French, for instance, were much less concerned to play to appearances by pretending to observe the demands of international law and Western morality. But the British had pleaded with the French to abide fabrications that would make their ignominious plans appear honorable (Goldsmith 2000, 89). Once the U.S. realized that Britain had been the mastermind of the fraudulence, it was difficult to avoid the conclusion that the British were untrustworthy liars who all along had been hiding something about their character. It became a narrative truth among American leaders that the British had a preference for lies over truth, and that underneath their veneer, the British had a hidden bellicose nature. In this way, 'Collusion' became fuel for that dissident "reality."

'Collusion' fueled the logic of bellicosity using another logic as well: The incredible shabbiness of the collusive lies the British invented—from the ridiculous pretext for invasion, to the obviously unacceptable nature of the ultimatum, to the half-baked military planning, to Eden's dismissive rudeness toward the Americans—all suggested that even as the British were trying to fool the Americans into accepting some legal basis for their action, they were so eager to get on with their show of force that they could not even take the time to construct persuasive lies (Neff 1981, 375). It seemed that Her Majesty's Government was so beholden to bellicose, aggressive urges that it was unable to mask them any more. In fact, Eisenhower marveled at how the British government was even keen to proceed with the invasion, even though the British people did not wholeheartedly back their government or even know about what had transpired.[25] In this sense, the "reality" of bellicosity was fueled by 'Collusion' less because of the forceful acts themselves than because of the urgency with which they were undertaken. It suggested that the character of the British leadership was constitutionally and insidiously aggressive rather than peace-loving.

Among authors narrating 'Collusion' as evidence of bellicosity and as a phrase-in-dispute of the Special Relationship were Eisenhower, Dulles, Allen Dulles, head of the CIA, and Vice President Richard Nixon in his capacity as head of the National Security Council. All of them inscribed links between phrases conjuring up collusion, phrases reflecting a bellicose disrespect for accountability to others, and phrases that highlighted the contradictions that such bellicosity and collusion entailed for the Special Relationship. As John Foster Dulles put it:

> We do not know where they stand nor are we consulted. The series of concerted moves among the British, French, and Israelis look like concerted planning. We are quite disturbed here over . . . a deliberate British purpose of keeping us completely in dark as to their intentions . . . . We have fought them off for three months against using force which they have been determined to do and now they are going ahead without us. I am fearful to know the real purposes . . . of the British. We are convinced American public opinion would not favor giving [in] to [the] British and French.[26]

In typical Dulles fashion, the derision is straightforward. Dulles represented the secretive, "concerted" efforts (that is, 'Collusion') as disturbing because the Americans were not "consulted." In fact, the U.S. was being deliberately "kept completely in the dark about their intentions." Given that the U.S. had "fought them off for three months against using force," and that "now they are going ahead without us," the specter of both deception and bellicosity was palpable in Dulles's remarks. Dulles reinforced this idea, linking "I am fearful to know the real purposes . . . of the British" to "we are convinced American public opinion would not favor giving [in] to [the] British and French" —a narrative move which indicated in a different way that he suspected the British of being untrustworthy, suspicious, and uncongenial to the U.S. He feared to know who the British really were, especially because it seemed likely to him that it would reveal a character that did not cohere with the values and goals of the U.S. or the Special Relationship.

Dulles' brother, then the head of the CIA, and therefore a central figure in the discovery of collusion, constructed an even more overtly dissident narrative when he described the secret meetings that had transpired among the British, French, and Israelis throughout October:

> What these governments decided on October 16 was to take the law into their own hands . . . the British accepted a situation in which the Israelis were to play the part of dues ex machina in the plot. They became accessories both before and after the fact. This amounted to constructive collusion on the British part. It is therefore disingenuous to believe that the British were unwitting tools of the French and Israeli principals and that they stumbled onto the scene at a late date without knowing what they were doing. Eden and Lloyd knew what they were getting themselves into . . . .

U.K. has taken pains to assert that its role against Egypt was not a consequence of an inexorable chain of commitments. The British . . . have vehemently denied that because they acted with the French they can be assumed to have connived with the Israelis before hand. Again, these ex post facto justifications are almost meaningless or at least very difficult to understand. . . . They shut out the U.S. from any knowledge of their actions after October 16 . . . . Statements calculated to deceive reflect a British desire to pretend that the conspiracy in which they were involved was not really of their choice. . . . Their statements are almost unbelievable.[27]

Crucial to this logic is the statement that the British had taken "the law into their own hands," a practice, which, especially in light of the logic of 'Nasser,' suggested bellicosity. But Allen Dulles also represented the British as untrustworthy ("their statements are almost unbelievable") and secretive ("They shut the U.S. out of any knowledge"). Together these links represented 'Collusion' as an indication of bellicosity and as an infidelity to the norms of openness; the phrase was simply incompatible with the "reality" of the Special Relationship.

As pungent as 'Collusion' was, it was not long before the British became wise to the blame that was being cast upon them. Eden's administration grimaced, but upheld their farce. They simply denied that they colluded to concoct their military scheme, hoping, as Eden put it, to "put on the best

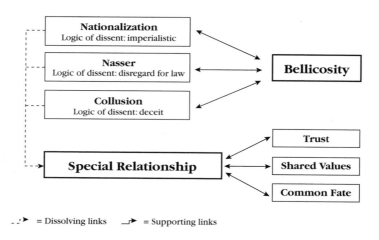

Figure 6–2 Interplay between "Realities" of British Bellicosity and Special Relationship

possible face." In the meantime, American confidence in their British allies fell off markedly. Between 'Nationalization,' 'Nasser,' and 'Collusion,' the very notion that the British American alliance was based on a Special Relationship was shut out in favor of one marred by British bellicosity.[28] The logic of the narrative "reality" of bellicosity and its effects on the Special Relationship can be viewed in (see Figure 6–2).

Specialness Dissolved

The phrases 'Dulles,' 'United Nations,' 'Economic Sanctions,' 'Nationalization,' 'Nasser,' and 'Collusion' all disputed the Special Relationship, but for different reasons. Each also lent language-power to the dissenting narrative "realities" of either American betrayal or British bellicosity; each "reality," in turn, disputed the Special Relationship as well. In the context of an already demagnetized attraction between the U.S. and Britain, the weight of all of this language-power militated against the Special Relationship in a cumulative way. Since there was no legitimate authority to defend the logic of we-ness that held the Special Relationship together, the dissident phrases and "realities" acquired credibility until finally the Special Relationship dissolved. The overall narrative process leading to the dissolution of the Special Relationship is sketched in Figure 6–3.

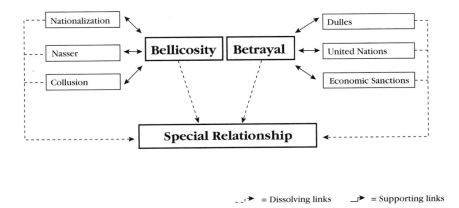

Figure 6–3 Dissolution of Special Relationship

As if to mark the dissolutionary moments of specialness, the historical record reveals that at various points during the course of events, Eisenhower telephoned Eden to unleash "tirades" and give Eden "unshirted hell" about how the Special Relationship was not special at all. The British were just "one among a number of allies" and "unworthy and unreliable allies" at that (Cooper 1978, 167; Risse-Kappen 1995, 95; Ovendale 1998, 118). The British marked the dissolution of specialness in their own way: as Sir Oliver Franks, the former U.K. Ambassador to U.S., described the triumph of the "reality" of betrayal over that of the Special Relationship, "it is as if we had lost a major battle without causalities. We were disemboweled" (Cooper 1978, 212). Macmillan put it differently; the rift between the two countries, he said, would take much longer to repair than it was possible for the world to accommodate (Cooper 1978, 254).

Once the intelligibility and logic of the links between Anglo-American shared values, trust, and common fate had eroded, so also did the Anglo-American security community order. All that was left was unshared or subjective British and American narratives of the "reality" of the other, but none about their mutual relationship. In the absence of shared self-other knowledge, Anglo-American order necessarily gave way to disorder. As Dulles mused, "never before in recent years had we faced a situation where we had no clear idea of the intentions of our British allies."[29] The sense of disorientation went both ways. As Dixon and Eden agreed, the department of state was behaving in a "fantastic" unfathomable manner. Said Dixon: "I simply cannot understand what the United States is thinking of."[30]

CHAPTER 7

Re-Production

The Suez Crisis precipitated an identity crisis for the Anglo-American we. It dissolved the instantiating narrative of that identity so that the previously shared representation of British and American self and other, intertwined in a trusting security relationship, was no longer shared. As we-ness broke down, neither the British nor the Americans knew what to expect from each other, and the stable expectations that had characterized the security community international order gave way to international disorder. But disorder did not prevail. Over the course of the crisis period, the very same authors who had dissolved the Special Relationship then turned around and re-produced that we-ness identity through the linguistic practice of fastening. More exactly, those who had been accused of being either bellicose Brits or disloyal Americans retaliated against that defamation by waging campaigns of representational force. Their campaigns were designed to reverse, or at least neutralize, each of the dissenting phrases that constituted those two slanderous "realities" (bellicosity and betrayal). Each campaign was successful. Thus, phrase by phrase, and one by one, those who had dissolved Special Relationship with dissident narratives were forced to backtrack on their own dissent until, ultimately, the logic of the six phrases that gave "reality" to bellicosity and betrayal had dissolved instead. The cumulative result was not just to re-produce the narrative "reality" of the Special Relationship, but also to re-produce the Anglo-American security community order of stable expectations for nonviolent behavior that had flowed from we-ness.

The East/West and Lion/Eagle Problem

Why would the very same actors who had so painstakingly narrated the "realties" of bellicosity and betrayal—those who had claimed such grievous alienation from and disillusionment with the Special Relationship—turn around and re-produce the "reality" of the very identity from which they had so adamantly tried to disentangle themselves? The answer hearkens back to theoretical arguments about agency and rationality (Chapter 4). States, as actors and agents of world politics, are not unitary, singular constructs with enduring, clear-cut, or obviously discernible interests. As beings and actors, states are the product of the complex interplay between the different identities that constitute their subjectivity. The will and capacity of states to make choices or decisions, to author particular narratives over others, and to act in certain ways rather than in others, are thus situated at the intersection of the various identity narratives that make up their Self. Depending on the potential for a domino effect among those narratives, in which the dissolution of one identity threatens to dissolve other identities, a state may experience the stakes bound up with preserving the status quo as high enough to prompt narrative action. When the stakes are so high that the state cannot bear the risk that its narrative action may fail to re-produce its Self, the most rational narrative choice is to fasten using representational force.

This, I propose, is just what happened for both the U.S. and Britain in the context of the Suez Crisis. The dissolution of the Special Relationship under the pressure of the dissident "realties" of bellicosity and betrayal threatened a central and, at the time, indispensable identity in the subjectivity of each Britain and the U.S.–each one's self/other* relationship with the Soviet Union. That is, the dissent that dissolved the Special Relationship also threatened the identity narrative of West in the East/West dichotomy that characterized the Cold War. In order for each to preserve that aspect of its Self as West and so, to continue to re-produce the dichotomous boundary that made sense of the Cold War, something had to be done to stop the impending domino effect created by the dissolution of the narrative of Special Relationship. However, that something had to be more than simply a bargain in which both sides agreed to drop their dissenting narratives of bellicosity and betrayal in favor of the status quo Special Relationship. The problem was that both the British and American identity narratives of Lion and Eagle were also connected—in a zero-sum way—to the East/West narrative. Since the two were fighting for the right to claim leadership of the very West that was now unsettled, abandoning the dissent that held the

---

*I deliberately shift from "self-other" to "self/other" to emphasize the importance of boundary and dichotomy between East and West.

other responsible for that unsettling was unacceptable. It would be tantamount to admitting that the other *was* a fit leader of the West (a Self-defeating prospect for either side).[1] The only option, then, was for each side to try to *force* the other to abandon its dissenting narrative of bellicosity or betrayal so that the "reality" of the West (and Special Relationship) could be shored up on terms favorable to its Self—Lion or Eagle. This domino effect between the dissolution of the Special Relationship and the unsettling of the West and Lion or Eagle is sketched in Figure 7–1.

Significantly, this account for why the U.S. and Britain decided to repair the Special Relationship (i.e., concerns about the identity domino effect) rests on claims about the demands of the Cold War international order; the U.S. and Britain repaired the Special Relationship because of the bipolar international structure. It is a commonly advanced and regularly accepted explanation, and yet, in most accounts that appeal to Cold War structures (such as the realist alliance approach described in Chapter 3), the bipolar structure under consideration is based on a distribution of material power. The logic typically proffered is that fear for physical survival in the face of the Soviet physical threat must have been what prompted the two countries

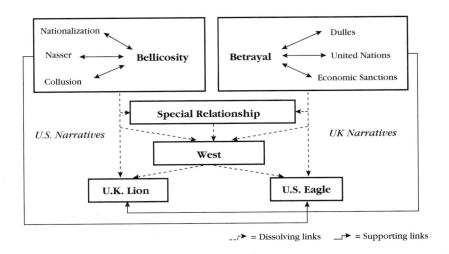

Figure 7–1 The West and the Lion/Eagle problem

to repair their relationship. In contrast, the reading I offer here treats bipolarity as a structure of self-other identities. As David Campbell (1992) explains, the Cold War was fundamentally an international order based not on action and reaction to material threats by states under anarchic conditions, but rather an international order characterized by the performances (or narrative actions, as Lyotard might call them) of states engaged in a ritualized process of forming and maintaining their Selves by delineating their identities from difference. As the U.S. and other states delineated themselves from the Soviet Union, the Cold War became a performance of the West. The "reality" of the West was narrated into existence both by creating the "reality" of the East and by erecting an ideological, political, and moral boundary between the East and West. The bipolar system was one based on bipolar identities; the pressure to repair the Special Relationship derived its strength from threats to the persistence of the "reality" of those identities.

To be sure, the distribution of material power between East and West was an ever-present factor in the Cold War identity performance. During the Suez Crisis, for instance, British and American leaders were troubled about how to understand and manage the material Reality of the evident Soviet development of an intercontinental ballistic missle (ICBM) (Paul 2000, 201). Tellingly, however, neither side knew quite what to make of that possibility. President Eisenhower was unsure whether the Russians really intended to pursue the military conquest of Western Europe with such an ICBM, and British Prime Minister Anthony Eden and the U.K.'s foreign secretary Selwyn Lloyd were equally uncertain. As they put it, there was no real fear that the "Soviets would make rocket attacks on British cities," but there was a high degree of uncertainty about just what such ICBMs could mean (Carlton 1989, 78; Chomsky 1993). In this way, the meaning of material power did not speak for itself. What gave it meaning was the shared self-other relationship between East and West; material conditions were simply foils for enacting the East/West relationship. In order to make sense of material Reality, the East/West relationship had to remain shared knowledge; the boundary had to remain clearly erected, stabilized, sustained, and performed. In this way, the Cold War was more fundamentally about policing the boundaries of the West in order to maintain the boundaries of the self in relation to other than it was about balancing material power.[2] To win the war meant simply to sustain the performance of self and other; to maintain the narrative realities of East and West.[3]

Yet, in order for East and West to remain stable, the Special Relationship had to be repaired. The Anglo-American Special Relationship, as the British and American disputants were quickly reminded, was not a stand-alone narrative "reality," unconnected from other key aspects of each side's sub-jectivity. The Special Relationship also functioned as a crucial phrase in the narrative that constituted the very West that the Cold War functioned to define and protect. As the Special Relationship dissolved, it unsettled the taken-for-granted truth of the West. It created an unanswerable question about who was "essentially" or "really" the West. Was it the U.S., with its commitment to rule of law? Or was it Britain, with its commitment to pro-tecting the world from the next possible Hitler? Anthony Nutting, Eden's protégé who ultimately resigned in disgust over the crisis, did so precisely because he could no longer recognize Britain as Western. Britain, he re-flected, "the champions of the rule of law, had applied the rule of the jun-gle . . . and with the Russians doing the same" (Nutting 1967, 139). In fact, because the "reality" of the West became too porous to distinguish it from the East, the whole logic of the Cold War—including the material practices of power balancing it justified—became tenuous as well. This logic and its trajectory were exemplified in the Soviet proposal that the U.S. and Soviet Union work together against Britain through the UN (See Chapter 5). The implication was clearly that the dissolution of the Special Relationship threatened a domino effect for the narrative and identity of the West, in-deed, for the whole logic of the narrative "reality" of a Cold War interna-tional order.

Of course, with the benefit of hindsight, American and British dissi-dents from the Special Relationship should have known that their dispu-tatious narrative practices would unsettle the West, the Cold War, and ultimately their Selves. The centrality of the phrase 'Special Relationship' to the logic that produced the narrative "reality" of the West should have been impossible to overlook. Such links had been forged regularly and fre-quently over the course of the early and mid-twentieth century by leaders in both the U.S. and Britain, as well as by authors from other countries such as Canada and Australia.[4] In fact, in various contexts the Special Relationship had been credited outright with making the West the social, economic, and political community that leads the civilized world (Gelber 1961; Mowrer 1961; Reynolds 1982; Danchev 1998; Kirby 2000).[5] Even Nasser recognized the links between the phrases 'Special Relationship' and 'West,' reportedly counting on his ability to divide the West by breaking down the Anglo-American Special Relationship. Doing so would enable him to avoid concerted retaliation by the West for his nationalization (Calvocoressi 1966, 48).

In the heat of the conflict, however, neither the U.S. nor Britain seemed to be particularly aware of just how entangled the narrative of the Special Relationship was with the maintenance of their identities as West in the Cold

War. For its part, the leadership of the U.S. seemed to believe that we-ness was expendable; that a relationship with Britain fashioned as a limited cooperative alliance (devoid of the demands of trust, shared values, and common fate) would be adequate for pursuing American interests and their underlying identities. For the most part, the U.S. envisioned a useful strategic relationship with Britain, but as the President noted to Dulles, only "we [the U.S.] provide the West's hope that some vestige of real political . . . union can be preserved" (Bowie 1989, 210–12; Baylis 1997, 86–7). In the American mind, the British were unconnected to the viability of the U.S. identity as West. The British had a similar take. To Eden and the majority of British citizens, "Britain was still a world power, only temporarily weakened by the impact of the war years" (Beloff 1989, 334). "Going it alone," without accountability to the Special Relationship, was thus simply a matter of righting things that had gone wrong (Nutting 1967, 70). Like the U.S. administration, the British government remained interested in sustaining a strategic alliance with the United States. But it was also broadly in agreement that the Special Relationship had nothing to do with the British interests and identities. As Harold Caccia put it to Selwyn Lloyd, "I doubt that we would lose much by snapping the sentimental ties."[6]

Both sides were quickly set straight about their misconception. Through a series of incidents, including that apparent American collaboration with the Soviet Union at the United Nations and the eerie coincidental timing of the British imperial operation in Egypt with the Soviet repression of Hungary, it became increasingly clear to both sides (and not just to Nutting) how perilously unsettled the West had become as a moral and ideological category. Ultimately, American and British leaders could not help but notice that it was the breakdown of the shared values of the Special Relationship that produced the ambiguity about what constituted West versus East, Good versus Bad, Us versus Them. After all, it was the very absence of any intersubjective narrative about what counted as West-Good-Us that rendered the dissident "reality" of bellicosity just as compelling as that of betrayal, and vice versa. By extension, the question of who belonged in the category of the West and on the "right" side of the Cold War—was it the U.S. or Britain?—was up for grabs just as soon as Special Relationship dissolved. Each side independently had the same realization, recognizing that the instability in subjectivity that it now experienced was rooted in the dissolution of the Special Relationship. Eisenhower's administration came around to the idea that a bare bones Anglo-American strategic alliance was inadequate, and instead "consideration of the Special Relationship began to weigh on Washington" more heavily (Hitchens 1990, 276). The British, too, became increasingly haunted by the loss of the sentimental ties they had previously dismissed as unlikely to make a difference (Ovendale 1998).

In this way, then, through the threatened domino effect between the demise of the Special Relationship and the demise of the West, the Cold War international order mattered for the preservation of the nonviolent Anglo-American order. The Cold War constituted and was constituted by the very identities and interests that had been put at risk by the Suez Crisis. In turn, both the British and Americans decided that re-producing the Special Relationship was imperative. They both realized that to do so, they needed to eradicate the "realities" of bellicosity and betrayal (and the constitutive phrases that had rendered them logical), thereby stopping the dissolutionary domino effect on the West at its source. But, significantly on this account, the respective British and American decisions to repair the Special Relationship had less to do with their material concerns about material bipolarity than with each state's anxious reaction to the possible erasure of crucial aspects of their subjectivity by the dissolution of the East/West identity bipolarity.

Yet there is a final curiosity in the situation: Given that both sets of statesmen realized the stakes bound up in saving the Special Relationship, why did they need to fasten with representational force? Why strategically choose this forceful linguistic weapon when, given the circumstances at that point in time, the two sides might have more easily voluntarily abandoned their dissent in order to reconstruct their narrative of we-ness friendship? But such an alternative was not an option. For either to revoke their dissent (that is, the phrases-in-dispute that constituted bellicosity and betrayal, respectively) they would have had to acknowledge those narrative "realities" as dissent rather than as truth. To acknowledge such a thing would have been tantamount to an apology for having disrupted the Special Relationship through the polemics of frivolous dissent. By extension, it would have been an admission of culpability for unsettling the West. Admitting responsibility for unsettling the West was beyond the realm of possibility for either side, since for both countries, the whole purpose for having become involved in the Suez Crisis in the first place was to demonstrate their prowess in managing the West. To accept blame—even implicitly—was unacceptable and would only have further unsettled the credibility of the narratives of Lion and Eagle. Put somewhat differently, unless a way could be found to eliminate bellicosity and betrayal (aside from acknowledging its own dissidence), in an awkward twist, one or both sides would have ended up defeating itself (or more accurately, its Self) in the zero-sum competition for the right to claim leadership in the West.

It seems that both the British and American leadership actually recognized this risk. As Anthony Nutting reflected on the eve of his frustrated resignation, the tragedy "could have engulfed them all [the British], nullifying . . . every principle for which Eden had stood and fought" (Nutting 1967,

138). If the British were to relent on claims to American betrayal (fueling British responsibility for unsettling the West), they would have provided a coup de grace to the demise of the representation of the Lion as a leader and still-great power. In its place would be a legitimate narrative of Britain as a self-glorifying has-been. "How," mused Nutting, "could we ever retrieve all that we had lost?" Perhaps, then, it was for the integrity of the identity of the Lion that Eden never, even on his deathbed, acknowledged any British wrongdoing. The Americans faced a similar problem. Revoking their narrative of British bellicosity would have only fueled the logic of betrayal, by indicating that the U.S. was irresponsible and fickle rather than a reliable leader of the West. Of course, this is precisely what the British had charged with such dissident phrases as 'Dulles' and 'United Nations.' Perhaps this conundrum hit home hardest for Eisenhower when Nasser commended him for "putting your principles before your friends."[7] It was a veiled way of thanking Eisenhower for his unfaithfulness to the West, but what Nasser actually clarified was that the risk to the Eagle of admitting any wrongdoing was simply too high to abide. Just like bellicosity, betrayal could not be acknowledged.

It was, as such, for the very same reasons that each side needed to eradicate the dissenting "realities" that neither could afford to revoke their own dissent.[8] There were just too many interconnected narratives, inscribing crucial identities in the complex that constituted British and American subjectivity. It appeared that the best bet for either side would be to *force* the other to abandon its dissent in the hope not only of re-producing the Special Relationship and settling the "reality" of the West, but also of maintaining some ground upon which to claim the continuing integrity of the Lion/Eagle. Getting rid of bellicosity and betrayal, that is, required deploying representational force.

The American Campaign

And deploy representational force is what the U.S. did. Faced with the increasingly compelling "reality" that the West was no longer "real"—at least in any definitive terms—and that the Eagle as leader of the West, and so the American Self, was therefore unsettled, the U.S. had to either wait for the British to voluntarily retract their narrative of betrayal (thereby incriminating themselves) or the American authors would have to force them to do so. With the stakes so high, the U.S. chose the latter. In practical terms that meant finding ways to delink the phrases-in-dispute 'Dulles,' 'United Nations,' and 'Economic Sanctions,' from the logic of betrayal while at the same time as re-producing the narrative of the Special Relationship so that the meaning of 'West' could be settled in a way that supported the Eagle.

For this purpose, Terror—the incorporation of dissent into the status quo—would be ideal. In one fell swoop, it could delink support from bellicosity and turn a phrase-in-dispute into a phrase-in-support of the Special Relationship; it could re-produce the Special Relationship, but as it did so, it could also define that Special Relationship in such a way as to advance the kind of West that the Eagle envisioned. As it turned out, the Americans were largely successful in devising compelling narratives of Terror, but in some cases they were unable to construct compelling enough traps. Although they were able to wield Terror over 'Dulles' and 'Economic Sanctions,' they had to settle for Exile, that is, exclusionary silence, in the case of 'United Nations.' 'United Nations' was thus simply erased as a relevant point of discussion in relation to the Special Relationship. Nevertheless, the end result was quite spectacular. The Americans effectively detached all logical support from the narrative of betrayal, and, on at least two scores, turned those detached phrases into support that re-produced the Special Relationship. In turn, those phrases contributed to settling the West and eradicated any logical contradictions in the narrative of the American identity as Eagle.

Dulles

The phrase-in-dispute 'Dulles' had become natural evidence of betrayal because, as the British narrated it, the phrase highlighted just how fickle and unreliable the U.S. was. Not only did 'Dulles' undermine the Special Relationship and muddy up the lines of what counted as West (Could a fickle, unreliable state still be an embodiment of Westernness?), but in turn, it put a serious kink in the logic that the Eagle was the pillar of Western leadership. For this reason, 'Dulles'—at least as it had been depicted by the British—needed to be eliminated. Key American authors, President Eisenhower and especially Dulles himself, did so through a thorough** campaign of narrative Terror against the subjectivity of the British dissidents who had constructed 'Dulles' in that detrimental way. The logic of that Terror rested on a trap that forced the British to accept that rather than temporizing and double-crossing, Dulles's diplomatic wrangling was actually the best thing that a loyal friend could do given the circumstances. Dulles had not betrayed the British. On the contrary, he had stood mightily

---

**By "thorough" I mean that for all the dissident authors that I identified in the primary resources that I had examined, every one capitulated to the American campaign of Terror. I do not present that exhaustive analysis here, but it can be found in Bially, 1998. This is also the case for the five other phrases-in-dispute.

vas an interpretation that not only made Dulles look like a
ich, by association, protected the logic of the West and the
gle.

⌐ne genius of this narrative was that the linguistic "gun," or trap the
Americans had set, jammed up the British precisely where they could not
afford to get stuck if they were to preserve the Lion aspect of their Self. The
trap, in other words, zeroed in on the intrasubjective vulnerabilities of the
British and effectively exploited them. In particular, what the Americans
knew and what the British unfortunately realized was that as an older
power, the British were at risk of seeming out of date with the demands of
the contemporary international system. As Dulles, himself, pointed out, if
the British were going to look like leaders they needed to be careful to stay
attuned to the larger contemporary international context. And yet, as he
also noted, the British seemed completely in the dark about the threat lurking on the figurative other side of the Middle East conflict. It was not
Nasser; it was the Soviet Union. In addition, the Soviet Union was not the
old imperialist Russian regime that the British were accustomed to dealing
with. Britain could not assume that it could do business with the Soviet
Union in the way that it had with the czars of old. The British now needed
to be prepared for much more (Drummond and Coblentz 1960, 163).

Substantively being prepared for doing business with the Soviets meant
learning how to get inside of the logic of the Soviet strategic vision and
work it against the Soviets to the advantage of the West. As Dulles noted,
because Britain seemed to have little inkling of what that Soviet vision was,
it was instead bumbling about in the dark. If the British were savvy at all
they would know that Soviets had a force-first doctrine of behavior and
that the West could not also follow such a doctrine. To be force-first, at best
would mean engaging the East on its own terms; at worse it would mean
blurring the differences between the East and the West. What the West
needed to do was to be smart, so what Britain needed to do, if it were to lead
the West well, was to differentiate itself by adopting a *peace-first* strategy; it
needed to wage peace.

Above all else, waging peace meant that force could not be used as a first
resort. Of course, before Dulles stepped in with his diplomatic tactics, the
use of force as a first resort appeared to be exactly where the British were
headed (Berding 1965, 133). Had the British continued down that path, argued Dulles, they would have revealed themselves as outdated, has-been
powers who thought that they were still dealing with imperial Russian
czars. Had he not intervened to stall for time through diplomatic tactics,
Dulles contended, the British would have impressed upon the Soviets and
other West-identified states the exact opposite of what was required for the

Lion to reclaim its prowess. In this way, Dulles had hardly betrayed the British—he had been their protective friend.

Dulles's logic offered the British a nonchoice; by calling up the need to wage peace in order to be savvy to the demands of the contemporary international system, Dulles made it impossible for the Lion to resist Terror without killing the Eagle aspect of its Self off. Once the British complied, 'Dulles' would become not merely a logical contradiction to betrayal, but a phrase-in-support of the Special Relationship. This American campaign of Terror over 'Dulles' can be schematized as Figure 7–2.

Dulles, joined by President Eisenhower, U.S. ambassador to the U.K. Winthrop Aldrich, and permanent U.S. ambassador to the UN Henry Cabot Lodge Jr., deployed this Terroristic structure in narratives in ways that forcefully incorporated the authors of the dissenting version of 'Dulles' back into the Special Relationship. Dulles, for instance, made this response to accusations that he had been anti-British in his diplomatic tactics.

> This was completely baseless. I have always recognized the need to work in the utmost cooperation with the British Foreign Office. I have great admiration for Britain . . . . As a lawyer I have esteemed Britain's devotion and contribution to law and order. It is true I have had a conflict of personality and views with Anthony Eden . . . . I came to admire and respect his ability and effective dedication to the cause of freedom in the world and unity between the free nations, particularly between the United States and the United Kingdom. (Berding 1965, 111)

In this narrative, Dulles shrewdly set his trap by linking his own vision of himself with phrases that depicted the British leadership as they *should be*: savvy to waging peace through "law" against the Soviet threat. In turn, Dulles confirmed 'Dulles' as a phrase-in-support of the Special Relationship through his final links to unity between the U.S. and the U.K. Analytically, this narrative can be parsed as Figure 7–3.

As the Americans had hoped, the British succumbed. They recognized that they no real choice but to accept the logic that Dulles had been their friend rather than their antagonist. Were the Lion to stand any chance at prevailing as a leader, it needed not only to command the respect of its enemies, but to demonstrate to other Western states that it was capable of managing contemporary conditions. Whether or not Dulles was actually right about the nature of the new Soviet threat, the importance of "law," and so the requirements of waging peace first, was irrelevant. The Lion needed to look as if it had thought about these many possibilities, as though the differences between old Russia and the new Soviets had not been overlooked by British strategists. To ensure this appearance, the best thing

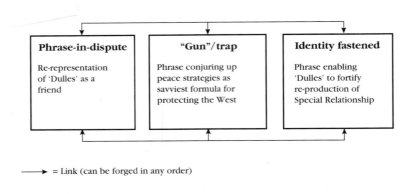

Phrase-in-dispute	**"Gun"/trap**	**Identity fastened**
Re-representation of 'Dulles' as a friend	Phrase conjuring up peace strategies as savviest formula for protecting the West	Phrase enabling 'Dulles' to fortify re-production of Special Relationship

⟶ = Link (can be forged in any order)

Figure 7–2 Terror of Dulles

would be to embrace the logic that Dulles presented about the purpose of his diplomacy. At least then it would remain a narrative *possibility* to represent Britain as a willing participant in diplomacy and so a country who tried to wage peace before resorting to force. By accepting 'Dulles' as a signifier for a friend rather than as a betrayer, Britain could retain the possibility of narrating its Self as a savvy power, adaptable to the changing international structure. If Britain rejected Dulles as a friend, the British Lion would be revealed as outmoded.

Selwyn Lloyd, previously one of Dulles's more vocal critics, offered the following narrative of compliance that mimicked precisely the structure of Terror that had been issued at him (see Figure 7–4):

> Dulles introduced his SCUA plan briefly . . . This was certainly the best speech which I ever heard him make. He pulled out all the stops. He spoke with emotion, apparent conviction, and sincerity . . . After, I had long talk with Dulles and we went over the ground again. He began by repeating that it was imperative that Nasser should lose as a result of Suez. The question was how to achieve that. War would make Nasser look like a hero. In spite of all the difficulties . . . Dulles made a notable speech, firmly on our side. He gave valuable help. (Lloyd 1978, 129)

(Note that SCUA was one of Dulles' allegedly temporizing tactics and part of what enabled the representation of Dulles in support of betrayal).

As Eden, Macmillan, and the coterie of British dissidents (including British ambassador to the U.S., Roger Makins) complied with the similar

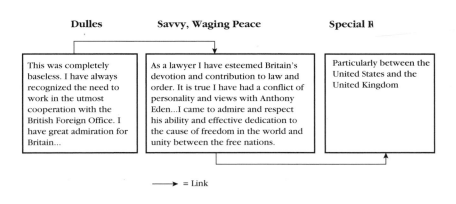

Dulles	Savvy, Waging Peace	Special R
This was completely baseless. I have always recognized the need to work in the utmost cooperation with the British Foreign Office. I have great admiration for Britain...	As a lawyer I have esteemed Britain's devotion and contribution to law and order. It is true I have had a conflict of personality and views with Anthony Eden...I came to admire and respect his ability and effective dedication to the cause of freedom in the world and unity between the free nations.	Particularly between the United States and the United Kingdom

⟶ = Link

Figure 7–3 Dulles's Terror of Dulles

nonchoice, the phrase 'Dulles' not only became delinked from betrayal but also inscribed more than ever as evidence of the Special Relationship. Indeed, after Dulles' death in 1959, when Macmillan became concerned about the onset of an era of precarious summit diplomacy with Kruschchev, he discussed the prospects with an American friend at 10 Downing Street.

"How much we shall miss Foster now," he said. The American asked him why. Anticipating the shape of events to come, Macmillan replied: "Very difficult negotiations lie ahead of us in the next few years. It is going to be necessary for the West to give some ground. Every inch we give will look like a capitulation. If we had Foster with us, everyone would know it was not. No one would be alarmed" (Drummond and Coblentz 1960, 240).

United Nations
Although the Terror of 'Dulles' was a great success, dealing with the phrase-in-dispute 'United Nations' proved more difficult. As British dissident authors had narrated it, the U.S. had used the United Nations to humiliate their best friends in the face of the international community. The UN antics that the U.S. engaged in surrounding the cease-fire and withdrawal were, as the British represented it, antithetical to the stuff of the Special Relationship. But the U.S. could not tolerate responsibility for the demise of the Special Relationship. Were the unsettling of the West to fall on its shoulders, the result would reverberate on—even topple—the Eagle. As with the phrase 'Dulles,' the Americans undertook to rewrite the meaning of 'United Nations' in a way that vindicated the U.S.

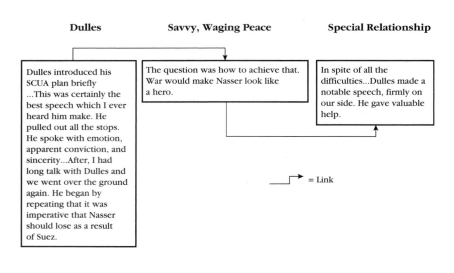

Figure 7–4 Lloyd's reply: Terror of Dulles

Terror would not work, however. First, no trap was compelling enough. No logic existed by which the American force-wielders could compel the British into accepting that the U.S. *had not* brandished the UN against them, or that their behavior at the UN had served the Special Relationship.[9] Yet, this is precisely what Terror would have had to do. Moreover, and more important from the perspective of the American identity, a successful campaign of Terror over 'United Nations' perversely worked against the integrity of the narrative of the Eagle. By convincing the British that the UN had not been used against them as punishment for unnecessarily using force in Suez, the logic of the American/Lion emphasis on waging peace would be undermined. A nation serious about waging peace, as the U.S. represented itself, *would* seek to use the UN to promote a quick, peaceful solution in lieu of threatened aggressive acts. It would demonstrate its very nature as a responsible leader. Had the Americans used Terror to force the British into a narrative "reality" in which the U.S. *had not* used the UN as a tool for peace against their British friends (and thereby, not humiliated them), then the Americans would be sacrificing the opportunity to fortify the Eagle. Indeed, the U.S. could even appear hypocritical about the need to wage peace, potentially feeding back into the "reality" of betrayal. The use of Terror was therefore out of the question.

Exile, however, was a more promising option. Deploying Exile would re-quire a compromise, but a compromise with a worthwhile payoff. The Americans would admit to having humiliated the British at the United Nations, but they could then pass off the blame for having had to do so to someone or something, so that the humiliation did not appear as a betrayal. When coupled with a trap that played on the internal vulnerabilities of the British subjectivity, a narrative structured as Exile would have the effect of forcing the British to drop the topic of 'United Nations' as a meaningful phrase for evaluating the integrity of the Special Relationship in the con-text of the Suez Crisis. In this way, even if the U.S. could not find a way to rewrite the United Nations in support of the Special Relationship, at least they could remove it as evidence of betrayal, and neutralize or silence its destabilizing effects. Such a move also would remove it as a disruptive force on the West while still allowing the Eagle to claim that it had waged peace through the UN during the Suez Crisis.

One vocal advocate of the Exile strategy was Lieutenat General C. P. Cabell, the acting director of the CIA. Writing in a Special National Intelligence Estimate, Cabell argued that "a U.S. effort to disassociate itself would provide some opportunities for efforts at conciliation and localiza-tion of the . . . considerable strain . . . on U.S. relationship with its princi-pal allies."[10] It was a difficult decision nevertheless. As the NSC minutes of November 1 reveal, Dulles and Senator Harold Stassen (who was more in favor of using force than Dulles was) engaged in a rather bitter discussion about how to frame the U.S. use of the UN in relation to the British. Ultimately, the two agreed that making the compromise entailed in Exile—an admission of humiliation—would allow the Eagle to claim success at waging peace through the UN "without drawing British blood."[11]

Finding a target on which to deflect responsibility for the American hu-miliation of the British was much less difficult than the decision about whether to do so in the first place. Just as the U.S. had appealed to the de-mands of the new-fangled Soviet threat (and the British apparent lack of savvy toward it) to Terrorize the British narrative of 'Dulles,' so also they did to Exile the British narrative of 'United Nations.' The Americans repeatedly called British attention to the Soviet insinuation that they would use nu-clear weapons to salvage their Middle East interests if they deemed it nec-essary (Eden 1960, 555).[12] Even as the U.S. did not seem to believe the Soviets would use those weapons, the U.S. played on the ambiguity sur-rounding those material conditions, constructing them, as Charles Bohlen, U.S. ambassador to the Soviet Union, put it "to enhance dramatic effect."[13] By exaggerating their concern about a Soviet nuclear response, the U.S. found a compelling justification for using extraordinary caution through whatever diplomatic means were available at the UN. As U.S. authors put it to the British in their narratives of Exile, although they may have humiliated the British with their approach to cease-fire and withdrawal, they wanted to give the Soviets no opportunity to quibble with how the situation in the Middle East was handled. They wanted to end the Suez affair as quickly as possible to get the Soviet finger "off of the button."[14]

The British had no choice but to succumb, abandoning the link between 'United Nations' and the "reality" of betrayal. The trap they fell victim to was the very same one that had worked for the U.S. in relation to the dissident version of 'Dulles': If the British rejected the idea that Soviet threat ought to be taken seriously and cautiously, they would also narrate the logic of their own unfitness to lead the West. They would be implicitly acknowledging that they were rigid, uncreative, or too ossified in their notions about leadership to recognize changing international conditions, and therefore incapable of coping with the Soviet threat. Thus, by constructing a narrative in which 'United Nations' was linked to both the Soviet threat and to a concern for savvy Western leadership, the American authors put a "gun" to the head of the Lion. Indeed, by linking the trap to phrases that conjured up the Special Relationship, this campaign of Exile ensured that 'United Nations' could no longer be used as a phrase-in-dispute of the Special Relationship or as a phrase-in-support of betrayal. The logic of this campaign is schematized in Figure 7–5.

Many American authors were involved in this campaign to Exile 'United Nations,' including Dulles, Lodge, Herbert Hoover Jr. (Undersecretary of State), and, most important, Eisenhower. For instance, Eisenhower revealed an anxious tone when he penned the following note to Eden in late October.

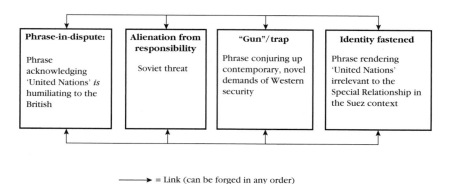

Figure 7–5 Exile of United Nations

Dear Anthony: I address you in this note not only as he
Majesty's government but as my long time friend who has,
believed in and worked for real Anglo-American understan
Egypt could very well ask the Soviets for help—and then
East fat would really be in the fire. It is this latter possibility that has
led us to insist that the West must ask for a United Nations examination and a possible intervention, for we may shortly find our-
selves not only at odds concerning what we should do, but
confronted with a de facto situation that would make all our present troubles look puny indeed. Because of all of these possibilities,
it seems to me of first importance that the U.K. and U.S. quickly and
clearly . . . find some way of concerting our ideas and plans so that
we may not, in any real crisis be powerless to act in concert because
of misunderstanding each other. I think that our two peoples . . .
have this clear understanding of our common or several viewpoints.
With warm personal regard. As Ever, Ike E.[15]

Eisenhower's letter can be recognized as Exile in Figure 7–6.

The trap, one to which the British ultimately had no choice but to succumb, was costly for the British. In accepting the American logic, the British
were forced to concede ground: Because 'United Nations' could no longer
signal betrayal, it further diminished British claims that the Americans had
been at fault in the rupture of the Special Relationship (and consequently at
fault for unsettling the West and acting as an irresponsible Eagle leader).

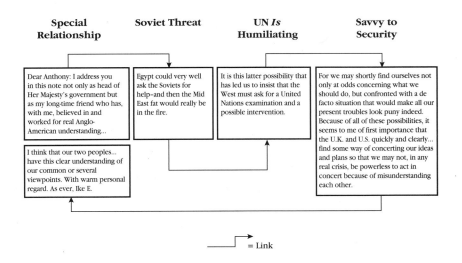

Figure 7–6 Eisenhower's Exile of United Nations

However, by succumbing to the trap, the British protected the Lion as best they could under the circumstances. With a "gun" to the head, the issue of relative identity gains between Lion and Eagle had to take a back seat to the absolute question of Self-preservation.[16] Precisely because 'United Nations' was Exiled, the U.S. could not use it against the Lion as evidence that the British had failed to recognize particular threats to the Western world. Once it had been silenced, in other words, 'United Nations' could not be used to strengthen the idea that the British were outdated. In succumbing to the force, the British kept the Lion from accumulating logical contradictions in its narrative. It was meager consolation, but the alternative was Self-destruction. Macmillan's acquiescence, analyzed in Figure 7–7, is indicative of the kind of narrative compliance the British authored.

> It is evident that the British government may be faced within the next few days of withdrawing from Egypt, having accomplished nothing. . . . The danger of course in the minds of the British Cabinet is . . . loss of prestige . . . while . . . the alternative would obviously involve the risk of bringing in the Russians and resulting in a third world war . . . The British Cabinet is beginning to . . . appreciate . . . immediate and intimate cooperation with the United States.[17]

As the humiliating American antics at the UN were unhinged from any connection to betrayal, the phrase no longer violated the logic of Special Relationship. UN simply disappeared from the Suez Crisis, and in this way no longer obstructed the re-production of we-ness or fastening of the security community. Most importantly for the U.S., United Nations no longer threatened a domino effect among the "realities" of betrayal, West, and Eagle.

Economic Sanctions

'Economic sanctions,' the remaining substantiating phrase in the narrative "reality" of betrayal, was represented by the British as evidence that the U.S. was a saboteur of the British, blackmailing them into accepting intolerable terms for withdrawal from the Canal Zone. In order to reverse, or at least put a stop to, the chain of narrative events between the dissolution of the Special Relationship and the kind of unsettling of the West that would cast aspersion on the Eagle, the U.S. needed to take forceful narrative action. The frontline American authors did so through a shrewd and ultimately successful campaign of Terror in which they rewrote the narrative of 'Economic Sanctions' in a way that depicted them as set of policies the U.S. had devised to help the British extricate themselves from a tight spot of their own making. American authors played strongly—and persuasively—

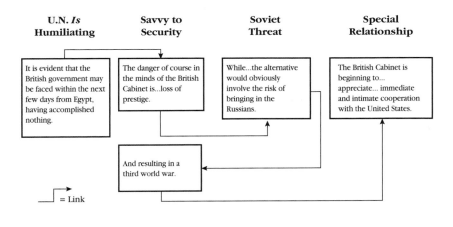

Figure 7–7 Macmillan's reply: Exile of United Nations

to the idea that the British operation in Suez was misconceived from its inception and doomed to failure. Rather than betray Britain, the U.S. had in fact saved the British from inevitable embarrassment. By forcing the British to withdraw before they made a mockery of themselves, the Americans had epitomized good friends.

The basis for this narrative and the effectiveness of its trap was rooted in two sources. The first was Eisenhower's military expertise. The president (a revered five-star general) was direct and vocal about his opinion that from a military perspective, the British mission was doomed to fail. He criticized the British for poorly planning and executing the mission.[18] But the inevitable failure would be more than just a matter of military efficiency and pride, Eisenhower pointed out. A slipshod operation would backfire in a way that was disastrous to British "prestige."[19] It would accomplish the exact opposite effect of what the Lion intended, making the British look more like foolish caricature than a powerful military leader. In fact, if that were to happen, it would no longer just be British prestige at stake; it would be the influence and perhaps even the very existence of the West as a whole. Speaking to Lloyd, Dulles passed along the message,

> It is the military estimate of President Eisenhower, who assuredly is well qualified to have an opinion, that military measures would start a war which would be extremely difficult to end and that before it

was ended the sympathies of all the Middle East, Asian, and African peoples would be irrevocably lost to the West—and lost to such an extent as to pose a grave problem for the next generation. If we do not retain the sympathy of those people they will, in all probability, go over to the Soviet Union.[20]

In short, if the British failed in the Middle East (particularly because their mission was not viable militarily), the West would fail there as well, the Soviet Union would benefit, and the British would be responsible for that.

At first, the British reaction—or at least the reaction of those close to Eden—was to stand firm against this logic. Britain had not yet failed and, Eden maintained, there was no problem with the mission. For the most part, Eden's allied commander-in-chief, General Sir Charles Keightley, agreed. The military planning was sound. What was more, there would have been no way for Eisenhower to know about the planning and intricacies (or lack thereof) of the British operation. (In fact, though he would not have admitted this, Eden often did not know them much before they happened either) (Kyle 1991, 335–40). Indeed Macmillan, it seems, had been expecting this kind of nay-saying and gloomy forecasting from the U.S., even preparing Eden for it. On September 18—a full five weeks before the Israeli invasion—Macmillan reminded Eden that "it is vital that the Americans should not think that we are weakening." As long as the British maintained a strong stature, the Americans would not be able to play into "defeatist elements" (Macmillan 1971, 128). The British, it seems, had clearly prepared themselves for withstanding that kind of a trap.

There was a second aspect to the situation, however, which, in combination with the speculative threat about Britain's military inadequacy, gave the U.S. far more leverage over the British. This was that by the time of the British occupation in early November, the domestic legitimacy of Eden's government was on the wane. Not long after Eisenhower had remarked on the mess the British were sure to make of their military mission, news broke at the BBC of just that: poor military planning, personnel shortfalls, and an increasingly "irascible" Eden (Kyle 1991, 337). British public support for the conservative government's policies crumbled fast. The Labour party, in a crusade led by Hugh Gaitskell, capitalized on the failing British "war" to cultivate even stronger-than-normal resistance from the opposition and the general public (Kyle 1991, 424). This cascaded into an unprecedented level of division within the Tory party, which split into loyalists and dissenters. Dissenters publicly disassociated themselves from Eden's government. For instance, Sir Walter Monkton, secretary of defense and cabinet member, purposely receded into the political woodwork, demoting himself to a lower post in order to avoid having to defend HMG's "inevitable" military operation (Kunz 1991, 129). Anthony Nutting simply resigned. All in all, as prominent Labour leader Aneurin Bevin colorfully put it, there was a "lingering stench of Suez about the place," and with a vote of confidence sure to be called in short order, the fall of the conservative government also seemed inevitable (Horne 1989, 9, quoting Bevin).

It was in this context of breaking news about the failing mission and an impending vote of no confidence, that the Americans made the British a narrative offer they could not refuse. The Americans represented the economic sanctions they had deployed, as designed specifically to provide a scapegoat for the Tory party so that the Her Majesty's Government could save face, withdraw from the canal gracefully, and survive the impending vote of no confidence. In short, the Tories could use the negative effects of American economic policies to their advantage by harping on the injustice of those tactics. It would provide an other or an enemy force around which the splintered conservative government could bond and rally the British public. Surely, in spite of all of their internal divisions, the Tories could nevertheless agree that the American misdeeds left them no choice but to agree to the cease-fire and withdrawal. In focusing on the American misdeeds, HMG could publicly blame its untimely withdrawal on the U.S., without ever having to acknowledge that the mission had been failing anyway. Attention focused on the rough edges and poor planning of the British operation could be diverted by fingers pointing instead at the inhospitable economic situation the Americans had created.

The benefits in this for the Americans were twofold. First, if the U.S. had deployed economic sanctions to help the British out of a tight spot of their own making, then the British could hardly use the phrase to animate a logic of betrayal. On the contrary, 'Economic Sanctions' were evidence of friendship and even a common fate.[21] It was a move that made the U.S. look more like an embodiment of the Special Relationship than a cause of its (and the West's) dissolution. The second benefit to the U.S. of accepting responsibility for the demise of the British mission was that it demonstrated to the international community the power the U.S. had over Britain. It revealed that the U.S. was the cleverer, stronger, and more capable of getting what it wanted. Economic sanctions would lend some credibility to the narrative of the Eagle as the more fit protector of the West, because it was through these sanctions that ultimately the U.S. had secured British withdrawal from the Canal.

The offer looked less enticing from the British side. Obviously fueling the notion that the Eagle was a more clever and fit protector of the West was antithetical to the British, mired as they were in the zero-sum game between the Lion and the Eagle. After such extensive efforts to protect the Lion from the aspersions cast through other American narratives, it would be a waste for the British to succumb to such logic. Of course, a scapegoat and an opportunity to win the vote of confidence was appealing to some Tories, but the future of the Lion as a player in the international system was not dependent on the future of Eden's government, and Macmillan more than anyone recognized this (Horne 1988, 415, 444). Eden's government did not need to survive in order for the Lion to survive. In fact, evidence suggests that Macmillan had often given Eden faulty advice and imperfect information—especially about the economic viability of the mission—in the hope of precipitating the demise of Eden's government that he may eventually take over (Horne 1988, 443; Ovendale 1998).[22] For Macmillan, then, to take the American deal would have little upside. It would perpetuate the status quo (for as long as Eden, now sick, was well enough to stay at his post),[23] and it would counterproductively fuel the "reality" of the Eagle as the powerbroker of the West.

But even Macmillan could not refuse; the Americans had constructed a trap that was a nonchoice. Eisenhower, who favored a continued conservative government with someone other than Eden at the head, made clear to the two likely conservative contenders for Eden's post, Macmillan and Rab Butler, that he and his people were poised to either help or hurt the conservative party in British politics. As Eisenhower put it to U.S. ambassador to the U.K. Winthrop Aldrich, if the conservatives acted sensibly "we can furnish a lot of fig leaves [with which to cover up]."[24] Conversely, if the British did not accept the American deal, Eisenhower and his people could exacerbate internal divisions and undermine the conservative position at home. Eisenhower, that is, would play the conservatives off against each other. He would, he threatened, exacerbate the intra-subjective tensions among them. Inasmuch as he could successfully do so, the whole conservative logic would fail, at best, seriously lengthening the amount of time before either Macmillan or Butler could take over.[25] Even worse, if the Labour party were to gain hold of the government because of Eisenhower's meddling in the internal divisions of the conservative party, then surely the cause of the Lion would be lost anyway. By this point in the crisis, most key authors in Labour were more accurately "American" than "British"—that is, they no longer had interest or desire in preserving the Lion. They were no longer dissidents fueling the logic of betrayal. As such a Labour victory threatened that whatever hard work the current conservative government had put into maintaining that identity as a part of British subjectivity would be for naught.

The trap as such was set: The remaining dissident British authors had the nonchoice to either accept the American scapegoat offer and survive domestically in the long run, or to reject it and fail domestically, as well as undermine the narrative logic of the Lion internationally. Said Eisenhower of this trap, "we are trying . . . to help them [Conservatives] permanently —which they don't seem to understand."[26]

Although Eisenhower initiated the logic of this Terror, illustrated in Figure 7-8, there were other authors as well. In this case, those included Aldrich and George M. Humphrey, secretary of the treasury (Dulles was in the hospital at this point). Humphrey, as representative of the treasury, was right in the thick of the dispute surrounding 'Economic Sanctions.' The narrative that follows is his (see Figure 7–9):

> The possibilities for good and for evil which could come out of the present situation were such that they could scarcely be exaggerated. The range was complete from great success to genuine disaster. In Britain, there was a terrific fight between the two wings of the conservative party. It was touch and go . . . . Anything the United States can do to help the Conservatives through their difficulties and to work out an acceptable Middle East settlement, we certainly ought to be prepared to do . . . this government should be prepared to give Butler*** everything that he asks of us . . . [after] the vote of confidence on a movement for censure on Wednesday parliament. [I am] anxious over Britain's financial and economic situation.[27]

The force of this logic was too much for the British to withstand. Of course, by this point in the crisis, there were only a few British dissenters left. Eden was recovering from illness and not actively participating in politics by this time, and no record exists of Rab Butler having exercised narrative voice in relation to this debate. However, Macmillan, Lloyd, and U.K. ambassador to the UN, Pierson Dixon, continued to defend the Lion, and so it is their submission to Terror that is most relevant. Most striking among them is Macmillan's reply, because he has often been reflected upon as having made the most curious "overnight switch from . . . foremost protagonist of intervention to . . . the leading influence for disengagement" (Fisher 1982, 169). Parliament member Brendan Bracken remarked that Macmillan had gone from "bellicose beyond description . . . wanting to tear Nasser's scalp off with his own fingernails . . . to the leader of the

---

***Eisenhower was trying to be agnostic over whether Butler or Macmillan would take over, but clearly, Humphrey had taken sides. Kyle (1991) 506.

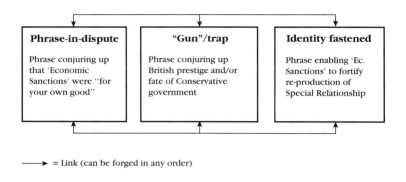

Figure 7–8 Terror of Economic Sanctions

bolters," an apologist for U.S. economic sanctions (Horne 1988, 440). Consider Macmillan's remarks in January, 1957 (see Figure 7–10).

> Washington had every right to refuse Britain a loan. That decision was at least understandable. . . . It also seemed effective. . . . Britain's financial position, unsustainable, was pivotal to the Government. . . . Suez had dealt a crushing blow to the Anglo-American friendship and leadership . . . . (Horne 1988, 444; Calhoun 1991, 492)

In the end, 'Economic Sanctions' became a phrase-in-support rather than a phrase-in-dispute of the Special Relationship. For one, the Americans held up their part of the deal, as Eisenhower intervened to help get the conservatives past the vote of censure. When Macmillan took over he noted in one breath that "curiously, the Suez debacle may have had little effect on the electoral fortunes of the conservative party," and in the next that Eisenhower was largely to credit for that.[28] As a result, the narrative of betrayal simply made no sense; in its place was the Special Relationship. As Dixon put it, "It was really an extraordinary situation in which we were quite incompetent. . . . Our best friends averted their gaze . . . Suez turned out surprisingly well in the longer run" (Dixon 1968, 277).

Indeed, all of the narrative evidence of betrayal was eradicated as phrases-in-dispute of the Special Relationship, and two of them had actually been transformed into support for it. It was as if betrayal had never happened. As Lloyd retrospectively claimed, throughout the crisis he had

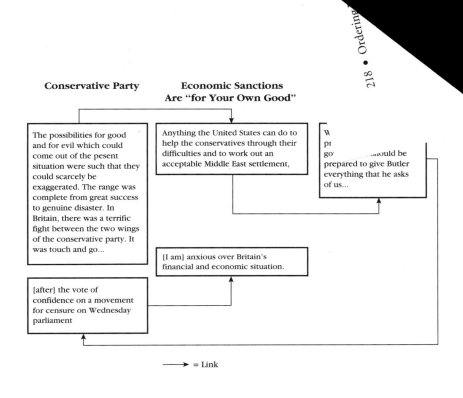

Conservative Party

Economic Sanctions Are "for Your Own Good"

The possibilities for good and for evil which could come out of the pesent situation were such that they could scarcely be exaggerated. The range was complete from great success to genuine disaster. In Britain, there was a terrific fight between the two wings of the conservative party. It was touch and go...

Anything the United States can do to help the conservatives through their difficulties and to work out an acceptable Middle East settlement,

W pr go _____ should be prepared to give Butler everything that he asks of us...

[I am] anxious over Britain's financial and economic situation.

[after] the vote of confidence on a movement for censure on Wednesday parliament

⟶ = Link

Figure 7–9 Humphrey's Terror of Economic Sanctions

"firmly believed in Anglo-American friendship" (Lloyd 1978, 234). In this way, we-ness was fastened and the Special Relationship was re-produced—at least from the American side.

The British Campaign

Ultimately, the Special Relationship was re-produced from the British side as well. The British had to get rid of the dissenting narrative "reality" of bellicosity, for not only did it compellingly represent Britain as un-Western (indeed, Soviet-like) in the context of the Cold War, but it made laughable any British claim to Lion-like prowess as a protector of the West. In order to get rid of bellicosity in a manner that put Britain firmly back on the Western side of the East/West divide, and which, therefore, did not *ipso facto* rule the Lion out of contention as leader of the West, the Special Relationship would have to be repaired and fastened in a congenial way. But because the U.S. would not—indeed, could not—give up its dissent, the British authors, too, appealed to representational force.

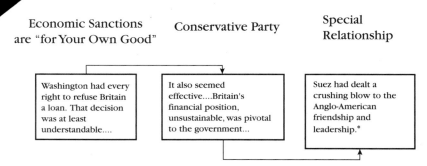

Economic Sanctions are "for Your Own Good"	Conservative Party	Special Relationship
Washington had every right to refuse Britain a loan. That decision was at least understandable....	It also seemed effective....Britain's financial position, unsustainable, was pivotal to the government...	Suez had dealt a crushing blow to the Anglo-American friendship and leadership.*

*This remark, which seems disparaging of the Special Relationship, takes on a different hue when linked to admission that Washington's decisions were understandable and that they had helped the UK. In this context, this remark becomes a lament and apology. This is clear in Macmillan's acknowledgement that Suez **had**—not **has**— dealt a crushing blow and that Britain's government gained.*

⌐➤ = Link

Figure 7–10 Macmillan's reply: Terror of Economic Sanctions

Toward the end of erasing bellicosity, British authors sought to forcefully delink the logic of the connections between the narrative of bellicosity and the phrases 'Nationalization,' 'Nasser,' and 'Collusion.' Although they were by and large successful in this effort, the British did have to rely more on Exile and make more compromises than the U.S. in its re-productive campaigns. Only 'Nasser' turned out to be a smooth campaign of Terror. In the case of 'Collusion,' the British had to resort to Exile, whereas in the case of 'Nationalization,' the force-wielding authors had to combine Terror and Exile into a two-step force process. Moreover, even after the British had eradicated bellicosity, they were still unable to render the logic of the Lion as a leader of the West credible. In that zero-sum competition, the U.S. won. Yet that failure was not due to the British having slid into the Eastern side of the East/West divide. One successful effect of the British campaigns of narrative force was that it stopped that particular domino effect at its source. The other was that the British had gone some way toward fastening we-ness and re-producing the Special Relationship on terms tolerable (if not ideal) to the British Self.

Nationalization

'Nationalization' became a phrase-in-dispute of the Special Relationship (and therefore of the West and the Lion) because the Americans had represented the British call to arms in response to Nasser's action as unthinking and imperialistic. This representation informed the logic that the British were Bellicose and of questionable moral character rather than law-abiding. In order to protect the Lion from such an undermining "reality," the British needed to find a way to prevent imperialism from entering into discussions of the British response to nationalization. In the event that they were able to do so, they would also be able to represent their reaction to nationalization as something other than bellicose, perhaps even as a reaction commensurable with Special Relationship. But it was to be a complex campaign.

Logically, there were two options for delinking 'Nationalization' from the narrative of bellicosity, and both required stepping back and coping with the phrase 'Imperialism.' In one strategy, British authors could have attempted to use Terror to force the Americans into accepting a representation of 'Imperialism' as a positive development for the West in the East/West conflict. For instance, the British might have constructed a representation of the importance of paternal care in which 'Imperialism' became a phrase signifying nurture and the strengthening of at-risk states; something akin to trusteeship. Such 'Imperialism' might be usefully juxtaposed with the Soviet ruthless and rapacious 'Imperialism.' If Terror of this sort were successful, the British reaction to nationalization with imperialist intentions could be understood as not bellicose at all, but rather as a smart move by the Lion in the struggle to differentiate the moral standards between East and West. But the problem with this approach was that it was not likely that the "Americans will come round" (Horne 1988, 419; Horne 1989, 22). It would have been exceptionally difficult to convince the Americans that imperialism, even of a nurturing and paternalistic sort, was a good thing. Anti-imperialism was simply too central to the American liberal conception of self-determination upon which crucial aspects of the Eagle were founded. Moreover, self-determination had become central to the whole logic of the United Nations and to most of the countries in the world. It would not be enough to trap the U.S. into accepting 'Imperialism;' the British would have had to Terrorize the meaning of that phrase for former colonies as well. It was a daunting prospect.[29]

The British adopted the second strategic option instead; they Exiled the phrase 'Imperialism' in a way that effectively committed Terror over the phrase 'Nationalization.' That is, they forced the U.S. to drop the topic of 'Imperialism' altogether so that they were free to renarrate 'Nationalization' as a phrase-in-support of the Special Relationship. (It was a campaign of Exile-Terror.) It worked like this: The British acknowledged how imperialist their force-pursuant reaction to nationalization must have looked, but they represented that imperialist appearance as an unfortunate and unavoidable externality of their necessary actions to save the West in the face of the building momentum of Soviet confidence. British authors, particularly Eden, Macmillan, and Lloyd—and in this case, the American Joint Chiefs of Staff[30]—constructed this story line by relying on the logic that using force was the only prudent response for dealing with the increasingly unpredictable Soviets. As the Soviets gained confidence, they would be more likely to take advantage of Nasser if he was left unchecked; and so rather than being imperialistic, the British were being cautious, concerned, and savvy Western leaders. The unpredictability of the Soviets left them no choice. If that meant enduring some ill-directed accusations about 'Imperialism' in the short run, well, the British were prepared for that. Tolerating that misconception was a small price to pay to effectively staving off any capricious developing threats to the West.

This clever logic served multiple purposes. First, it rendered 'Imperialism' irrelevant to the whole Suez affair because on this view, 'Imperialism' was *not really* what the British were up to—that was an understandable though wrongheaded conclusion others were likely to draw. Second, because this narrative pitched the British as willing to incur the ill-directed accusations of the rest of the international community in order to protect the West against the Soviets, it shored up the logic that the Lion was not only savvy to the requirements of coping with the demands of the contemporary international system (something which the U.S. had raised questions about), but that the Lion was selfless and courageous. In other words, at the same time that 'Imperialism' was Exiled from the discussion altogether the logic of that Exile helped fasten the narrative of the Lion. Third, and importantly, this Exile of 'Imperialism' completely reversed the significance of the phrase 'Nationalization' in relation to the "reality" of the Special Relationship. Rather than fueling a logic of bellicosity, a reflection of depraved moral character, the British reaction to nationalization became logically represented as a selfless attempt to *defend* the West and preserve its prestige against the deceptive, volatile Soviets. 'Nationalization,' that is, came to signify an effort to preserve the integrity of the shared values that the British and Americans hoped to inculcate in world politics. In this way, Exiling 'Imperialism' effectively Terrorized 'Nationalization' and so contributed to the fastening of the Special Relationship.[31]

The Americans could not resist. Even though the core logic of the Eagle rested on incredible antipathy toward any apparent affront to self-determination, and even though accepting this British Exile-Terror would lend more credibility to the Lion as a fit leader than the U.S. would have liked, the cost of resisting was too high to bear. The British had built a rather impossible trap that played on the intra-subjective vulnerabilities of the American Self. Were the U.S. to reject the logic that the British were acting out of moral fortitude and a keen perception of the range of potential Soviet reactions to the power vacuum in the Middle East, the U.S. would also inadvertently send a message to Europe and NATO that it did not take seriously any moral and strategic logic other than its own. It would create the impression across Europe that as the Western leader, the U.S. would not be an "open hegemon." It would not listen and take account of the perceptions and concerns of its allies (Deudney and Ikenberry 1999). Instead, ironically, it would appear as a quasi-imperialist hegemony with Europe and the members of NATO as its subjects. Such a representation would hardly inspire confidence that the Eagle could responsibly lead the West in a fair, reliable manner. The nonchoice then was to succumb to the Exile of 'Imperialism' and Terror of 'Nationalization,' or to inadvertently represent the very logic of betrayal, fickleness, and irresponsibility that was so damaging to the Eagle in the first place. The logic of the Exile-Terror is schematized in Figure 7–11.

Eden, who perhaps had the most attachment to imperialism and bore the most responsibility for Britain's allegedly bellicose reaction to nationalization, narrated one instance of Exile-Terror in a letter to Eisenhower on October 30, 1956 (see Figure 7–12).

> We are well aware that no real settlement of Middle Eastern problems is possible except through the closest cooperation between our two countries. Our two governments have tried. . . . This seems like an opportunity for a fresh start. I can assure you that any action which we may have to take to follow up the Declaration is not part of a harking back to the old colonial and occupational concepts. We are most anxious to avoid this impression. Nothing could have prevented this volcano from erupting somewhere. But when the dust settles there may well be a chance for our doing really constructive pieces of work together and thereby strengthening the weakest point in the line against Communism.[32]

The logical trap entailed by this Exile-Terror left the Americans with the nonchoice of relinquishing their dissent over 'Nationalization' (and silencing the very topic of 'Imperialism') or alienating the very European allies who were indispensable to the validation of the Eagle as leader. Eisenhower and Dulles, as it turns out, were already worried about the delicate internal politics of NATO, and so this trap found fertile ground. In fact, Eisenhower confided in Dulles that he was concerned that if the U.S.

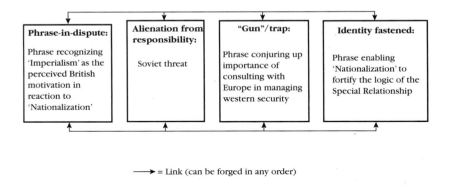

Figure 7-11 Exile-Terror of Nationalization

appeared to dominate decision making, it would be difficult to make NATO an effective institution whose members could take each other into confidence. Dulles agreed. He was fearful that a U.S. dismissal of Britain's input about the nature of the Soviet threat might set a precedent of European mistrust for the U.S. In that case, NATO would weaken with the net effect of undermining the U.S.'s own subjectivity, which required heading up a unified Western alliance.[33] American Ambassador to France, C. Douglas Dillon confirmed these fears when he reported:

> Suez developments have tended to impair . . . confidence in NATO and to make serious the possibility of a strong grouping in Europe which would be able to deal directly and on even terms with both U.S. and USSR. Much as we favor principle of European unity, I think that we should view with grave concern the development of a European Union in which the leading foreign policy figures are . . . anti-American. Such a Western European union however is the type toward which . . . opinion is tending to veer as they continue to feel let down by U.S. in . . . Suez. Even if such a situation should eventuate, historical and cultural ties to U.S. would remain far stronger than to USSR. But situation would certainly be more favorable to USSR than to anything we have previously thought of.[34]

Dillon crystallized the nonchoice the Americans faced: If they alienated Europeans further, NATO would weaken and so too would the West. It

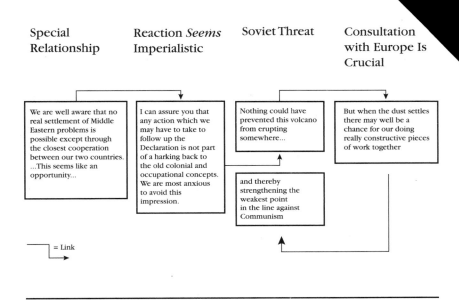

Special Relationship

Reaction *Seems* Imperialistic

Soviet Threat

Consultation with Europe Is Crucial

We are well aware that no real settlement of Middle Eastern problems is possible except through the closest cooperation between our two countries. ...This seems like an opportunity...

I can assure you that any action which we may have to take to follow up the Declaration is not part of a harking back to the old colonial and occupational concepts. We are most anxious to avoid this impression.

Nothing could have prevented this volcano from erupting somewhere...

and thereby strengthening the weakest point in the line against Communism

But when the dust settles there may well be a chance for our doing really constructive pieces of work together

= Link

Figure 7–12 Eden's Exile-Terror of Nationalization

might even drive some European countries to the Soviets. Surely that would be the final blow to the logic of any American Eagle leading the West forward. Even the Joint Chiefs of Staff warned the Eisenhower administration, pointing out that the U.S. should be very careful about a "decrease in Western prestige" and "jeopardizing" U.S. military, political, and economic interests "throughout the world."[35]

Rather than pulling the trigger of the "gun" pointed at the head of the Eagle and the West, American dissidents chose to succumb to the British campaign of force. Although Dulles and Eisenhower were obviously crucial dissidents, so, too, in this case, was Vice President Richard Nixon. He authored the following acquiescent narrative in January 1957 (see Figure 7–13).

> We are proud of our association with Britain and France and our common dedication to the principles of freedom and justice which joined us together as allies in both World War I and World War II. We recognize that they were confronted with a series of aggressive acts short of the use of force; in addition to an ominous military build-up in a nation which they believed threatened their vital interests. In that no mans land between war and peace, it is difficult to decide which is the best course of action. (Lucas 1991, 319)

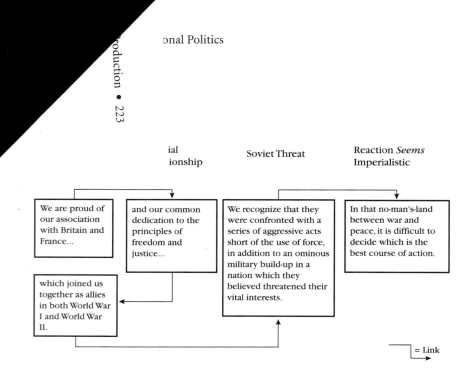

ial   Soviet Threat   Reaction *Seems*
ionship   Imperialistic

Figure 7–13 Nixon's reply: Exile-Terror of Nationalization

One final caveat about the British campaign of force over nationalization is worth noting. Although it was hugely successful in removing support for the narrative links between 'Nationalization' and the "reality" of bellicosity, and replacing them with links which reinforced the Special Relationship, the British never did succeed in convincing the Americans that, after all, force *was* the appropriate way to strategize against the unpredictable Soviets. The Americans accepted that the British forceful reaction to nationalization was *intended* in the best interest of the West and the Special Relationship. However, this did not mean that the Americans ever came to agree that this was, in fact, the best way to protect the West. The distinction lies in the Americans having been forced to accept the well-meaning British intention versus their continued disagreement about the appropriate strategy for realizing that intention. Although the former disrupted the Special Relationship, the latter enabled the Anglo-American we by reinvesting the British with trust in their character to adopt, in Nixon's words, "the best course of action" under the "difficult" conditions of the "no-man's-land between war and peace."

Nasser

Beyond 'Nationalization,' there was the problem of 'Nasse
American authors had represented the British rendering of 'N
portunistic and disregarding of the law. As such, Nasser fueled the logic of
bellicosity; it became a phrase-in-dispute of the Special Relationship and it
contributed to the unsettling of the West. Because Britain was busy representing the U.S. as too fickle, self-centered, and irresponsible to lead the
West, it would be counterproductive to Britain's own identity as Lion and
Western to allow this narrative of British opportunism and lawlessness fester. So they embarked on a campaign of Terror designed to turn 'Nasser'
from a phrase-in-dispute into a phrase-in-support of the Special
Relationship. If the British could force the United States to abandon its dissent and accept that Nasser was a dictator of Hitler-like proportion, then
the British impulse to use force would no longer seem opportunistic and
bellicose. Certainly a threat of Hitler-like proportions did not deserve pa-
tience and the benefit of rule of law. As Lloyd reminded Eisenhower, "we
had lost countless lives and spent the accumulated wealth of more than a
century to defend freedom" from Hitler (Lloyd 1978, 90). Hitler-like dictators thus stood outside of moral and legal standards because the cost of appeasing them was simply too high. In light of this, if the British prevented
another Hitler they would be anything but bellicose; they would be champions of the West, protecting it from aggression and occupation, and so
safeguarding the values and institutions so treasured by the Anglo-
American way. Through this logic both the representation of the Lion and
the Special Relationship could prosper in relation to the phrase 'Nasser.'

Fortunately for the British, the trap necessary to make this campaign of
Terror work was neither complicated to construct nor too unlikely to succeed, so there was never a question of needing to settle for Exile.
Specifically, the British trapped the Americans into accepting their version
of Nasser by embedding their representation of the Hitler-like dictator
within a context of the security of Europe and the threat of World War III.
Lloyd reasoned that a "megalomaniac dictator" left "unchecked" could do
"infinite damage to Western interest[s]," and in a firm tone he added that this
should be enough to "make the U.S. understand." If the U.S. chose to reject
the British view of 'Nasser,' it would appear insensitive to the security dilemmas faced by others—particularly the Europeans (Lloyd 1978, 80, 90–91).
Macmillan agreed. Quite directly, he informed Dulles of this, asking him to
pass on this message to Eisenhower who "as a former [sic] commander in
chief should fully appreciate the European position"[36] (See Figure 7–14).

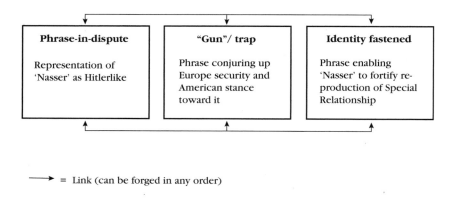

= Link (can be forged in any order)

Figure 7–14 Terror of Nasser

Logically, the U.S. as the Eagle could not safeguard its own identity and still allow itself to appear isolationist or disregardful of European concerns. The Americans, trapped once again by the requirement of appearing as an open hegemon, were faced with a nonchoice between abandoning their dissident definition of 'Nasser' (in exchange for one that supported Anglo-American Special Relationship instead of bellicosity) and inadvertently admitting that they were indifferent toward the security of Europe. The nonchoice they made was to acknowledge that the British were right; Nasser *was* Hitler-like and the British had not been opportunistic or bellicose. In this choice they avoided pulling the trigger of the "gun" pointed at the Eagle's head.

As a model of this logic, consider Eden's September 6, 1956 letter to Eisenhower, illustrated in Figure 7–15.

> Dear Friend. What should the next step be? You suggest that this is where we diverge. If that is so I think that the divergence springs from a difference in our assessment of Nasser . . . . May I set out our view of the position.[37] In the 1930's Hitler established his position by a series of carefully planned movements. These began with the occupation of the Rhineland and were followed by successive acts of aggression against . . . the West. His actions were tolerated and excused by the majority of the population of Western Europe. It was argued either that Hitler had committed no act of aggression against anyone or that it was impossible to prove that he had any ulterior designs . . . In more recent years Russia has attempted similar

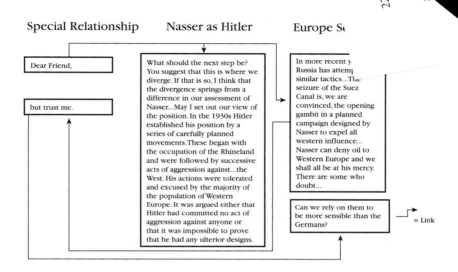

Special Relationship   Nasser as Hitler   Europe S(

Dear Friend,

but trust me.

What should the next step be? You suggest that this is where we diverge. If that is so, I think that the divergence springs from a difference in our assessment of Nasser...May I set out our view of the position. In the 1930s Hitler established his position by a series of carefully planned movements. These began with the occupation of the Rhineland and were followed by successive acts of aggression against...the West. His actions were tolerated and excused by the majority of the population of Western Europe. It was argued either that Hitler had committed no act of aggression against anyone or that it was impossible to prove that he had any ulterior designs.

In more recent y Russia has attemp similar tactics...The seizure of the Suez Canal is, we are convinced, the opening gambit in a planned campaign designed by Nasser to expel all western influence... Nasser can deny oil to Western Europe and we shall all be at his mercy. There are some who doubt...

Can we rely on them to be more sensible than the Germans?

= Link

Figure 7–15 Eden's Terror of Nasser

tactics. . . . The seizure of the Suez Canal is, we are convinced, the opening gambit in a planned campaign designed by Nasser to expel all western influence. . . . Nasser can deny oil to Western Europe and we shall all be at his mercy. There are some who doubt . . . but trust me. Can we rely on them to be more sensible than the Germans?[38]

With such narrative guns being wielded also by Macmillan and Lloyd, American dissidents succumbed. In fact, part of what makes this particular campaign of Terror so interesting is why the American dissidents felt the force of these particular "guns" to the extent that they did. After all, the British had used nearly the same trap in their campaign over 'Imperialism,' and in that case, they were only able to accomplish Exile. In the case of Nasser, however, the trap conjuring up European security was effective at Terror. The question is why there was such a difference in the trapping effects of this threat to subjectivity.

In significant part, the answer has to do with the discursive context: When it came to 'Imperialism,' the narrative "reality" of much of world opinion was already settled in a way that backed the U.S. representation of that phrase. So in order for Britain to renarrate 'Imperialism' to signify *nething good* for the West and the Special Relationship (Terror), it would also have had to find traps to ensnare the authors of that virtually worldwide narrative "reality." Put differently, in the case of 'Imperialism,' the British would have been using Terror to fasten a *dissenting* narrative (their own representation of 'Imperialism') rather than to fasten the status quo (which was more akin to the U.S. representation). Because the weight of narrative legitimacy was on the side of the U.S., any identity within American subjectivity that was linked to that status quo representation of 'Imperialism' was protected by the weight of its narrative legitimacy around the world. So putting a "gun" to the head of that subject would be much harder. It was a tougher trap to construct.

But in the case of 'Nasser,' there was no status quo representation at all, no less a status quo that favored the American interpretation (Heikal 1986). World opinion about what to make of Nasser was an unsettled narrative in its own right, which made it much easier for the British to trap the American subjectivity in a vulnerable position. For this reason, virtually the same trap that had only been enough for Exile in the case of 'Imperialism' became effective for Terror in the case of Nasser. Indeed, the Americans fretted about the status of the Eagle. Loy Henderson, U.S. diplomat in the U.K., reversed his objection to the British representation of Nasser, urging Dulles to as well. He pointed out that "we must be sympathetic and responsive to British concerns" because who knew "what Nasser might certainly harden into."[39] Robert Murphy, deputy undersecretary of state expressed a similar concern: "Nasser intends . . . to wield power without limit. . . . The U.S. should agree with the U.K."[40] In turn, Eisenhower and Dulles also revoked their dissent.[41]

Most interesting in this context is what became of Henry Byorade's dissent (see Chapter 6). As the U.S. ambassador in Cairo, Byorade's dissenting voice was originally quite powerful, coming as it did from an author involved in a personal relationship with Nasser. And yet, Byorade retired as the ambassador to Egypt before the British could complete their campaign of Terror. The British could have simply ignored Byorade's dissident voice because, by retiring, Byorade effectively silenced himself. Yet they did not. Vigilant about ensuring that 'Nasser' not resurface in a way that would contribute to the Lion's already significant problems, Lloyd looked to Raymond Hare, Byorade's replacement, to tie up the loose ends of dissent, narrating Terror to ensure that Hare adopted the sympathetic representation. It is not clear whether in the absence of Terror Hare would have been a dissident from the British version of 'Nasser.' What does seem clear, though, is that as the front-line author responsible for depicting Nasser's character to the American government, the British were concerned to guarantee Hare's compliance. As Hare narrated that compliance, it followed the logic of British Terror precisely (see Figure 7–16).

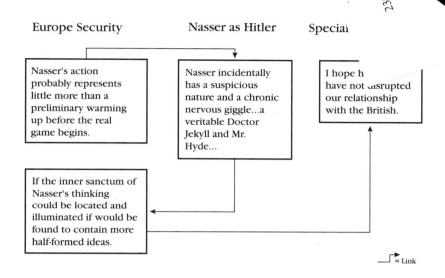

Figure 7–16 Hare's reply: Terror of Nasser

> Nasser's action probably represents little more than a preliminary warming up before the real game begins . . . Nasser incidentally has a suspicious nature and a chronic nervous giggle . . . a veritable Doctor Jeckyll and Mr. Hyde. . . . If the inner sanctum of Nasser's thinking could be located and illuminated it would be found to contain more half-formed ideas . . . I hope his plans have not disrupted our relationship with the British.[42]

In the end, 'Nasser' was no longer admissible evidence for logic of British bellicosity. In fact, the phrase became completely consistent with the logic of a representation in which the British had acted in keeping with the West and the Special Relationship, and so 'Nasser' was removed as a point of concern for the Lion. It is noteworthy though, that like with 'Nationalization,' the successful British campaign of narrative force did not translate into an American endorsement of the British *policy* of actually using physical force against Nasser. It simply meant that the Americans no longer interpreted the use of force in Egypt as bellicose if it was justified in reference to Nasser's *character*. Accepting that using force on Nasser would not be bellicose did not mean that there were not better strategies to pursue; the

...nericans still found many reasons why a Hitler-like character did not necessarily require force. It just meant that when the British chose to justify their use of force in relation to Nasser's threat potential, that logic no longer mattered as a breach of the shared values embodied in Special Relationship. And it also meant that the British Lion was no longer in danger of being misunderstood as opportunistic. Dulles summed it all up in one of his narrative recants of dissent:

> I told them I agreed that Nasser is the worst we've had so far; Hitlerite personality . . . We are finally convinced that he is an extremely dangerous fanatic. If he can get by with the action the British and French are probably right in their appraisal of the consequences . . . Nasser is a wild man brandishing an ax and they did not have to wait for the blow to fall. If this happened it could have had serious effect for some time upon good relations between our countries . . . [43]

Collusion

But the British were not yet clear of responsibility for bellicosity, unsettling the West, or therefore, of risks to the Lion. 'Collusion' still had to be addressed. Narrating in reference to the British secret collaboration with the French and Israelis, the Americans had represented the phrase 'Collusion' as an indication that the true British character was aggressive, deceitful, and untrustworthy. Aside from all the now familiar problems of such a representation for unsettling the West and undermining the Lion, 'Collusion' was also a representation that had accumulated the weight of international legitimacy. The Soviets, for one, had a stake in this American authored phrase-in-dispute because it could be used to support the Soviet identity as the Bear.[44] Specifically, Soviet Prime Minister Marshal Nikolai Bulganin took advantage of the disunity created by 'Collusion' to try to assert "fellow-superpower status" (Kyle 1991, 457). He appealed to Eisenhower to collaborate with the Soviet Union in "a joint and immediate" use of force against the British and French in the Middle East (Frankland 1960, 292–4). Many members of the United Nations General Assembly (including former colonies of France and Britain) also found nourishment for their respective identities in the logic of 'Collusion.'[45] So between the threats that 'Collusion' created for British subjectivity and its ever-increasing legitimacy as an international "reality," this particular phrase-in-dispute became a menacing problem and a significant burden for the British.

Yet the British persevered in their efforts to salvage the Lion. They rose to the challenge of reinscribing 'Collusion' with considerable though, not complete, success. The campaign of force they deployed was not ultimately successful at preventing the demise of Britain as a legitimate Western leader —on the contrary, the phrase 'Collusion' is often associated with such representations as "the Lion's last roar" and so became something of the final straw for the Lion (Cooper 1978; Heikal 1986; Lucas 1996; Moser 1999). But British authors did manage to successfully silence 'Collusion' so that it became irrelevant to the status of Special Relationship. In this way, the British lost the battle of preserving the subjectivity that they were trying to preserve in the first place (Lion), but their forceful efforts still contributed to fastening of we-ness and so the re-production of the Anglo-American security community.

Charting that campaign of force was a complex process for the British. At first, Lloyd encouraged his cohorts to consider the possibility of Terror. He held out hope that they could redefine 'Collusion' so that it would be illogical in relation to bellicosity but supportive of Special Relationship. Toward that end, he suggested a representation that depicted the collusive use of force as an accident. The idea was to narrate the British involvement in the planning of force not as a finished decision but as a process through which the British inadvertently and unknowingly came to use force in Egypt as a result of trickery by the French. The British had not "inexorably committed" themselves to using force, argued Lloyd, and so collusion should be seen as an honest mistake. As he put it, "There was nothing fraudulent or disreputable about any of our objectives or motives" (Lloyd 1978, 249–50). If the Americans could be forced into accepting this representation, the idea of premeditated deceit could be neutralized, bellicosity delegitimized, and the integrity of Anglo-American shared values and the Special Relationship preserved.

However, Terror never took. In fact, Lloyd never even got as far as devising a trap. Perhaps it was the discursive weight of the many other international identities that had become bound up with the American version of 'Collusion' that discouraged the British from embarking on Terror; or perhaps it was that many Britons themselves were simply astounded by their own government. After all, multiple harmful events occurred simultaneously that conspired against Lloyd's narrative of guileless innocence—the weapons transfers between France and Israel, the discovery of British presence at the secret planning meeting at Sevres, Nutting's resignation without explanation, and the normally progovernment papers (including the *Daily Telegraph, The Times,* and the *News Chronicle*) publicized their serious reservations about their government's Middle East "adventure." The *Daily Mail* even went so far as to challenge the government to certify its innocence.[46] Whatever the combination of events, there was certainly no shortage of obstacles to overcome, and so Lloyd and his fellow British authors—primarily

Eden, Macmillan and ambassador to the U.S. Roger Makins—never did converge on a trap, nor did they disseminate Lloyd's narrative. Instead, they turned to Exile.

Exile of 'Collusion' delinked that phrase-in-dispute from bellicosity, in effect silencing it as a phrase-in-dispute of Special Relationship. This also had the effect of neutralizing the unsettling effects of 'Collusion' on the West and the Lion. Front-line British authors accomplished Exile through narratives that depicted British deceit as undertaken for the benefit of protecting Eisenhower during the critical period just prior to the American election. The logic was quite irresistible to Eisenhower's administration: The British would accept that they had given the appearance of 'Collusion' with the French and Israelis. At the same time, however, they would contend that they had risked that appearance to protect Eisenhower from having appeared as though *he* had known about the use of force. After all, if anyone in the U.S. or abroad suspected that Eisenhower actually knew in advance about the invasion of Egypt, then Eisenhower would appear complicitous in the wrongdoing. In this way, given that Britain was committed to using force anyway, secrecy in its planning with the French and Israelis was the best possible protection the British could offer their American friends. As Eden put it in a letter to Eisenhower, "after a few days, you will be in a position to act with renewed authority. I beg you to believe that what we are doing now will in our view facilitate your action."[47] In this way, the British passed responsibility for their secretive activities onto Eisenhower's election. By Exiling 'Collusion,' this particular incident no longer fueled the narrative "reality" of bellicosity.

In order to render this logic a coercive nonchoice for American dissidents, British authors built a trap that promised to unsettle and even erase the carefully crafted image of the Eisenhower presidency and the members of its administration. More exactly, even though Eisenhower is reported to have been willing to sacrifice the election for his principles,[48] he and his staff were fearful for the legacy of his presidency should he lose the election due to suspicions that he knew of the planned invasion. Such suspicions would cast a dark cloud over the historical memory of the entire administration. After all, Eisenhower's administration put a premium on his identity as the Peace President and his strategists had even convinced him to campaign on the Suez issue as the Peace President (Kingseed 1995, 98–9). So were it to appear that Eisenhower had known about the plans of invasion but done nothing to stop it, then 'Peace President' would hardly be a credible phrase to narrate of the memory of the Eisenhower years.

Part of what made the reference to the Peace President so potent as a trap was that there was increasing public speculation (particularly by the British themselves) that Eisenhower *had* in fact known about the invasion plans.

For instance, Macmillan intimated that he and the president had discussed the invasion. "Eisenhower," he said, "didn't wish to be informed when we took the final action" (Macmillan 1971, 136). Although Eisenhower maintained a posture of innocence and seemed genuinely surprised by the British action, the possibility that he knew about it in advance is real—and was compelling at the time. It is true, for instance, that the British and Americans usually shared information. Although there was allegedly a blackout of communications between the two countries just prior to the invasion, and although the British evidently planted some false intelligence to dupe the U.S., a number of credible testimonies have indicated that enough accurate intelligence filtered through earlier that Eisenhower should have known. In fact, Allen Dulles, the intelligence community, and the national security counsel are all on record suggesting from very early on that some foul play was developing. And yet Eisenhower and Foster Dulles never followed it up.[49] Both were acutely aware that at certain turns in the course of the crisis, they could have interpreted the British intentions more accurately. This realization had them rather concerned (Horne 1988, 438). If this rumor became "reality," it would appear not just that Eisenhower had been deceitful in his lack of commitment to his own pretensions at justice and peace, but that he was a blatant liar whose word could not be trusted. Ironically, in other words, Eisenhower might have been accused of bellicosity. It was a narrative "gun" held to the Self-conception of the Eisenhower administration. This logic is illustrated in Figure 7–17. Lloyd, Eden, Macmillan, and Makins spared no effort in wielding that force.[50]

In his memoirs, Lloyd reconstructed his narrative Exile of 'Collusion' (see Figure 7–18):

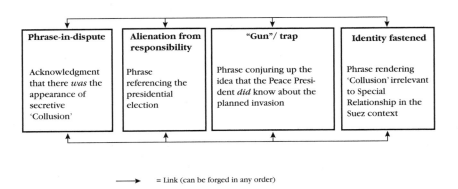

Phrase-in-dispute	Alienation from responsibility	"Gun"/ trap	Identity fastened
Acknowledgment that there *was* the appearance of secretive 'Collusion'	Phrase referencing the presidential election	Phrase conjuring up the idea that the Peace President *did* know about the planned invasion	Phrase rendering 'Collusion' irrelevant to Special Relationship in the Suez context

⟶ = Link (can be forged in any order)

Figure 7–17 Exile of Collusion

Eisenhower's mind was concentrated on an election campaign, appearing as the candidate who could preserve the peace of the world ... I am sure Eisenhower must have feared such a trend and been desperately anxious to preserve his image as the man of peace, the great soldier who had indeed beaten his sword into a ploughshare.

It was considered whether our action would cause offense to the United States. It was felt that in view of their situation they had no reason to complain although no doubt they would make disapproving noises. Eventually it was agreed, without dissent, that if Israel attacked we would act as Eden proposed.

The argument that we ought not offend the Americans was not conclusive ... it would be easier for them if we did not tell them beforehand ... If he was not told beforehand, he could grumble afterwards but not lose face. Between our interests and our friend's interests there was a balance to be found. (Lloyd 1978, 168, 189, 193)

Dissident American authors of collusion succumbed to this logic. By choosing to agree that Britain's deception was a way of protecting Eisenhower, the whole administration could publicly claim innocence and its identity as Peace President without fear that voices would be raised to the contrary. Dulles (who aside from Eisenhower himself was the member of the administration most invested in the Peace Presidency) replied as follows to the Exile of 'Collusion' (see Figure 7–19):

Macmillan recognized that there had been a certain loss of confidence on the part of the President, myself, and others because of the Suez operation and the deception practiced upon us in that connection ... He personally was very unhappy with the way the matter was handled, but ... did not disguise the fact that he had always favored strong action and the point was the manner and timing, particularly vis-à-vis the United States ... as if they told us their plans, we might then feel we had to raise objections or else be a party to what might seem and improper use of force.[51]

Eisenhower, Allen Dulles, and Nixon all authored similar submissions to Exile. Interestingly, Eisenhower also authored a different kind of response, one that never even mentioned the 'Collusion.' Instead of excusing the British their deceitful collusion in light of the protection it offered the president, Eisenhower dropped the notion of deception and 'Collusion' altogether by speaking instead of the war. In this way, Eisenhower's narrative enacted the very silence to which he was agreeing and as he did, he reproduced the Special Relationship.

I was as delighted at the end of the war in the Middle East as I was about my own electoral victory ... congratulated Eden over the

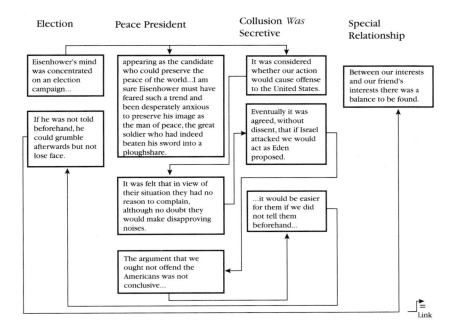

Figure 7–18 Lloyd's Exile of Collusion

telephone and cabled him afterwards. *Obviously now want the Special Relationship reestablished. After all it had only been like a family spat.* (Calhoun 1991, 495, my emphasis)

Now, with bellicosity out of the way, the British responsibility for that family spat—and so for its reverberations on the West—was removed. The narrative of the Special Relationship would no longer be unsettled by that logic.

The Fastened We

Bellicosity and betrayal had dissolved the Special Relationship, but through deliberate campaigns of Terror and Exile directed at the constitutive phrases of those two dissident "realities," British and American authors turned around and dissolved bellicosity and betrayal. In the process, they fastened the Special Relationship by re-producing the logic of we-ness that

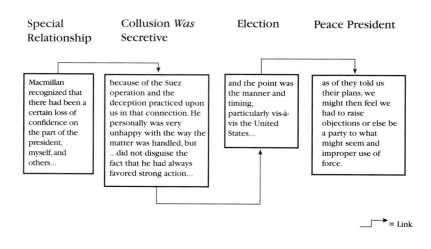

Special Relationship	Collusion *Was* Secretive	Election	Peace President

Macmillan recognized that there had been a certain loss of confidence on the part of the president, myself, and others...

because of the Suez operation and the deception practiced upon us in that connection. He personally was very unhappy with the way the matter was handled, but ...did not disguise the fact that he had always favored strong action...

and the point was the manner and timing, particularly vis-á-vis the United States...

as of they told us their plans, we might then feel we had to raise objections or else be a party to what might seem and improper use of force.

⌐→ = Link

Figure 7–19 Dulles's reply: Exile of Collusion

made it an intelligible narrative. From the American side, the disjuncture over Suez was never forgotten, but the damage to the Special Relationship was. As Eisenhower reflected, "you cannot resort to force in international relationships because of your fear of what might happen in the future . . . (but) quite naturally, Britain not only has been, but must be our best friend in the world."[52] Macmillan, Lloyd, and even Eden—all of whose political legacy depended on assigning blame to the United States—remember Suez similarly. As Macmillan and Lloyd told the British cabinet in 1957, "when the history of Suez crisis is written it will be a history of British patriotism" for the West and a successful "regaining of the Special Relationship with the United States (Ovendale 1998, 120–22)."

As we-ness was fastened, it became real as a lived experience between the two states. Shared understandings for stable expectations and behaviors of nonviolence between the U.S. and Britain became reliable once again. Indeed, the connection between the re-production of the Special Relationship and the reconstruction of the security community was openly acknowledged. Both the U.S. State department and the British Foreign Office were vocal and explicit about linking "ties of language, culture, and common ideas" to the continued mutual security between the U.S. and Britain. Both countries recognized the occasionally "irksome" and often "inconvenient" normative demands of consultation and openness, but both also recognized that it brought them "the security without which we cannot prosper."[53] Indeed, even while Britain was, with American encouragement, "moving toward (the European) continent" and even while the U.S. was cultivating its nuclear leadership, both still kept "looking back at" the U.S.-U.K. Special Relationship for "affirmation and renewal" of their mutual security and as a basis for the collaborative security alliance of the West.[54] The Anglo-American security community order, based on shared self-other understandings of trust and common security fate, was "real" once again. Identity, re-produced through representational force over the course of the crisis, had forced order back upon disorder.

Conclusion

CHAPTER 8
Re-Turn to Identity

In 1956, the Anglo-American international order broke down into international disorder. On both sides of the Atlantic, leadership and bureaucrats were at a loss about what to expect from the other. However, over the course of the Suez Crisis, Anglo-American disorder was molded back into a security community; back into an order of stable expectations for nonviolent behavior between the U.S. and Britain. The question—the Suez Puzzle—is how uncertainty and confusion was replaced with reliable shared Anglo-American expectations and behaviors. The answer, I have argued, rests with Anglo-American we-ness identity. Whereas neither power politics nor common interests were sufficient to impose order on the relationship between the U.S. and Britain from within the context of the Suez disorder, shared Anglo-American self-other understandings of common values, trust, and security fate were. We-ness gave the two states directions about what to expect from each other and how to behave.

IR scholars interested in the international identity-international order connection, and historians of Anglo-American relations alike have long believed that we-ness is the solution to the Suez Puzzle. But attempts to establish this empirically and theoretically have come up short. Empirically, the problem has been that the Suez incident was nothing if not an identity crisis between the U.S. and Britain. The Anglo-American Special Relationship was demagnetized and then dissolved through a rancorous process of mutual dissociation. Moreover, it was nothing other than the dissolution of the Special Relationship that created Anglo-American disorder in the first place. So how could it be that we-ness imposed order on that disorder when the failure of we-ness precipitated the disorder to begin with? Empirically

241

ness did not exist at the time. At the least it is awkward to claim that it was the source of the revived security community.

For its part, identity theory has not been much help in sorting through this conundrum. In fact, the most popular identity theories used in IR—primordialism, social identity theory (SIT), and constructivism—have simply failed to take on the issue of how identities that break down are repaired, especially during unsettled times. As such, the belief that we-ness was the source of the Anglo-American security community during the Suez Crisis has amounted to a leap of faith; an empirically and analytically uncorroborated conviction.

But when the Suez Puzzle is analyzed through the lens of a postconstructivist conception of identity, the intuition that Anglo-American we-ness was the source of sustained Anglo-American nonviolent order acquires a theoretical apparatus that can make sense of the empirical conundrum. Conceiving of identity as indistinguishable from the ongoing, power-laden, agent-owned narrative process that constitutes it, the postconstructivist account treats international identity as at once contingent upon the vicissitudes of the international environment and at the same time an agent-driven process that is produced and re-produced through its members' will to narrate it. This conception makes it theoretically possible to account for both the breakdown and the repair of identities over time, even in crises. It counsels that identities are active, lived experiences built by their members rather than passive constructs formed and maintained only when they are facilitated by external conditions outside of actors' control. Furthermore, this theoretic logic draws attention to otherwise overlooked empirical processes at work in the Anglo-American case—the dynamics by which British and American authors first dissolved their own we-ness, precipitating the breakdown of the security community and disorder, and then, re-produced their order by deploying their language-power to force back upon each other the "reality" of shared self-other understandings. In short, what is novel is not the conclusion that we-ness was the source of the Anglo-American security community; what is novel is the account of how that was empirically and theoretically possible. We-ness, re-produced as it was by representational force, forced order.

Given that a postconstructivist approach to identity can solve the Suez Puzzle and sustain the logic of identity as a source of the Anglo-American order, the postconstructivist theoretical framework renews the call for an identity turn in international order. The identity turn, understood as an identity-first analytical and practical approach to international order, seems at first blush to promise significant revision of how scholars and practitioners think about international order by shifting attention away from power politics and common interests. But so far that shift has not delivered on the promise, because in the final analysis most conceptions of identity have gone the way of the very power-politics and common-interests approaches they seek to move beyond; they too fail to sustain the logic of sourceness or sufficiency for imposing order upon disorder. As such, there has been little reason to take the identity turn any more seriously than other alternatives as a basis for theoretical models and policy practice. But because the postconstructivist conception of identity *does* sustain the logic of sourceness, it raises anew the need to explore what international order looks like through an identity lens—but specifically through a postconstructivist identity lens.

In the remainder of this book, I return to the identity turn, engaging it this time through a postconstructivist lens. I do not seek to establish on empirical grounds the degree to which a postconstructivist identity turn is necessary but rather to explore what it might look like. In particular, I sketch key ideas along three axes: theoretical, historical, and practical. I argue that for each of these domains, a postconstructivist stance emboldens some exceptional shifts of perspective quite beyond anything offered by power politics, common interests, or even conventional constructivist identity models of international order. By treating identity as an ongoing, power-laden, agent-owned narrative process, everything changes—from the theoretical frameworks best suited to thinking about the dynamics of international order to the history of international order and to the strategic practices that would best serve statesmen who fantasize about ordering international politics.

In Theory

At base, an identity turn in the theory of international order means modeling international order in reference to shared self-other understandings. Because shared self-other understandings are simply ideas socially or intersubjectively held among actors, an identity turn demands an idealist theoretical stance. Idealism, as Alexander Wendt explains, is an approach to the study of international politics in which the researcher maintains a conviction that international politics are more fundamentally "constituted by ideas rather than material forces." It means, that is, adopting an ideas-first perspective (Wendt 1999, 24–25). Idealism is purposefully minimalist as a guide to theory building (i.e., it is not normative, utopian, or substantive in its content). And yet it translates into a fairly dramatic turn away from the standard or traditional courses of theorizing in IR. It excludes not only power-political and most common-interests models of order (because ideas are secondary to material forces), but also any kind of primordial or SIT conception of identity as the foundation for a model of order. The former has no theory of how ideas work, and the latter is too focused on individual cognition to offer theoretic leverage over the intersubjectivity, or sharedness, of ideas and identity (Chapter 2). On these criteria only, constructivism and postconstructivism qualify as idealist approaches to international theory, and so only they can animate an identity-turn.

But the demands of idealism can be fleshed out more precisely than a mere call to put ideas first. In fact, because of the injunction to put ideas first, idealism demands at least four specific theoretical shifts: an appreciation of understanding as methodologically prior to explanation; a conception of ideas as power; attentiveness to process and agency; and a coherent account of how particular ideas become platforms for particular state actions. Yet when taken together, these specific demands add up to an idealist theory that, in the end, conventional constructivism cannot fully accommodate. The postconstructivist approach to modeling identity and international order can and therefore offers a better idealist theory.

1. The Importance of Interpretative Understanding

Idealist theory requires that scholars reject the dichotomy between explaining and understanding (Hollis and Smith 1991). As traditionally understood, explanation is a method for uncovering generalized laws about the workings of the international political world—in this case, international order—whereas understanding is a method for illuminating particular pockets of international order from the inside in terms of what they mean to those involved. Whereas explanation is generally equated with scientific causal inference (King, Keohane, and Verba 1994), understanding is generally associated with interpretation (Baylis and Smith 2001). But particularly in the American academy, where scientific study is valued so disproportionately over context and interpretation, the explaining and understanding classification scheme has become a standard tool for implicitly, and sometimes explicitly, legitimating certain bodies of scholarship over others (von Wright 1971; King et al. 1994). In fact, it is fair to say that although the two approaches are ostensibly separate but equal, the culture of IR, thoroughly imbued as it is with aspirations of natural science or at least economics, has constituted the two approaches into a dichotomy in which explaining is privileged over understanding.

But studies that pursue understanding are the key to putting ideas first. Ideas, after all, are intangibles, and as social scientists are quick to note, devising methodologies and measurements that appear to live up to the "epistemologically exacting" standards required of social science explanation becomes increasingly more difficult as variables become more ideational and less concrete (Ferguson and Mansbach 1996, xiii). In fact, the only way to operationalize such intangibles is through interpretation. Of course, interpretation is a form of understanding because interpretations cannot, strictly speaking, be falsified (except perhaps for the most mundane and politically uninteresting interpretations). As such, social scientists tend to dismiss ideas-first studies as invalid.[1]

But idealists reach a different conclusion. Given that ideas are prior to tangible variables as components of international politics, they argue that understanding must be more fundamental than explanation for comprehending international politics. Indeed, on an idealist read, material variables become unintelligible without adequate attention to the ideas that give them meaning. In this way, understanding is prior to, continuous with, and necessary for explanation (Wendt 2000, 172). Ironically it follows that any allegedly scientific explanation of international order that fails to offer adequate interpretative understanding of the social meanings that signify the variables involved in its causal scenario will, over time, become unconvincing. After all, the social meanings assigned to tangible things change over time such that the role of a "thing" in causing some outcome changes as well. Jens Bartelson (1995) makes this point eloquently in his genealogy of the different meanings of sovereignty over time; as the meaning of sovereignty changed, so too did its political effects. In the same spirit, Barkin and Cronin (1994) have called for a treatment of sovereignty, not as a given, but as a changeable construct that must be understood before it is used to explain. Idealism, and thus an identity turn, means recognizing this dependence of explanation (social science) on understanding (interpretation).

Of course, neither power-politics nor common-interests models of order take interpretation or understanding seriously. Informed as they are by neorealism and neoliberalism, they are focused on social scientific explanation and are often resistant to understanding as a legitimate form of research (Rengger 2000, 17).[2] Both the conventional-constructivist and postconstructivist-identity accounts fare much better on this score. Both begin with an appreciation for interpretation as the first methodological step for comprehending international life. In this way, both pass the first test of idealism.

2. Ideas and Power

But conventional constructivism fails the second. Idealism amounts to more than just an appreciation for interpretation. It is also a theoretical perspective on ideas themselves. More exactly, idealism sees ideas as having teeth, being heavy, or, put less poetically, as having independent weight in the world as "causes."[3] This view challenges traditional international theory —even common-interests theory—in which ideas are taken as ephemeral, without bite, and light in weight (Goldstein and Keohane 1993). They are not assigned any wherewithal in the production of order. Rather, that wherewithal goes to power—the material, physical, heavy, and tangible stuff that makes states behave in certain ways. This dichotomy, between power as heavy and foundational to order and ideas as light and dispensable for order, means that whenever ideas and power face off as explanations, power wins. Thus, any theory that abides by this dichotomy cannot by definition be idealist; it cannot put ideas first in the analysis of international order. Idealism as such requires breaking down the distinction between ideas and power so as to conceptualize ideas in a way that recognizes them as expressions of power in their own right; as heavy, with teeth, and primary in the processes by which international order is produced.

Conventional constructivist theory does not thoroughly challenge the dichotomy between ideas and power. Even as it puts ideas before material power, it still refuses the notion that ideas themselves are a source of power. For instance, Wendt argues that ideas shape how states perceive each other and so what they make of each others' power. Thus, friends are less likely to see each others' military capabilities as threatening. But the idea (friendship) is not itself an expression of power. Power is vested in material loci such as military forces (Wendt 1999, 25). In this way, theoretically ideas might come before material power, but an idea itself expresses no power of its own. Others who rely upon constructivist theory abide by a similar dichotomy between ideas and power. Margaret Keck and Kathryn Sikkink (1998) look to the softer forms of power, such as persuasion or manipulation, to explain how ideas stick (See also Finnemore 1996). On their view, the idea of human rights, for instance, has no power of its own. What makes human rights compelling are the tangible material incentives and goals that advocates tap into when pitching that idea to an audience.[4] Power as such is transmitted through material, physical, or otherwise tangible vehicles, not through the ideas themselves.[5] In its failure to rethink the relationship between ideas and power, constructivism embraces something less than idealism in its theoretical model of international order.

A postconstructivist framework does challenge the dichotomy between ideas and power, and so by extension it sustains a more thorough-going idealism in its theoretical apparatus. On this conception, ideas *are* power because language, the mode of their very formulation, expression, and communication, creates "reality." In other words, the postconstructivist approach conceptualizes ideas as embodiments and manifestations of language-power. Significantly, because language-power is expressed in reference to subjectivity and not to material incentives, ideas acquire a heaviness that does not necessarily depend on material conditions. For instance, Richard Price (1998) (aspects of whose work I would characterize as postconstructivist in spirit) argues that the power of an idea can come from its association with other ideas; that is, by being *grafted* together. In this way, Price suggests that an idea's power is a function of the sociolinguistic context into which it is narratively situated. Ideas, in this way, can be a source of compulsion in their own right. They need not be grafted to allegedly objective, exogenously given, unchallenged "realities."

Of course, much remains to be said about the different types of language-power that can be used to express ideas (representational force, persuasion, authority, and so on), as well as about their respective capacities to oblige or compel under varying conditions (settled or unsettled). But a postconstructivist identity turn entails the conceptual apparatus for exploring such questions. In this way, a postconstructivist identity turn facilitates idealist thinking about international order beyond what can be offered by other approaches.

3. Process and Agency

Beyond the entreaty to interpretation and a rethinking of the relationship between ideas and power, idealism calls for deeper theoretical engagement with the notion of process and the issues of agency that arise from it. The logic here is that because idealism theorizes about ideas as the basis of international order, and because ideas are no more or less permanent than the expressions of language-power through which they are constituted, idealist theories need to capture international order in a way that recognizes its ever-changeable nature. But idealist scholars themselves tend to reify, bracket, or otherwise overlook the fluidity of the very components that constitute order—from the ideas that constitute the "realities" of identities to the "realities" themselves, to the orders they engender, and so on (for a good discussion see Bleiker 2000, 15–16). Thus, for an idealist theory to remain attentive to this mutability, some safeguard must be built in against the tendency to reify, and it is in this respect that thinking in terms of process is useful. By explicitly theorizing the "stuff" that goes into the production of international order not as variables but as ongoing "functionally linked occurrences," it becomes much more difficult to take for granted any given aspect of its meaning and effect (Jackson and Nexon 1999, 302). One must constantly look at the relevant processes to keep track of their form and character, and so their effects on international order.

Virtually nothing is processual about power-politics and common-interest models of order. The meaning of military power, state interests, anarchy, and other key variables are taken as given and unchanging, which makes disorder or a lack of shared understandings theoretically impossible (on their own terms) (Chapter 2). By contrast, at least on the face of it, constructivism seems highly processual and idealist. After all, its conception of identity is just that: an ongoing process and one that is allegedly never reified. But, as Maja Zehfuss points out, the extent of processuality admissible in the constructivist model is, in spite of intentions, actually rather limited.

Nonprocess "givens" are built into the theory—for instance, the assumption that international identity forms in a context of settled basic truths about states—that "exclude certain processes entailed in the construction of identity from view" (Zehfuss 2001, 316). In the end, constructivism reifies aspects of identity so that its idealism does not go "all the way down." An identity turn informed by constructivism thus, would, in an ironic similarity to power politics and common-interests theories, yield models of order that lack sensitivity to changing conditions.

The postconstructivist approach invites process into everything about identity and, indeed, about order more generally. In fact, it even conceives of *international order* itself as a process—because identity is inextricable from the process by which it is produced, and because identity is a source of order. This may seem counterintuitive because order is often associated with stasis; it is, after all, about *stable* shared understandings. But precisely because maintaining stability of shared understandings is an ongoing process of re-producing over and again the same intersubjective knowledge, order too ought to be thought of as indistinguishable from the complex of processes by which it is constructed. A postconstructivist stance is attentive to this, and so an identity turn informed by it is likely to promote theorizing far more conscientious of the character of the complex of processes that constitute a given order, and of perturbations to it that could lead to its disruption, transformation, or even collapse.[6] A process focus, as such, makes not just for deeper idealism; it also broadens the conceptual and empirical tools available for capturing the passages between stability, instability, change, and disorder in international politics.

It is important, though, that precisely because idealism demands process-orientation, it also demands renewed attention to agency. One cannot think for long about the world as constituted of ideas, and ideas as constituted by processes, without asking who starts, stops, and controls those processes in the first place. Constructivism allows questions of agency to recede into the background by chalking up identity formation processes to automatic, remote dynamics that just happen under the right conditions. A postconstructivist stance, in contrast, grapples with the question of how people acquire the desire and will to initiate, sustain, stop, and manage processes. In this way, an identity turn informed by postconstructivism is likely to lead IR theory into an era of renewed exploration of agency, conceptualizing it as endogenous to process, and yet formative of it (Chapter 3, Emirbayer and Mische 1998, 963; Jackson and Nexon 1999, 318; Bleiker 2000).

4. Ideas and State Action

A last requirement of idealist theory—and so of an identity turn—is in some ways so elementary and assumed that it is forgotten. An idealist theory must be analytically sophisticated enough to fluently translate between particular ideas and the state actions to which they allegedly give rise. After all, the whole point of an identity turn in the study of international order is to provide better leverage on the question of how that connection between ideas and action works. In concrete terms, this means any acceptable idealist theory needs a compelling account of how the whole array of different identities (enmity, rivalry, friendship, and so on) give rise to the particular orderly expectations and behaviors with which they are correlated (power politics, cooperation, nonviolence, and so on).

To be sure, constructivists have been at the forefront in heightening awareness in IR of the constitutive effect of ideas for state action. In light of this, it is a bit surprising to realize that the constructivist account of identity does not pass this test of a coherent theory of the ideas-action connection. As it turns out, the theoretic apparatus employed by constructivism fails to provide a compelling model of the process by which the international identity of enmity could impel states to deploy power politics with each other.[7] As Wendt notes, enmity and power politics is a hard case for constructivism because constructivism takes identity-formation as a communal learning process; a passive development of shared culture and ideas (Wendt 1999, 164). This is a problem because it suggests on the one hand that enmity identity develops among states through some kind of societal learning and sharing, but on the other that enmity identity produced by that "soft" process is posited to drive states to power-political actions against each other. Enmity evokes state actions that are destructive of the very community that formed that identity in the first place. In this way, the constructivist account of the relationship between ideas and state action encompasses a logical ellipses regarding the idea of enmity: It leaves unanswered important questions about just how these states, who so communally collaborate in the signification of each other, come to fear each other as credible threats to each others' survival.[8]

A postconstructivist approach to international identity entails no awkward mismatch between its account of how states come to share self-other understandings of enmity and the claim that enmity leads to power-political behaviors. After all, from this view, sharing is not some benign cultural evolution, nor is it a passive by-product of fortuitous interactions. It is an active performance and production by states that use their power (language-power) to create particular, shared self-other understandings that they believe will serve their Self-interests (i.e., subjectivity). In this way, the process by which states come to share ideas is not evocative of a romantic community but of a political struggle—fraught and power-laden. In short, the process of attaining self-other understandings of enmity may itself be representationally hostile and forceful. In this way, it need not sit in tension with the hostile, forceful, and even physically violent actions to which it is expected to give rise.

Of course, given a view of international identity as power-laden and fraught, it may be that on the postconstructivist account, the hard case is explaining the transition from prosocial or "nice" ideas/identities to prosocial or "nice" state actions like cooperation and nonviolence. The objection here might be that if identities are the product of language-power and Self-interest, then a logical ellipses emerges surrounding how, for instance, a forcefully fastened we identity could engender such community-oriented behaviors as nonviolence.[9] The question, more succinctly, is how those forced against their will into we-ness can be expected to come to treat each other nonviolently? But because representational force leaves its victims with no choice but to comply, no real logical problem exist here at all. As long as states are effectively trapped into we-ness, and as long as they are Self-interested, it makes sense to think that those states would act in keeping with we-ness. That is, as long as the power politics of identity have been properly deployed, states will live the experience of we-ness, even if they do not feel it (Chapter 4). In this way, the account of the relationship between ideas and action offered in postconstructivist idealism is more internally coherent than that offered by the conventional variant, making it a more compelling idealist theory.

An Unusual Alliance

One final theoretic turn is implied by postconstructivism, which emerges especially from the preceding reflections on the postconstructivist view of the relationship between ideas and action. This is the possibility of theoretic cross-fertilization between realism and postconstructivism. In particular, it is interesting to note that the postconstructivist account formulates the relationship between ideas and state action in a logically parallel fashion to the way that various realists formulate the relationship between material conditions and state action (Waltz 1979; Morgenthau 2003). In both theories, power impels states to act in particular manners by playing on their interests. Of course, on the realist account, power is mediated through material means and impels state action by playing on states' exogenously given physical or material interests, whereas on the postconstructivist account, power is mediated through the language that expresses ideas and impels state action by playing on states' endogenously constituted subjective (Self) interests. Clearly, each highlights different expressions of power and different kinds of state interests. Yet the correspondence of logic is undeniable. Both put power and interests at the core of their accounts of how states get from disorder to order.

These logical similarities suggest that beyond the theoretic emphases on ideas as power, process, agency, and sources of state action, one significant way in which a postconstructivist identity turn in IR theory can embolden theoretic change is by prompting mutual engagement between the seemingly disparate realist and postconstructivist approaches. For instance, such collaboration might usefully center on the continuities and relationship between ideational and material power. Given that these issues were very much a concern of classical realists like Machiavelli and Carr, a postconstructivist identity turn in theory may end up looking, in some respects, very much like a sophisticated return to the classical realist roots of IR; to a realist or coercive constructivism (Barkin 2003; Jackson and Krebs 2003).

In History

An identity turn, however, calls for more than just a reorientation in the theories of international order; it also calls for a rereading of the history of international order. The purpose of international history is to represent a course of events in a way that allows one to "remember"[10] some aspect of the international world, as well as to draw lessons from it about the present and future of international politics. But as historians are quick to note, it is impossible to represent a course of events or draw out lessons about it without some theory, implicitly or explicitly held, to guide one's thinking about what mattered in that course of events to begin with (Gaddis 2001). Theory is thus central to history; it shapes the way history is written. Given this, and the dominance of power-politics and common-interest theories of international order, it is no surprise that historically oriented IR scholars have tended to write histories of international orders that sketch the saga of the various balances of power and overlapping of interests among states (Kennedy 1989). And yet, because theory shapes history, as theories change, so ought history. At issue is how a postconstructivist identity turn in theory would change the histories of international order, and what that would mean for how we remember the world and learn from it.

My suggestion is that a postconstructivist identity turn would make for *better* histories of international order. Good history rests on at least three qualities—richness, coherence, and fertility for drawing "particular generalizations" (context-specific generalizations).[11] And yet, as historian Edward Ingram notes, good history is seldom written because history requires theory, and theories more often than not function like "suits of armor." Speaking specifically of power-politics theories, but lamenting about theory in general, Ingram notes that scholars can become so restricted by their theoretical suits of armor that they lose track of the story they are trying to tell. In his colorful words, the armor is so restrictive that it gives "not an inch to accommodate the size and figure of the wearer." The result is a story not about the event itself but about the theory. Writing such histories, he continues, is dangerous, not only because they inscribe collective international memories of events that are (usually accidentally) biased and careless, but also because the lessons to be gleaned from them are too spare, repetitive, and generalized to be useful (Ingram 2001, 251).[12]

Ingram's point—especially about careless memories and overly generalized lessons—is particularly well illustrated in the current debate among historically oriented IR scholars about how to best to tell the story of the end of Cold War international order. As that discussion has been formulated, Soviet new thinking signified the beginning of the end of the Cold War order, and so the question is what led to new thinking. Scholars from all walks of theoretical life have proffered stories. And yet, as Ingram would likely note, most have adopted suit-of-armor theories that have prevented them from writing a rich, coherent history, fertile with useful particular generalizations for the future.

Consider for instance, Steven Brooks and William Wohlforth, who writing through the lens of a power-politics theory, tell a story that chalks up new thinking to a set of strategic plans formulated among Soviet leaders about how to adapt to the adverse changes in material circumstances in the 1980s. New thinking happened, they argue, simply because the Soviet leadership realized that it could no longer realistically balance the U.S. (Brooks and Wohlforth 2000, 45). In contrast, Janice Gross Stein reads the end of the Cold War order through a common-interests lens. She argues that, on the contrary, new thinking was not a concession to power politics, but rather a result of changes in the Soviet leadership's conception of how to protect state interests. As Gorbachev learned more and more about Soviet security in the context of an interdependent world, he came to think (and so taught others in the government) that the nuclear security dilemma and the Soviet economy were better managed through cooperation than through competition (Stein 1994). So whereas Brooks and Wohlforth draw on power political theory to tell a story that encourages a collective memory of the end of the Cold War as a Soviet defeat, Stein draws on common-interests theory to inscribe a memory of the end of the Cold War as a moment of Soviet enlightenment. Whereas Brooks and Wohlforth imply a generalized lesson fully consistent with their power-politics theory—that statesmen can order international politics by manipulating the distribution of power—Stein concludes with a generalized lesson that statesmen can order international politics by developing regimes and institutions to augment harmonies of interests.

So which history is better? Neither is good history. In both cases, the theoretical perspectives have become suits of armor to the extent that neither story, collective memory, nor lesson really has anything to do with the event itself. Each is merely a reflection of the theory. The suit-of-armor quality of these histories is betrayed by the fact that substantively, both stories about the end of the Cold War can be traced back to the same factors (the manner in which Soviet leadership coped with changing material conditions in a context of anarchy and a security dilemma[13]), and yet each draws upon different kinds of evidence.[14] In fact, each explicitly refuses to engage the other's evidence, setting up their study instead as a response to a challenge from other theoretical camps.[15] That both fail to integrate extant, interesting, and largely complementary evidentiary material available in the historical record simply because it does not enhance their theoretical agenda confirms Ingram's point. In these cases, suit-of-armor theories produced biased stories and memories that in the end are not about the end of the Cold War, but about power politics and common interests, respectively. Indeed, the disconnection of these stories from the events surrounding the end of the Cold War is further highlighted by the fact that neither authors draws *particular generalizations* from their histories. For both, the implications are universal and general and little (if at all) related to the Cold War.

So how does one get away from such a theoretical suit of armor in writing history? The problem is not with the authors. It is with the theories themselves. Power politics and common interests are ahistorical theories; they are not context-bound, but universalizing. So the alternative, proposes Ingram, is to find a theory that is more context-bound and that actually believes that the world is an empirical puzzle rather than *just* a theoretical one; a theory that works less like a suit of armor and more like a "whale bone corset." Such a theory is so nimble that its conceptual apparatus "has no shape and cannot stand alone," yet is just constricting enough that when the "ungainly flesh" of the untold story of an international order steps into it, it is transformed into a rich but coherent history. When that happens, not only can the collective memories inscribed be accepted as careful, but it becomes possible to draw "particular generalizations," rather than universalizing lessons, about the international order (Ingram 2001, 251).

The question then, is how close various identity theories can come to providing a whalebone corset theory for representing, remembering, and learning about international order in a particularistically generalized way. Primordialist and SIT identity theories, it seems, come no closer to the whalebone ideal than either power-politics or common-interests theories. Like those, neither primordialism nor SIT takes context seriously. Instead, each is built upon too many unquestioned universal givens about how self and other relate and about how that relation bears on order. Constructivism appears more promising. Rooted as it is in the particular social constructions of self and other that underwrite international order, it allows the researcher to pursue a richer story that can coherently accommodate the "complex interaction of ideational and material structures in influencing state behavior" (Herman 1996, 273). But in the end, it seems, even constructivist theory can be too constricting to facilitate good history.

Consider Robert Herman's constructivist history of the end of the Cold War. As his story goes, new thinking (or the end of the Cold War) began with a shift in the self-other understandings of the East toward the West. As the East changed its view of the West, so too did Gorbachev and the Soviet leadership change their interpretations of the particular demands of the structural material constraints of which Brooks and Wohlforth and Stein write. In this way, Herman not only grapples with the factors upon which power-politics and common-interests histories focus, but also moves beyond them. Indeed, in evidentiary terms, Herman calls attention to something that both Brooks and Wohlforth, and Stein omit from their stories: the emergence of a cadre of "idealist"[16] Soviet scientists and other specialists whose interactions with pro-reform Westerners attuned them to what life could look like without the "absurdity and irrationality" of the Soviet system. Through their interactions, the idealists learned that they wanted a "normal country," one that would be admissible into the world of civilized nations. Over time this idealist cadre penetrated policy circles, forming a group whose primary intentions were to "reverse the arms race and eradicate the political sources of military conflict" by "inject[ing] normative criteria into the formulation and conduct of foreign policy." They became the new thinkers. In this way, new thinking was first and foremost an embodiment of a new Soviet identity in relation to the West, and that identity came to shape strategic and instrumental concerns.

Much about Herman's story suggests that it is good history. It is rich and complex, involving a multiplicity of processes, factors, and variables, and yet, it is still coherent, inscribing a nuanced memory of how the Cold War ended. Rather than the simplistic power-politics memory of Soviet defeat or the equally simplistic common-interest memory of Soviet self-enlightenment, Herman's story offers a complex memory of the end of the Cold War as a social transformation at the international level that came to bear in tangible political ways on the domestic structure of Soviet society. Herman's story also offers up more embedded or particularistic lessons than either power-politics or common-interests versions. Rather than pinpointing certain specific behaviors as productive of international order, Herman's lesson is that a big part of what underwrites international order is the specific, contextually embedded content—or lack thereof—of international communication, transnational linkages, and the collective learning they engender. With its nuanced and embedded approach, Herman's account surely comes closer to Ingram's ideal.

But the constructivist theoretical framework that Herman uses to structure his story still ends up requiring him to exclude rather important information. Consider Herman's treatment of the process of identity change. Although he holds out the shift in the content of Soviet identity as the source of the end of the Cold War, Herman offers only the most surface discussion of the specific underlying processes by which the old Soviet identity dissolved and the new, more West-friendly one was produced. His story is simply that Western-Soviet interaction activated a Soviet desire to be more Western, normal, and civilized. But entirely omitted is any consideration of *how* that desire was activated. What exactly happened over the course of interaction between Westerners and the Soviet specialists that made the latter come to see their country as less than normal and civilized in the first place? Herman offers no answer. In fact, his silence implies an assumption that the meaning of normality and civility were somehow obvious or settled, so that simply by interacting, the Soviets could come to see the absurdity and irrationality of their own country. They could be "magnetically attracted" to the ways of the West.

Ultimately, it is an empirical question as to whether there were shared prior settled truths between the West and the Soviet Union about the character of normality, civility, absurdity, and rationality. But Herman never delves into that aspect of the history. In this regard, his theory takes over the story; the constructivist refusal to take the process all the way down—the refusal to disrupt certain truths or givens about the world—guides Herman to take the settledness of meanings between the West and Soviet Union for granted.[17]

Of course, no account can include everything and disrupt every assumption. If it did, it would not likely be intelligible (Bially Mattern 2001). But in a case such as this, where the whole point is to tell the history of some moment of change in international order, the framework should not skimp when it comes to forcing the historian to wrestle with as many of the dimensions as possible that contributed to the change itself (Ferguson and Mansbach 1996, 4; Ackerly and True 2001). Indeed, in this case it seems obvious that Herman's story would have benefited from a more flexible theory. Given the ideological conflict between the U.S. and Soviets over what a good society should look like lo those many Cold War years, it seems egregious to assume that they shared settled basic truths about the meaning of normality, civility, absurdity, and rationality. Read through an ideological lens, the whole Cold War conflict was precisely about the lack of those shared meanings. In this light, it seems likely that yet a richer, more coherent history, memory, and set of particular generalizations could be drawn from the Cold War were it read through an even less restrictive theory; a postconstructivist theory.

A postconstructivist account of identity works like a whale bone corset—it gives shape without becoming the story itself. On one hand, a postconstructivist approach imbues a story about international order with coherence by directing the historian to focus on the underlying processes of identity production, dissolution, and re-production. But on the other hand, because its theoretic apparatus for investigating those processes involves nothing more than context-specific narratives, processes, and agents, the content, trajectory, and effects of these processes are entirely dependent on the ungainly flesh of the particular event or international order under exploration. Hence, the theory highlights particular points of inquiry—language-power and states' Self-interests in the process of identity production—but it makes no general assumptions about what kinds language-power and state interests will fuel a given process under varying circumstances.[18] Nothing is assumed exogenously. Because of this whale-bone-like construction, a postconstructivist theory is likely to produce good history—history in which the theory is not the story itself; in which the story is rich, coherent, and fertile as a resource for particular generalization.

So what might a postconstructivist rereading of the end of the Cold War look like? The answer, of course, depends entirely upon what the empirical record reveals. But an historian reading that event through a postconstructivist identity lens would be guided to think about the event in terms of the changing content and linguistic structure of the shared narrative "realities" of East-West identity. Thus, he might begin by asking about the content of the shared East-West narratives during the Cold War; when and how (through what linguistic processes) those changed, and when and how those changes produced changes in the narrative "reality" of the Soviet identity vis-à-vis the West. One might begin, for instance, by exploring whether there was, as Herman implies, a shared Western-Soviet settled basic narrative truth about what counted as a normal society. If such a settled truth did exist, did it magnetically attract the idealist Soviets to the West, leading them to dissent from the old Soviet narrative "reality" of Self? Or did the Soviet idealists argue or bargain with the West over the content of the new identity? Alternatively, what if there was no shared narrative "reality" of normalcy and civility during the Cold War? In that case, a historian would have to consider the kind of linguistic exchanges that occurred during the Soviet/Western interactions to discern what led the Soviets to share the Western version of those phrases. Did Westerners use a power politics of identity to force the Soviet specialists into sharing an appreciation for the Western lifestyle, and so into a more conciliatory identity? Or perhaps it was the Soviets who, for reasons related to emerging subjectivity, forced the West into accepting that the Soviets could aspire to a Western-style identity.[19] The possibilities go on. But what is clear, is that the relevant questions and so the story told, the content of the memory, and the particular generalizations to be drawn depend entirely upon the trajectories determined by the empirical record.

It is this quality that makes postconstructivism a whale-bone corset theory of international order, allowing the shape of its wearer (the empirical record) to determine the story, the memory it inscribes, and so the particular generalizations that can be drawn from it. A postconstructivist identity turn, that is, promises better histories of international order.

In Practice

A third dimension of an identity turn is the one with which this study began —its practical implications. The study of international order is not just about knowledge for knowledge's sake. As Yale Ferguson and Richard Mansbach write (1996, 7), IR scholars are "up to their ears in 'reality' and they hope their scholarship will have an impact on society." The question is, what kind of impact on the "reality" of international order might be produced by a postconstructivist identity turn? This is a tricky question, as it turns out, because the potential impact on practice of any model of international order is entirely circumscribed by the willingness of policymakers and theoreticians to talk with each other. And yet, communication between scholars and practitioners of international politics is, to put it mildly, spotty. During very stable international periods, policymakers seem to scoff at most theory as the stuff of unacceptable fantasy, too disconnected from the here-and-now of day-to-day international politics to be useful (Jentleson 2002).[20] During less stable periods, though, theory becomes quite popular with practitioners. Big changes in the world call for big visions and so during those times members of the policy community often turn full face to the fantasies offered by theory, even internalizing and adopting those fantasies themselves. In this way the extent to which an identity turn can matter for the practice of international order is, at the most basic level, contingent on big changes and open minds among policymakers.

It is opportune, then, that the contemporary era of international political order is precisely one of big changes and open minds. At the end of the Cold War, a veritable call for proposals went out around the United States as the (elder) Bush and then Clinton administrations hunted around for visions of international order that could be parlayed into plans of action.[21] As President Bush famously proclaimed, it was time for a New "World"[22] Order; a "sweeping transformation of the agenda for cooperative international action" with America at the helm. It was nothing if not an invitation for theorists to offer up fantasies that could inform practice. Of course, the U.S. was not the only country cultivating fantasies about Self-serving worldwide international orders at the end of the Cold War. Chinese leaders envisioned a new international order that was multipolar in orientation, and one in which China could play an autonomous role as a major power.[23] Many of the less-developed regions of the world proffered visions that rested not on fantasies about shifts in power polarity, but on fantasies about increased commitment to and constraint by rule of law and property rights at both the domestic and international levels.[24] The European vision was much more complex and multifaceted. That fantasy was of an international order that would control "disputed frontiers and restless minorities," extricate NATO from the shadow of American power,[25] and transform Europe into a unified center with an international strategic role.[26] And of course, any variety of nonstate actors—from transnational advocacy groups (like human rights activists) to transnational criminal organizations (both economic, like transnational mafias, and political, like Al Qaeda) —had their own fantasies about how the world ought to be re-ordered. But irrespective of the content of each fantasy, the end of the Cold War was viewed as an opportunity to re-order international politics.

This willingness to entertain fantasies and visions about ordering international politics largely persists among statesmen today. Perhaps this is because, as many have noted, no worldwide international order has ever really taken root as a replacement for the bipolar Cold War order.* Rather, the contemporary international world is populated by multiple regional and issue-based international orders. Indeed, the very persistence of the phrase "post-Cold War" (now often appended with "post-9/11") as a descriptor of the contemporary order signifies above all the inability of any particular state, including the U.S., to seize leadership, spread its visions, and construct a new "world" order with its own specific signifying name. Although the U.S. has certainly made more progress toward this end than others, the effective implementation and settling of its fantasized order into "reality" is constantly being unsettled by dissident narratives from all corners—including its own longstanding allies in Europe (most vociferously over the 2003 war in Iraq).

Although likely multiple explanations exist for the failures to settle new "realities" of international order—political, sociological, material—some part of the reason lies with the existence of inadequate plans for how to implement the various visions. After all, translating visions or fantasies about international order into political "realities" requires a plan of action, and the more those plans are rooted in compelling theories and studies about

---

*Though Steven G. Brooks and William Wohlforth appear to be trying to make systemic "unipolar vision" stick, Wohlforth (1994, 1999), Brooks and Wohlforth (2000, 2002). Michael Ignatieff (2002, 2003) is working on making a "neoimperialist vision" stick.

the sources of international order, the more dependable they are likely to be as blueprints for how to build the order in question. But because the theoretically flawed and historically limited power-politics and common-interests models have dominated IR scholarship, when practitioners have looked to scholars for visions of order and insight about how to implement them, they have been offered inadequate tools. A postconstructivist identity turn may well provide better blueprints and tools for those statesmen who seek translate fantasies about international order into lived "realities."

As a foil against which to make this point, consider one of the most popular fantasies about an international order, which has been circulating in the United States since the early 1990s: the vision of a worldwide international order predicated on a democratic peace. The democratic peace theory, inspired philosophically by Kant's notion of perpetual peace, holds that democratic countries do not wage war on one another because of the structure of their democratic governments and because they share democratic norms, values, and culture.[27] Supported as it is by considerable (though not uncontested) empirical evidence, the democratic peace thesis was embraced as a pillar of American foreign policy by President Clinton in his 1994 State of the Union address. His argument was that ultimately spreading democracy "would be the best strategy to insure our security" because it would lead to international order populated by states that understand and share American values (Owen 1994). It would be an order, that is, that would work to the advantage of American national interests. Although current U.S. President George W. Bush was initially less captivated by the democratic peace idea than was Clinton, the core insight that democracies can co-exist more peacefully and securely has become deeply ingrained in American policy consciousness. Indeed, even Bush now conceptualizes the reconstruction of postwar Afghanistan and Iraq as exercises in promoting a democratic international order.[28] In policy circles, as such, questions about the veracity of the democratic peace theory have been eclipsed by ponderings on the next step—on *how* to effectively spread democracies (Lynn-Jones 1998; Corothers 1999).

But academic IR has offered little in the way of good advice on this score. A power-politics model of international order is purposefully unenlightening on the question of how to spread democracy. Indeed, it simply counsels against spreading the democratic peace because, as the realist model holds, the only way to arrive at stable shared understandings (international order) is through threats and use of force. Thus, the idea that somehow democracies can transcend anarchy and its relentlessly competitive demands because of common norms and institutional constraints makes little sense. So, as self-identified "hyper-realist" Christopher Layne has argued, any attempt to spread democracy should be rejected. Such an attempt, in his view, is more likely to provoke war than peace (Layne 1994).

In fairness, power-politics models do have more active advice to offer practitioners when it comes to making a "reality" out of other types of fantasy international orders. For instance, one of George W. Bush's fantasies has been a worldwide international order based on a universally shared understanding (and practice) that no state harbor, tolerate, or otherwise aid terrorists.** The Bush administration's plan for enacting this order appears to have been informed directly by realist logic: The administration has waged a war on terrorism that relies on power-political threat systems, direct military force, and realist metaphors of defeat. The intention has been to inculcate compliance with the envisioned terror-free order in at least two types of actors: other governments, who would presumably be scared into giving up terrorists and the illicit arms industries upon which terrorists feed; and the terrorists themselves, who hopefully would be rooted out through military force.[29]

Yet the record of success for this type of order-building strategy has been thin, to say the least. For one, not all states suspected of harboring terrorists or in other ways aiding their purposes have been cowed by the threat of American military might—most notably Saddam Hussein's Iraq, which was undeterred by Bush's threats (eventually to the point of its own demise).[30] In fact, even American allies—particularly France and Germany—have remained unconvinced that Bush's realist policies were the most effective way to achieve compliance with the desired order.[31] What is more, the terrorists themselves have not been cowed into compliance by the U.S. strategy. After their bombardment by American troops, Al Qaeda operatives in Afghanistan simply fled to Pakistan, and more recently, to Europe, where they have reinforced their ranks by partnering with other dissident groups, who were clearly no more deterred by the specter of the U.S. than was Al Qaeda.[32] Indeed, Al Qaeda and its associated cells continue a fairly rigorous schedule of terrorist activities around the globe in spite Bush's promise of military annihilation.[33] Evidently the threat of physical[34] death at the hand of the American military holds little or no coercive power over them and the various states that still knowingly harbor them.

But a power-politics approach to constructing international order could not have anticipated this aberration in rationality, because the assumption that material threats under anarchy speak for themselves in the same way to all actors obscures the notion that threats of force mean different things

---

**By terrorism I refer the physical act, not Terror the discursive linking strategy. However, I make no effort to define which physical acts count as terrorism because, as Oliverio (1998) notes, the referent of the term is best understood as a political decision by the state.

to different actors. As a result, power politics has proven less than efficacious as a plan of action for constructing a terrorist-free international
order. The point travels: As a plan of action for ordering international politics more generally, power politics will only be efficacious under conditions that perfectly approximate the highly restrictive assumptions of
realist theory.

The common-interests model hardly fares better. Certainly when it comes
to offering a plan of action for spreading the democratic peace, such models
offer supportive, practical ideas. In particular, the premise of common-
interests approaches—that international order can emerge when states recognize their common interests in some outcome—logically implies that an
attempt to construct an international order of democracy involves educat-
ing nondemocratic regimes about their own interest in pro-democracy re-
forms. In service of this effort, international institutions are thought to be
rather useful tools. For instance, one familiar scheme inspired by a common-interest model is to use international economic institutions as leverage to promote democracy. For the U.S., this means making trade relations
contingent on a better human rights record (as in China), or using economic sanctions to foment revolt against a totalitarian military regime
(Haiti, Cuba). But whatever the particular point of leverage, the idea is to
hold a state's material interests hostage until it realizes that it is in their interest to adopt democracy. Other international institutions can be lever-
aged as well—universal human rights, for example, in the preservation of
which all peoples are taken to have a common interest. Humanitarian military interventions are undertaken in the name of universal human rights
to protect those common interests. They are often followed by nation
(re)building efforts in order to institutionalize the kind of democratic conditions that would prevent another breach of human rights.

The problem with these various approaches is that interests—material
ones or in preserving human rights—are not exogenously given or universally common among states and peoples, and so many of these plans of action simply fail in practice. Consider, for instance, the economic sanctions
imposed on Haiti in the early 1990s. These were designed to coerce the
delegitimated military government into relinquishing power, but as a point
of leverage for tapping into the interests of the Haitian military and elite,
they simply did not work. The country's leadership did not see the economic livelihood of their populace as a major concern or interest of theirs.[35]
The same problem plagued the Clinton administration's attempt to link
human rights to trade in China—the Chinese leadership apparently had a
stronger interest in retaining domestic control than in better access to U.S.
markets (Gilley 1998).[36] Finally, humanitarian intervention, as a method

for protecting the universal institution of human rights, has often back-fired. In the Somali case, for instance, the purpose of delivering humanitarian aid was so strongly resisted by the fighting warlord factions that American military personnel perished in the process of trying to get aid through. Clearly, those warlords did not hold in common with the U.S. an interest in preserving the basic rights of the Somali people. The nation-building projects that follow humanitarian interventions have not fared much better, regularly failing to consolidate into stable democracies. As Thomas Corothers argues (1999), imposing democratic institutions upon a people is doomed to fail, an insight that suggests that it is not all that easy edify people as to their interest in free and fair elections, freedom of expression, and other key tenets of what it means to be a democratic state.*** In these ways, even though many practical suggestions can be mined from a common-interests approach to democratic international order, the logic of a common-interest model is too simplistic to translate those suggestions into effectual practices for the construction of international order.

So can an identity approach do any better? To be certain, an identity model would point practitioners in a different direction. Because the logic of an identity model (whether primordial, SIT, conventional, or postconstructivist) is that shared self-other understandings constitute states so that they know what to expect from each other, the basic practical insight is that democracy ought to be treated as a particular kind of self-other understanding. Constructing a democratic and peaceful international order means spreading that identity. Importantly, then, the goal should not be to build a specific set of democratic institutions per se, but to constitute others (nondemocratic regimes) so that they share with self (democracies) the core values and ideas that make democracies nonviolent in the first place. This means inculcating nondemocratic states with democratic political culture. Once the peoples of that nondemocratic state identify with the tenets of democratic political culture, presumably behavior will follow; they will implement their own democratic institutions from below rather than having them imposed from outside. In short then, constructing a democratic peace is just like constructing an international security community (indeed, the former is a subtype of the latter); it is about cultivating a shared set of democracy-friendly values and understandings among democratic and nondemocratic states. The rest will take care of itself.

***Interestingly, this is something that George H. W. Bush realized would be a problem in Iraq and it is one of the reasons he abstained, as he puts it, from "going the invasion route." As Bush and Scowcroft (1998, 489), wrote, "Had we gone the invasion route, the United States could conceivably still be an occupying power in a bitterly hostile land."

It is important to note that in practical terms, the whole logic of any identity approach to spreading democracy rides on the capacity of the "spreader" (the U.S. in the current context) to implement policies that cultivate democratic-leaning shared self-other understandings with non-democracies. But what kinds of policies might those be? Each identity theory implies a different course of action. If one seeks to answer this question by drawing on primordial theory, no advice can be gleaned at all, because on that view, identities are pregiven and immutable. The practical upshot is that a democratic identity has no way to spread. The logic of SIT substantively offers nothing as well. Although it allows for the possibility that nondemocracy outgroup states can become part of the democracy in-group, how that happens and how that political culture "takes" is entirely untheorized. As such, SIT offers no practical advice about how to order international politics.

The constructivist identity model supplies some slightly more developed options, but these end up unsatisfyingly vague. Given its emphasis on interaction and social learning for identity-formation, the constructivist account counsels only that in practical terms, states must engage with the regimes they wish to transform. But exactly how those interactions can be set up in a way that nondemocratic regimes learn what the U.S. wants them to is pretty much anyone's guess. The lack of specificity on this score can again be traced back to the assumption that some kind of magnetic attraction will do the work—that nondemocracies will be magnetically attracted to what the U.S. has to teach them about democratic values.[37] But if American engagement with China is any indicator, magnetism is mythical. The leadership of China continues to resist democratic ideas and values even as its interactions with the West increase. Though some are optimistic that a dialogic engagement with China has produced progress toward a stable U.S.-Chinese international order, this order does nothing to help realize the fantasy of a worldwide democratic peace order. It is its own pocket of order based on mutual recognition of difference (Lynch 2002). As laudable as such a vision for international order might be, it gets practitioners who are interested in spreading of a worldwide democratic peace no closer to their goal.

A postconstructivist conception of identity may. The promise of this model of identity is that it implies particular tactics through which politicians and others who speak on behalf of the U.S. can actively steer the content of the identity that their targets learn over the course of interaction. More exactly, given that identity is inextricable from the power-laden narratives that represent it, teaching a democratic identity to a nondemocratic state should at base be a matter of statesmen deploying the most effective form of language-power possible in the narratives they use to represent the phrase 'Democracy' to their targets. That is, practitioners can narrate the "reality" of democracy in ways that persuade, manipulate, demand, or otherwise use their language-power to talk leaders and bureaucrats of a target state into the democratic community. At the extreme, this means that practitioners might even try to fasten democratic identity by using Terror and Exile to trap the resistant dissidents in nondemocratic regimes into accepting and living the experience of democratic political identity. In fact, depending on how serious the U.S. gets about spreading democratic identity, it may be the most efficient course of action to resort straight out to such strategies of representational force. After all, because it leaves its victims no choice but to comply, effectively deployed Terror and Exile would surely augment the likelihood of success of a campaign intended to spread democratic identity.

If this is not a very normatively appealing prospect (I address this issue below) it nevertheless has a substantial precedent as a commonly deployed and rather efficacious scheme among advertisers. More exactly, advertisers have taken to using what Douglas Walton calls scare tactics to narrate television, radio, and print commercials such that targeted subject-types (i.e., homosexuals, Hispanics, women, or politically incorrect white males) cannot simultaneously preserve their sense of Self and still ignore the product being advertised (Walton 2000). Scare tactics, in this way, are a form of Terror. Another precedent for using representational force as a practical means to a fantasized end can be found in the abortion debate in the United States. That discourse is replete with both Terror and Exile. Although it is not clear how effective these strategies have been at forcing pro-life advocates to switch to pro-choice or vice-versa, or even just at silencing the opposition, it remains that both sides deploy dehumanizing stereotypes to at least attempt to trap the other into abiding their perspectives (Brennan 1995). Thus, however unprecedented it may be as an openly acknowledged and embraced foreign policy strategy, the use of representational force is not only practiced as a policy in other political and social domains, but, at least in the case of advertising, it has proven to be rather effective. It may well be for ordering international politics as well.

Finally, even though Terror and Exile may be the most surefire way to spread democratic identity, there is no necessary reason why a state should not seek to do so through Tolerance; that is, by using nonforceful forms of language-power. In fact, under very settled conditions, persuasive, authoritative, or other Tolerant forms of language-power may be just as good or better. For instance, in target countries like Pakistan where some political leaders and bureaucrats have a collective memory of democracy, or perhaps even a faction of sympathetic democratic-leaning authors in the ranks of their own leadership, Tolerance may well do the trick.**** However, in the absence of relevant shared settled truths, the U.S. will lack both the authority to dictate the identity of its target and the kind of common lifeworld required to persuade through argument. In the case of strongly dissident nondemocratic regimes that share no basic truths about the value of democracy (for instance, Saudi Arabia), a power politics of identity offers a new approach to spreading a democratic peace. Either way, for those who deign to translate their fantasy international orders—whether worldwide or regional—into actual orders, novel and potentially effective tactics can be gleaned from a postconstructivist identity turn.

Conclusion: Turn to Ethics

But should those tactics actually be gleaned and deployed? Left unspoken in the preceding discussion—indeed, in this study as well as in the study of international order, more generally—is the question of whether states *should* be trying to construct nationally advantageous international orders. This question applies regardless of whether the preferred tactic for such an endeavor is material power politics, leveraging common interests, spreading identity though nonforceful forms of language-power, or forcing it through concerted campaigns of representational force. But for a variety of often contradictory reasons, such questions are seldom asked. These reasons range from straightforward assertions that no place exists in international politics for concerns about what is right or what *ought* to be done (Carr 1964), to insinuations that because international order is a normative good so its construction must be as well (discussed in Chapter 2), and to claims that, anyway, it does not matter whether it is right or wrong because in the end, international order is exogenously given (it can only be tinkered with, not voluntarily constructed) (Waltz 1979). But whatever the reason, the normative validity of the aspiration, no less the practice, of constructing a nationally advantageous international order has rarely been challenged.

****In a different example, it will be fascinating to see what forms of language-power states openly or surreptitiously use to deal the variety of current phrases-in-dispute of the Western international order—for instance, "Old Europe" and "New Europe." These dissident phrases, first authored by U.S. Secretary of Defense Donald Rumsfeld, signify France and Germany as "outside of the center of gravity" in NATO and international order, and Britain and the 13 EU new members as inside of it. But as of this writing the prior settled foundations of Western international order are not so unsettled as to make Terror and Exile the only linking option for dealing with such dissident narratives. On these phrases-in-dispute, "Outrage at 'Old Europe' remarks" (January 23, 2003) and "New Europe Backs EU on Iraq (February 19, 2003) both available at http://news.bbc.co.uk/2/hi/europe/.

And yet, above all else, the message to be drawn from this study is that international order can be socially constructed by the linguistic practices of intentional agents. International order is not dictated by the nature of anarchy, nor does it arise out of the discovery of naturally overlapping interests among states, nor does it just magnetically spread among states. It is constructed by people, acting on behalf of states, who make choices about when, how, and why to do it. But to acknowledge this is to admit the need for further reflection on the value of making certain choices and taking certain actions over others. In other words, because a postconstructivist identity turn in the study of international order highlights people—authors—and their choices, it does more than just demand a turn in theory, history, and the practice of international order. It demands a turn to ethics as well.

An ethical turn in the study of international order would center on investigations into whether it is morally defensible for states to seek to construct their preferred international orders, and how to do so in the most morally defensible manner. Of course, discussions of this sort have been going on for a long time among scholars, but insofar as the study and practice of international order has been disconnected from normative reflections upon it, the wisdom offered by these scholars has mostly fallen on deaf ears. Although a thorough review of this interesting literature is not possible here, constructing international order has generally been depicted as morally problematic by any variety of thinkers, including postmodernists, who view constructing order as oppressive and violent (Connolly 1991; Campbell and Shapiro 1999), Marxist and Gramscians who view it as alienating (Cox 1987; Robinson 1996), feminists who view it as unjustly exclusionary (Tronto 1993; Ackerly and True 2001) and proponents of the English School who view it as possibly damaging to the moral covenant of state sovereignty (Jackson 2000). However, these concerns are balanced with a healthy appreciation for the potentially deleterious effects of global disorder and isolation, which, aside from being potentially just as disorienting, exclusionary, and intolerant, are generally (though not always)[38] also more physically violent than the fantasy international orders envisioned by any given state (Baumann 1988, 1992).

In light of the recognition that moral ills exist to both order and disorder, one strain of discussion has been dedicated primarily to developing visions for the most morally defensible international order. But there has been little progress on what that order might be. Some argue that a unipolar world, in which a hegemonic U.S. polices the rest of the world "with an iron fist covered in a velvet glove" would be the most stable, and therefore peaceful, order (Brooks and Wohlforth 2002, 30). Inasmuch as that hegemony were open, in the sense of being relatively responsive to its subjects, it would be morally defensible (Ikenberry 2001). But no matter how velvety the glove or how responsive to its subjects, moral objections are easily raised that such a hegemony is a form of soft (or even hard) international authoritarianism. Other visions are similarly subject to moral disapprobation. For instance, Charles Beitz has famously advocated a cosmopolitan international order based on rules of distributive justice (Beitz 1999), while David Held has proffered a move to a cosmopolitan democracy; a world in which political decision making is internationalized and democratized (Held 1995). But Hedley Bull objects to visions that minimize state sovereignty because without state sovereignty "people's welfare and entitlements" diminish (Caney 2001, 268). Michael Walzer implies a similar perspective, suggesting that a balance of power, populated by sovereign, distinct states actors, is most morally appealing because it is (on his view) least oppressive toward different cultures (Walzer 1983). As an alternative to all of these visions, one might look to security communities; after all, they create nonviolent domains without either power balancing or the dispersion of juridical sovereignty. However, using the Anglo-American case as an indicator, it seems that states do not just naturally gravitate into security communities. Inasmuch as the sharedness of we-ness rests on a power politics of identity—on systematically deployed Terror and Exile—even the security community entails some normatively troubling dimensions.

Indeed, representational force *should* be recognized as normatively troubling. Certainly the form of power and mode of oppression wielded by Terror and Exile are not physically harmful (though they may be a precursor to physical harm in some instances).[39] So Terror should not be confused with physical terrorism,[40] and Exile should not be confused with the physical banishment of physical bodies. Representational force may, as Dennis Wrong notes, bear some interesting and important relationships to physical force, but the two are not interchangeable (Wrong 1988). And yet, taken on its own terms, representational force has morally pernicious effects that should not be overlooked simply because they are not physical. Representational force squelches voices of difference, creates oppression, and facilitates entitlement selectively. What is more, because it does so bluntly, nonnegotiably, and for self-interested purposes, it looks strikingly similar to hegemonic authoritarianism, only in this case exercised on an ideational level. It follows then that inasmuch as the unipolar American vision is morally objectionable, so should be any order underwritten by a power politics of identity. The latter may be more appealing in relative terms, but it would be ethically inappropriate to ignore its moral pitfalls.

Given the difficulty of envisioning an international order that is beyond moral reproach, more recent normative work on international order has not asked "is the vision morally defensible," but "was the vision arrived at through a morally defensible process?" (Linklater 1998; Crawford 2000) The goal of this work has been to derive a morally defensible process for constructing a vision of international order. As Neta Crawford envisions it, such a process would need to be not only international (between states) but inclusive of all interested parties, including individuals in civil society. Substantively, the process would be a dialogue and argument among these parties in which they abide by a set of discourse ethics that, among other things, allows only persuasive forms of language-power into the discussion. In this way, representational force and all its attending moral dilemmas are ruled out so that those involved can gradually come to settle without coercion on the covenants that they will allow to govern the terms of their expectations and behaviors (Crawford 2002, Chapter 9). But as Crawford is careful to note, the appropriate conditions for this discursive democracy are extremely limited in world politics, a point which raises the further question of how such conditions might emerge in the first place. It is a question that runs headlong into the specter of representational force, because constructing a settled foundation from which to engage in persuasive dialogue requires crafting order out of disorder. In this way, the very possibility of discourse ethics may be indebted at some important level to representational force. Voices are squelched, differences excluded, and privileges meted out before the dialogue even begins.[41]

How then to get away from representational force in the construction of international order? One possibility is to abandon the quest for international order altogether. This kind of suggestion has been the domain of postmodern ethics. For instance, Lyotard's postmodern ethics jettisons the notion of totalizing orders in favor of particularistic, interpersonal relationships. Those may occur across time and space (and so globally), but they are only moral if the authors of the relationships script their interactions using Tolerance. That is, subjects must maintain an ever open-minded approach to the other such that no specific interpretation is demanded or offered. In practical terms, this is an order in which the shared understanding is of mutual hands-off (Lyotard and Thébaud 1985).

This of course creates a serious problem in terms of helping or caring for others, which is troubling, especially during times of tragedy. As David Campbell has mused with obvious consternation, it offers no option but to wait for the carnage to subside (Campbell 1994).[42] What is more, it is unclear that an order based on postmodern ethics would avoid the pitfall of representational force any more than do particular substantive visions or discourse ethics. After all, in the very process of articulating his vision, Lyotard himself deploys representational force—he Exiles by assumption the views of such classical realists as Carr and Machiavelli, which hold that representational force need not always be a moral negative. Indeed, it is a curious, undefended, and unchallenged presumption in postmodern ethics and poststructuralist philosophical thought, more generally, that power is a moral bad. Perhaps then this is where a postconstructivist identity turn in ethics might begin; by delving more deeply into the moral logic of representational force.

was Saddam Hussein better than dispersed anarchistic power?

Endnotes

Chapter 1

1. Bush's statement made January 21, 2001; Jiang's statement made July 16, 2001. Emphasis added in both quotes.
2. The term "fantasy" is regularly used by foreign affairs strategists themselves to describe grand visions for political control. For instance see Byman, Pollack and Rose (1999) . However the word also, usefully in my view, evokes a host of psychological and sociopolitical possibilities (Todorov 1973; Kristeva 1984).
3. The trend began in 1989 with newspaper editorials calling for vision and imagination in foreign policy. George H. W. Bush's New World Order speech, March 6, 1991, lent official legitimacy to the call for fantasies.
4. These questions do presuppose that it is politically, socially, and normatively acceptable to seek to do so in the first place. I am less sanguine about this prospect and address the political, social, and normative questions throughout this study and in the conclusion.
5. For a discussion of Hu's fantasy of a multipolar order in which China holds great power status see Medeiros and Fravel (2003)
6. One might also think of this as an epistemic order though in the context of IR scholarship using this language risks confusion with Haas' notion of epistemic communities (groups of experts). See for instance the Special Issue of *International Organization*, Vol. 46, No. 1, "Knowledge, Power, and International Policy Coordination," Winter, 1992.
7. "Putin reassures Jiang about Bush", June 19, 2001, http://dailynews.muzi.com/ll/english/1077525.shtml. On Hu's continuation of this effort see "Beijing Analysts View Inside Story of President's Visit to Russia, France" BBC Monitoring Global News Wire-Asia Africa Intelligence, May 31, 2003. On Chinese aspirations to turn the Association of Asian Parliaments into a foundation for multipolarity, and the expected failure of that effort, see P. Parameswaran "China's Wu Bangguo calls for New Global Order based on Equality," Agence France-Press, September 1, 2003.
8. For brevity, I use the term "international identity" interchangeably with "identity" and "international order" interchangeably with "order." When referring to the thesis of this study however I am referring specifically to international identity and international order.
9. Which is not to imply any necessary normative improvement surrounding spreading identity. I discuss this later.
10. Though I am skeptical of this since physical survival does not seem to be among the values of many terrorists, particularly radical Islamic fundamentalists.

271

11. For instance the Bush Administration's 2003 appeal to the UN for multilateral assistance in the post-war reconstruct of Iraq sends a confusing message about unilateralism.

12. This ambiguity about the way that China is constructing its self-other relationship to the United States is captured by Alastair Iain Johnston (2003) 56, when he states that China may be more status quo oriented though "it (China) is not necessarily . . . more benign" or averse to revisionism.

13. Using identity to theorize the constitution of the modern states' system (as Reus-Smith and Philpot do) is clearly related to this project, in which I use international identity to theorize international order. However, the former projects focus on connecting identities and norms held by actors that existed prior to states to the production of the states system. This project *begins* with states and looks at how their identities with each other (international identities) produce specific configurations of expectations and behaviors among them (international order).

14. Neither he nor any other constructivist addresses the question of whether new identities can form during crises.

15. In fact, as Lyotard argues, there is never real settledness in any relationship. While I am sympathetic to this position, I assume for the sake of argument and for the purposes of this work that settledness is possible, though I focus on identity formation and maintenance during unsettled times.

16. I explore the particular conditions under which crises would create such a resonance for actors in Chapter 4.

17. I purposely write the word re-production rather than reproduction or (re)production. I avoid reproduction because the term conjures up feminist theory and I have not explored the gendered aspects of this practice (although there surely are such aspects). I avoid (re)production since this configuration is associated with poststructural deconstruction, which I argue in Chapter 4 is not the intention of the postconstructivist approach I adopt here.

18. Language-power is related to discursive power but because discourse and language are not interchangeable ideas, the two should not be conflated. Discourse is one communicative configuration that rests upon language. Thus, language-power is more basic than discursive power.

19. There are constructivists that have already relaxed the assumptions of settledness and emphasized various forms of language-power, but they have not recognized the importance of their frameworks for theorizing the identity-order connection. They also implicitly second the view that identity is passively produced. For instance, see Kratochwil (1989), Onuf (1989). An exception is Richard Price (1997), a work which I would describe as postconstructivist in spirit.

20. Especially Jacques Derrida (1978).

21. Thus although security communities are sometimes defined simply as regimes of nonviolence, for Adler and Barnett, and for this study, they are defined as regimes of nonviolence that are underwritten by the particular international identity of we-ness.

22. Allen (1955), Bartlett (1992), Dobson (1995), Baylis (1997), Danchev (1998), Dumbrell (2001).

23. Memorandum of Discussion at the 302nd Meeting of the National Security Council, Washington, D.C., November 1, 1956, Eisenhower Library, Whitman File, NSC Records; Memorandum of a Conversation among the President, the Secretary of State, and the Undersecretary of State (Hoover), White House, October 31, 1956, Eisenhower Library, Dulles papers, Meetings with the President.

Chapter 2

1. A poignant example of this can be found in Harry Harding's open forum talk to practitioners at the Department of State in April 2002, where he began with three different definitions and sources of international order commonly found in the discipline.

2. Similar arguments about mining consistencies among apparently incommensurable histories of ideas can be found in Lustick (1996) 616, Isacoff (2002) 229–32.

3. Many other types of orders can emerge as well; this is not an exhaustive list. Clearly the presence, absence, and content of international order can be shaped by or even indebted to the other actors in world politics. Thus, distinguishing orders on the basis of the actors within in them is more for heuristic purposes than it is to imply a number of discrete, non-interactive orders among global actors. But regardless of the degree to which other orders shape or determine international order, there does seem to be a special sphere of social relationships among states that is different from their relationships with other actors. Finally, although the focus of this study is international order, I in no way mean to subscribe to the view that it is the most important order in world politics.

4. The notion that the content of behaviors and expectations are not significant may on some readings seem to depart importantly from Hedley Bull's popular conception of order as a substantive set of cooperative agreements among states', Bull (1977). But since there is nothing that rules out thick cooperative expectations and behaviors these conceptions or models need not be thought of as incommensurable. Moreover, as Hoffmann notes, Bull himself believed that shared understandings amounted to substantive cooperation. When read this way, the account presented here coheres perfectly to Bull (Hoffman, 1990).

5. Hegemonic wars are expected at predictable intervals.

6. Specifically when combined with necessity.

7. Actually he also suggests love. But love *qua* love has never been taken seriously as an underpinning of international order, even, as it turns out, by Boulding himself. He mentions it merely as a foil for highlighting the constraints of anarchy. Cited in Rapoport (1999) 3.

8. In fact, they would argue that power politics are *the* source of international order. In this sense realists are actually making an argument for sufficiency and necessity, meaning not only that all power politics produce orders but that all orders entail power politics. This covering-law formulation is captured by Mearsheimer in his claim that international orders that rest upon anything other than power politics are "a false promise," Mearsheimer (1995). However, given that sourceness demands only the easier case of sufficiency, and that, as I argue, power politics fails even on that score, I do not take on the stronger claim in the text. However, arguing against the necessity of power politics is not hard. As I argue later, since anarchy is not inevitably competitive then the inevitability of these forceful threat systems is a myth. International orders exist in which power politics, as realists understand them, have no discernible role. The Anglo-American security community is a case in point. Thus, power politics cannot be necessary for international order.

9. As Walton (2000: 46) notes, not all threats are forceful.

10. This is intended as an illustrative (not exhaustive) list of nonforceful forms of power.

11. Schelling sees coercion not as a form of power in its own right but rather as a mode for deploying force. Dennis Wrong agrees, arguing that the only way to understand coercion is as an adjective, which modifies the noun (a form of power) or an adverb, which modifies the verb describing the way in which power was used, Wrong (1988) 31–2.

12. Although there are very important distinctions among "critical" theorists, in this context I use the phrase to denote a commitment to the view that state behaviors and expectations are socially constructed, as is in most cases, the state itself, Cox (1987), Wendt (1992), Cronin (1999), Stevens (1999) .

13. PRO FIO 371/120314 /AU1013/54 , minutes by AN MacClearly 21 November 1956.

14. After all, even where extenuating external conditions (like a bipolar nuclear race) make an alliance between states of different civilizations possible, the mistrust between "us" and "them" would make it impossible to develop we-ness. In turn, expectations for nonviolence would not be reliable or stable.

15. Though their we-ness is itself generating an ASEAN way or a shared civilization, Kuhonta (2002).

16. The following discussion is indebted to Hogg and Terry (2001). Fearon (1999) refers to this as personal identity, but in deference to the primary sources in the SIT literature I use the self-concept terminology.

17. He treats security communities and cooperative regimes as synonymous. He argues that it was through such a process of ingroup expansion that former enemies France and Germany became part of the same security community (249–50).

18. This phrase is Smith's (2000).

19. I develop this "almost" issue, and with it the idea of weak constructivism, in the next section.
20. As opposed to discovery. See first footnote in Chapter 1, Toward an Identity Turn?
21. Adler and Barnett do not use the phrase "framing" in *Security Communities* but they do describe this process.
22. Wendt (1999) 246–78 introduces an argument about the Hobbesian culture of anarchy in order to make just this point.
23. In fact, as William Connolly (1991) suggests, all forms of power are powerful only in light of the shared beliefs of their effectiveness between power-wielder and subordinate. So, even if one were to challenge the requirement of authority as the basis for identity formation, the critique of an ever-receding horizon of shared values would persist.
24. For a different formulation of the same idea see Bransen (2001).
25. In this sense crises are neither objective events that arise under some regular, identifiable set of external conditions, such as sudden changes in material structures (Gourevitch 1986; Ikenberry 2001) nor intersubjective events in which all sides agree on the need to redefine the relationships.
26. A scientific definition of this process reflects the same idea: demagnetization is the removal of the ferromagnetic properties of a body by disordering the domain structure. One method of achieving this is to insert the body within a coil through which an alternating current is flowing; as the magnitude of the current is reduced to zero, the domains are left with no predominant direction of magnetization. *A Dictionary of Science*, Oxford University Press, Market House Books Ltd. 1999.

Chapter 3

1. One might alternatively illustrate this same point through any number of other unsolved problems, like the end of the Cold War, the expansion of NATO, the nuclear taboo, and so on.
2. Scholars regularly use the phrase security community to refer to any behaviorally nonviolent order (for instance, NAFTA) but only those that are nonviolent as a result of we-ness are properly security communities. So while the NAFTA countries are nonviolent among each other, their relationships do not constitute a security community because the U.S.-Mexico relationship lacks the common values and trust that are part of we-ness, Gonzalez and Haggard (1998).
3. David Cannadine (1999) has pointed out that historians and other academics play a role in producing the magnetism and unifying bonds among the political leadership as they construct the stories permissive of trust among political elite.
4. Although it should not be forgotten that the Americans supported European colonial territories as late as 1950, Curtis (1998) 11.
5. It was possible to read the logic of isolationism as supportive of democratic rule of law (because it was an American policy driven by popular domestic consensus) and as revering democratic freedom (because it left determination of other nations up to them). The British disliked this reading of isolationism, but its logic was sound.
6. Recent years have been challenging for the Special Relationship, Rachman (2001), but its representation at leadership and bureaucratic levels as shared values, trust, and common security fate persists. As Alan Dobson puts it, "the quality of the relationship does not have to be devalued just because it operates at a less exalted level in world affairs," Dobson (1995) 168. For an overview of the contemporary Special Relationship and security community see Dumbrell (2001).
7. As Dumbrell (2001) 12, citing Stephen Krasner, points out, "very powerful nations . . . are able to indulge cultural preferences beyond immediate power interests." In the case of Britain, the U.S. certainly did.
8. This refusal to acknowledge the absence of Anglo-American self-other understandings of each other as democracy is an example of how the constructivist almost-all-the-way-down approach to identity produces incapacity to imagine disorder (Chapter 2).

9. In fact, it appeals to we-ness between the U.S. and all its Western allies, which is a far more robust claim about identity than I have advanced here. My claim has been that we-ness between the U.S. and Britain protected the other allies from violence in this case.

Chapter 4

1. I use the word "language" in the broadest sense. Languages do not have to be constituted of the signs of verbal or written words; languages can also be gestures, art, or other forms of expression as long as they are collective sign systems, meaning that they are socially shared.
2. While this notion of language-power may sound more familiar as discursive power, I want to make a distinction between them for the purposes of this study for two reasons. For one, I have been unable to find any compelling and uniform definition of discourse that did not reduce it to a system of signs embedded in a culture, which on a poststructuralist view is precisely what language is. See Bleiker (2000) 220-221. Second, and more interestingly, often among scholars the notion of discursive power is understood as Foucault (1977) meant it: focused primarily on how collectively established sign systems construct subjects. But for that kind of analysis the sign system is considered extant; it is like a settled foundation. Of course, since I am interested in how identities form during unsettled times—times when sign systems are disrupted—I am more interested in how agents (in this case states) can produce the collective sign systems that then produce them as situated in some shared self-other relationship. But it is true that in both cases the idea is that language produces "reality" and is an expression of power. I am grateful to François Debrix for bringing this issue to my attention.
3. Lyotard, whose version of poststructuralism animates most of this study, is a case in point. Lyotard never lost sight of the author/agent in every speaker/writer.
4. Foucault, among other poststructuralists, actually left traces of human agency in their works (particularly in the call for dissent) but resisted developing those traces systematically.
5. One of Bleiker's main contributions is to offer a theoretical basis for the agency implicit Foucaultian thought. In its focus on sociolinguistic constructions *and* agency, Bleiker's work offers an analysis that I would characterize as postconstructivist.
6. Though which is better at it is something I do not investigate since the concern of this study is unsettled times.
7. Though there is significant debate about whether or not this kind of statement even counts as a speech act, Recanati (1987).
8. In fact, for Lyotard (1988), all times are unsettled times because there is never perfectly shared knowledge. There is always an unspoken and unrepresentable difference in the genres that subjects use to speak. Trying to settle them means trying to navigate *le differend* and so doing constitutes force. While I intuitively agree with Lyotard, I suspend this possibility for the purposes of this study in which it would get me too far off the topic to demonstrate the point empirically. This bracketing of degree to which the world is perpetually unsettled —and so accepting for argument sake that settledness may actually exist—marks a significant departure in this work from Lyotard's philosophy. However, given Lyotard's own intention to treat authorship as infinitely open to revision and interpretation ("a message in a bottle," Lyotard and Thébaud 1985) my "cafeteria style" approach to appropriating his work is probably not philosophically objectionable.
9. Another way to put this: power in general is relational and that is why its "verve" breaks down when relationships between actors break down. What makes representational force able to function in spite of this is that during unsettled times when relations break down it exploits the relations between different aspects of a person's Self.
10 It is also possible that states can even prevent a breakdown by using representational force to maintain an identity when a crisis begins. However, I bracket this possibility in this work because understanding this would require a theory about actors' foresight into how the breakdown of identity might affect them and thus give them reason to fasten it before it breaks down. It may be possible to construct such a theory, but that merits independent study.

11. An objection here might be that it is not identity doing the order-producing work but representational force (and so identity is not a source of order). However, this is an incorrect characterization because where representational force is used to fasten identity, it is not the force that tells states what to expect and how to behave (order). It is the content of what is being fastened—in the case of we-ness, the particular shared values and trust in the domain of security. Representational force is used to stabilize that shared vision, but it is the vision itself (or at least the representation of that vision as articulated by even dissenting victims of force) that demands particular expectations and behaviors or order. In this sense, representational force occupies the same role as authority and magnetism in the constructivist account of the security community. All are preconditions but not sufficient conditions for nonviolent order. Nonviolence is rooted in the content of what is learned, framed, or fastened.

12. Of course, representational force and the power politics of identity do not promise physical death the way coercive force does, a point that is normatively important. Though this may mean that representational force is more normatively attractive, threats of damage to the Self are surely as real as threats of damage to the body. As Dennis Wrong puts it, "it is plainly not true that 'sticks and stones can break my bones but names can never hurt me'" Wrong (1988) 28. Ernst Haas (1982) notes that this holds true and has political import even in international relationships.

13. Nutting (1967) 70 discusses this.

14. And of course there is significant debate about whether these conditions are even met among states during settled times since the appeal to coercive forms of persuasion often pollutes these idealized versions of argument, see Crawford (2002).

15. The discussion below draws primarily on *Le Differend* though in some instances from *The Postmodern Condition* or *Just Gaming*. I differentiate the sources throughout the discussion.

16. Metaphor, for instance, would make no sense without a prior narrative. Metaphor is a representative genre in which one phenomenon is understood with reference to the qualities of another. Consider the notion of "spending time", which metaphorically reflects time as an economy; it is something we can waste, budget, invest, squander. But without a narrative to imbue these signified concepts (economy, waste, etc.) with some meaning the metaphor itself is meaningless. Narrative must come first. For an interesting look at metaphor in IR, see Chilton (1996).

17. For another, highly convincing treatment of identity as a narrative construct see Neumann (1999).

18. In fact, he discusses Tolerance without naming it, probably to avoid the kind of forceful settling of knowledge against which Tolerance stands. In doing so I have, again, departed significantly from Lyotard's own narrative.

19. Terror is Lyotard's word. I discuss this below. I derive the phrase Exile from Richard Ashley's (1988) notion of reduction. Lyotard scholars will be sensitive to the fact that Terror can encompass Exile. However, Lyotard does not spell this out explicitly and since neutralizing threats by externalizing difference is so critical to producing identity, it is analytically useful to draw it out in as a separate strategy.

20. Many others have made this same observation that terror is a function of psychologically rooted anxiety as much as of physically rooted anxiety. See Bloch and Reddaway (1977), Derrida (1978), Glass (1989), Feldman (1991), Caruth (1996), Oliverio (1998) Wrong (1988).

21. A Habermasian discursive democracy is a communicative institution in which an actor is required to crystallize his reasons and interest. This structural requirement implies a particular type of calculus in which an actor will prefer narrative choices that give others the opportunity to engage in a clarifying dialogue, Warren (1995) 179. Nevertheless, the actor has his reasons and interests prior to his arrival in the discursive democratic institution and, as such, at the end of the day he can flout the rationality bestowed by the institution, in that case making choices that would change the communicative institution. Indeed, one might reasonably speculate that the reason Habermas conceptualizes the ideal speech situation so rigidly is to prevent "runaway" agents who would choose a form of narrative that changes the structure.

22. Patrick Jackson and Daniel Nexon (1999) 318 conceptualize it in a similar way, though calling up network or relational rather than narrative theory. Agency and rationality are situated within the network of relations in which a Self is embedded.
23. This is what Adler and Barnett (2000) 325 seem to be hoping for when they propose that "practices" can fix identity without entailing representational force.
24. Which sounds ironically intolerant.

Chapter 5

1. My guess is that Lyotard would probably have been critical of the degree to which I have imposed order on this history since to do so may easily be a form of Terror. Depending on how my narrative is constructed (in terms of my descriptive phrases of the crisis and the manner in which I link them together) my story may force one reading of the history over another. In fact, recognizing this as I do while simultaneously struggling to find a way of telling this story that is both attentive to readers' need for historical contours and bearings is what leads me to a main point of my conclusion: that Tolerance is impossible to achieve; it is only an ethical ideal. For a work captures well this notion of the messiness of life in a still-readable form see Bleiker (2000).
2. Elsewhere I have developed criteria for the systematization of this analysis, which I have used to present the evidence here. See Bially (1998).
3. John Kentleton (1987) 175, points out that Britain may have ceased to be a world power in 1945, but for another ten years the country could believe it was one. During the Suez Crisis that changed. Indeed, Robert Murphy, U.S. deputy undersecretary of state, is noted as saying that Eden went blind into Suez because he seemed unable to grasp just "how much Britain's power had diminished in relation to the United States and Russia," Love (1969) 372.
4. Memorandum of Discussion at the 295th Meeting of the National Security Council, Washington, August 30, 1956, Eisenhower Library, Whitman File, NSC records, document 149.
5. Memorandum of a Conversation, British Foreign Office, London, August 1, 1956, Department of State, Central Files, 974.7301/7–3156.
6. Carl W. McCardle of the Senior Staff of Advisers in the Delegation at the Suez Canal Conference to the Secretary of State, London, August 21, 1956, in Department of State Central Files, 974.701/8 –2156.
7. Letter from the British ambassador to the Secretary of State, Washington, September 10, 1956, in Department of State Central Files.
8. One concern with that course of action was that there was no one in the progressive camp of Egyptian politics who could weld the heterogeneous Opposition Party together sufficiently to carry out a successful coup against Nasser.
9. Memorandum of Discussion at the 295th Meeting of the National Security Council, Washington, August 30, 1956, Eisenhower Library, Whitman File, NSC records, document 149.
10. Before the invasion of the canal most senior British officials did not even know what was happening. No justificatory representation is thus available for that time.
11. Draft Message from President Eisenhower to Prime Minister Eden, Washington, September 8, 1956, Eisenhower Library, Dulles Papers, Misc. Papers-U.K. (Suez Crisis).
12. Humphrey's characterization in Minutes of the Second Meeting of the Delegation to the General Assembly, Two Park Avenue, New York, November 15, Department of State Files.
13. Draft Message from President Eisenhower to Prime Minister Eden, Washington, September 8, 1956, Eisenhower Library, Dulles Papers, Misc. Papers- U.K. (Suez Crisis).
14. Of course, Dulles's righteousness could be selective. He was known to sacrifice his moral and religious ideals for personal power and success. See Berding (1965).
15. Telegram from the Department of State to the Embassy in the United Kingdom. Washington, July 30, 1956, 12:59pm. From Department of State Central Files, 974.7301/7–3056.
16. The French had their own reasons for this move; for a discussion of French interests see Bell (1997).
17. Message from President Eisenhower to Prime Minister Eden. September 2, 1956. In Eisenhower Library, Whitman File, International File.

18. Message from Foreign Secretary Lloyd to Secretary of State Dulles, London, September 7, 1956, in Department of State, Presidential Correspondence; Lot 66 D 204 U.K. Official Correspondence.

19. Israel had perennial disputes with Egypt over the activities of *fedayeen* in border areas and the Egyptian economic blockade of Israel. It became particularly concerned when Nasser, who repeatedly rallied for the destruction of Israel, began to rearm the Egyptian army. Accordingly, right after the nationalization of the Canal, and in addition to its negotiations with Britain, France had also initiated secret negotiations with Israel. Later, France combined its talks with both countries so that in the final stages, all the three countries worked together to devise a plan for a joint operation against Egypt.

20. Eisenhower Papers, Ann Whitman Series, DDE Diaries, Box 19, October 1956.

21. Memorandum by the President, Washington, November 1, 1956. Eisenhower Library, Dulles Papers, White House Memoranda.

22. Memorandum of a Conversation, Secretary Dulles's Room, Walter Reed Hospital, Washington, November 7, 1956, Eisenhower Library, Dulles Papers, Meetings with the President.

23. It has frequently been suggested that collusion was doomed to be discovered because of the ignorance of British military strategists, who should have known that the complexity of the mission would be a dead giveaway of prior planning, Calvocoressi (1966), Love, Carlton (1989), Kyle (1991).

24. Memorandum of Discussion at the 302nd Meeting of the National Security Council, Washington, November 1, 1956, in Eisenhower Library, Whitman File, NSC Records.

25. United States Department of State, Foreign Relations of the United States, 1955–1957, Doc. 482, p. 957.

26. United States Department of State, Foreign Relations of the United States, 1955–1957, fn to Doc. 527, p. 1029.

27. United States Department of State, Foreign Relations of the United States, 1955–1957, Doc. 531, p. 1033; Doc. 532, p. 1034.

28. Memorandum of a telephone conversation between President Eisenhower in Washington and Prime Minister Eden in London, Nov 7, 1956, Eisenhower Library, Whitman File, Eisenhower Diaries.

29. Memorandum for the Record by the President's Staff Secretary, Washington November 7, 1956, Eisenhower Library, Whitman Files, Eisenhower Diaries.

30. Memorandum of a Conversation, Secretary Dulles's Room, Walter Reed Hospital, Washington, November 7, 1956, Eisenhower Library, Dulles Papers, Meetings with the President. This ultimatum is offered in United States Department of State, *Foreign Relations of the United States, 1955–1957*, Doc. 545, p. 1056.

31. Memorandum of a Conversation between Prime Minister Eden and Secretary of State Dulles, 10 Downing Street, London, August 1, 1956, 12:45 pm, Department of State, Central Files, 971.7301/8–156.

32. Memorandum of a Conversation, Department of State, Washington, August 3, 1956, Department of State, Central Files, 974.7301/8–356.

33. Memorandum of a Conference with the President, White House, Washington, October 30, 1956, Eisenhower Library, Whitman Files, Eisenhower Diaries.

34. Memorandum for the Chancellor, 31 October 1956, T236/4188, PRO.

35. According to Calhoun (1991) 491, "In fact the Federal Reserve Bank did not hold any foreign currencies in 1956, and it had nothing to do with the attack on sterling. Neither did the U.S. treasury. Some of its major sellers were not American at all. India was off-loading pounds in the American currency markets. So were the Middle Eastern oil states. Even Communist China managed to sell some of its sterling holdings via U.S. intermediaries. Once it was obvious the pound was under pressure, of course, American bankers felt they too had to cut their losses and dump sterling."

Chapter 6

1. I do not explore the type of language-power expressed in each narrative of the phrases-in-dispute because that would entail theorizing the structure of all sorts of language-power beyond representational force. It would be fascinating to know, but since the purpose here is to explore the effects of representational force for re-producing identity—rather than for all sorts of language-power for producing dissent—I bracket this issue for this study.
2. Presidential historians have since revised this view of Eisenhower, though, and it is now thought that he had much more control over Dulles than it appeared at the time, Kingseed (1995).
3. Letter from Foreign Secretary Lloyd to Secretary of State Dulles, London, October 15, 1956, Eisenhower Library, Dulles Papers, Misc. papers—U.K. (Suez).
4. Memorandum from the Secretary of State's Special Assistant for Intelligence to the Secretary of State, Washington, December 5, "Record of Events Leading to the Israeli and Anglo-French Attacks on Egypt in Late October 1956," Department of State, s/p files: Lot 66 D487.
5. Memorandum of a Discussion at the 302nd meeting of the National Security Council, November 1, in Eisenhower Library, Whitman Files, NSC Records.
6. Memorandum of Discussion at the 305th Meeting of the National Security Council, Washington, November 30, Eisenhower Library Whitman Files, NSC records.
7. Letter from the British ambassador to the Secretary of State, Washington, September 10, 1956, Department of State Central Files.
8. By this time there was such dissent within the British ranks that fewer were willing to fight for the logic of the Lion. I return to this in Chapter 7.
9. Interestingly, revisionist readings note that it is not at all clear that the British economy would not have been able to withstand the pressure of either economic or oil sanctions. Macmillan is thought to have purposefully misinformed the cabinet in order to precipitate the downfall of Eden, Ovendale (1998).
10. Memorandum of a Conference with the President, White House, Washington July 31, 1956, 9:45am. Eisenhower Library, Ann Whitman File, Eisenhower Diaries.
11. Memorandum of Discussion at the 295th Meeting of the National Security Council, Washington, August 30, 1956, Eisenhower Library, Whitman File, NSC records, document 149; Carl W. McCardle of the Senior Staff of Advisers in the Delegation at the Suez Canal Conference to the Secretary of State, London, August 21, 1956, in Department of State Central Files, 974.701/8 –2156; Letter from the British ambassador to the Secretary of State, Washington, September 10, 1956, in Department of State Central Files.
12. Memorandum of a Conference with the President, White House, July 31, 1956, 9:45 A.M., Eisenhower Library, Ann Whitman Files, Eisenhower Diaries.
13. Although Dulles was the more vocal and emphatic in expressing his opinions, both he and Eisenhower represented the West as the God-fearing, moral high ground in the battle and the Soviet Union as a place of infectious, atheistic decay. Eisenhower was "an unwavering and unequivocal supporter" who agreed with the "fundamental rightness" of Dulles's policies, Drummond and Coblentz (1960) 190.
14. Humphrey especially in Memorandum of a Conference with the President, White House, July 31, 1956, 9:45 A.M., Eisenhower Library, Ann Whitman Files, Eisenhower Diaries.
15. Memorandum of a Conference with the President, White House, Washington, October 30, Eisenhower Library, Whitman Files, Eisenhower Diaries.
16. Memorandum of Discussion at the 302nd Meeting of the National Security Council in Washington, November 1, Eisenhower Library, Whitman File, NSC Records.
17. For a good statement of British perspectives on American anticolonialism see Colonial Office brief on "British Colonial Policy & United States Attitude," in Perth to Prime Minister., PM (57), February 1957. PRO CO 967/309 .
18. Memorandum of Discussion at the 295th Meeting of the National Security Council, Washington, August 30, 1956, Eisenhower Library, Whitman File, NSC Records.
19. Humphrey's characterization in Minutes of the Second Meeting of the Delegation to the General Assembly, Two Park Avenue, New York, November 15, Department of State Files.

20. James (1986) 459. Also Louise Richardson (1996) 35, writes, "British Chiefs of Staff and American Charge d'Affairs were under the impression Nasser shouldn't be allowed to get away with it, but the group recognized that the action might be legal."
21. Telegram from the Embassy in Egypt to the Embassy in the United Kingdom, Cairo, August 1, Department of State, Central Files, 396.1–LO/8–156.
22. Telegram from the Embassy in Egypt to the Department of State, Cairo, August 4th, 1956, 4 A.M., Department of State Central Files, 974.7301/8 –456.
23. Draft Telegram from the Embassy in the United Kingdom to the Department of State, Department of State Central Files, 974.7301/9 –1156.
24. Middle East Center Archive, St. Anthony's College, Oxford, Monroe Papers, John Hamilton interview with Elizabeth Monroe, September 1959.
25. Memorandum, November 5, 1956, Concerning Conference with the President November 4, 1956. Eisenhower Library, Ann Whitman Files, Eisenhower Diaries, box 19.
26. Memorandum of Discussion at the 302nd Meeting of the National Security Council, Washington, November 1, Eisenhower Library, Whitman File, NSC Records; Memorandum of a Conversation among the President, the Secretary of State, and the Undersecretary of State (Hoover) White House, October 31, 1956, Eisenhower Library, Dulles papers, Meetings with the President.
27. Department of State, s/p files: Lot 66 D487
28. Department of State, s/p files: Lot 66 D487
29. Memorandum of a discussion at the 299th Meeting of the National Security Council, Washington, October 4, in Eisenhower Library, Whitman File, NSC records.
30. Telegram 444 from USUN, October 30, Department of State, Central Files, 684A.86/10 – 3056.

Chapter 7

1. Of course, Britain was unsuccessful at eradicating the representation of the Suez Crisis as "the Lion's last roar" but nevertheless it sought to do so, Cooper (1978), Lucas (1996).
2. In this regard, it is interesting to note that at the time, most of the discourse about the Cold War was very much ideological and identity-driven in its substantive focus. Very few discussions in the documents I examined addressed particular substantive material threats. Throughout the 1950s the American basic national security policy was entirely framed around the need to protect individual liberty, religious commitment, and moral truths from the moral, political, and religious bankruptcy of the Soviet regime, Campbell (1992) 30. In Britain, the East/West conflict was pitched differently, but in no less ideological or identity-driven terms. British policymakers internalized the Cold War as an opportunity to bring "civilization" to as much of the world as possible through re-establishment of British imperial rule. Epstein (1964) 44–45, Kent (1993), Greenwood (1999). Either way, both the U.S. and Britain conceived of the Cold War as a rivalry of ideas about such dualities as right/wrong, good/bad, and us/them.
3. This dichotomy implies that when the Cold War ended in 1990, we all lost—not just the Soviet Union. George Arbatov, the chief America-watcher for the USA Institute in Moscow, recognized this in 1989 when he said, "We are going to do a terrible thing to you. We are going to deprive you of an enemy." Jonathon Kaufman Boston Globe, November 12, 1989, p. 1.
4. The documents produced in connection with the Menzies mission are loaded with such linkages by non-U.S. and non-British authors. See, for instance, the The Evatt Collection, Secret cables Menzies/Nasser Sep 1956, External Affairs-Suez Crisis, Flinders University of South Australia Library.
5. There are also countless primary resources in which key leaders are found remarking on the central role of Anglo-American cooperation for preserving the free world. For instance, see President Eisenhower and Harold Macmillan, Declaration of Common Purpose, October 1957. Commonwealth Survey, 29 October 1957, 943–4.
6. AU 1051/53, "The Present State of Anglo-United States Relations," Sir Harold Caccia to Mr. Selwyn Lloyd, Washington, 28 December 1956 (received 1 January 1957). Public Record Office, PREM 11/2189.

7. Hare's Oral History transcript at the Eisenhower Library, quoted in Kingseed (1995) 144.
8. A more recent international conundrum regarding the acceptance of blame occurred surrounding the collision of U.S. surveillance plane with a Chinese fighter plane in April 2001.
9. The likely reason that it was too hard to construct a compelling trap of this sort was because so many other nations at the United Nations agreed with the British view on the American behavior. The U.S. would have had to invest energy in Terrorizing those nations as well. It is not to say, however, that others thought the U.S. was wrong to use the UN against the British as they did. Most favored the U.S. maneuvers. But most did also understand Britain's humiliation. See Heller (2001) 42–52.
10. Special National Intelligence Report: Probable Repercussions of British-French Military Action in the Suez Crisis, September 5, 1956.
11. Foreign Relations of the United States, 1955–1957, Volume 16, Suez Crisis July 26–December 31, 1956 (Washington: Department of State) p.912–915. This is a fascinating exchange worthy of its own analysis.
12. Also in primary documents, Message from Prime Minister Eden to President Eisenhower, October 1, 1956, Eisenhower Library, Whitman File, International File.
13. Telegram from the embassy in the Soviet Union to the Department of State, Moscow, November 5, Department of State, Central Files, 674.84A/11–556.
14. *Ibid,* and Memorandum of a Discussion at the 302nd Meeting of the National Security Council, Washington, November 1. Eisenhower Library, Whitman File, NSC Records.
15. Message from President Eisenhower to Prime Minister Eden, Washington, October 30, 1956, Department of State, Central Files, 684A.86/10–3056.
16. The allusion to relative versus absolute gains in the neorealist-neoliberal debate is intentional but transposed to an ideational level. As I argue in Chapters 2, 4, and 8, the dynamics of identity production and re-production are rather similar to power politics as understood by the realist and neoliberals, but applied at the level of identity.
17. Telegram from the Embassy in the United Kingdom to the Department of State, London, November 19, Department of State Central Files, 974.7301/11–1956.
18. Letter from President Eisenhower to Swede Hazlett, Eisenhower Library, Whitman Files, Eisenhower Diaries, November 2, 1956.
19. Memorandum of a Conference with the President, White House, Washington, October 29,1956. Eisenhower Library, Whitman File, Eisenhower Diaries.
20. Memorandum of a Conversation, Secretary Dulles' Suite, Waldorf Astoria, New York, October 5, 1956, Department of State Central Files, 974.7301/10–556.
21. The cleverness of the American logic is worth some appreciation because, after all, the Americans had forced the British to accept a representation of 'Economic Sanctions' as beneficial to Special Relationship by deploying the very same logic that the British had used to depict that phrase as a threat to Special Relationship. That is, both sets of authors identified economic sanctions as the reason for the demise of the British operation, but the Americans carried this representation to a different logical conclusion.
22. Macmillan (1971) 109–10 tries to rebut that he ignored these warnings by arguing that he had calculated on the basis of them. But then on page 163, he admits to having "miscalculated." These miscalculations have since been treated as purposeful.
23. At the time, there was still belief that Eden would return to power if he could demonstrate that he could "lead a vigorous, progressive, efficient government." Indeed, Eden himself argued that there were "tasks aplenty" and that he was "reinvigorated to solve them" (*The Times*, December, 15, 1956, quoted in Kyle, 1991).
24. Memorandum of a Telephone Conversation, Eisenhower/Aldrich November 20, 1956, Dwight D. Eisenhower Diaries, Box 19, Eisenhower Library Abilene.
25. Memorandum of a Conference with the President, Humphrey Hoover, Allen Dulles, Radford et. al. November 21, 1956, Dwight D. Eisenhower Diaries, Box
26. Memorandum of a Telephone Conversation Between the President in Augusta, Georgia and the Secretary of State in Key West, Florida, November 27, 1956, Eisenhower Library, Whitman File, Eisenhower Diaries; Memorandum of a Conference with the President, White House, Washington, November 20, 1956, Eisenhower Library, Whitman File, Eisenhower Diaries; Memorandum of a Conference with the President, White House, November 27, 1956, Eisenhower Library, Whitman Files, Eisenhower Diaries.

27 Memorandum of Discussion at the 305th Meeting of the National Security Council, Washington, November 30, Security Council, Washington, November 15, Eisenhower Library, Whitman Files, NSC Records.

28. PROT236/4190, 24 November 1956.

29. For an interesting discussion of the difficulties of justifying trusteeship-type imperialism in the international context, see Paris (2003)

30. The JCS identities and interests made them more Lion-like than Eagle-like in the Suez context. They sustained an interest in keeping military force in the core of American foreign policy.

31. Contrast to "straight" cases of Exile in which the phrase-in-dispute ('Nationalization' in this case) simply become irrelevant to the status quo narrative being fastened (Special Relationship).

32. Message from Prime Minister Eden to President Eisenhower, October 30, 1956, Eisenhower Library, Whitman File.

33. Memorandum of a Conversation Between the President and the Secretary of State, Secretary Dulles's Room, Walter Reed Hospital, Washington, November 12, 1956, Eisenhower Library, Dulles Papers, Meetings with the President.

34. Telegram from the Embassy in France to the Department of State, Paris, October 6, 1956, Department of State Central Files, 974.7301/10–656.

35. Memorandum from the Joint Chiefs of Staff to the Secretary of Defense, Washington, August 3, 1956, Eisenhower Library, Dulles Papers, White House Telephone Conversations.

36. Telegram from the Embassy in the United Kingdom to the Department of State, Department of State Central Files, 674.84A/7–3156

37. It is interesting to note that Eden poses this as a question "May I . . . " but punctuates it with a period rather than a question mark. Certainly it is punctuation that demands its listener's attention rather than requests it. Eden also punctuates "Dear Friend" with a period rather than a comma, as if it is an assertion that must be the final word.

38. Message from Prime Minister Eden to President Eisenhower, September 6, 1956, Eisenhower Library, Whitman File, International File.

39. Telegram to State Department, September 19, 1956, Department of State Central Files, 974.7301/9–1156.

40. Paper by the Undersecretary of State's Special Assistant, Washington, August 4, 2956, Department of State NEA Files: Lot59 D18 OMEGA—Memos etc. from July 1–August 31, 1956.

41. See Memorandum of a Conversation Among the President, the Secretary of State and the Under Secretary of State (Hoover), White House, Washington, September 6, 1956, Eisenhower Library, Dulles Papers, Meetings with the President; Letter from President Eisenhower to Swede Hazlett, Washington, November 2, 1956, Eisenhower Library, Whitman File Eisenhower Diaries

42. Hare (1993) 112 p.112; Telegram from the Embassy in Egypt to the Department of State, Cairo, December 16, Department of State Central Files, 674.00/12–1656.

43. Memorandum of a Conversation Among the President, the Secretary of State and the Under Secretary of State (Hoover), White House, Washington, September 6, 1956, Eisenhower Library, Dulles Papers, Meetings with the President.

44. On "the Bear" as the identity of the Soviet Union and the process of its narration during Suez, see Love (1969) 225–261, Kyle 456–60.

45. Communiqués between Sir Pierson Dixon, U.K. ambassador to the UN and the British Foreign office provide a useful view on how the British perceived the hostility of the General Assembly toward their collusion. See Foreign Office 371/121746/VR1074/452, telephone calls between Dixon and Foreign Office on October 31 and November 1, 1956. See also Gorst and Kelly (2000).

46. Daily Mail, October 13, 1956.

47. Message from Prime Minister to President Eisenhower, November 5, 1956, Eisenhower Library, Whitman File, International File.

48. For example, "President said in this matter he does not care in the slightest whether he is re-elected or not. He feels we must make good on our word . . ." In Memorandum of a Conference with the President, White House, Washington, October 29, 1956, Eisenhower

Library, Whitman File, Eisenhower Diaries. See also Eisenhower to Gruenther, November 2, 1956 in Eisenhower Correspondence Series, Box 1 Gruenther Papers, EL.

49. See for example, Annex to Watch Committee Report No. 318, CIA Files Top Secret, September 20, 1956.

50. For other narratives of Exile over 'Collusion,' see Macmillan, Fisher (1982), Horne (1988), Lucas (1991) ; Message from Prime Minister to President Eisenhower, November 5, Eisenhower Library, Whitman File, International File; Dulles, J. F. (November 24, 1956). Memorandum of a Telephone Conversation Between Secretary of State Dulles and Harold Macmillan, November 24, 1956, Eisenhower Library, Dulles papers, Misc. papers, U.K.

51. *Memorandum of a Telephone Conversation Between Secretary of State Dulles and Harold Macmillan, November 24, 1956,* Eisenhower Library, Dulles Papers, Misc. Papers—U.K; Lucas 320

52. Letter from President Eisenhower to Swede Hazlett, Washington, November 2, Eisenhower Library, Whitman File Eisenhower Diaries.

53. SC (58) 8 Steering committee, Planning paper on interdependence, 27 January 1958. Public Record Office, FO 371/132330, excerpted in Baylis (1997) 84–104 84–104.

54. Scope paper prepared in the Department of State, Washington, 20 April 1962, for Prime Minister Macmillan's visit to Washington, 27–9 April 1962. Foreign Relations of the United States, 1961–63, Vol. XIII, pp. 1064–8; President Kennedy and Prime Minister Macmillan, "Statement on Nuclear Defense Systems" from their joint statement at Nassau, 21 December 1962. Public Papers of the President (1962) pp. 908–10

Chapter 8

1. Which is ironic because generally those research designs that are accepted as explanatory in character also fail to live up to the epistemologically exacting standards of positivist science, Kosso (1992).

2. Exceptions can be found in the English School tradition, which explicitly prefers an interpretive approach over a scientific (empiricist, positivist) method. See Dunne (1998) 7–9.

3. It is important to keep in mind here that causes come in multiple forms, many of which are not covering laws. See Chapter 2.

4. Adler and Barnett (1998) do the same with magnetism. They indicate that magnetic power is activated when states acquire an interest in achieving the physical security and material wealth that they see in specific other states. See alo Checkel (1999).

5. For a similar observation about constructivist idealism, see Payne (2001).

6. In this way, it is possible to dismiss objections that processualizing order collapses the distinction between periods of stability and moments of change in global politics. Processualizing order attunes researchers to the particular configurations underlying the maintenance of an order and so highlights when change is occurring.

7. Constructivism does a better job at navigating the passage between prosocial identities and prosocial behaviors because it is at least logically consistent to think that a communal sharing of ideas can lead to certain prosocial state behaviors.

8. Wendt (1999) 272–8 tries to solve this problem with the concept of internalization but this just creates the same problem at a different level. Internalization is a form of sharing, or intersubjective knowledge. The question then is how that sharing is produced, and that question is left unanswered. In solving this, some engagement with the power entailed by ideas would be helpful. But as I have argued, constructivism treats ideas and power as distinct.

9. Though it is also worth recalling that from a postconstructivist perspective not all identities —prosocial or antisocial—are produced through forceful forms of language-power. It is possible, for instance, that during settled times, we-ness may be produced through magnetism, persuasion, or some other form of language-power, which sits in seemingly less awkward tension with behaviors of nonviolence.

10. In quotes because it is a memory that often has never been lived in the present.

11. I extrapolate these criteria from Edward Ingram (2001) but the phrase "particular generalization" is from John Lewis Gaddis (2001).

12. Ingram also makes the interesting observation that in some way realists in IR are postmodern in their intellectual stance because theory is everything and the world can be molded to fit it. It is a provocative and compelling point.

13. Of course, they tell their stories with different emphases: Brooks and Wohlforth emphasize actors' deductive rationality in the face of that context, whereas Stein emphasizes their inductive instrumentality.

14. Stein was writing before the evidence upon which Brooks and Wohlforth draw was available, but even in 1994 there was evidence that the Soviet economic decline was pressing. In the case of Brooks and Wohlforth's evidentiary oversights, the case is unambiguous. As Robert English (2002) notes, they unjustifiably rely on a woefully circumscribed data set which obviously limits the nature of the story they could tell.

15. Stein sets hers up as challenge to neorealist structuralism, whereas Brooks and Wohlforth pitch theirs as a rebuttal to the notion that realism cannot explain the end of the Cold War.

16. Not in Wendt's minimalist sense of the word, but normatively.

17. Which is frustratingly inconsistent because Herman sets out to challenge the fixity of material interests (273) only to turn around and assume fixity of ideational values and interests.

18. Even the theoretical claim that representational force is the only way to fasten an identity during crises ends up being context-contingent because the use of this form of language-power depends upon the context-contingent desire of subjects to survive.

19. The U.S. was trying to sustain the East as enemy so that the West could remain meaningful. Allowing the East to redefine normalcy in a Western manner would muddy that boundary. Perhaps, then, the East used Terror and Exile to force the West to comply. Campbell (1992) offers a version of Cold War history that is congenial to this possibility.

20. An exception is deterrence theory, which achieved the height of its popularity during the very stable years of the Cold War order.

21. David Boren of the New York Times warned that the end of the Cold War was a crossroads in international order and "those who mill around at the crossroads do so at their own peril" (New York Times, 1/2/89, p. A16). Indeed, even the notoriously realist former secretary of state Henry Kissinger recognized the end of the Cold War as a situation of extraordinary fluidity in international politics. As he referred to it, it is "a period pregnant with possibilities" (Quoted in Don Oberdorfer, Washington Post, 5/7/89, p. 1).

22. Strictly speaking, it was a new international order because Bush envisaged it between states. From now on when I say "new world order" I am using the colloquialism of the time to refer to the new international order (Barry James, International Herald Tribune, 1/19/90, p. 5).

23. "China and the International Order," Harry Harding, Elliott School of International Affairs, The George Washington University, Remarks to the Open Forum, Washington, DC, April 3, 2002, at www.state.gov/s/p/of/proc/tr/11589.htm; "The Anti-Terrorist Coalition: A 'New World Order' Redux?" By Robert M. Cutler, October 15, 2001, at www.fpif.org/commentary/0110coalit_body.html.

24. Hernando de Soto, "The Mystery of Capital," 21st Annual Morgenthau Memorial Lecture on Ethics and Foreign Policy, May 8, 2002, at www.carnegiecouncil.org/about/morgenthau02.html.

25. Michael Howard, Manchester Guardian Weekly, 3/25/90, p. 11.

26. Francois Heisbourg, Independent, 12/28/90, p. 21; Dominique Moisi, International Herald Tribune, 3/24–25/90, p. 6.

27. The literature on the democratic peace, both supportive and critical, is now voluminous. The original ideas were introduced by Doyle (1986), Russett (1993). For useful overviews of the current discussion see, Brown, Lynn-Jones, and Miller (1996), Elman (1997)

28. See, for instance, the text of Bush's speech on November 6, 2003 in the East Room, "President Bush Signs Funding for Troops and Reconstruction in Iraq and Afghanistan, www.georgewbush.com/News/read.aspx?ID=2092.

29. Andrew F. Tully, "U.S.: Bush Asks World to Back Campaign Against Terror," Radio Free Europe/Radio Liberty, September 21, 2001, www.rferl.org/nca/features/2001/09/21092001105708.asp

30. Recent events suggest that, in the end, there was no connection between Saddam Hussein's regime in Iraq and Al Qaeda terrorists. But the point remains that in the face of American threats of military action, Saddam Hussein did not adopt a conciliatory stance toward the United States.

31. Though Britain remains firmly behind the U.S.
32. Tim McGirk, "Al Qaeda"s new hideouts" Time, July 29, 2002; Antony Barnett, Jason Burke and Zoe Smith "Terror cells regroup—and now their target is Europe" January 11, 2004.
33. For instance, the Middle East, Turkey, and Morroco.
34. As opposed to subjective death, which I suspect is likely to hold greater sway over terrorists (see Chapter 3).
35. William Robinson (1996) 304, who takes a more cynical view, also notes that the U.S. was violating its own embargo. His conclusion is that the agenda was not to spread democracy but to install a capitalist class.
36. Indeed, that China is now a member of the WTO on terms that make no regard for human rights almost mocks the very effort.
37. It is perhaps in recognition of this fact that President George W. Bush has decided to focus on increasing interactions among individuals in democratic and nondemocratic nations. He has called upon individual American citizens as national servants who might join the Peace Corps and teach peoples abroad how to be more American-friendly. "Bush Urges Volunteerism As a Way to Fight Evil," January 31, 2002 on CNN; online at www.cnn.com/2002/ALLPOLITICS/01/30/bush.sou.1408/?related.
38. An exception would be the international order envisioned by the Nazis. Moreover, it is important to keep in mind that disorder need not mean physical violence, though by definition disorder implies that no shared understandings exist to militate against it or render it predictable (Chapter 2).
39. Lyotard (1988) implies a link between Terror and the Holocaust.
40. Indeed, even physical terror is not necessarily terrorism, Byford (2002).
41. This kind of objection to discourse ethics is precisely what characterizes the Habermas/Lyotard debate in political theory. See Poster (1998).
42. Though the solutions he suggests in his own work violate their own principles.

Bibliography

Acharya, A. (2001). *Constructing a Security Community in Southeast Asia: Asean and the Problem of Regional Order*. London and New York: Routledge.

Ackerly, B. and J. True (2001). *Transnational Justice: The Contribution of Feminism to Critical International Relations Theory*. Workshop on Justice and Globalization, Center for International Studies, University of Southern California.

Adler, E. and M. Barnett (1996). "Governing Anarchy: A Research Agenda for the Study of Security Communities." *Ethics and International Affairs* 10: 63–98.

Adler, E. and M. N. Barnett, Eds. (1998). *Security Communities*. Cambridge, England: Cambridge University Press.

Adler, E. and M. Barnett (2000). "Taking Identity and Our Critics Seriously." *Cooperation and Conflict* 35(3): 321–330.

Adler, P. (1981). *Momentum: A Theory of Social Action*. Beverly Hills, CA: Sage.

Agger, B. (1992). *Cultural Studies as Critical Theory*. London: Praeger.

Agnew, J. and S. Corbridge (1995). *Mastering Space*. London: Routledge.

Aldrich, R. J. (1998). "British Intelligence and the Anglo-American Special Relationship During the Cold War." *Review of International Studies* 24: 331–351.

Allen, H. C. (1955). *Great Britain and the United States: A History of Anglo-American Relations*. New York: St. Martin's Press.

Ashley, R. (1988). "Untying the Sovereign State: A Double Reading of the Anarchy Problematic." *Millennium* 17(2): 227–262.

Ashmore, R. D. and L. J. Jussim (1997). *Self and Identity : Fundamental Issues*. New York: Oxford University Press.

Austin, J. L. (1961). *How to Do Things with Words*. New York: Oxford University Press.

Axelrod, R. (1984). *The Evolution of Cooperation*. New York: Basic Books.

Baldwin, D., Ed. (1993). *Neorealism and Neoliberalism*. New York: Columbia University Press.

Barkin, J. S. (2003). "Realist Constructivism." *International Studies Review* 5(3): 325–342.

Barkin, S. and B. Cronin (1994). "The State and the Nation: Changing Norms and the Rules of Sovereignty in International Relations." *International Organization* 48(1): 107–130.

Barnett, M. (1998). *Dialogues in Arab Politics*. New York: Columbia University Press.

Barnett, M. (1999). "Culture, Strategy and Foreign Policy Change: Israel's Road to Oslo." *European Journal of International Relations* 5(1): 5–36.

Bartelson, J. (1995). *A Genealogy of Sovereignty*. Cambridge, England: Cambridge University Press.

Barthes, R. (1977). "The Death of the Author." In *Image, Music, Text* (S. Heath, Trans., pp. 142–148). New York: Hill and Wang.

Bartlett, C. J. (1992). *The Special Relationship: A Political History of Anglo-American Relations.* New York: Longman.

Baumann, Z. (1988). *Life in Fragments.* New York: Blackwell.

Baumann, Z. (1992). *Intimations of Postmodernity.* London: Routledge.

Baylis, J. (1997). *Anglo-American Relations Since 1939.* Manchester, England: Manchester University Press.

Baylis, J. and S. Smith (2001). *The Globalization of World Politics.* New York: Oxford University Press.

Behnke, A. (2001). "Grand Theory in the Age of Its Impossibility: Contemplations on Alexander Wendt." *Cooperation and Conflict* 36(1): 121–134.

Beitz, C. (1999). *Political Theory and International Relations.* Princeton, NJ: Princeton University Press.

Bell, P. H. (1997). *France and Britain 1940–1994: The Long Separation.* Essex, England: Addison Wesley Longman.

Beloff, L. (1989). "The Crisis and Its Consequences for the British Conservative Party." In W. R. Louis and R. Owen (Eds.), *Suez 1956: The Crisis and Its Consequences.* Oxford, England: Clarendon Press.

Berding, A. H. (1965). *Dulles on Diplomacy.* New York: D. Van Nostrand.

Bhabha, H. K. (1990). "Dissemination: Time, Narrative, and the Margins of the Modern Nation." In H. K. Bhabha (Ed.), *Nation and Narration.* London: Routledge.

Bially, J. (1998). *The Power Politics of Identity.* Doctoral dissertation, Yale University.

Bially Mattern, J. (2001). *Subjects of Reflection: Feminist Critical Method and the (Re)Production of Exclusion.* Working paper. University of Southern California, School for International Studies.

Bially Mattern, J. (2003). "The Difference That Language-Power Makes: Solving the Puzzle of the Suez Crisis." In F. Debrix (Ed.), *Language, Power, and Agency in a Constructed World.* Armonk, ME: Sharpe.

Bleiker, R. (2000). *Popular Dissent, Human Agency, and Global Politics.* Cambridge, England and New York: Cambridge University Press.

Bloch, S. and P. Reddaway (1977). *Psychiatric Terror: How Soviet Psychology Is Used to Suppress Dissent.* New York: Basic Books.

Bowie, R. and R. Immerman (1998). *Waging Peace: How Eisenhower Shaped Enduring Cold War Strategy.* Oxford, England: Oxford University Press.

Bowie, R. R. (1989). "Eisenhower, Dulles, and the Suez Crisis." In W. R. Louis and R. Owen (Eds.), *Suez 1956: The Crisis and Its Consequences.* Oxford, England: Clarendon Press.

Bransen, J. (2001). "On Exploring Normative Constraints in New Situations." *Inquiry* 44(43–62).

Brennan, W. (1995). *Dehumanizing the Vulnerable: When Word Games Take Lives.* Chicago: Loyola University Press.

Brooks, S. G. and W. C. Wohlforth (2000). "Power, Globalization, and the End of the Cold War: Re-Evaluating a Landmark Case for Ideas." *International Security* 25(3): 5–53.

Brooks, S. G. and W. C. Wohlforth (2002). "American Primacy in Perspective." *Foreign Affairs* 81(4): 20–33.

Brown, M. E., S. M. Lynn-Jones, et al. (Eds.) (1996). *Debating the Democratic Peace: An International Security Reader.* Cambridge, MA: MIT Press.

Brubaker, R. and F. Cooper (2000). "Beyond Identity." *Theory and Soceity* 29: 1–47.

Bukovansky, M. (2002). *Legitimacy and Power Politics : The American and French Revolutions in International Political Culture.* Princeton, NJ: Princeton University Press.

Bull, H. (1976). "Martin Wight and the Theory of International Relations." *British Journal of International Studies* 2: 101–116.

Bull, H. (1977). *The Anarchical Society.* New York: Columbia University Press.

Bush, G. H. and B. Scowcroft (1998). *A World Transformed.* New York: Vintage.

Butler, J. (1997). *The Psychic Life of Power.* New York: Routledge.

Buzan, B. (1993). "From International System to International Society: Structural Realism and Regime Theory Meet the English School." *International Organization* 47(3): 327–352.

Byford, G. (2002). "The Wrong War." *Foreign Affairs* 81(4): 34–43.

Byman, D., K. Pollack, et al. (1999). "The Rollback Fantasy." *Foreign Affairs* 78(1): 24–41.

Calhoun, D. F. (1991). *Hungary and Suez, 1956: An Exploration of Who Makes History*. Lanham, MD: University Press of America.

Calvocoressi, P. (1966). *Suez: Ten Years After*. New York: Pantheon.

Campbell, D. (1992). *Writing Security: United States Foreign Policy and the Politics of Identity*. Minneapolis: University of Minnesota Press.

Campbell, D. (1994). "The Deterritorialization of Responsibility: Levinas, Derrida, and Ethics after the End of Philosophy." *Alternatives* 19: 455–484.

Campbell, D. and M. Shapiro (1999). *Moral Spaces: Rethinking Ethics and World Politics*. Minneapolis: University of Minnesota.

Caney, S. (2001). "British Perspectives on Internationalism, Justice, and Sovereignty: From the English School to Cosmopolitan Democracy." *The European Legacy* 6(2): 265–275.

Cannadine, D. (1999). "Historians as Diplomats? Roger B. Merriman, George M. Trevelyan, and Anglo-American Relations." *New England Quarterly: A Historical Review of New England Life and Letters* 72(2): 207–231.

Carlton, D. (1989). *Britain and the Suez Crisis*. New York and Oxford: Blackwell.

Carr, E. H. (1964). *The Twenty Years' Crisis, 1919–1939: An Introduction to the Study of International Relations*. New York: Harper & Row.

Caruth, C. (1996). *Unclaimed Experience, Trauma, Narrative, and History*. Baltimore, MD: Johns Hopkins University Press.

Cederman, L. E. (2001). "Back to Kant: Reinterpreting the Democratic Peace as a Macrohistorical Learning Process." *American Political Science Review* 95(1): 15–31.

Chai, S. K. (2001). *Choosing an Identity: A General Model of Preference and Belief Formation*. Ann Arbor: University of Michigan Press.

Checkel, J. T. (1999). "Norms, Institutions, and National Identity in Contemporary Europe." *International Studies Quarterly* 43: 83–144.

Checkel, J. T. (2001). "Why Comply? Social Learning and European Identity Change." *International Organization* 55(3): 553–588.

Chilton, P. (1996). *Security Metaphors: Cold War Discourse from Containment to Common House*. New York: Peter Lang.

Chomsky, N. (1993). *What Uncle Sam Really Wants*. Tucson, AZ: Odonian Press.

Churchill, W. (1974). "The Sinews of Peace." In R. R. James (Ed.), *Winston S. Churchill: His Complete Speeches 1897–1963. Vol. vii: 1943–1949*. New York: Chelsea House Publishers.

Claude, I. (1984). *Swords in Plowshares: The Problems and Progress of International Organization*. New York: McGraw Hill.

Cobley, P. (2001). *Narrative*. London: Routledge.

Connelly, M. (2002). *A Diplomatic Revolution: Algeria's Fight for Independence and the Origins of the Post-Cold War Era*. Oxford, England and New York: Oxford University Press.

Connolly, W. (1991). *Identity/Difference*. Ithaca, NY: Cornell University Press.

Connolly, W. E. (1974). *The Terms of Political Discourse*. Princeton, NJ: Princeton University Press.

Cooper, C. L. (1978). *The Lion's Last Roar: Suez, 1956*. New York: Harper and Row.

Corlett, W. (1989). *Community without Unity: A Politics of Derridean Extravagance*. Durham, NC: Duke University Press.

Corothers, T. (1999). *Aiding Democracy Abroad: The Learning Curve*. Washington DC, Carnegie Endowment for International Peace.

Cox, R. (1987). *Production, Power, and World Order*. New York: Columbia University Press.

Crawford, N. C. (2000). "The Passion of World Politics: Propositions on Emotions and Emotional Relationships." *International Security* 24(4): 116–156.

Crawford, N. C. (2002). *Argument and Change in World Politics*. Cambridge, England: Cambridge University Press.

Cronin, B. (1999). *Community under Anarchy: Transnational Identity and the Evolution of Cooperation*. New York: Columbia University Press.

Cronin, J. (2000). "Convergence by Conviction: Politics and Economics in the Emergence of the Anglo-American Model." *Journal of Social History* 33(4): 781–804.

Cruz, C. (2000). "Identity and Persuasion: How Nations Remember Their Pasts and Make Their Futures." *World Politics* 52(3): 275–312.

Curtis, M. (1998). *The Great Deception: Anglo-American Power and World Order*. London: Pluto Press.

Danchev, A. (1996). "The Special Relationship." *International Affairs* 72(4): 737–750.

Danchev, A. (1998). *On Specialness*. New York: St. Martin's Press.

Der Derian, J. (1988). "Philosophical Traditions in International Relations." *Millennium* 17(2): 189–193.

Derrida, J. (1978). "Violence and Metaphysics: An Essay on the Thought of Emmanuel Levinas." *Writing and Difference*. Chicago: University of Chicago Press.

Derrida, J. (1978). *Writing and Difference*. Chicago: University of Chicago Press.

Dessler, D. (1999). "Constructivism within a Positive Social Science." *Review of International Studies* 25: 123–137.

Deudney, D. and J. G. Ikenberry (1999). "The Nature and Sources of Liberal International Order." *Review of International Studies* 25: 179–196.

Deutsch, K., R. A. Burrell, et al. (1957). *Political Community and the North Atlantic Area*. Princeton, NJ: Princeton University Press.

Dimbleby, D. and D. Reynolds (1988). *An Ocean Apart: The Relationship between Britain and America in the Twentieth Century*. New York: Random House.

Dixon, P. (1968). *Double Diplomacy: The Life of Sir Pierson Dixon*. London: Hutchison.

Dobson, A. P. (1995). *Anglo-American Relations in the Twentieth Century: Of Friendship, Conflict, and the Rise and Decline of Superpowers*. London and New York: Routledge.

Doty, R. (1997). "Aporia: A Critical Exploration of the Agent-Structure Problematique in International Relations." *European Journal of International Relations* 3(3).

Doty, R. (2000). "Desire All the Way Down." *Review of International Studies* 26: 137–139.

Doyle, M. (1986). "Liberalism and World Politics." *American Political Science Review* 80(4): 1151–1169.

Drezner, D. W. (2000). "Bargaining, Enforcement, and Multilateral Sanctions: When Is Cooperation Counterproductive?" *International Organization* 54(1): 73–102.

Drummond, R. and G. Coblentz (1960). *Duel at the Brink*. New York: Doubleday.

Dumbrell, J. (2001). *A Special Relationship: Anglo-American Relations in the Cold War and After*. New York: St. Martin's Press.

Dunne, T. (1998). *Inventing International Society: History of the English School*. New York: St. Martin's Press.

Duportail, G. F. (2000). "The Interpretation of Meaning and Common Sense—Reflections on the Subjectivity of Language." *Revue De Metaphysique Et De Morale* 105(2): 199–213.

Eden, A. (1960). *Full Circle: The Memoirs of Anthony Eden*. Boston: Houghton Mifflin.

Elman, M. F. (Ed.) (1997). *Paths to Peace: Is Democracy the Answer?* Cambridge, MA: MIT Press.

Elster, J. (1989). *The Cement of Society*. Cambridge, England: Cambridge University Press.

Elster, J. (1996). "Strategic Uses of Argument." In K. J. Arrow (Ed.), *Barriers to Conflict Resolution*. New York: WW Norton.

Emirbayer, M. and A. Mische (1998). "What Is Agency?" *American Journal of Sociology* 103(4): 962–1023.

English, R. D. (2002). "Power, Ideas, and New Evidence on the Cold War's End: A Reply to Brooks and Wohlforth." *International Security* 26(4): 70–92.

Epstein (1964). *British Politics in the Suez Crisis*. Champagne-Urbana: University of Illinois Press.

Falk, R. (1993). *Explorations at the Edge of Time: The Prospects for World Order*. Philadelphia, PA: Temple University Press.

Fearon, J. D. (1999). *What Is Identity (as We Now Use the Word)?* Unpublished manuscript, Stanford University, Stanford, CA.

Fearon, J. D. and A. Wendt (2002). "Rationalism Versus Constructivism: A Skeptical View." In W. Carlnaes, T. Risse, and B. Simmons (Eds.), *Handbook of International Relations*. Thousand Oaks, CA: Sage.

Fearon, J. D. and D. D. Laitin (2000). "Violence and the Social Construction of Ethnic Identity." *International Organization* 54(4): 845–877.

Feldman, A. (1991). *Formations of Violence: The Narrative of the Body and Political Terror in Northern Ireland*. Chicago: University of Chicago Press.

Ferguson, Y. H. and R. W. Mansbach (1996). *Polities: Authority, Identities, and Change*. Columbia: University of South Carolina Press.

Fierke, K. M. (2002). "Links across the Abyss: Language and Logic in International Relations." *International Studies Quarterly* 46: 331–354.

Finer, H. (1964). *Dulles over Suez*. Chicago: Quadrangle Books.

Finnemore, M. (1996). *National Interests in International Society*. Ithaca, NY: Cornell University Press.

Finnemore, M. and K. Sikkink (1998). "International Norm Dynamics and Political Change." *International Organization* 52(4): 887–918.

Fisher, N. (1982). *Harold Macmillan*. London: Weidenfeld & Nicholson.

Foucault, M. (1977). *Power/Knowledge*. Hempstead, England: Harvester.

Foucault, M. (1978). *The History of Sexuality, Volume 1*. New York: Random House.

Foucault, M. (1983). "The Subject and Power." In H. L. Dreyfus and P. Rabinow (Eds.), *Michel Foucault: Beyond Structuralism and Hermeneutics*. Chicago: University of Chicago Press.

Frankland, N. (Ed.) (1960). *Documents on International Relations*. London: RIIA/Oxford University Press.

Gaddis, J. L. (2001). "In Defense of Particular Generalization: Rewriting Cold War History, Rethinking International Relations Theory." In C. Elman and M. F. Elman (Eds.), *Bridges and Boundaries: Historians, Political Scientists and the Study of International Relations* (pp. 301–326). Cambridge, MA: Belfer Center for Science and International Affairs.

Garvey, T. G. (2000). "The Value of Opacity: A Bakhtinian Analysis of Habermas's Discourse Ethics." *Philosophy and Rhetoric* 33(4): 370–390.

Gelber, L. (1938). *The Rise of Anglo-American Friendship: A Study in World Politics, 1891–1906*. London: Oxford University Press.

Gelber, L. (1961). *America in Britain's Place: The Leadership of the West and Anglo-American Unity*. London: Allen & Unwin.

Gilley, B. (1998). *Tiger on the Brink: Jiang Zemin and China's New Elite*. Berkeley: University of California Press.

Gilpin, R. (1981). *War and Change in World Politics*. Cambridge, England and New York: Cambridge University Press.

Glass, J. M. (1989). *Private Terror/Public Life: Psychosis and the Politics of Community*. Ithaca, NY: Cornell University Press.

Goldsmith, C. (2000). "In the Know? Sir Gladwyn Jebb, Ambassador to France." In S. Kelly and A. Gorst (Eds.), *Whitehall and the Suez Crisis* (pp. 79–97). London: Frank Cass Publishers.

Goldstein, J. and R. Keohane (1993). *Ideas and Foreign Policy*. Ithaca, NY: Cornell University Press.

Gonzalez, G. and S. Haggard (1998). "The United States and Mexico: A Pluralistic Security Community?" In E. Adler and M. Barnett (Eds.), *Security Communities*. Cambridge, England: Cambridge University Press.

Goodin, R. E. and G. Brennan (2001). "Bargaining over Beliefs." *Ethics* 111(January): 256–277.

Gorst, A. and L. Johnman (1997). *The Suez Crisis*. London, New York: Routledge.

Gorst, A. and S. Kelly (2000). *Whitehall and the Suez Crisis*. London: Frank Cass.

Gourevitch, P. (1986). *Politics in Hard Times*. Ithaca, NY: Cornell.

Greenblatt, S. (1991). *Marvelous Possessions: The Wonder of the New World*. Chicago: University of Chicago Press.

Greenwood, S. (1999). *Britain and the Cold War*. London: St. Martin's Press.

Grieco, J. (1988). "Anarchy and the Limits of Cooperation." *International Organization* 42: 485–507.

Guthrie, E. F. (1935). "The Crisis Concept in the Approach to the Problem of Personality." *Social Forces* 3(13): 383–390.

Haas, E. (1982). "Words Can Hurt You: Or Who Said What to Whom About Regimes." *International Organization* 36(2): 207–243.

Habermas, J. (1990). "Discourse Ethics: Notes on a Program of Philosophical Justification." In *Moral Consciousness and Communicative Action* (pp. 43–115). Cambridge, MA: MIT Press.

Habermas, J. (1996). *Between Facts and Norms: Contributions to a Discourse Theory of Law and Democracy*. Cambridge, MA: MIT Press.

Habermas, J. (2000). *The Philosophical Discourse of Modernity*. Cambridge, MA: MIT Press.

Hahn, P. (2000). "Discord or Accomodation? Britain and the United States in World Affairs, 1945–92." In F. M. Leventhal and L. A. Quinault (Eds.), *Anglo-American Attitudes*, (pp. 276–293). Aldershot, England: Ashgate.

Hall, R. B. (1997). "Moral Authority as a Power Resource." *International Organization* 51(4): 591–622.

Hall, R. B. (1999). *National Collective Identity*. New York: Colombia University Press.

Harding, H. (2002). *China and the International Order*. Open Forum, State Department, Washington DC.

Hare, P. J. (1993). *Diplomatic Chronicles of the Middle East: A Biography of Ambassador Raymond A. Hare*. Ann Arbor: University of Michigan Press.

Hathaway, R. M. (1981). *Ambiguous Partnership: Britain and American, 1944–1947*. New York: Columbia University Press.

Heikal, M. (1986). *Cutting the Lion's Tail: Suez through Egyptian Eyes*. New York: Morrow/Avon.

Held, D. (1995). *Democracy and the Global Order : From the Modern State to Cosmopolitan Governance*. Stanford, CA: Stanford University Press.

Heller, P. B. (2001). *The United Nations Under Dag Hammarskjold*. Lanham, MD: Scarecrow Press.

Hempel, C. G. (1966). *Philosophy of Natural Science*. Englewood Cliffs, NJ: Prentice-Hall.

Henderson, M. (1999, July 21). "Britain Blocked Secret U.S. Plan to Save Belsen Jews." *Times* (London).

Herman, D. (2001). "Sciences of the Text." *Postmodern Culture* 11(3): http://muse.jhu.edu/journals/postmoder_culture/v011/11.3herman.html.

Herman, R. G. (1996). "Identity, Norms, and National Security: The Soviet Foreign Policy Revolution and the End of the Cold War." In P. Katzenstein (Ed.), *The Culture of National Security: Norms and Identity in World Politics* (pp. 272–316). New York: Columbia University Press.

Hitchens, C. (1990). *Blood, Class, and Nostalgia: Anglo-American Ironies*. New York: Farrar, Strauss, and Giroux.

Hoffman, S. (1990). "International Society." In R. Vincent and J. Miller (Eds.), *Order and Violence: Hedley Bull and International Relations* (pp. 13–37). London: Oxford University Press.

Hogg, M. A. and D. Abrams (1990). *Social Identifications: A Social Psychology of Intergroup Relations and Group Processes*. New York: Routledge.

Hogg, M. A. and D. J. Terry (2001). "Social Identity Processes in Organizational Contexts." In M. A. Hogg and D. J. Terry (Eds.), *Social Identity Processes in Organizational Contexts*, Philadelphia, PA: Psychology Press.

Hollis, M. and S. Smith (1991). *Explaining and Understanding International Relations*. Oxford, England: Clarendon Press.

Horne, A. (1988). *Macmillan*. London: Macmillan.

Horne, A. (1989). *Macmillan II*. London: Macmillan.

Huntington, S. (1993). "The Clash of Civilizations." *Foreign Affairs* 73(3).

Huntington, S. P. (1996). *The Clash of Civilizations and the Remaking of World Order*. New York: Simon & Schuster.

Hurrell, A. (2001). "Keeping History, Law and Political Philosophy Firmly within the English School." *Review of International Studies* 27(3): 489–494.

Hymans, J. E. C. (2000). *Taking the Plunge: Emotion and Identity in the Decision to Build Nuclear Weapons*. Unpublished manuscript delivered to American Political Science Association, Washington DC.

Ignatieff, M. (2002, July 28). "Nation Building Lite." *New York Times Magazine*.

Ignatieff, M. (2003, January 5). "American Empire: The Burdes." *New York Times Magazine*.

Ikenberry, G. J. (2001). *After Victory: Institutions, Strategic Restraint, and the Rebuilding of Order after Major Wars*. Princeton, NJ: Princeton University Press.

Ikenberry, G. K. (1998–1999). "Institutions, Strategic Restraint, and the Persistence of American Postwar Order." *International Security* 23(3): 58–72.

Immerman, R. (1998). *John Foster Dulles: Piety, Pragmatism, and Power in U.S. Foreign Policy (Biographies in American Foreign Policy)*. Wilmington, DE: Scholarly Resources.

Ingram, E. (2001). "Hegemony, Global Reach, and World Power: Great Britain's Long Cycle." In C. Elman and M. F. Elman (Eds.), *Bridges and Boundaries: Historians, Political Scientists and the Study of International Relations* (223–251). Cambridge, MA: Belfer Center for Science and International Affairs.

Isacoff, J. B. (2002). "Revising War: The Historical Problem in International Relations." Doctoral dissertation, University of Pennsylvania.

Jackson, P. T. and D. H. Nexon (1999). "Relations before States: Substance, Process and the Study of World Politics." *European Journal of International Relations* 5(3): 291–332.

Jackson, P. T. and R. R. Krebs (2003). *Twisting Tongues and Twisting Arms: The Power of Political Rhetoric*. Unpublished manuscript delivered to American Political Science Association, Philadelphia, PA.

Jackson, R. (2000). *The Global Covenant: Human Conduct in a World of States*. Oxford, England: Oxford University Press.

James, R. R. (1986). *Anthony Eden*. London: Weidenfeld and Nicolson.

Jentleson, B. W. (2002). "The Need for Praxis: Bringing Policy Relevance Back In." *International Security* 26(4): 169–183.

Jervis, R. (1985). "From Balance to Concert: A Study of International Security Cooperation." In K. A. Oye (Ed.), *Cooperation under Anarchy* (58–79). Princeton, NJ: Princeton University Press.

Johnston, A. I. (2003). "Is China a Status Quo Power?" *International Security* 27(4): 5–56.

Jones, M. (2003). "Anglo-American Relations after Suez, the Rise and Decline of the Working Group Experiment, and the French Challenge to Nato, 1957–59." *Diplomacy and Statecraft* 14(1): 49–79.

Jones, P. (1997). *America and the British Labor Party: The Special Relationship at Work*. New York: St. Martin's Press.

Joynt, C. B. (1967). "John Foster Dulles and the Suez Crisis." In G. Grob (Ed.), *Statesmen and Statecraft of the Modern West: Essays in Honor of Dwight E. Lee and H. Donaldson Jordan*. Barre, MA: Barre Publishers.

Kahl, C. H. (1998). "Constructing a Separate Peace: Constructivism, Collective Liberal Identity, and Democratic Peace." *Security Studies* 8(2).

Katzenstein, P. (Ed.) (1996). *The Culture of National Security*. New York: Columbia University Press.

Keck, M. E. and K. Sikkink (1998). *Activists Beyond Borders: Advocacy Networks in International Politics*. Ithaca, NY: Cornell University Press.

Kecskés, G. (2001). "The Suez Crisis and the 1956 Hungarian Revolution." *East European Quarterly* 35(1): 47–58.

Kennedy, P. (1989). *The Rise and Fall of the Great Powers*. New York: Random House.

Kent, J. (1993). *British Imperial Strategy and the Origins of the Cold War, 1944–49*. London: Leicester University Press.

Kentelton, J. (1987). "Eisenhower, Churchill, and the Balance of Terror." In J. Krieg, (Ed.), *Dwight D. Eisenhower, Soldier, President, Statesman*. Westport, CT: Greenwood Press.

Keohane, R. O. (1984). *After Hegemony*. New York: Columbia University Press.

King, G., R. O. Keohane, et al. (1994). *Designing Social Inquiry: Scientific Inference in Qualitative Research*. Princeton, NJ: Princeton University Press.

Kingseed, C. C. (1995). *Eisenhower and the Suez Crisis of 1956*. Baton Rouge: Louisana State University Press.

Kirby, D. (2000). "Divinely Sanctioned: The Anglo-American Cold War Alliance and the Defence of Western Civilization and Christianity, 1945–48." *Journal of Contemporary History* 35(3): 385–412.

Koh, T. and A. Acharya (1998). *The Quest for World Order: Perspectives of a Pragmatic Idealist*. Singapore: Times Academic Press.

Kosso, P. (1992). *Reading the Book of Nature: An Introduction to the Philosophy of Science*. Cambridge, England: Cambridge University Press.

Krasner, S. D. (1982). "Regimes and the Limits of Realism: Regimes as Autonomous Variables." *International Organization* 36(2): 497–510.

Kratochwil, F. (1989). *Rules, Norms, and Decisions: On the Conditions of Practical and Legal Reasoning in International Relations and Domestic Affairs*. Cambridge, England: Cambridge University Press.

Kristeva, J. (1984). *Revolution in Poetic Language*. New York: Columbia University Press.

Kubalkova, V., N. G. Onuf, et al. (1998). *International Relations in a Constructed World*. Armonk, NY: ME Sharpe.

Kuhonta, E. (2002). *The Makings of an Illiberal Peace: Asean and the Evolution of a Security Community*. Unpublished manuscript, Princeton University, Princeton, NJ.

Kunz, D. (1991). *The Economic Diplomacy of the Suez Crisis*. Chapel Hill: University of North Carolina Press.

Kupchan, C. (1998). "After Pax Americana: Benign Power, Regional Integration, and the Sources of a Stable Multipolarity." *International Security* 23(2): 40–79.

Kyle, K. (1991). *Suez*. New York: St. Martin's Press.

Labov, W. (1989). "Exact Description of the Speech Community: Short a in Philadelphia." In R. Fasold and D. Schiffrin (Eds.), *Language Change and Variation* (pp. 1–57). Amsterdam: Benjamins.

Lader, P. (1998, June 12). "Lessons from Walking." John C. Whitehead Lecture, The Royal Institute of International Affairs, London.

Lash, J. (1971). *Roosevelt and Churchill, 1939–1941: The Partnership That Saved the West*. New York: Norton.

Layne, C. (1994). "Kant or Cant: The Myth of the Democratic Peace." *International Security* 19(2): 5–49.

Legro, J. and P. Kowert (1996). Norms, Identity, and Their Limits. In P. Katzenstein (Ed.), *The Culture of National Security: Norms and Identity in World Politics* (pp. 451–497). New York: Columbia University Press.

LeMahieu, D. (2000). "America and the Representation of British History in Film and Television." In F. M. Leventhal and R. Quinault (Eds.), *Anglo-American Attitudes* (261–275). Burlington, VT: Ashgate.

Linklater, A. (1998). *The Transformation of Political Community: Ethical Foundations of the Post-Westphalian Era*. Columbia: University of South Carolina Press.

Lloyd, S. (1978). *Suez 1956 : A Personal Account*. London: Cape.

Love, K. (1969). *Suez: The Twice-Fought War*. New York: McGraw-Hill.

Lucas, S. (1991). *Divided We Stand, Britain, the U.S. and the Suez Crisis*. London: Hodder-Stoughton Press.

Lucas, S. (1996). *Britain and Suez: The Lion's Last Roar*. Manchester, England: Manchester University Press.

Lustick, I. S. (1996). "History, Historiography, and Political Science: Multiple Records and the Problem of Selection Bias." *American Political Science Review* 90(3).

Lynch, M. (2002). "Why Engage? China and the Logic of Communicative Engagement." *European Journal of International Relations* 8(2): 187–230.

Lynn-Jones, S. M. (1998). *Why the United States Should Spread Democracy*. Working papers. 1–30. Belfer Center for Science and International Affairs, Cambridge, MA.

Lyotard, J. F. (1979). *The Postmodern Condition: A Report on Knowledge*. Minneapolis: University of Minnesota Press.

Lyotard, J. F. (1988). *Le Differend*. Minneapolis: University of Minnesota Press.

Lyotard, J. F. and J. L. Thébaud (1985). *Just Gaming*. Minneapolis: University of Minnesota Press.

Machiavelli, N., Ed. (1984). *The Prince*. New York: Bantam Classics.

MacKinnon, N. J. (1994). *Symbolic Interactionism as Affect Control*. Albany, NY: SUNY Press.

Macmillan, H. (1971). *Riding the Storm: 1956–1959*. New York: Harper and Row.

Marks, F. W. (1993). *Power and Peace: the Diplomacy of John Foster Dulles*. Westport, CT: Praeger.

Martel, G. (2000). "Decolonization after Suez: Retreat or Rationalization." *Australian Journal of Politics and History* 46(4): 403–417.

Mattli, W. (1999). *The Logic of Regional Integration: Europe and Beyond*. Cambridge, London and New York: Cambridge University Press.

Maynard, D. W. and T. P. Wilson (1980). "On the Reification of Social Structure." *Current Perspectives in Social Theory* 1: 287–232.

McKinley and R. Little (1986). *Global Problems and World Order*. London: Frances Pinter.

Mearsheimer, J. J. (1995). "The False Promise of International Institutions." *International Security* 19(3): 5–49.

Mearsheimer, J. J. (2001). *The Tragedy of Great Power Politics*. New York: Norton.

Medeiros, E. and T. M. Fravel (2003). "China's New Diplomacy." *Foreign Affairs* 82(6): FIND.

Mercer, J. (1995). "Anarchy and Identity." *International Organization* 49(2): 229–252.

Meyers, D. T. (1994). *Subjectivity and Subjection*. London: Routledge.

Montgomery, A. H. (2002). *Cooperation under Fire: Institutional and Cultural Dynamics During War*. Unpublished manuscript, Stanford University, Stanford, CA.

Morgenthau, H. J. (1948). *Politics among Nations: The Struggle for Power and Peace*. New York: Alfred A. Knopf.

Morgenthau, H. J. (1951). *In Defense of the National Interest: A Critical Examination of American Foreign Policy*. New York: Knopf.

Morgenthau, H. J. (2003). "The Moral Blindness of Scientific Man." In R. Art and R. Jervis (Eds.), *International Politics: Enduring Concepts and Contemporary Issues* (pp. 7–16). Boston: Longman Publishers.

Mosely, L. (1978). *Dulles: Biography of Elanor, Allen, and John Foster Dulles and Their Family Network*. New York: Dial Press.

Moser, J. E. (1999). *Twisting the Lion's Tale: American Anglophobia between the World Wars*. New York: New York University Press.

Mouzelis, N. (1993). "The Poverty of Sociological Theory." *Sociology* 27(4): 675–695.

Mowrer, E. A. (1961). *An End to Make Believe*. New York: Duell, Sloan & Pearce.

Murphy, R. (1964). *Diplomat among Warriors*. Garden City, NY: Doubleday.

Murray, A. (1999). *The United States, Great Britain, and the Middle East: Discourse and Dissidents*. Boulder, CO: Social Science Monographs.

Myers-Scotton, C. and A. Bolonyai (2001). "Calculating Speakers: Codeswitching in a Rational Choice Model." *Language in Society* 30: 1–28.

Neff, D. (1981). *Warriors at Suez*. New York: Linden Press/Simon and Schuster.

Neumann, I. (1999). *Uses of the Other*. Minneapolis: University of Minnesota Press.

Neustadt, R. E. (1970). *Alliance Politics*. New York: Columbia University Press.

Nicholas, H. G. (1975). *The United States and Britain*. Chicago: University of Chicago Press.

Nutting, A. (1967). *No End of a Lesson: The Story of Suez*. New York: C. N. Potter.

Oliverio, A. (1998). *The State of Terror*. Albany, NY: SUNY Press.

Onuf, N. (1989). *World of Our Making: Rules and Rule in Social Theory and International Relations*. Columbia: University of South Carolina Press.

Onuf, N. (2003). "Parsing Personal Identity: Self, Other, Agent." In F. Debrix (Ed.), *Language, Agency, and Politics in a Constructed World*. Armonk, NY: ME Sharp.

Ovendale, R. (1985). *The English Speaking Alliance: Britain, the United States, the Dominions and the Cold War 1945–51*. London: George Allen and Unwin.

Ovendale, R. (1998). *Anglo-American Relations in the Twentieth Century*. New York: St. Martin's Press.

Owen, J. M. (1994). "How Liberalism Produces the Democratic Peace." *International Security* 19(2): 87–125.

Oye, K. (1985). "Explaining Cooperation under Anarchy: Hypotheses and Strategies." In K. Oye (Ed.), *Cooperation under Anarchy* (pp. 1–24). Princeton, NJ: Princeton University Press.

Palan, R. (2000). "A World of Their Making: An Evaluation of the Constructivist Critique in International Relations." *Review of International Studies* 26: 575–598.

Paris, R. (2003). "Peacekeeping and the Constraints of Global Culture." *European Journal of International Relations* 9(3): 441–473.

Parmar, I. (1995). *Special Interests, the State and the Anglo-American Alliance, 1939–1945*. London: Frank Cass.

Paul, S. H. (2000). *Nuclear Rivals*. Columbus: Ohio State University Press.

Payne, R. A. (2001). "Persuasion, Frames, and Norm Construction." *European Journal of International Relations* 7(1): 37–61.

Peceny, M. (2000). "International Relations in a Constructed World." *American Political Science Review* 94(1): 243–244.

Philpot, D. (2001). *Revolutions in Sovereignty: How Ideas Shaped Modern International Relations*. Princeton, NJ: Princeton University Press.

Pietroski, P. M. (2000). *Causing Actions*. Oxford, England: Oxford University Press.

Poster, M. (1998). "Postmodernity and the Politics of Multiculturalism: The Lyotard-Habermas Debate over Social Theory." In J. J. Goux and P. R. Wood (Eds.), *Terror and Consensus: The Vicissitudes of French Thought*. Stanford, CA: Stanford University Press.

Powell, R. (1993). "Absolute and Relative Gains in International Relations Theory." In D. Baldwin (Ed.), *Neorealism and Neoliberalism: The Contemporary Debate* (pp. 209–233). New York: Columbia University Press.

Powell, R. (1999). *In the Shadow of Power*. Princeton, NJ: Princeton University Press.

Price, R. (1997). *The Chemical Weapons Taboo*. Ithaca, NY: Cornell University Press.

Price, R. (1998). "Reversing the Gun Sights: Transnational Civil Society Targets Land Mines." *International Organization* 52(3): 613–644.

Price, R. and C. Reus-Smit (1998). "Dangerous Liaisons? Critical International Relations Theory and Constructivism." *European Journal of International Relations* 4(3): 259–294.

Rachman, G. (2001). "Is the Anglo-American Relationship Still Special?" *Washington Quarterly* 24(2): 7–18.

Ragin, C. C. (2000). *Fuzzy-Set Social Science*. Chicago: University of Chicago Press.

Raiffa, H. (1982). *The Art and Science of Negotiation*. Cambridge, MA: Harvard University Press.

Rapoport, A. (1999). "Conceptions of World Order." In A. W. Dorn (Ed.), *World Order for a New Millennium: Political, Cultural, and Spiritual Approaches to Building Peace* (3–15). New York: St. Martin's Press.

Recanati, F. (1987). *Meaning and Force: The Pragmatics of Peformative Utterances*. Cambridge, England: Cambridge University Press.

Rengger, N. (2000). *International Relations, Political Theory, and the Problem of Order*. New York: Routledge.

Rescher, N. (1996). *Process Philosophy: An Introduction to Process Philosophy*. Albany, NY: State University Press.

Reus-Smit, C. (1999). *The Moral Purpose of the State: Culture, Social Identity, and Institutional Rationality in International Relations*. Princeton, NJ: Princeton University Press.

Reynolds, D. (1981). *The Creation of the Anglo-American Alliance, 1937–41: A Study in Competitive Cooperation*. London: Europa Publications.

Richardson, J. E. (2001). "'Now Is the Time to Put an End to All This': Argumentative Discourse Theory and 'Letters to the Editor.'" *Discourse and Society* 12(2): 143–168.

Richardson, L. (1996). *When Allies Differ: Anglo-American Relations During the Suez and Falklands Crisis*. New York: St. Martin's Press.

Risse, T. (2000). "Let's Argue!: Communicative Action in World Politics." *International Organization* 54(1): 1–40.

Risse-Kappen, T. (1995). *Cooperation among Democracies*. Princeton, NJ: Princeton University Press.

Roberts, P. (1997). "The Anglo-American Theme." *Diplomatic History* 21(3): 333–364.

Robinson, W. P. and H. Tajfel (1996). *Social Groups and Identities: Developing the Legacy of Henri Tajfel*. Oxford, England and Boston: Butterworth-Heinemann.

Rogers, W. D. (1986). "The 'Unspecial Relationship' in Latin America." In W. Louis and H. Bull (Eds.), *The "Special Relationship" in Anglo-American Relations since 1945* (pp. 341–353). Oxford, England: Oxford University Press.

Rosenberg, J. P. (1987). "The Foreign Policy Making Process." In J. Krieg (Ed.), *Dwight D. Eisenhower, Soldier, President, Statesman*. Westport, CT: Greenwood Press.

Ruggie, J. G. (1998). *Constructing the World Polity: Essays on International Institutionalization*. New York: Routledge.

Russett, B. (1993). *Grasping the Democratic Peace*. Princeton, NJ: Princeton University Press.

Russett, B. (1998). "A Neo-Kantian Perspective: Democracy, Interdependence and International Organization." In E. Adler (Ed.), *Security Communities*, (pp. 368–394). Cambridge, England: Cambridge University Press.

Said, E. (1978). *Orientalism*. London: Penguin.

Schedler, A. (2000). "Common Sense without Common Ground: The Concept of Democratic Transition in Mexican Politics." *Mexican Studies-Estudios Mexicanos* 16(2): 325–345.

Schelling, T. C. (1966). *Arms and Influence*. New Haven, CT: Yale University Press.

Schimmelfennig, F. (1998). "Nato, Germany, and the United States: A Constructivist Explanation." *Security Studies* 8(2).

Schoppa, L. J. (1999). "The Social Context in Coercive International Bargaining." *International Organization* 53(2): 307–342.

Schweller, R. (2001). "The Problem of International Order Revisited: A Review Essay." *International Security* 26(1).

Seib, P. (1998). *Taken for Granted*. Westport, CT: Praeger.

Shapiro, M. (1989). "Textualizing Global Politics." In J. Der Derian and M. Shapiro (Eds.), *International/Intertextual Relatons: Postmodern Readings of World Politics*. Lexington, MA: Lexington Books.

Shaw, T. (1996). *Eden, Suez, and the Mass Media: Propaganda and Persuasion During the Suez Crisis*. London: IB Tauris.

Slaughter, A. M. (1997). "The Real New World Order." *Foreign Affairs* 76(5): 183–197.

Smith, G. (1990). *Reagan and Thatcher*. London: The Bodley Head.

Smith, S. (2000). "Wendt's World." *Review of International Studies* 26(1): 151–163.

Stafford, D. (2000). *Roosevelt and Churchill: Men of Secrets*. New York: The Overlook Press.

Stein, A. (1993). "Coordination and Collaboration: Regimes in an Anarchic World." In D. Baldwin (Ed.), *Neorealism and Neoliberalism*. New York: Columbia University Press.

Stein, J. G. (1994). "Political Learning by Doing: Gorbachev as Uncommitted Thinker and Motivated Learner." *International Organization* 48(2): 155–184.

Stevens, J. (1999). *Reproducing the State*. Princeton, NJ: Princeton University Press.

Swidler, A. (1986). "Culture in Action: Symbols and Strategies." *American Sociological Review* 51(2): 273–286.

Sylvester, C. (2002). *Feminist International Relations: An Unfinished Journey*. Cambridge, England and New York: Cambridge University Press.

Tajfel, H. (1978). *Differentiation between Social Groups: Studies in the Social Psychology of Intergroup Relations*. London and New York: Academic Press.

Todorov, T. (1973). *The Fantastic*. Cleveland, OH: Case Western Reserve University Press.

Tronto, J. (1993). *Moral Boundaries: A Political Argument for an Ethic of Care*. New York: Routledge.

Turner, A. C. (1971). *The Unique Partnership*. New York: Pegasus.

Van Pelt, T. (2000). "Otherness." *Postmodern Culture* 10(2).

von Wright, G. H. (1971). *Understanding and Explanation*. Ithaca, NY: Cornell University Press.

Walker, R. (1990). "Security, Sovereignty, and the Challenge of World Politics." *Alternatives* 15: 3–27.

Walker, R. (1992). *Inside/Outside: International Relations as Political Theory*. Cambridge, MA: Cambridge University Press.

Walt, S. M. (1987). *The Origins of Alliances*. Ithaca, NY: Cornell University Press.

Walton, D. (2000). *Scare Tactics: Arguments That Appeal to Fear and Threats*. Dordrecht, The Netherlands: Kluwer Press.

Waltz, K. N. (1979). *Theory of International Politics*. Reading, MA: Addison-Wesley Publishing Company.

Walzer, M. (1983). *Spheres of Justice: A Defense of Pluralism and Equality*. New York: Basic Books.

Warren, M. E. (1995). "The Self in Discursive Democracy." In S. K. White (Ed.), *The Cambridge Companion to Habermas* (pp. 167–200). New York: Cambridge University Press.

Weber, C. (1995). *Simulating Sovereignty: Intervention, the State and Symbolic Exchange*. Cambridge, England: Cambridge University Press.

Weissman, D. (2000). *A Social Ontology*. New Haven, CT: Yale University Press.

Wendt, A. (1987). "The Agent-Structure Problem in International Relations." *International Organization* 41(3): 335–370.

Wendt, A. (1992). "Anarchy Is What States Make of It: The Social Construction of Power Politics." *International Organization* 46(2): 393–425.

Wendt, A. (1996). "Collective Identity Formation and the International State." *American Political Science Review* 90(2): 384–396.

Wendt, A. (1999). *Social Theory of International Politics*. Cambridge, England: Cambridge University Press.

Wendt, A. (2000). "On the Via Media: A Response to the Critics." *Review of International Studies* 26(1): 165–180.

White, H. (1987a). *The Content of the Form*. Baltimore, MD: Johns Hopkins University Press.

White, H. (1987b). "The Value of Narrativity in the Representation of Reality." In H. White (Ed.), *The Content of the Form*. Baltimore, MD: Johns Hopkins University Press.

Williams, M. C. (2001). "The Discipline of the Democratic Peace: Kant, Liberalism and the Social Construction of Security Communities." *European Journal of International Relations* 7(4): 525–553.

Williams, M. C. and I. B. Neumann (2000). "From Alliance to Security Community: Nato, Russia, and the Power of Identity." *Millennium-Journal of International Studies* 29(2): 357–387.

Wittgenstein, L. (1958). *Philosophical Investigations*. Oxford, England: Basil Blackwell.

Wohlforth, W. C. (1994). "Realism and the End of the Cold War." *International Security* 19(3): 91–129.

Wohlforth, W. C. (1999). "The Stability of a Unipolar World." *International Security* 24(1): 5–41.

Woods, R. B. (1990). *A Changing of the Guard: Anglo-American Relations 1941–1946*. Chapel Hill: University of North Carolina Press.

Wrong, D. (1988). *Power: Its Forms and Bases*. Chicago: University of Chicago Press.

Wrong, D. (1994). *The Problem of Order*. New York: Free Press.

Young, O. (1989). *International Cooperation: Building Regimes for Natural Resources and the Environment*. Ithaca, NY: Cornell University Press.

Zehfuss, M. (2001). "Constructivism and Identity: A Dangerous Liaison." *European Journal of International Relations* 7(3): 315–348.

Index